OXFORD MONOGRAPHS ON M

Music in the English Courtly Masque

Music in the English Courtly Masque
1604–1640

PETER WALLS

CLARENDON PRESS · OXFORD

This book has been printed digitally and produced in a standard design
in order to ensure its continuing availability

OXFORD

UNIVERSITY PRESS

Great Clarendon Street, Oxford OX2 6DP
Oxford University Press is a department of the University of Oxford.
It furthers the University's objective of excellence in research, scholarship,
and education by publishing worldwide in

Oxford New York

Athens Auckland Bangkok Bogotá Buenos Aires Cape Town
Chennai Dar es Salaam Delhi Florence Hong Kong Istanbul Karachi
Kolkata Kuala Lumpur Madrid Melbourne Mexico City Mumbai
Nairobi Paris São Paulo Singapore Taipei Tokyo Toronto Warsaw

with associated companies in Berlin Ibadan

Oxford is a registered trade mark of Oxford University Press
in the UK and certain other countries

Published in the United States
by Oxford University Press Inc., New York

© Peter Walls 1996

ISBN 0-19-816141-7

FOR HELEN

Preface

This book is about the character and function of music in the masque. Like many others, I was drawn to the masque in the first place because of its interest as a multimedia form involving some of the greatest artists of early seventeenth-century England. On the face of it, poetry, drama, scenic design, music, and dance were united in a single endeavour. But the preparation of a court masque does not seem to have involved an orderly sequence of tasks carried out within a clearly defined hierarchy (librettist—composer—director—designer—conductor—performers). With music and dance in particular we get a picture of a looser collaboration between various groups with overlapping responsibilities. The challenge for the poet must partly have been to know how to harness what he knew these people were likely to come up with to his own artistic ends. This, and the mixing of professional musicians with courtier participants, makes the whole question of how music contributed to the masque's 'meaning' fascinatingly unruly.

I have tried to embrace these complications. In the following chapters, musical and literary discussion is combined with historical enquiry in what I hope is an illuminating way. I wanted to give the ideal a chance—to see how the different elements in the masque could be integrated to produce a coherent vision of a model human society. The primary task was one of conveying a sufficiently strong sense of what masque music was actually like— no easy matter, given the forms in which the sources have survived. But then, I also wanted to give a sense of the fragility of that vision, of the way in which the actual circumstances of masque performances allowed for a very much less elevated view of what was going on. Even in the early years of the seventeenth century there was open disagreement about whether the masque was a serious artistic endeavour or entertainment of the most ephemeral kind.

Until relatively recently, musicological research on the masque has been preoccupied with identifying music used in the original performances (a frequently misguided pursuit). J. C. Meagher's *Method and Meaning in Jonson's Masques* (1966) included a useful chapter on music outlining the intellectual context for its use. In 1970 Murray Lefkowitz edited *Trois Masques à la cour de Charles 1er d'Angleterre*, which made available almost all the William Lawes masque music (but included with it—amongst music intended for processions, antimasques, and revels—some compositions of too intimate or contrapunt-ally elaborate a character to have had any possible connection with the masque).

This book started out as a revision of a D.Phil. thesis. Since that thesis was completed (in 1976), a number of important studies of the masque and of seventeenth-century English music and history have appeared. It will be clear, I hope, from my footnotes and bibliography that I have benefited both from the information and the stimulation that these have provided. This is, how-ever, the first full study devoted to the music in court masques—though Mary Chan's *Music in the Theatre of Ben Jonson* has several chapters on Jonson's masques, and David Lindley included a chapter on Campion's masques in his book on the poet-composer. Most of the music discussed here is now available in a single volume, Andrew Sabol's *Four Hundred Songs and Dances from the Stuart Masque*. Without wishing to seem ungrateful for this very useful anthology, I should add a word of caution for those who use it alongside this book. In my view, the suggested contexts for dance tunes are unreliable (for reasons explained in Chapter 3) and some of Sabol's editorial practices seem misleading (in particular, his alteration of note-values as a way of indicating the significance of time signatures and his provision of over-active continuo realizations of unfigured basses).

This book covers the period from the accession of James I until the beginning of the civil war. It deals only with masques at court and their first cousins—masques in the Inns of Court and the houses of the great. One of my main reasons for defining the scope in this way is that I wanted to stay as close to actual music as I could. While the survival rate of (particularly) vocal settings for the court masque is not terribly high, it is infinitely better than for other forms of entertainment that have some affinity with the masque. So, I have not dealt with the masque in the sixteenth century, with garden enter-tainments, entertainments at Oxford or Cambridge, masques in plays, Caroline pastorals, or what W. J. Lawrence termed 'substantive theatre masques' (productions—like the Middleton play quoted in the Introduc-tion—purporting to give the patrons of the public theatres vicarious experi-ence of a court masque). The first three chapters are concerned primarily with the Jacobean masque—though Caroline productions are freely referred to where they continue to illustrate features evident in the earlier period. Chapters 4 to 6 then deal only with features of Caroline masques which are new or distinctive. Earlier versions of sections of Chapters 1, 2, 4, and 7 have appeared in the articles listed under my name in the Bibliography.

The Helmholtz system is used for indicating pitch in the text. In summary tables (but not the text) I have used upper-case letters to indicate major keys and lower-case letters for minor keys. Quotations preserve original spelling wherever possible. Line (or page) references following quotations from masque texts are from currently available modern editions (and those used for this purpose are indicated in the Appendix). After the initial reference, works are cited in the notes by author and abbreviated title only; full references will be found in the Bibliography. In citing seventeenth-century documents reproduced in modern publications I have, wherever practicable, given footnote references to the original documents as well as to the secondary sources from which they are quoted. I have given all dates as in the English calendar but with the year starting on 1 January; consequently a reference to Twelfth Night 1618 (OS), would appear as 6 January 1619. The only exceptions to this rule are in direct quotation (where any ambiguity is always clarified) and in citing title-pages of masque texts (in the Appendix and Bibliography).

I have received microfilms from a number of libraries and had the pleasure of working in many others. I should like to express my thanks to the staff of those institutions—mostly represented by the RISM sigla in my list of abbreviations. To that list, however, I should add the Pendlebury Library in Cambridge, the Music Faculty Library in Oxford, the library of Worcester College, Oxford, the Courtauld Institute Library, and the Alexander Turnbull and Victoria University libraries in Wellington, New Zealand. I wish to thank the Board of Victoria University Press, the Internal Grants Committee, and the Leave Committee at Victoria University for their generous support for my work. The book was completed during a year at Clare Hall in Cambridge, and I should like to express my gratitude to the President and Fellows for ensuring that the college was such a congenial research base. I have been helped by many friends and colleagues. In particular, from the first phase of my interest in the masque, I should like to record my gratitude to Don (D. F.) McKenzie (who introduced me to the genre), to the late Frederick Sternfeld (who supervised my thesis), and to thank John Caldwell, and Roger Savage (whose kindness in reading and reacting to what I wrote was enormously helpful). I have been grateful for help on specific matters from Christy Anderson, Suzanne Aspden, Gioia Brunoro, Barry Empson, Greer Garden, Penny Gouk, Kate Harris (Librarian and Archivist at Longleat House), Stoddart Lincoln, G. H. Mandelbrote (of the Royal Commission on Historical Manuscripts), Samantha Owens, Robert Spencer, and Robert Thompson. Carol Marsh and Ken Pierce have provided me with useful comment on some of the dance sections of the book. Lynn Hulse has been generous in making her work on music in aristocratic households available to me. I have had many fruitful discussions with Peter Holman, who has always been willing to share research materials. I should like to thank Bruce Phillips for his patience and encouragement, and the other editorial staff at Oxford University Press who have given advice. In particular, Bonnie Blackburn and Leofranc Holford-Strevens have (amongst other things) elucidated many points in my transcription and translation of early seventeenth-century European languages. Finally, my greatest debt is to my wife, Kathryn, not just for her unfailing support but more specifically for her willingness to turn aside from her own work to help with matters of both style and content.

Contents

List of Plates

(between 172 and 173)

List of Tables

List of Music Examples

Abbreviations

AM	*Acta Musicologica*
BM	T. J. B. Spencer and S. Wells (eds.), *A Book of Masques in Honour of Allardyce Nicoll* (Cambridge, 1967)
CEKM	Corpus of Early Keyboard Music
CSPD	*Calendar of State Papers, Domestic Series*
CVSP	*Calendar of Venetian State Papers*
ELR	*English Literary Renaissance*
ELS, I	The English Lute Songs, first series
ELS, II	The English Lute Songs, second series
EM	*Early Music*
Grove 6	S. Sadie (ed.), *The New Grove Dictionary of Music and Musicians*, 20 vols. (London, 1980)
H&S	*Ben Jonson*, ed. C. H. Herford and P. and E. Simpson, 11 vols. (Oxford, 1925–52)
JRMA	*Journal of the Royal Musical Association*
MB	Musica Britannica
Mf	*Die Musikforschung*
ML	*Music and Letters*
MR	*The Music Review*
MSC	*Malone Society Collections*
NQ	*Notes and Queries*
NS	New Style (date)
O&S	S. Orgel and R. Strong, *Inigo Jones: The Theatre of the Stuart Court*, 2 vols. (London, 1973)
OED	*The Oxford English Dictionary*
OS	Old Style (date)
PRMA	*Proceedings of the Royal Musical Association*
RD	*Renaissance Drama*, new series
RdM	*Revue de Musicologie*

RECM	A. Ashbee, *Records of English Court Music*, 6 vols. (Snodland, 1986–91; Aldershot, 1991–2)
RES	*Review of English Studies*
RMARC	*Royal Musical Association Research Chronicle*
RORD	*Research Opportunities in Renaissance Drama*
S + number	The number of a piece in A. Sabol, *Four Hundred Songs and Dances from the Stuart Masque* (Hanover and London, 1978–82)
TLS	*The Times Literary Supplement*

RISM LIBRARY SIGLA

IRELAND
EIRE–Dtc	Dublin, Trinity College

FRANCE
F–Pm	Paris, Bibliothèque Mazarine
F–Pn	Paris, Bibliothèque Nationale

GERMANY
D–Kl	Kassel, Landesbibliothek und Murhardsche Bibliothek der Stadt Kassel
D–Lr	Lüneburg, Ratsbücherei

GREAT BRITAIN
GB–AB	Aberystwyth, National Library of Wales
GB–Ce	Cambridge, Emmanuel College
GB–Cf	Cambridge, Fitzwilliam Museum
GB–Cu	Cambridge University Library
GB–Eu	Edinburgh University Library
GB–Lbl	London, British Library
GB–Llp	London, Lambeth Palace Library
GB–Lpro	London, Public Record Office
GB–Lva	London, Victoria and Albert Museum
GB–NO	Nottingham University Library
GB–Ob	Oxford, Bodleian Library
GB–Och	Oxford, Christ Church

ITALY
I–Vnm	Venice, Biblioteca Nazionale Marciana

SWEDEN
S–Sk	Stockholm, Kungliga Biblioteket
S–Uu	Uppsala, Universitetsbibliuteket

UNITED STATES OF AMERICA
US–NYp	New York, Public Library at Lincoln Center
US–NYpm	New York, Pierpont Morgan Library
US–SM	San Marino (California), Henry E. Huntington Library

Introduction

> This our Device we do not call a play,
> Because we breake the Stages Lawes to day . . .
> You shall perceive by what comes first in sight,
> It was intended for a Royall Night
> There's one houres words, the rest in Songs & Dances.[1]

Middleton and Rowley's *Courtly Masque* would not, in fact, have given its audience at the Swan a very accurate picture of what real masques were like, but the prologue is absolutely right in suggesting that the balance between spoken drama and music (and I include dance here) would have been very much in music's favour. When masques at court feature in seventeenth-century letters and chronicles, music and dancing attract at least as much comment as the visual spectacle and rather more than the literary device. The entry about *The Masque of Blackness* in the Revels Book for 1605 simply reads: 'On Twelfe Night The Queens Maties Maske of Moures wth Aleven Ladies of honno^r to Accumpayney her mat^{ie} wch cam in great showes of devises wch they satt In wth excellent musik.'[2] And when the Venetian ambassador reported on *The Masque of Beauty*, he described the stage machinery as miraculous, marvelled at the quantity and beauty of the lights, and noted that 'the music and dance [were] most sumptuous';[3] not a word about the poetry or the dramatic structure. And yet the masque has been regarded first and foremost as a literary genre. This is primarily due to the dominating position of masque texts in our total picture of these entertainments. Texts are, of course, vitally important; it is through the unfolding of the literary device that the masque as a whole is given shape, and the music in particular endowed with significance. The constant use of musical imagery might be seen as

---

[1] T. Middleton and W. Rowley, *A Courtly Masque: The Device called the World Tost at Tennis* (London, 1620), prologue. My attention was drawn to this prologue by K. Sturgess, *Jacobean Private Theatre* (London, 1987), 160. See also E. Welsford, *The Court Masque* (Cambridge, 1927; repr. New York, 1962), 213–14; W. J. Lawrence, 'Early Substantive Theatre Masques', *TLS*, 8 Dec. 1921, 814, and id., 'The Origins of the Substantive Theatre Masque', *Pre-Restoration Stage Studies* (1927), 334–6.

[2] Revels Book 1605, fo. 2^v; cited in H&S, x. 445.

[3] *CVSP*, xi. 86; cited in H&S, x. 457.

an attempt to relate the masque's thematic concerns to the music actually performed.

By the end of the first decade of the seventeenth century, the court masque had acquired a classic structure, thanks largely to Ben Jonson's vision of the relationship between its form and function. Poetry, music, and visual spectacle were united through the device of the masque in projecting a coherent ideology for the early Stuart court. Or at least that was how it was supposed to be. Not everybody saw the point. Some of Jonson's fellow dramatists showed impatience or amusement with his elevated view of the masque's function, and many more of his contemporaries seem to have regarded masque nights as purely social occasions in which the device provided an incidental framework for dancing.

A great deal of music was performed during the presentation of a masque at court. When the king entered the masquing room and took his seat on the chair of state, loud music—a wind consort—was heard. The performance which followed usually fell into two parts: an antimasque and a main masque. The grotesque or comic antimasque always contained at least one dance and sometimes included singing. When this world of misrule or vulgarity vanished (at a visually spectacular moment known as the transformation scene), more loud music was heard. The masquers (courtiers, and not professional actors and dancers like the performers in the antimasque) were revealed and came forward to music. They danced several (usually two or three) newly choreographed set dances, each of which would be introduced in song. Movement of the masquers within the performing area might occasion more instrumental music. Another song would introduce the revels, in which the masquers 'took out' members of the audience to dance with them. After several hours of social dancing, one last song, and possibly a final set dance, brought the entertainment to a close. While the variations on that pattern were manifold, the sense of a common matrix underlying the masques of the early Stuart period is nevertheless very strong.

The amount of time devoted to musical performance of one kind or another during a masque stands out in the following hypothetical and very approximate timetable (justified in the closing pages of this book) of the main subdivisions just described. Middleton's *Courtly Masque* prologue, if anything, underestimates the extent to which song and, more particularly, dance overwhelmed spoken drama:

> 9.00 p.m.   loud music
>
> 9.03 p.m.   ANTIMASQUE
>   [song]
>   dance
>
> 9.15 p.m.   TRANSFORMATION SCENE (loud music)
>   MAIN MASQUE

> song → set dance
> song → set dance
> [song → set dance]

9.45 p.m.   revels

1.00 a.m.   [closing song and/or dance]

The antimasque in the Jacobean period was performed entirely by professional actors and dancers. Since it was normal in antimasques for the same
people both to dance and to take speaking roles, we may assume that the
dancing-masters (who are mentioned from time to time as participants) were
joined by the actors. Actors had a reputation, in any case, as skilled dancers.
Until 1614 at the Globe (and longer in other theatres) plays concluded with
a jig—a comic song-and-dance routine which must have exploited skills very
like those needed in the antimasques. (Thomas Platter's account of seeing
Julius Caesar in 1599 mentions that 'When the play was over they danced
marvellously and gracefully together as is their wont, two dressed as men and
two as women.'[4])

Professional actors were also prominent in the main masque as presenters,
the speaking roles which moved the action forward. Some also sang. 'When
all the ages of the earth' in *The Masque of Queens* was performed by 'that most
excellent *tenor* voyce, and exact Singer (her Ma[ties] seruant, *mr. Io. Allin*)' (ll.
740–1). John Alleyn was again acknowledged—alongside Nicholas Lanier—
for singing in *The Somerset Masque*. He was a member of Shakespeare's
company, not part of the musical establishment. The references to him in
masque texts present an interesting picture of collaboration between actors
and musicians.

As in the public theatres, the professionals who did the singing were all
male. This has one rather unusual aspect, however, since they were often
assigned female roles. It is easy to understand Jacobean audiences coping
with the unbroken voices of the 'little eyases'[5] who played female characters
in ordinary drama, but the practice in the masque of having adult males
impersonating female deities (and not singing as falsettists) adds another
dimension to the audiences' willing suspension of disbelief. Nicholas Lanier
(a tenor) sang the role of Eternity in *The Somerset Masque*, wearing 'a long
blew Taffata robe, painted with Starres, and on her head a Crowne'. (*The
Triumph of Peace*, discussed in Chapter 4, provides other striking examples.)
This—like the linking of heroic roles in *opera seria* to soprano voices (often
female when castrati were unavailable)—suggests that modern attitudes towards credible dramatic representation are irrelevant and that we should do

---

[4] Quoted by A. Gurr, *Playgoing in Shakespeare's London* (Cambridge, 1987), 213.
[5] See *Hamlet*, II. ii. The *OED* gives 'A young hawk taken from the nest for the purpose of training, or
one whose training is incomplete' as the primary meaning of 'Eyas'.

better to think about voice-types in relation to character status rather than gender.

But that, too, may be an oversimplification, since the masque provides the first English evidence of women singing dramatic roles in public (that is, if we discount the case of Moll Frith dressed as a man and causing scandal at the Fortune by sitting on the edge of the stage and singing to her lute). In *Tempe Restor'd* Nicholas Lanier (as the Highest Sphere) was joined by Madame Coniacke as Circe and Mistress Shepherd as Harmony. Nothing is known about these two trail-blazing women; their names seem just a little improbable—pseudonyms, perhaps, to avoid public opprobrium.[6] Some factions clearly were not ready for them. As is well known, the participation of Queen Henrietta Maria and her ladies in pastoral dramas at court provoked a diatribe from William Prynne in *Histrio-Mastix* (1633) which led to his losing his right ear and (of more significance for the masque) being expelled from Lincoln's Inn.[7]

The participation of women as masquers was a different matter (though this was a subtlety Prynne did not appreciate). The whole point was to have courtiers or the ladies of the court at the centre of masque. They danced (but did not sing or speak) characterized in roles intended to be seen as projections of their actual status and function in society. Stephen Orgel explains the importance of this congruity between role and performer by contrasting it with the position of the professionals in the antimasque:

A masquer's disguise is a representation of the courtier beneath. He retains his personality and hence his position in the social hierarchy. His audience affirms his equality with them by consenting to join the dance. This is the climax of the Jacobean masque . . . But a professional dancer is like an actor; he plays any part; he can assume all personalities because he has none of his own . . . his persona is not a *representation* of the reality beneath, but the reality itself. When an actor unmasks the revelation is trivial. We see a person who is no person . . . who has been performing an *impersonation*. . . . The courtier's unmasking is the point of the masque, through which its significance is extended out beyond the boundary of the stage into the real world . . .[8]

We shall be very much concerned with what might be described as the interface between the masque's imaginative integrity and the real world. In

---

[6] It has been suggested to me that Madame Coniacke was a member of Henrietta Maria's household. The 'Estat des offitiers et serviteurs de la Royne' (GB-Lpro, SP 16 3 173) and 'L'Etat de la maison de la Royne d'Angleterre' (GB-Lpro, SP 16 3 175) include no such name, though the latter has some women grouped anonymously as 'Six femmes de Chambre, Une Lavanderie', etc.

[7] Prynne 'translates' St Basil (Commentary upon Essay 5) in support of his opposition to women singing: 'What a miserable Spectacle is it to chaste and wel-mannered eyes, to see a woman, not to follow her needle or distaffe, but to sing to a Lute? not to be knowne by her owne husband, but to be often veiwed by others as a publike whore: not to modulate or sing a Psalme of confession, but to sing songs inticing unto lust: not to supplicate to God, but willingly to hasten unto Hell: not to goe diligently to the Church of God, but to with-draw others with her selfe from thence & c'; *Histrio-Mastix: The Players Scourge, or Actors Tragedie* (London, 1633), 277.

[8] S. Orgel, *The Jonsonian Masque* (Cambridge, Mass., 1965), 117–18.

various ways, the creators, participants, and audiences all recognized that this relationship was distinctive. As we shall see in Chapter 1, their awareness of this (often only implicit) accounts to a large extent for the form in which texts and musical sources have been preserved. And this in turn gives rise to some of the most interesting (and sometimes frustrating) problems which are explored in subsequent chapters, where a picture needs to be built up from diverse pieces of evidence which are neither complete nor obediently complementary. This is perhaps most obvious in Chapter 4, which in part attempts to disentangle the records produced by four Inns of Court collaborating on the production of *The Triumph of Peace* (1634). The rewards here are obvious: the accumulated memoranda help illuminate one of the most precious musical sources for the Stuart masque, the William Lawes autograph, GB-Ob, MS Mus. Sch. b. 2. Not until the final chapter do I confront what must surely have seemed in the early seventeenth century the most obvious difficulty in trying to draw members of the court into the kind of self-regarding heroic allegory that we find in the masque: the whole enterprise presupposed that persona and reality *are* essentially compatible. Whether or not these people lived up to the values and ideals attributed to them by the masque devices would be scarcely relevant here except that their behaviour does have some bearing on the kind of dancing seen in the revels.

The group of people who are of most interest in this book, however, are not the masquers, but the professional musicians and dancers. Except for those considered in Chapter 7 (Masques away from Whitehall), these were mainly members of the court musical establishment in its richest and most active period. In addition to the singers of the Chapel Royal, James I employed about forty musicians, and the number rose to an average of sixty-five under Charles I. They did not normally perform as a single ensemble *except* in such grand occasions as court masques. Other members of the royal family—notably the Queen and the Prince of Wales—retained their own musicians, many of them of exceptional quality. Some indication of the strength of Prince Henry's musical establishment is given in Chapter 8. After his death, many of these musicians were taken into Prince Charles's household (when that was officially formed in 1616) and were joined by other illustrious figures (like, in 1618, Giovanni Coprario). The households of the children and wives of the first two Stuarts have a particular interest because of their concentration of highly favoured foreign musicians, who must have played a role in familiarizing their English colleagues with Continental styles.[9]

What this all adds up to is quite remarkable: a large group of highly skilled executants with a number of very gifted composers in their midst who seem to have both valued their own distinctively English musical traditions

---

[9] For an overview of the royal music and its place in the musical life of London, see my 'London 1603–49', in C. Price (ed.), *The Early Baroque Era*, Man and Music series (London, 1993), 276–81.

and been open to innovation from abroad. Given that kind of strength, it is little wonder that seventeenth-century observers wrote with as much enthusiasm about the music of the masque as they did about its other dimensions.

1

Texts, Scores, and Musicians

Speculative and Practical Music in the Masque

> The fingers of the Powres aboue, do tune
> The harmony of this Peace . . .
> (*Cymbeline* v. v. 466–7)

The soothsayer's comment on the final reconciliation in *Cymbeline* comes after the descent of Jupiter in the vision scene; like so many of the climactic moments in Shakespeare's late plays, it is shaped by the court masque. This is not simply a matter of borrowing clearly recognizable elements from masque devices, but a way of using these features to allude to the ethos of the masque—an assertion that just, benevolent, and cohesive human government participates in a much larger order. The image of such government as divinely inspired music permeates masque texts in the Jacobean and Caroline period—and it endows the music heard in those entertainments with an immediate and vital significance.

In Samuel Daniel's *Vision of the Twelve Goddesses* (the first full masque of James I's reign), Iris describes Britain as 'the Land of ciuil Musick and of rest' (l. 259). The phrase, associating music with order in society, indicates succinctly the symbolic importance music assumed in the Stuart masque. Jonson often uses a similar form of expression; in *The Irish Masque* a Bard is told:

> This is that IAMES of which long since thou sung'st,
> Should end our countreyes most vnnaturall broyles;
> And if her eare, then deafned with the drum,
> Would stoupe but to the musique of his peace,
> Shee need not with the spheares change harmony.   (ll. 156–60)

'The music of his peace' is a key phrase—and it comes at the climax and turning-point of the sentence. The same phrase reappears in two later masques. The herald in *News from the New World* proclaims to the king that the masquers move 'to the musicke of your peace' (l. 314). In *Pan's Anniversary* all the bravest spirits of Arcadia discuss what rites would befit 'the Musique of his peace' (l. 68). The idea is returned to later in the masque when a shepherd encourages the masquers to dance:

> And come you prime Arcadians forth, that taught
> By P A N the rites of true societie,
> From his loud Musicke, all your manners wraught,
> And made your Common-wealth a harmonie . . . (ll.159–62)

Pan represents the king, and the masquers' dancing will express a social harmony with its source in his good government.

Sometimes the constituents of this concord are specified. In *Hymenaei*, Hymen speaks in praise of union for bringing 'eu'rie discord in true musique' (l. 102), and Reason exclaims, 'all is *peace*, and *loue* and *faith*, and *blisse*: What *harmony* like this?' (ll. 326–7). In *Love Restored*, Cupid enumerates the elements which make up the harmony the audience will see in the masquers' dancing:

> As *musique* them in forme shall put,
> So will they keep their measures true,
> And make still their proportions new,
> Till all become one *harmonie*,
> Of *honor*, and of *courtesie*,
> True *valure*, and *vrbanitie*,
> Of *confidence*, *alacritie*,
> Of *promptnesse*, and of *industrie*,
> *Habilitie*, *Realitie*.
> Nor shall those graces euer quit your Court . . . (ll. 260–9)

Civil music, the harmony of the commonwealth, 'the well-set partes of our affections and our harts',[1]—such phrases are only the most obvious expressions of a set of ideas which recur again and again in masque texts. They exist in a context where actual music could be heard as illustration or even manifestation of princely harmony. The music of the king's peace was not just a figure of speech, since the concept implies a humanist acceptance of the notion that (unheard) musical harmony informs a healthy body or a well-governed body politic. Such ideas derive from *musica speculativa*—the theories describing the ultimate position of music in the created universe transmitted from ancient Greek sources to the mainstream of Western European thought by Boethius in the early sixth century.

The most basic tenet of speculative music is that music is divided into three species, *musica mundana*, *musica humana*, and *musica instrumentalis*. *Musica mundana* is the harmony of the well-ordered motions of the universe evident in the music of the spheres. *Musica humana* characterizes a physically and mentally healthy body—a microcosmic parallel to the macrocosmic harmony of *musica mundana*. This harmony of a human body supplied a model for the body politic. It is here that the idea of the harmony of a peaceful and well-governed state (an idea that pervades masque texts) fits into the scheme of things. *Musica instrumentalis* is the music we hear; performed by singers and instrumentalists, it is governed by the rules of practical music. These three

---

[1] *Tethys Festival*, ll. 335–6.

species were understood, not as separate phenomena, but as different aspects or manifestations of a universal harmony. Normally only *musica instrumentalis*, the most inconsequential of the three, was thought capable of being heard by our imperfect human faculties.[2]

Humanist writers also placed a great deal of emphasis on the affective power of music as it was summed up in the Orpheus, Arion, and Amphion myths. Practical music, *musica instrumentalis*, could by a kind of sympathetic vibration influence the harmony of creation. The effects of music were such that, by playing in the right modes, a skilled musician could incite men to war, placate them once their anger was aroused, or cure a distempered body. We are familiar with these ideas through Shakespeare's plays. Lorenzo's warning not to trust the man 'that hath no music in himself', Ulysses' perception of the state as an instrument that needs to be kept well in tune, or the physician's use of music to treat the ailing Lear all arise from this context. One of the tidiest literary summaries of music's place in creation and its affective power is Ben Jonson's first epigram addressed to Alfonso Ferrabosco II, a poem which has obvious circumstantial links with the masque:

> To vrge, my lou'd ALPHONSO, that bold fame
>   Of building townes, and making wilde beasts tame
> Which *Musick* had; or speake her knowne effects
>   That shee remoueth cares, sadnesse eiects,
> Declineth anger, perswades clemencie,
>   Doth sweeten mirth, and heighten pietie,
> And is t'a body, often, ill inclin'd,
>   No lesse a sou'raigne cure, then to the mind;
> T'alledge, that greatest men were not asham'd
>   Of old, euen by her practise, to be fam'd;
> To say, indeed, shee were the soule of heauen,
>   That the eight spheare, no lesse, then planets seauen,
> Mou'd, by her order, And the ninth, more high,
>   Including all, were thence call'd harmonie:
> I, yet, had vtter'd nothing, on thy part,
>   When these were but the praises of the Art.
> But when I haue said, The proofes of all these bee
>   Shed in the Songs; 'tis true: but short of thee.[3]

Jonson's strategy here is to challenge received doctrine. His compliment to Ferrabosco is rooted in the recognition of an ultimate separation between the music we hear (the music Ferrabosco composed) and what we can know about (but scarcely experience)—music's place in the world order. The poem

---

[2] A full discussion of speculative music may be found in J. Hollander, *The Untuning of the Sky: Ideas of Music in English Poetry 1500–1700* (Princeton, 1961), esp. chs. 2 and 4. See also the chapter on music in J. C. Meagher, *Method and Meaning in Jonson's Masques* (Notre Dame, Ind., 1966); G. Finney, *Musical Backgrounds for English Literature: 1580–1650* (New Brunswick, NJ, 1962); and J. Hutton, 'Some English Poems in Praise of Music', *English Miscellany*, 2 (1951), 1–63.

[3] H&S, viii. 82.

contends that Ferrabosco's music is more rewarding than that described in Neoplatonic theory. Jonson's capacity to play with these ideas is itself testimony to their currency. In the masque, the relationship between these different species of music—heard and unheard—is crucial. Music is omnipresent and, as we have seen, the texts invite the audience to relate what they have heard to the ideal of social harmony. Even the absence of music (in parts of the antimasque, for instance) draws significance from these doctrines. Music both expresses and induces social integrity; it is both image and agent of social cohesion.

A direct relationship between speculative and practical music is asserted through the kind of dramatic roles given to performing musicians. Those who sang and played in the main masque were invariably characterized as figures with special insight and powers. They were portrayed in a way which gave their utterances an oracular weight. There were two principal means by which this was done; first, by representing musicians as priestly figures, and secondly by identifying them as poets. Quite often the two suggestions were combined. In *The Masque of Beauty*, Vulturnus announced that

> Hither, as to their new *Elysium*,
> The spirits of the antique *Greekes* are come,
> *Poets* and *Singe[r]s, Linus, Orpheus* all
> That haue excell'd in knowledge musicall . . .   (ll. 136–9)

The musicians who then appeared 'represented the *Shades* of the olde *Poets*, and were attir'd in a *Priest*-like habit of *Crimson*, and *Purple*, with *Laurell* gyrlonds' (l. 245 ff.). The fusion of poet, priest, and musician in this characterization has a basis in humanist attitudes to the place of poetry in human society. Since these attitudes provide a basis for so much that we shall see about the characterization of musicians in the masque, they are worth exploring further.

Humanist writers habitually insisted on the common identity of poets and musicians. Jonson glossed the lines just quoted, 'So *Terence* and the Ancients called *Poesy, Artem musicam*'. William Webbe and Thomas Campion both refer to the Terence maxim. When Campion came to state the same commonplace, he explained it by referring to *musica mundana*: 'The world is made by Simmetry and proportion, and is in that respect compared to Musick, and Musick to Poetry: for *Terence* saith, speaking of Poets, *artem qui tractant musicam*, confounding musick and Poesy together.'[4] If the link between poet and musician seemed clear, so too did that between poet and priest. It was often pointed out that the Latin word *vates* used for poet and priest implicitly recognized that poets had a prophetic and normative function in society. Sir Philip Sidney affirmed that since poets 'range, onely rayned with learned discretion, into the diuine consideration of what may be and should be', they

---

⁴ *Observations on the Art of English Poesie* (1602), in *The Works of Thomas Campion*, ed. W. R. Davis (London, 1969), 293. Webbe, *A Discourse on English Poesy* (1586) may be found in G. Smith (ed.), *Elizabethan Critical Essays*, 2 vols. (London, 1904), i. 226–302.

may therefore 'iustly be termed *Vates*'.[5] All these strands come together in George Puttenham's *Arte of English Poesie* (1598). He writes that 'Poets were the first . . . Musitiens of the world', has a chapter entitled 'How poets were the first priests; the first prophets; the first legislators and politicians in the world', and cites as his prime examples the poet-musicians Orpheus and Arion. Orpheus, he says, 'by his discreete and wholsome lessons vttered in harmonie and with melodious instruments . . . brought the rude and sauage people to a more civill and orderly life'.[6] This triple identification of poet, musician, and priest, or (to put it another way) the acceptance of the idea that musicians were poets who 'spoke' with the special authority of the *vates*, points to the centrality of music in the masque.

Some of the simplest identifications of poet and musician come in Caroline masques. In *Albion's Triumph* one group of musicians appeared as '*Orpheus, Amphion, Arion,* and three old Poets and Musicians more' (p. 77). There is, too, a chorus of Poets in Davenant's *Temple of Love*. More interesting, however, is that a double suggestion of Orphic and priest-like status was made in masque after masque. In *Love Freed from Ignorance and Folly*, the captive Love (who must solve the Sphinx's riddle to be free) complains that Ignorance

> Thinkes she doth her selfe aduance,
> If of problemes cleare, shee make
> Riddles, and the sense forsake,
> Which came gentle from the Muses,
> Till her vttring, it abuses.   (ll. 235–9)

The insight necessary to untangle the enigma comes, significantly, in a song. And the musicians who perform it are depicted as the Muses' Priests.[7]

Musicians are presented as priests in many other masques—they are Hymen's priests in *The Haddington Masque*, Jove's in *The Masque of the Inner Temple and Gray's Inn*, and Pan's in *Pan's Anniversary*. In *The Memorable Masque* the 'choice musicians of our kingdom' were 'attired like Virginian priests, by whom the sun is there adored, and therefore called the Phoebades' (p. 439). The Chorus in *Time Vindicated* is described simply as 'certaine Votaries' (l. 273), while in *Love's Triumph through Callipolis* (though not actually called priests) they 'walke about with their censers' (l. 82). *Albion's Triumph* has a chorus of 'High Priests and Sacrificers' (p. 85). In Davenant's *Temple of Love* the musicians are 'Brachmani'[8] and 'Priests of the Temple of Love', and

[5] *An Apology for Poetry* (1595), in Smith (ed.), *Elizabethan Critical Essays*, i. 159.

[6] *The Arte of English Poesie* (1589) in Smith (ed.), *Elizabethan Critical Essays*, ii. 6 and 8.

[7] The riddle in this masque, like the one in *The Masque of Blackness* (ll. 189 ff.), has at its heart the analogy between James I and the sun.

[8] In Bryskett's *Discourse of Civill Life* (London, 1606), 163, Edmund Spenser comments on the wisdom of the Brachmani: 'M. *Spenser* then said If it be true that you say, by Philosophie we must learne to know our selues, how happened it, that the Brachmani men of so great fame, as you know, in *India*, would admit none to be their schollers in Philosophy, if they had not first learned to know them selues: as if they had concluded, that such knowledge came not from Philosophie, but appertained to some other skill or science.'

in *The Triumphs of the Prince d'Amour* there were—in successive sections of the main masque—Priests of Mars, Venus, and Apollo.[9] Bulstrode Whitelocke described the musicians in *The Triumph of Peace* as being 'in the habits of heathen priests'.[10]

The text of *The Triumph of Peace* gives a more complicated account than this. It describes musicians 'like priests and sibyls, sons and daughters of Harmony, some with coronets, others with wreaths of laurel and myrtle . . .' (ll. 85ff.). Here we have something more than the representation of musicians as priests—a conflation of priests and sibyls with the sons and daughters of harmony, This intermingling of musical and priestly properties has ample precedent. In *The Somerset Masque*, the Orphic guise of the musicians is given a specifically musical slant, and they appear as 'Harmony with nine Musitians more, in long Taffata robes and caps of Tinsell, with Garlands guilt, playing and singing' (p. 272). This variation can be seen in other masques. In *Neptune's Triumph* Jonson prescribed that '*Apollo*, with *Mercury*, some *Muses* & the Goddesse *Harmony*, make the musique' (ll. 335–7).[11] The same idea reappears in *Tempe Restored* where '*Harmony* comes foorth attended by a *Chorus* of Musique' (p. 98).[12] In these cases the implications of the characterization are that the music performed in the main masque approaches harmonic perfection and that the words sung have a more than mortal authority.

Occasionally musicians were dignified in other ways: in *Hymenaei* they appeared as 'spirites of the ayre' (l. 222), and in *Oberon* there are fairy musicians. One final (if rather peripheral) example serves to illustrate how well established the convention of musicians-as-priests became. In *The Masque of Flowers* the musicians are introduced as, 'The Garden-gods, in number twelve, apparelled in long robes of green rich taffeta, caps on their heads and chaplets of flowers' (ll. 307–9). But later in the text the writer slips into referring to these Garden Gods simply as 'the Priests' (l. 350).

Attitudes to the Masque

The musician as *vates* fits easily into a view of the masque which saw it as a vehicle for projecting a social vision (or, more crudely, for propaganda). Jonson's clearest statement of his view of the masque's didactic potential comes in a note entitled 'To Make the Spectators vnderstanders' which prefaces the text of *Love's Triumph through Callipolis*:

---

[9] In the pastoral *Florimène* (1635), the musicians are Priests of Dian with an Arch Flamine and Sacrificers; see S. Orgel, 'Florimène and the Ante-Masques', *RD* 4 (1971), 135–53.

[10] GB-Lbl, Add. MS 53726, fo. 91.

[11] In the 1625 revision of this masque as *The Fortunate Isles* this was reduced to 'APOLLO with *Harmony*, and the spirits of *Musique*' (ll. 445–6).

[12] Yet another group of musicians in this masque are depicted as 'the eight spheres' (p. 99). So tangible a representation of the ineffable subverts rather than supports the concept *musica mundana*—but this will be taken up in Ch. 5.

. . . all Repræsentations, especially those of this nature in court, publique Spectacles, eyther haue bene, or ought to be the mirrors of mans life, whose ends, for the excellence of their exhibiters (as being the donatiues, of great Princes, to their people) ought alwayes to carry a mixture of profit, with them, no lesse then delight . . .   (ll. 1–7)

The Horatian ideal of combining instruction with pleasure was, for Jonson as for other Renaissance writers, an essential characteristic of all poetry.[13] We may deduce that the masque, like poetry, could offer 'to mankinde a certaine rule, and Patterne of living well, and happily, disposing us to all Civill offices of Society'.[14] But the masque had a more specialized social function in that it emphasized the role of the king, who, by preserving order and dispensing wisdom and justice, safeguarded the good society. Such a view inevitably made the writer of the text a central, controlling, figure in the invention of the masque.

Occasionally, other masque writers went out of their way to make it clear that they did not accept Jonson's priorities. In *Tethys Festival*, Samuel Daniel declared that 'in these things wherein the onely life consists in shew; the arte and inuention of the Architect giues the greatest grace, and is of most importance: ours, the least part and of least note in the time of the performance thereof . . .' (Preface, ll. 74–8). Daniel was the first of the masque writers to accept Inigo Jones as the senior partner in a working relationship. Inigo Jones himself provided the most pithy statement of the anti-Jonsonian position in *Tempe Restored*, where he declared that 'indeed these showes are nothing else, but pictures with Light and Motion' (p. 94).

It might be thought that such a view would produce something very different from the morally serious Jonsonian masque. But there was a stronger, non–aesthetic principle which ensured at least a superficial similarity: masques, as Lysippus put it in Beaumont and Fletcher's *Maid's Tragedy*,

> . . . must commend their king, and speake in praise
> Of the assembly, blesse the Bride and Bridegroom
> In person of some god; they're tied to rules
> Of flatterie.   (i. i. 8)

No writer responding to a commission from the court for a masque could afford to move too far away from the Jonsonian model, so perfectly adapted to the representation of king and court as the embodiment of wisdom, honour, and virtue. In the final analysis, skilful flattery and normative eulogy may be indistinguishable.

In the performance of a Jonsonian masque the court was first presented with and then drawn into a vision of an exemplary human society. Jonson habitually suggested that a kind of miracle occurred. Often this was achieved

---

[13] See Horace, *Ars poetica* 343, 'Omne tulit punctum qui miscuit utile dulci.'
[14] Jonson, *Discoveries*, ll. 2386–8, in H&S, viii. 636.

simply by his use of prepositions to link the different elements on the title-page: 'THE GOLDEN AGE RESTOR'D In a Maske at Court, 1615, by the Lords, and Gentlemen, the Kings seruants'.[15] That rather equivocal phrasing is quite typical. Often it seems that some ellipsis is hinted at: 'LOVE [was] RESTORED, In a Masque at Court, by Gentlemen the KINGS *Seruants*', or 'MERCVRIE [was] VINDICATED FROM THE ALCHEMISTS AT COURT, By Gentlemen the Kings Seruants'.

This meeting of real and ideal was provided for by the carefully contrived links between the event to be celebrated and the device of the masque. When, for example, Prince Charles returned from his expedition to Spain, the court prepared to celebrate *Neptune's Triumph for the Return of Albion*.[16] In more distracted times, this congruity between invention and reality became more a matter of polemics and hysterical assertion, so that when Charles I was having to cope with fierce criticism of his rule, and in particular with an attack upon his indulgence in masques, he responded by ordering the inns of court to produce the most lavish masque of all, defiantly entitled *The Triumph of Peace*. By 1640 such a response was scarcely possible, and the nation's troubles are openly acknowledged even in the main masque of *Salmacida Spolia*:

> O who but he, could thus endure
> To live, and governe in a sulleine age,
> When it is harder far to cure
> The Peoples folly than resist their rage?   (ll. 176–9)[17]

In a well-known passage in the prefatory section of *Hymenaei*, Jonson set forth his view of the ideal relationship between a masque device ('more remou'd mysteries') and the actual circumstances of its performance ('present occasions'):

This it is hath made the most royall *Princes*, and greatest *persons* (who are commonly the *personaters* of these *actions*) not onely studious of riches, and magnificence in the outward celebration, or shew; (which rightly becomes them) but curious after the most high, and heartie *inuentions*, to furnish the inward parts: (and those grounded vpon *antiquitie*, and solide learnings) which, though their *voyce* be taught to sound to present occasions, their *sense*, or doth, or should always lay hold on more remou'd *mysteries*.   (ll. 10–19)

A similar resolve to make the masque begin from—but then transcend—the circumstances which occasioned it can be seen in George Chapman's preface to *The Memorable Masque of the Middle Temple and Lincoln's Inn*: 'all these courtly, and honoring inuentions (hauing Poesie, and Oration in them, and a

[15] Title-page in the 1616 Folio.

[16] There are a number of detailed studies of the relationship between 'present occasions' and 'more removed mysteries'. See, for example, the articles by Leah Marcus listed in the Bibliography, and the chapter on masques in D. Lindley, *Thomas Campion* (Leiden, 1986).

[17] C. V. Wedgwood, in 'The Last Masque', *Truth and Opinion* (London, 1960), 143–55, sets out to recreate imaginatively the atmosphere of mixed political tension and reckless folly in which *Salmacida Spolia* took place.

fountaine, to be exprest, from whence their Riuers flow) should expressiuely-arise out of the places, and persons for and by whome they are presented; without which limits, they are luxurious and vaine'.[18] The implications of those statements could be summarized in two propositions: that the masque is a potentially didactic form, and that each masque, being linked to a unique occasion, has no enduring dramatic life. Of those two propositions, the former may have been, as we have seen, a matter of some dispute, while the latter represents a generally held point of view in the early seventeenth century.

To begin with, no court masque was ever intended to have a life beyond the situation which formed it. The care with which 'more remou'd mysteries' were related to 'present occasions' made a series of performances or revivals of masque productiotions impossible and pointless. (Moreover, courtier-masquers—unlike a company of actors—would not be available for more than one or two performances.) There were, in fact, a few masques which did receive more than one performance. Between 1615 and 1620 the Christmas season masques at court tended to be given two performances—though this started in an unplanned way with *The Golden Age Restored* being repeated two nights after the first performance simply because 'it was so well liked and applauded'.[19] There are several examples of Inns of Court masques which, having been performed 'at home', were taken to Whitehall a few days later. In these cases, the dates of the two performances were so close that no gap could open up between the device of the masque and the circumstances of its presentation. *The Temple of Love* received four performances in 1635, but Martin Butler has argued that the main reason for this was Queen Henrietta Maria's conviction that this entertainment did have an urgent message for the court just at that time.[20] These repetitions are all exceptions which prove the rule.

It is largely because the masque was so transient that it could be used as an image of vanity. The following poem, for example, responds cynically to the masque's concern with hierarchy:

> Life is a Maske disguis'd & puft with pleasures,
> Whose ground is but a common Cinque-pace.
> The meaner sort doe onely tread the measures,
> High lofty trickes note those of higher place.[21]

In the aftermath of the wave of criticism aroused by the extravagance of the 1611 masques (*Oberon* and *Love Freed from Ignorance and Folly*), Jonson devised an antimasque for *Love Restored* which tackled the objections directly (if only

[18] From the Description preceding the masque text, ll. 185–9.
[19] John Chamberlain, quoted H&S, x. 553.
[20] M. Butler, *Theatre and Crisis 1632–42* (Cambridge, 1984), 29–30.
[21] GB-Ob, MS Rawl. poet. 26, fo. 13. Decorum is upset here. It is those of higher place who might be expected to dance the measures. The meaner sort might attempt high lofty tricks (see below, pp. 114–16). The conceits in this poem have not been rigorously worked out; the cinque-pace or galliard, for example, is not built on a ground.

by trying to discredit the motives of those voicing them). It is the miserly
Plutus, god of money, who complains about the expense and, in doing
so, emphasizes the masque's ephemeral character: 'I tell thee, I will haue no
more masquing; I will not buy a false, and fleeting delight so deare: The
merry madnesse of one hower shall not cost me the repentance of an age . . .'
(ll. 34–6).

Whatever their point of view, all commentators acknowledged the un-
deniable fact of the masque's transience. Hence the masque on Twelfth
Night would come and go, and for those few hours something quite remarkable might take place in the masquing hall, but after that it became, to use
Campion's words, like a 'golden dream', quite irretrievable. At the end of
Hymenaei Jonson voiced his regret that this was so: 'Onely the enuie was, that
it lasted not still, or (now it is past) cannot by imagination, much lesse
description, be recouered to a part of that *spirit* it had in the gliding by' (ll.
576–9). The realization that the masque enjoyed only a fleeting existence was
beautifully expressed by Samuel Daniel in one of the songs for *Tethys Festival*:

> Are they shadowes that we see?
> And can shadowes pleasure giue?
> Pleasures onely shadowes bee
> Cast by bodies we conceiue,
> And are made the thinges we deeme,
> In those figures which they seem.
> But these pleasures vanish fast,
> Which by shadowes are exprest:
> Pleasures are not, if they last,
> In their passing, is their best.
> Glory is most bright and gay
> In a flash, and so away.
> Feed apace then greedy eyes
> On the wonder you behold.
> Take it sodaine as it flies
> Though you take it not to hold:
> When your eyes haue done their part,
> Thought must length it in the hart.   (ll. 341–58)

Davenant ended his text of *The Triumphs of the Prince d'Amour* with yet
another statement of the masque's transience: 'Thus, as all Pleasures and
Triumphs are full of haste, and aptest to decay, this had an end, yet may live
mention'd a while if the envie of such as were absent do not rebuke the
courteous memory of those who vouchsaf'd to enjoy it.' This was clearly
regarded as a 1636 event not capable of revival at another time. Bulstrode
Whitelocke concludes his reminiscences about *The Triumph of Peace* with what
seems by now an almost inevitable reference to its transience. For the puritan
Whitelocke, though, it becomes an expression of ambivalence. This whole
episode which had given him an immense amount of enjoyment was like all

the pleasures of this world: 'Thus was this earthly Pomp and Glory, if not Vanity, soon past over and gone, as if it had never been.'[22]

Prospero's comments about the 'insubstantial pageant' he conjures up for Ferdinand and Miranda are the most evocative (and, naturally, the best known) expression of ideas which are truisms about the masque's impermanence:

> Our Reuels now are ended. These our actors,
> (As I foretold you) were all Spirits, and
> Are melted into Ayre, into thin Ayre,
> And like the baselesse fabricke of this vision
> The Clowd-capt Towres, the gorgeous Pallaces,
> The solemne Temples, the great Globe it selfe,
> Yea, all which it inherit, shall dissolue,
> And like this insubstantiall Pageant faded
> Leaue not a racke behinde: we are such stuffe
> As dreames are made on; and our little life
> Is rounded with a sleepe . . .   (*The Tempest*, IV. i. 148–58)

The individual elements of Prospero's vision—the towers, palaces, and especially the temples—are all familiar masque settings, and in their insubstantiality they reflect not only the impermanence of theatrical props but the dream-like quality of the whole experience. The masque, more than any other dramatic form, is a perfect image for the transience of human endeavour.

The Nature of Masque Texts

In *The Characters of Two Royall Masques* (1608) Jonson justifed the printing of masque texts as an attempt to prevent the imaginative element from following the spectacular show into oblivion:

The honor, and splendor of these *spectacles* was such in the performance, as could those houres haue lasted, this of mine, now, had been a most vnprofitable worke. But (when it is the fate, euen of the greatest, and most absolute births, to need, and borrow a life of posteritie) little had beene done to the studie of *magnificence* in these, if presently with the rage of the people, who (as a part of greatnesse) are priuiledged by custome, to deface their *carkasses*, the *spirits* had also perished. In dutie, therefore, to that *Maiestie*, who gaue them their authoritie, and grace . . . I adde this later hand, to redeeme them as well from Ignorance, as Enuie, two common euills, the one of *censure*, the other of *obliuion*.   (ll. 1–14)

The texts themselves characteristically acknowledge the masque's transience in their use of the past tense to describe the action. They are essentially reports of past events. The title-page and running-titles of both Campion's *Lord Hay's Masque* and his *Somerset Masque* read simply *The Description of a Maske*; such a title could accurately be applied to the texts of most Stuart court

---

[22] 'Annales', GB-Lbl, Add. MS 53726, fo. 91.

masques. They are essentially authorial accounts of performances. In other words, they are not scripts. Since they were not printed with revived productions in mind, we find in them (quite lengthy) descriptions of action (rather than stage *directions*). It is, of course, true that even play texts in this period were not printed to make the work available to acting companies. Yet in both genesis and their final format play texts do tend to be more like prescriptions for (repeatable) performances than—as with masque texts— descriptions of unique events.[23]

It is interesting to consider just to what extent these texts are what they claim to be—records of actual presentations. The fact that masque texts are authorial reports is not quite the advantage it might seem in seeking to establish what actually happened musically at a performance. Different authors may have had different priorities in preparing a text for publication, and they showed varying degrees of interest in the musical aspects of the production. As might be expected, Campion is the writer who (especially in his first masque text) is most eager to detail the nature and disposition of musical resources. His account of *The Lord Hay's Masque* seems all the more reliable for his willingness to acknowledge imperfections (even if only in a marginal gloss). There were, he tells us, problems with the machinery: 'Either by the simplicity, negligence, or conspiracy of the painter, the passing away of the trees was somewhat hazarded; the patterne of them the same day having bene showne with much admiration, and the 9 trees beeing left unsett together even to the same night' (p. 222 n.). In *The Somerset Masque*, Campion again complained that the visual elements fell short of what had been intended. This time his anger is directed at Constantine de Servi:

The work-manship whereof was vndertaken by M. *Constantine* an Italian, Architect to our late Prince *Henry*: but he, being too much of him selfe, and no way to be drawne to impart his intentions, fayled so farre in the assurance he gaue, that the mayne inuention, even at the last cast, was of force drawne into a farre narrower compasse then was from the beginning intended . . . (p. 268)

Clearly these are not idealized accounts (unlike so many other quasi-official descriptions of court entertainments). Yet Campion's complaints about the visual side of the masques (outside his control) does not guarantee objectivity in his reporting on the success of the music (where his own reputation was at stake).

There are a few details reported in Beaumont's text of *The Masque of the Inner Temple and Gray's Inn* which make it clear that it is a real account of the performance. Some of this has a direct bearing on the music: 'The perpetual laughter and applause was above the music . . . It pleased his Majesty to call for it again at the end, as he did likewise for the first anti-masque, but one of the Statues by that time was undressed' (ll. 241–8). This does give us a real insight into the conditions under which these performances took place. No other text

---

[23] On the interest in *reading* play texts, see Butler, *Theatre and Crisis*, 105–6.

acknowledges the problems of audibility in relation to the music, yet it would be surprising if *The Masque of the Inner Temple and Gray's Inn* were a special case. A disgruntled account of the Merchant Taylors' entertainment for James I in 1607 complained that not only did the musicians charge too much for their services but that they could not be heard:

At the upper end of the Hall there was set a chair of Estate, where his Majesty sat and viewed the Hall; and a very proper child, well spoken, being clothed like an Angel of gladness, with a taper of frankincense burning in his hand, delivered a short Speech containing 18 verses, devised by Mr. Ben Jonson, which pleased his Majesty marvelously well; and upon either side of the Hall, in the windows near the upper end, were galleries or seats, made for music, in either of which were seven singular choice musicians playing on their lutes, and in the ship, which did hang aloft in the Hall, three rare men, and very skilful who song to his Majesty; and over the King, sonnetts and loude musique, wherein it is to be remembered, that the multitude and noyse was so great, that the lutes nor songs could hardly be heard or understood . . .[24]

This entertainment was clearly less structured than a masque and it is likely that this encouraged informal behaviour in the audience, but even so this report reminds us that the opulent musical resources in the masque might at times have been needed for sheer audibility.

Early on in his masque-writing career Jonson was occasionally prepared to admit deficiencies in the production. Like Campion, he was unhappy with the work of the painters for the *Masque of Beauty*, but he insisted that their bad workmanship 'must not bee imputed a crime either to the inuention, or designe' (ll. 275–6). This is a vital qualification. It would be true to say that Jonson was generally more concerned with communicating the invention than he was with providing an accurate picture of what took place. His marginal glosses are not (like Campion's) used to note technical hitches; rather he uses them to cite authorities for symbolic details in his device. In attempting to redeem his masques from censure and oblivion, he seems to have been concerned above all to preserve the integrity of the imaginative concept rather than to report on the vicissitudes of particular productions. What he reveals about the music is less likely to be there 'for the record' than for what it contributes to the dramatic device.

On two occasions Jonson does make a distinction between what he wants us to read in the text—as a properly shaped literary conception—and what actually happened in performance. He tells us that only one stanza of the long epithalamion which concludes *Hymenaei* was actually sung in the masque. Of the similar epithalamion at the end of *The Haddington Masque* he writes: 'Here, the musicians attir'd in yellow, with wreathes of *marioram*, and veiles, like H Y M E N S *priests*, sung the first staffe of the following *Epithalamion*: which,

---

[24] From the records of the Merchant Taylors' Company; quoted J. Nichols (ed.), *The Progresses, Processions, and Magnificent Festivities of King James the First*, 4 vols. (London, 1828), ii. 137–8.

because it was sung in pieces, betweene the *daunces*, shew'd to be so many seuerall *songs*; but was made to be read an intire *Poeme*' (ll. 338–42). Like most masque texts, this is an authorial report printed after the performance.

Not all published masques are like this, however. There is a small but important group of texts which were clearly prepared *before* the performances. The function of these appears to have been analogous to so many early opera libretti: little books available during the performance to enable the audience to follow better what was happening. Obviously in these the invention is all, and there can be no question of reporting what actually happened.

Every Jonson masque appears in his *Works*. Masques up to *Mercury Vindicated* were printed in the first Folio of 1616 and the rest appeared in the later 1640 Folio (see Table 1.1). Where there is also an earlier copy of a Jonson masque than the Folio edition, it often seems that the copy was prepared for the night of the performance itself. This was certainly the case with the surviving manuscript for *The Masque of Blackness* which was given to the Queen for the performance on 6 January 1605. As one might expect, what happens on stage is described in this manuscript in the present tense, while the Quarto printed after the event and the Folio both use the past tense to describe action, scenes, and costumes.[25] The amount of actual description is much less in the queen's manuscript than in the printed text, where Jonson was attempting to supply what the eye could no longer see. And Jonson's contemporaries did treat this text as a *report*. Dudley Carleton wrote to Chamberlain the day after the performance of *The Masque of Blackness* to let him know what it was like. His letter begins 'The maske at night requires much labor to be well described; but there is a pamflet in press wch will saue me that paynes.'[26] The manuscript of *Pleasure Reconciled to Virtue* is a beautifully neat copy by Ralph Crane which, like the manuscript of *The Masque of Blackness*, has all the marks of being a presentation copy prepared for the night of the masque; it too uses the present tense.

Some quarto editions printed in the year of the masque's performance seem designed to fulfil the same kind of function as these manuscripts. They are distinguished by their use of the present tense in descriptive passages, by the absence of an imprint on the title-page, and by the lack of any reference acknowledging the work of Jonson, Jones, or any other person whose imagination and skill contributed to the entertainment.[27] There are five quartos which fall into this category, and for two of them at least, there is positive evidence that they were prepared in advance of the performance. The title-page of *Neptune's Triumph* claims that it was 'celebrated in a Masque at the

---

[25] The manuscript of *The Masque of Queens* is a holograph prepared for Prince Henry after the performance and uses the past tense throughout. Detailed descriptions of these manuscripts and early printed texts may be found in the textual notes which precede the edition of each masque in H&S, vii.

[26] GB-Lpro, SP 14 12 6; quoted in H&S, x. 449. What the 'little pamphlet' was is not clear; Jonson did not print the text of this masque until *The Characters of two Royall Masques* (1608).

[27] But see below (p. 36) for the *Masque of Augurs*.

TABLE I.I. *Extant texts for Jonson's masques*

Q = quarto edition printed in the same year as the masque
F = either 1616 or 1640 Folio of Jonson's *Works*
[F] = Folio text set from the quarto text (according to Herford and Simpson)
12° = duodecimo edition
Quartos marked with an asterisk (*) have neither imprint, nor any reference on their title-pages to Ben Jonson, Inigo Jones, or any other inventor.
Editions italicized (e.g. *F*) have descriptive sections in the present tense.

1605	*Masque of Blackness*	Q	F	MS
1606	*Hymenaei*	Q	F	
1608	*Masque of Beauty*	Q	F	
	Haddington Masque	Q	F	
1609	*Masque of Queens*	Q	F	MS
1611	*Oberon*		F	
	Love Freed		F	
1612	*Love Restored*		F[a]	
1613	*Irish Masque*		F[b]	
1615	*Golden Age Restored*		F	
1616	*Christmas his Masque*		F	MS[c]
	Mercury Vindicated (first Folio printed)		F[d]	
1617	*Lovers Made Men*	*Q	F	
	Vision of Delight		F	
1618	*Pleasure Reconciled*		F	MS
	For Wales		F[d]	
1620	*News from the New World*		F	
	Pan's Anniversary		F	
1621	*Gypsies Metamorphosed*[e]	12° (1640)	F	MSS
1622	*Masque of Augurs*	*Q	F	
1623	*Time Vindicated*	*Q	F	
1624	*Neptune's Triumph*	*Q	[F]	
1625	*The Fortunate Isles*	*Q	[F]	
1630	*Chloridia*	*Q[f]	F	
1631	*Love's Triumph*	Q	[F]	
1640	(second Folio printed)			

[a] Has no description of action, but one (play-like) stage-direction (ll. 207–8).
[b] Changes to present tense at l. 173.
[c] Songs and speeches only.
[d] Vacillates between past and present tenses in descriptive sections.
[e] The textual situation for *The Gypsies Metamorphosed* is especially complicated; see H&S, vii. 541 ff. and W. W. Greg, *Jonson's Masque of Gipsies in the Burley, Belvoir and Windsor Versions* (London, 1952).
[f] Author not acknowledged on title-page.

Court on Twelfth Night 1623', whereas the actual performance was deferred because of squabbles amongst the ambassadors who might have been invited. The Quarto for *The Fortunate Isles* prepared for the following year is more cautious about the date, and claims only that the masque was 'disign'd for the

Court, on the Twelfth Night 1624' (i.e. 1625 NS) when, in fact, it took place. Obviously both of these must have been printed before the projected date of performance. Sir John Ashburnham wrote to Elizabeth of Bohemia just four days after the performance of *Chloridia* enclosing a copy of the text. The timing—and the format of the quarto—suggest that this too must have been available at the performance.

We need to be very conscious of the nature of these various types of text in assessing the evidence they provide about music. With Jonson and, to a less marked extent, with other writers almost every musical reference is there to make a literary point; it is this which may account for its inclusion in the text (where other aspects of the music are ignored). Masque texts range between being literary artefacts and reports of events at court. While most have elements of both types, the particular blend varies from text to text.

There are other kinds of documentary sources, of course. Observer's reports, however, vary in their usefulness depending on the particular writer's interests. Some are interested in the masque only as an occasion for ambassadorial intrigue, while others have positions to defend which may well restrict the detail they report. Howes, in his continuation of Stow's *Chronicle*, for example, seems anxious to give a generally favourable picture of everything that went on under the auspices of the court, and his comments about music in the masques are vague and uncritical. (Howes saw *Oberon* as a gratuitous combination of 'excellent scenes, ingenious speeches, rare songs, and a great varietie of most delicate music'.)[28]

While the transience of masque performances prompted (or was used to justify) the printing of masque texts, there was unfortunately no corresponding impulse to preserve the music. This is perhaps surprising in view of the fact that on the Continent the music for at least a few notable court entertainments was published for exactly the same reasons as masque texts—to provide a record of an occasion which had been a splendid demonstration of courtly magnificence and sophistication. The published accounts of the *Balet comique de la Royne* (1581) and the *Balet de la Délivrance de Renaud* (1617) include vocal music. In Italy a set of partbooks for the music of the 1589 Florentine intermedii was published.[29] Caccini's music for *Il Rapimento di Cefalo* ('rappresentato nello sposalizio della Cristianissima Maria Medici Regina di Francia, e di Nauarra') was appended to *Le Nuove Musiche* (1601) and both he and Peri published their scores for *Euridice*.[30] The best-known case of this kind is the 1607 score for Monteverdi's *Orfeo* (where the list of instruments may be read as a statement about the magnificence of the Mantuan court, rather than a list of requirements for future users).

---

[28] Quoted by Nichols, *Progresses of James I*, ii. 375.

[29] *Intermedii et concerti, fatti per la commedia rappresentata in Firenze, nelle nozze del Serenissimo Don Ferdinando Medici, e Madama Christiana di Lorena, Gran Duchi di Toscana* (Venice, 1591).

[30] *Le Nuove Musiche*, 19 ff.; the *Euridice* scores were both published in 1600.

Musical Sources for the Jacobean Masque

The survival of masque music was mostly a matter of chance. Rarely was it preserved *because* it was masque music. There are three quarto editions of masque texts which stand out as exceptions to this: the beautifully printed editions of Campion's *Lord Hay's Masque* (1607) and his *Somerset Masque* (1613), and some copies of *The Masque of Flowers* (1614). But in these cases the choice of songs and the way in which they were printed demonstrate that any lasting appeal of masque music was seen to depend on its adaptability. The justification for setting the music down seems to have been not so much to provide a musical record which would complement the literary one, as to supply a few pieces for amateur diversion. Of all the songs performed in *The Masque of Flowers* it is not any of the five which were dignified enough to warrant the title of 'Cantus' in the text which were printed, but one which is in a popular style, the 'Catch/Freeman's song' from the section of the masque described as 'The Antic-Masque of the Song'.

Five songs were printed at the back of *The Lord Hay's Masque*. A note following them, however, makes it clear that they have been adapted for amateur enjoyment: 'These Songes were vsed in the Maske, whereof the first two Ayres were made by M. *Campion*, the third and last by M. *Lupo*, the fourth by M. *Tho. Giles*, and though the last three Ayres were deuised onely for dauncing, yet they are here set forth with words that they may be sung to the Lute or Violl' (p. 230). In other words, only the first two bear much resemblance to their original form. The others were not songs at all, but dance tunes which have now been given words. These added texts celebrate the joy of a kingdom whose ruler ensures the peace which makes such festivities possible:

> Shewes & nightly reuels, signes of ioy and peace,
> Fill royall Britaines court while cruell warre farre off doth rage,
>   for euer hence exiled . . .   (p. 229)[31]

But despite their masque-like theme, the expressed intention of the words is to present the dance tunes in a form which would make them suitable for use in contexts unconnected with the masque itself.

The songs printed with the *Somerset Masque* are advertised in the text in a very similar fashion: 'AYRES, made by seuerall Authors: And Sung in the

---

[31] Some years later, Thomas Carew also expressed the association of good and peaceful government with revelry:

> Let us that in myrtle bowers sit
> Under secure shades, use the benefit
> Of peace and plenty, which the blessed hand
> Of our good King, gives this obdurate land;
> Let us of Revels sing . . .

'An Elegy on the Death of the King of Sweden' (1632), in *The Poems of Thomas Carew*, ed. R. Dunlap (Oxford, 1949), 75, ll. 45–9.

Maske at the Marriage of the Right Honourable ROBERT, Earle of *Somerset*, and the Right Noble and Lady FRANCES HOWARD. Set forth for the lute and Base Violl, and may be exprest by a single voyce, to eyther of those instruments' (p. 277). One of these songs ('Bring away this Sacred Tree') is prefaced in the text by the words, 'Eternitie Singes Alone' and was, according to a note with the music, 'made and exprest by Mr. *Nicholas Laneir*'. The remaining three songs carry the inscription 'composed by Mr. *Coprario* and sung by Mr. *Iohn Allen* and Mr. *Laneir*'. For two of them, there is nothing in the text to indicate that they were not sung as solos (as the rubric just quoted implies), but the remaining song, 'While dancing rests', appears to have undergone quite extensive modification in order to present it in this form. If the text itself is correct, then this was a song 'of three partes, with a Chorus of fiue partes'. Moreover, the words themselves indicate that each stanza finished with a musical echo effect. The setting printed at the back of the text, however, is a solo ayre without provision for either chorus or echo. No settings were printed for the other songs in this masque, all of which required several voices; it seems that they may have been left out simply because they were not so readily adaptable for a single voice with lute accompaniment. (Similarly, the only songs not extant for *The Masque of Beauty* are those which, according to the text, required more than one voice.)

The printed text of *The Somerset Masque* provides a further example of the fortuitous survival of masque music. The beautiful song from *The Lords' Masque*, 'Woo her and win her', was printed with these other songs for apparently no better reason than to complete a gathering in the printed book. It is introduced by a note saying 'Song, made by *Th. Campion*, and sung in the Lords Maske at the *Count Palatines* Marriage, we haue here added, to fill vp these emptie Pages' (Pl. 1).

Campion does seem to have been one of the few people interested in seeing masque songs in print. He may have had a hand in the publication of *The Ayres that were Sung and Played at Brougham Castle in Westmerland in the King's Entertainment* (1618)—the only volume of songs ever devoted to music from such an entertainment. The music is by George Mason and John Earsden but Campion was called upon as someone with extensive masque experience to write the text and, it seems, to direct the entertainment.[32]

Buried amongst the treasures in Dowland's four published books of ayres are a handful of songs which seem to have originated in masques or similar entertainments.[33] Most are earlier than 1603, but there are three masque songs

[32] For details of Campion's involvement see R. T. Spence, 'A Royal Progress in the North', *Northern History*, 27 (1991), 59 *et passim*; and I. Spink, 'Campion's Entertainment at Brougham Castle, 1617', *Music in English Renaissance Drama*, ed. J. H. Long (Lexington, Ky., 1968), 57–74. The entertainment is discussed below, pp. 269–72.

[33] See D. Poulton, *Dowland* (2nd edn.; London, 1982), 267, 272, 276, and 309. It seems unlikely, however, that 'Come yee heavy states of night'—no. 14 in *The Second Book of Songs or Ayres* (1600)—could have been a masque song, as Poulton suggests; it may have come from a play. No. 22 in the same volume, 'Humour what mak'st thou here', and no. 3 of *The Third and Last Book of Songs or Ayres* (1603), 'Behold

in *The Pilgrimes Solace* (1612). Their exact provenance is unknown, but it seems possible that they were written for the wedding celebrations of Lord Howard de Walden, which were to have taken place in January 1611 (but were postponed until March in the following year).[34] The words of both 'Welcome black night' and 'Cease these false sports' (labelled as the first and second parts of a song pair) identify them as masque epithalamia. 'Cease these false Sports', for example, contains the stanza:

> Good night, yet virgin Bride,
> But looke ere day be spide,
> You change that fruitlesse name,
> Least you your sex defame,
> Fear not *Hymens* peaceful war,
> You'le conquer though you subdued are . . .

The similarity to Jonson's 'Why stays the Bridegroom' from *The Haddington Masque* is striking:

> Good-night, whilst yet we may
> Good-night, to you a *virgin*, say:
> To morrow, rise the same
> Your *mother* is, and vse a *nobler* name.
> Speed well in HYMEN's warre,
> That, what you are,
> By your perfection, wee
> And all may see.   (ll. 417–24)

The third song in the group, 'Up Merry Mates', is also a recognizable masque type, combining a nautical theme with an exhortation to sing and dance:

> Vp merry mates, to *Neptunes* prayse,
> Your voices high aduance:
> The watrie nymphs shall dance,
> And *Eolus* shall whistle to your layes . . .

The words, and indeed the style of the setting for these opening few lines, invite comparison with Coprario's lively sailors' song 'Come ashore, come merry mates', which was heard in 1614 at the end of *The Somerset Masque*. Apart from some of the rather undistinguished Brougham Castle *Ayres*, these Dowland songs are the only surviving settings from the Jacobean period which include solo and choral sections. Yet it is clear from masque texts that such settings must have been a feature of virtually every production.

The most extensive printed collection of vocal music for the Jacobean masque is Alfonso Ferrabosco II's *Ayres* of 1609, which includes amongst its

a wonder here', almost certainly do originate in a masque or courtly entertainment. E. Doughtie, *Lyrics from English Airs 1596–1622* (Cambridge, Mass., 1970), 513, suggests that this last song could have come from 'A deuice made by the Earle of Essex for the entertainment of the Queene'.

[34] See Poulton, *Dowland*, 310.

twenty-five songs eight from masques by Jonson and three other songs from an unidentified courtly entertainment.[35] The volume arises out of the milieu of the courtly masque: there are commendatory verses by Jonson (the epigram quoted above) and Campion, and it is dedicated to his pupil Prince Henry, for whom, in the same year, Jonson had prepared ('according to yo⟨r⟩ gracious command, and a desire borne out of iudgment')[36] a holograph copy of his *Masque of Queens*.[37]

Ferrabosco's songs do not appear to have undergone the rearranging that was evident in those printed with Campion's masque. In every case, the direction in the text that a particular song was sung by a soprano or tenor corresponds with the clef used in the music. The only song which stands out in this respect is 'Why stays the bridegroom to invade her' from *The Haddington Masque* (1608). This is, in fact, one stanza of the seven-stanza Epithalamion mentioned above. Jonson tells us that the song was 'varied with voyces, onely keeping the same *Chorus*' (ll. 345–6). The refrain 'Shine HESPERVS, Shine forth, thou wished *starre*' which ends each stanza (and was presumably sung by the Chorus Jonson refers to) is simply left out. Hence, although there is none of the adaptation of 'full' songs into solo ayres which characterized the published songs from Campion's masques, the same principle still applies. The only masque music by Ferrabosco which survives are solo ayres suitable for domestic use; anything involving larger resources has disappeared.

Another way in which masque songs were given a life after the revels was through the provision of new sets of words which freed them from the particularity of a unique masque occasion. Campion's song from *The Lord Hay's Masque*, 'Move now with measured sound', uses a melody which Campion later published in *Two Bookes of Ayres* (c.1613) with a completely different set of words ('The peaceful western wind'). Both poems have (in all but one stanza) a relaxed and joyous tone, and they fit equally well with Campion's graceful melody. There is even a link between the two lyrics, since one celebrates the new life which the western wind brings in the spring, while the other instigates the dancing of golden trees in the presence of Zephyrus. Despite this possible allusion from one lyric to the other, the contrast between the two poems is illuminating. The masque song is a public epithalamion:

> Yet neerer *Phoebus* throne
>   Mete on your winding waies,
> Your Brydall mirth make knowne
>   In your high-graced *Hayes*.
> Let Hymen lead your sliding rounds, & guide them with his light,
> While we do Io Hymen sing in honour of this night,

---

[35] Songs 12–14 ('Sing we then heroic grace', 'Sing the riches of his skill', and 'Sing the nobless of his race') were clearly intended to be sung continuously. In the British Library copy of the *Ayres* a note reading 'A Comp[limen]t to ye Prince' is written above Song 12.

[36] *The Masque of Queens*, ll. 34–5.   [37] On Prince Henry's interest in masques, see below p. 314.

Ioyne three by three, for so the night by triple spel decrees,
Now to release *Apollos* knights from these enchanted trees.   (p. 221)

The songbook lyric, on the other hand, is quite personal, especially in the last stanza where the singer complains that he stands outside the happy and festive mood of his surroundings:

> If all things life present,
>   Why die my comforts then?
>   Why suffers my content?
>   Am I the worst of men?
> O, beautie, be not thou accus'd
>   Too iustly in this case:
> Vnkindly if true loue be vs'd,
>   'Twill yeeld thee little grace.   (p. 100)[38]

This reversal at the end of the poem is a typical Campion device, but it is particularly interesting here since it points up the contrast between the impersonal celebratory nature of the masque version (which could not very well survive outside the masque context) and the intimate and personal vein of the ayre published later (in a more universally viable form). The same situation exists for another of the songs from a Campion masque, 'Come away, bring thy golden theft' from *The Lords' Masque*, which is so similar metrically to 'Come away, arm'd with loves delights' (in the *Second Book of Ayres*) that they must have shared the same setting. Once again, the words for the masque song are too closely related to the masque device to make much sense in another context:

> Come away; bring thy golden theft,
>   Bring, bright *Prometheus*, all thy lights;
> Thy fires from Heau'n bereft
>   Shew now to humane sights.
> Come quickly, come: thy stars to our stars straight present,
> For pleasure being too much defer'd, loseth her best content.   (p. 252)

The version in the *Second Book of Ayres* (published about the same time as the masque) reapplies phrases like 'come quickly, come' to a self-sufficient conceit about love's transitoriness:

> Come away, arm'd with loues delights,
>   The sprite full graces bring with thee,
> When loues longing fights,
>   They must the sticklers be.
> Come quickly, come, the promis'd houre is wel-nye spent
> And pleasure being too much deferr'd looseth her best content.   (p. 108)[39]

---

[38] The difference in the form of this stanza from that of the masque song is explained by the fact that only the first half of the setting is repeated in 'The peaceful western wind', whereas both halves of the setting are repeated to accommodate the words of the masque song.

[39] P. Vivian first pointed out the strong similarity between these two songs; W. R. Davis suggested that

This setting, like the other songs in the volume, is for three voices, but Campion points out in his preface that he had not originally conceived them like that. They were, he writes, 'for the most part framed at first for one voyce with the Lute, or Violl, but upon occasion, they have since beene filled with more parts, which who so please may use, who like not may leave'. The added voices are first and foremost to discourage those who were in the habit of improvising inner parts 'to the perverting of the whole harmonie'.[40] In 'Come away' the extra parts are quite inappropriate since they work against the song's declamatory features; they owe nothing to the masque context and everything to the need to make the song acceptable for domestic use.

Lanier's 'Bring away this Sacred Tree' is found in several manuscript sources with a set of words which turn a song relating to a very specific moment in the masque into a conventional complaint against women's cruelty:

Masque text	Independent ayre
Bring away this Sacred Tree,	Weep no more my wearied eyes,
The Tree of Grace, and Bountie,	Leave off your sad lamenting,
Set it in Bel-Annas eye,	Cease my voice your mournful cries,
For she, she, only she	Since she, she, cruel she,
Can all knotted spels unty.	Pleasure takes in my tormenting.
(p.272)	

The version of the setting printed with the text of *The Somerset Masque* is the only one with the masque words. It should be said, though, that the manuscript sources of 'Weep no more' do not unequivocally establish a date later than the masque for this version. It is, of course, possible that Lanier or Campion adapted an existing song for the masque rather than the other way around. However, the setting is remarkable for its bold declamation—something which the masque context is likely to have inspired (whereas it seems too neutral in tone to have been prompted by a set of words as emotionally charged as the 'Weep no more' lyric).[41]

I should mention one more very curious example of an adapted masque lyric (this time without musical setting). In *Love Freed from Ignorance and Folly*, one of the Muses' Priests sings a song celebrating the fact that the liberated lovers can now appreciate the wit, grace, and beauty of the Daughters of the Morn with whom they dance:

O what a fault, nay, what a sinne
In *Fate*, or *Fortune* had it beene,

---

they shared a common setting. See *Campion's Works*, ed. P. Vivian (Oxford, 1909), 365 and *Thomas Campion*, ed. Davis, 108.

[40] *Thomas Campion*, ed. Davis, 55.

[41] 'Weep no more' is found in three manuscripts: GB-Cf, MS 52. D. 25 (the 'John Bull manuscript') which has songs added *c.*1620; EIRE-Dtc, MS F. 5. 13 (for which see below, p. 73); and US-NYp, MS Drexel 4527. The song appears in I. Spink (ed.), *English Songs 1625–1660*, MB 33 (London, 1971), 1.

So much beautie to haue lost!
Could the world with all her cost
Haue redeem'd it? CHO. {No, no, no.   (ll. 338–42)

Two Bodleian manuscripts (both collections of early seventeenth-century poetry) contain that song as the first stanza of a poem with the title 'On his mistris yᵗ had yᵉ smale pox'. The second stanza of this poem, which completely reverses the mood of the masque version, runs as follows:

unmanerly disease yᵗ durst
threaten yᵗ face yᵗ ere first
askd leaue of nature who had spent
such paynes to make it excellent
& soe estemed it . . .[42]

Something rather different from an instinct to preserve masque lyrics must lie behind this parody, which reapplies the untroubled lines from the Platonic playground of the masque to one of the very down-to-earth threats of seventeenth-century life.

Like the songs, masque dances have mostly survived in forms which give very little information about the way they would have been performed in the masque itself. They found their way into various collections of virginal, lute, or consort music. The Fitzwilliam Virginal Book, the Margaret Board Lute Book, and GB-Lbl, Add. MS 38539 (known as John Sturt's Lute Book) are just a few examples of sources rich in masque dance tunes which betray scarcely any hint of their original context. The earliest masque dances to be printed were those from *The Masque of Queens* which Robert Dowland included in *Varietie of Lute Lessons* (1609).

By far the largest collection of masque dances is the set of treble and bass partbooks now bound together as GB-Lbl, Add. MS 10444. This, too, is the source which appears to be most directly related to the invention of the masques themselves (as distinct from collections which contain arrangements of masque dances as instrumental pieces). Pamela Willets identified the partbooks as having once belonged to Sir Nicholas Le Strange, who copied the treble volume himself (while leaving the bass parts to a less able assistant).[43] The collection begins with twenty-six tunes which are not from masques, including pieces by Gibbons (an instrumental version of 'The Silver Swan'), Dowland, and Bull. Then—after two blank leaves—a fresh start has been made with a group of tunes numbered from '1' to '139'.[44] The vast majority

---

[42] GB-Ob, MS CCC. 328, fo. 88 (and MS Eng. Poet. e. 14, fo. 11ᵛ).

[43] P. J. Willets, 'Sir Nicholas Le Strange's Collection of Masque Music', *British Museum Quarterly*, 29 (1965), 79–81.

[44] In describing this manuscript I have ignored the later Matthew Locke pieces in a completely different hand which have been bound in with it. Various writers (most seriously Sabol) have assigned their own numbers to the Add. MS 10444 masque dances. This is a pity since, apart from a couple of minor problems (where a dance has not been copied into both parts), the manuscript's own numbers work perfectly well. Throughout this book, I refer to all Add. MS 10444 tunes by their manuscript numbers, but give Sabol's numbers in brackets.

of these have titles which identify them as masque dances; in actual performances they would have been played by various ensembles (whose makeup, as
we shall see in Chapter 3, depended on such factors as whether they were
masque or antimasque dances). Peter Holman and John Ward have argued
that the bare two-part character of these versions (not yet fleshed out in
arrangements for the ensembles which would eventually play them) suggests
that Le Strange probably acquired his material from a dancing-master.[45] This
seems a likely explanation for the form of Add. 10444—though it leaves
unexplained why there is a bass part at all when the majority of dance sources
suggest that dancing-masters choreographed and taught from treble parts
alone.[46]

Le Strange had connections with two Inns of Court—the most obvious
places in which he could have met dancing-masters with access to such
material. He was admitted to Gray's Inn in 1617 (though he was too young
to be a student there at that time) and in 1624 he became a bencher at
Lincoln's Inn. Pamela Willets originally proposed that Le Strange copied his
dances during his Lincoln's Inn years, in other words, in the mid-1620s. More
recently, however, she has raised the possibility—suggested by the unformed
character of the hand in the treble part of Add. 10444—that the collection
could have been compiled before then.[47] The fact that the final four pieces in
the manuscript all have concordances in Brade's 1617 anthology (see below)
may indicate that, if not Add. 10444 itself, Le Strange's source may have been
assembled before 1620.

The only printed book to concentrate explicitly on instrumental music for
the masque is John Adson's *Courtly Masquing Ayres* (1621) which, according to
its title-page, is 'Composed to 5. and 6. Parts for *Violins, Consorts,* and *Cornets*'.
There are twenty-one five-part and ten six-part pieces; the Ayres from no. 19
to the end of the collection are designated as being 'for Cornets and Sagbuts'
(that is, all of the six-part pieces and the last three five-part pieces). The
individual ayres have no titles and Adson reveals almost nothing about their
history. He makes a rather equivocal statement in his dedication to Buckingham that 'They are all (for the most part) *Courtly Masquing Ayres,* framed only

---

[45] J. Ward, 'Newly Devis'd Measures for Jacobean Masques', *AM* 60 (1988), 111–42; P. Holman, *Four
and Twenty Fiddlers: The Violin at the English Court 1540–1690* (Oxford, 1993), 186–96. Both Ward and
Holman imply that the provision of a continuo part for the two selections of dances which Bernard Thomas
and I edited for London Pro Musica edition—*Twenty-one Masque Dances* (1974) and *Twenty-five Masque
Dances* (1985)—was somehow inappropriate since there is nothing missing from the collection as it stands.
That, however, is not the same thing as claiming that the collection is 'complete' in all senses. Now, no
less than in the 17th c., these tunes must be regarded almost as raw material; all were 'set' for the specific
ensembles used in the masque, and—as we see in this chapter—many were adapted as stand-alone
instrumental pieces. As the introductions to our editions make clear, the provision of a continuo part can
thus be seen to stand in a long tradition of adaptation.

[46] The Inner Temple dancing-master Robert Holeman seemed to have worked from simple tunes alone,
and we know that Praetorius received only treble lines from the dancing-master Anthoine Emeraud for the
French *ballet de cour* airs included in *Terpsichore*; see below, 110 and 238.

[47] Pamela Willets made this suggestion at a combined meeting of the Viola da Gamba and Lute Societies
in November 1992.

for *Instruments*; of which kinde, these are the first that haue beene euer Printed . . .'.[48] The 'framing for instruments' might, in fact, correspond quite closely to the arrangements used in masque performance. All the tunes which concordances with Add. MS 10444 show to have been definitely drawn from masque dance repertoire occur in the first section of Adson's collection.[49] Since the court violin band was a five-part ensemble, these arrangements are probably very like the ones used by those players in masque performances. The lack of concordances for the six-part pieces suggests that they form part of a different repertoire; six-part arrangements of this kind are characteristic of the court wind ensmbles.[50] Adson himself was a wind-player active in the London Waits at the time his publication appeared. (He was appointed to the King's Musick in 1633 as a musician for the flute and cornet.) It may be that in the second half of his *Courtly Masquing Ayres* we have some of the pieces played by the wind ensembles before the beginning of masque performances.

Another very sizeable collection of masque dances in five-part arrangements was published by William Brade in Hamburg in 1617. The full title-page emphasizes that these tunes are presented in a form which makes them useful for domestic entertainment, but revealingly it adds that they are especially suitable for violins: 'Newe ausserlesene liebliche Branden, Intraden, Mascharaden, Balletten, All'manden, Couranten, Volten, Auffzüge und frembde Tänze, Sampt schönen lieblichen Frühlings vnd Sommers Blümlein; Mit fünff Stimmen: Auff allerley musicalischen Instrumenten, Insonderheit auff Fiolen zugebrauchen. Zuvor in Druck niemals außgangen. Durch WILHELM BRADE Englisch.'[51] Brade's arrangements—like Adson's—are probably very much along the lines of those actually used by the violin ensemble in court masques. There are twenty pieces which have concordances with English masque sources and others which look stylistically very similar. One of the most striking features of Brade's selection is the number of concordances for some of his tunes. (No. 31, 'Der Erste Mascharada der Pfaltzgraffen', exists in a dozen other versions.)[52] He seems to have selected the most popular tunes from the masque dance repertoire.

Four years after Brade's partbooks were published, another expatriate Englishman, Thomas Simpson, produced a similar collection in Hamburg. His title, *Taffel Consort*, once again suggests its domestic applicability. Simpson's very attractive arrangements are in four parts with two frequently crossing treble lines—a departure from the disposition of the court violin ensemble.

---

[48] Sig. A2. It should be noted that there is no evidence for a 1611 edition of *Courtly Masquing Ayres*, referred to in the *Grove 6* Adson article and by various other writers earlier this century. (The *Grove 6* article also gives the date of the real edition wrongly as 1622.)

[49] That is, all the five-part pieces except numbers 6, 14, 16, 17, 18, and 20.

[50] See T. Dart, 'The Repertory of the Royal Wind Music', *GSJ* 11 (1958), 70–2.

[51] 'New selected delightful branles, entries, masques, ballets, allemands, courants, la voltas, processions, and foreign dances together with pleasing spring and summer flowers; in five parts for all kinds of musical instruments, especially violins; which have never before appeared in print; by William Brade, English.'

[52] These, and in particular the problems raised by their conflicting titles, are discussed below, pp. 146–7.

Ex. 1.1. Maurice Webster, 'Mascarada', bars 22–35, from Simpson, *Taffel Consort* (1621)

There are, too, far fewer definite English masque tunes in *Taffel Consort* than in Brade. Versions of two 'Temple' masques, of 'The Cadua', and of the dance called 'The Satyres Masque' in Add. MS 10444 (the latter with an attribution to Robert Johnson) are included, and one of the pieces called 'Maske' and ascribed to Giles Farnaby in the Fitzwilliam Virginal Book appears in Simpson as a 'Mascarada' of uncertain authorship.[53] Otherwise there are several other tunes called 'Mascarada' but written by composers (N. Bleier and Maurice Webster) who have no known connection with the English masque (at least not as early as 1621). The Webster 'Mascarada' even seems to have been modelled in part on the Robert Johnson piece since they share one quite unusual gesture—compare Ex. 1.1 with bars 9–20 of Ex. 8.1 (below, p. 318). How all this English material reached Germany is something of a mystery. It may have arrived with the groups of itinerant English actors who performed

---

[53] Add. MS 10444, no. 41 (S 92), 'The Third of the Temple', corresponds to the last two strains only of Simpson 44, 'Mascarada, Incert. Aut'; no. 40 (S 91), 'The Second of the Temple', corresponds to Simpson 32, 'Mascarada, Incert. Aut'; no. 32 (S 83), 'The Cadua', corresponds to Simpson no. 50, 'Aria' attributed to R.B.; no. 56 (S 107), 'The Satyres Masque', corresponds to no. 24 (untitled) in Simpson. The Farnaby 'Maske' is no. 194 in the Fitzwilliam Virginal Book, and no. 31 in Simpson (where it is described as being of 'Incert. Aut.').

(amongst other things) corrupt versions of Shakespeare's plays and who were known for their musical skills.[54]

These sources allow us to build up a reasonable picture of what masque dances were like. GB-Lbl, Add. MS 10444 is invaluable simply as a very sizeable repository of this repertoire. As we shall see, it provides a great deal of information about the structure of individual dances and of sets of dances. The five-part masque dances found in Adson and Brade (and, to some extent, the four-part versions in Simpson) allow us to see something of the progress from very basic dancing-masters' tunes to more sophisticated arrangements prepared for performance by the King's Musick in masque performances.

Throughout the period covered by this book it remains true that the vast majority of music survives divorced from its original context and arranged for utterly different circumstances and resources. In looking at its use in the masque, an element of imaginative reconstruction is always needed. One enormously important musical source from the Caroline period—the William Lawes autograph manuscript GB-Ob, Mus. Sch. b. 2—stands out for the way in which it does relate directly to the masque productions themselves. Other Caroline sources present problems which are distinctly different from anything in the earlier period. These will be examined in Chapter 4.

Composers and the Court Masque

There is another aspect of the masque's genesis which prevents us from assuming too readily that the music and the other elements of the entertainment shared the kind of unity of purpose found in the libretto and score of an opera. The production of a court masque involved not just the collaboration of librettist and musician, or even of librettist, designer, and musician, since what we might think of as the composer's role was subdivided among several people.

Just how complex the network of collaborators could be can be seen from the text of *Hymenaei* (1606), the first of Jonson's masques to appear in print. It is this text which most fully acknowledges that the masque achieves something quite unique through the fusion of its constituent arts. In the Quarto edition—he apparently felt less generous by the time the 1616 Folio was being prepared—Jonson gives unstinting credit to Inigo Jones, but then goes on to acknowledge Ferrabosco's contribution even more warmly:

And here . . . I doe for honours sake, and the pledge of our Friendship, name Ma. ALPHONSO FERABOSCO, a Man, planted by himselfe, in that divine *Spheare*; & mastring all the spirits of *Musique*: To whose iudicall Care, and as absolute Performance, were committed all those Difficulties both of *Song*, and otherwise. Wherein,

---

[54] See J. Limon, *Gentlemen of a Company: English Players in Central and Eastern Europe, 1590–1660* (Cambridge, 1985), 8, 16–19; also E. K. Chambers, *The Elizabethan Stage*, 4 vols. (Oxford, 1923), ii. 270–94, and Albert Cohn, *Shakespeare in Germany in the Sixteenth and Seventeenth Centuries* (London, 1865), especially pp. lxxx and lxxxi.

what his Merit made to the *Soule* of our *Invention*, would aske to be exprest in Tunes, no lesse ravishing then his. *Vertuous* friend, take well this abrupt testimonie, and thinke whose it is: It cannot be Flatterie, in me, who never did it to *Great ones*; and lesse then Love, and Truth it is not, where it is done out of *Knowledge*.   (following line 678)

Ferrabosco is thanked first and foremost for aiding the 'soul' of the invention; Jonson implies an ideal partnership. The two commendatory poems in hon-our of Ferrabosco confirm that Jonson genuinely esteemed his collaborator.[55] It is true that if any one composer were to be singled out as having an importance in the developing Jonsonian masque somehow equivalent to Jones as designer, it would have to be Alfonso Ferrabosco. But—despite the potentially all-embracing pair of words, 'and otherwise', in that accolade—Ferrabosco cannot be regarded as 'the composer' of *Hymenaei* or, for that matter, of any other masque. Immediately following the tribute to Ferrabosco, Jonson goes on to acknowledge another musician:

The Daunces were both made, and taught by Maister THOMAS GILES; and cannot bee more approv'd, then they did themselves: Nor doe I want the will, but the skill to commend such *Subtilties*: of which the *Spheare*, wherein they were acted, is best able to iudge.

Acknowledgements in masque texts are rather haphazard. In the Jacobean period, nobody except Jonson ever thought to give credit to specific musi-cians within the text itself (although, as we have seen, Campion identifies the composers of the songs and dances he appended to the texts of *The Lord Hay's Masque* and *The Somerset Masque*). Even Jonson's attributions are relatively few.

Where Jonson does acknowledge a composer, he invariably treats the composition of vocal music and the creation of the dances as quite distinct activities (as in the case of *Hymenaei*). Despite the fact that Ferrabosco wrote five beautiful songs for *The Masque of Beauty* (1608), Jonson mentions only Thomas Giles in that text, saying that he took the part of Vulturnus and 'made the *Daunces*' (l. 296). From the text of *The Haddington Masque* (1608) we learn that Giles shared the 'making' of the dances with Jeremy Herne and that 'the tunes were M. ALPHONSO FERRABOSCO'S' (ll. 351–2). Jonson's wording seems ambiguous, but the one extant song setting for *The Haddington Masque* and the pattern established in other masques suggests that by 'tunes' Jonson meant songs.

The Masque of Queens (1609) is richest in musical attributions, and these are dispersed through the text at the appropriate points. (We have seen in the Introduction that these acknowledgements include praise for John Alleyn's singing.) The gestures in the antimasque dance of witches 'were excellently

---

[55] These poems appeared with Ferrabosco's two 1609 publications, the *Ayres* and *Lessons for 1. 2. and 3. Viols*.

imitated by the Maker of the *Daunce*, M'. *Hierome Herne*, whose right it is, here to be nam'd' (ll. 351–3). Much later (l. 756), Jonson identifies the 'author' of the third of the masquers' set dances as Thomas Giles. Finally (l. 762), he pays tribute to 'my excellent Friend *Alfonso Ferrabosco*' for the composition of the songs.

Modern readers might well feel that it was an artist's 'right . . . to be nam'd'—but Jonson was merely employing a form of hyperbole in praising Herne. Not even Jonson himself appears to have had such a right. Masque texts often give prominence to the names of the nobility honoured by the performance, but they are usually unforthcoming about those who devised different aspects of the entertainment.

'Making' dances involved writing the music and providing appropriate choreography. The form of words might seem ambiguous, but the dance music by Thomas Giles printed with *The Lord Hay's Masque* is itself evidence that the composition of dance tunes and the devising of choreography for them must have been regarded as two aspects of one task.

'Make' as a term seems now to have a rather naïve (or perhaps *faux naïf*) ring to it, but in the early seventeenth century it was synonymous with 'compose'. Parts of Campion's *New Way of Making Fowre Parts in Counterpoint* were taken over by Coprario, who called his manuscript treatise 'Rules How to Compose'. Campion himself used the terms interchangeably; he writes that the first of the *Somerset Masque* songs was '*made* . . . by Mr. Nicholas Lanier', while the last three 'were *composed* by Mr. Coprario' (my italics).[56] In the 1617 Quarto of *Lovers Made Men*, Nicholas Lanier is credited with having '*made* both the Scene, and the Musicke' (l. 28).[57] 'Maker' as a word for poet was seen to have a very respectable lineage, and Jonson, particularly, could not have used it without being aware of this kind of resonance. In *Timber or Discoveries* he makes numerous references to the derivation of the word 'poet' from the Greek word meaning 'maker'.[58] The verb 'make' obviously bore the same connotations as 'create' does now.

Although he praises one of Thomas Giles's dances in *The Masque of Queens* by saying (apparently referring to the combination of music and movement) that 'a more numerous composition could not be seene', it is not until 1622 that Jonson uses the verb 'composed' in its modern sense. The Quarto text of

---

[56] See below, p. 270, for the use of the word 'compose' meaning to write the text.

[57] The controversy surrounding the attribution of *stylo recitativo* composition to Nicholas Lanier in this masque is explored below (pp. 86–9). The italics in the quotations here are mine.

[58] 'A Poet is that, which by the *Greekes* is call'd . . . a Maker or a fainer: His Art, an Art of imitation or faining; expressing the life of man in fit measure, numbers, and harmony according to *Aristotle*'; H&S, viii. 635, 637, 638, and 639. Sidney's enthusiasm for the word is even stronger (*An Apology for Poetry*, in Smith (ed.), *Elizabethan Critical Essays*, i. 155): 'The Greekes called him a Poet, which name hath, as the most excellent, gone thorough other Languages. It commeth of this word *Poiein*, which is to make: wherein I know not, whether by lucke or wisedome, wee Englishmen haue mette with the Greeke in calling him a maker: which name, how high and incomparable a title it is, I had rather were knowne by marking the scope of other Sciences then by my partiall allegation.'

The Masque of Augurs (1622) has (in one state only) the sentence '*The* Musique [was] *compos'd by that excellent paire of Kinsemen, M^r.* ALPHONSO FERRABOSCO, *and M^r.* NICHOLAS LANIER.'[59]

These texts point towards a norm for the early Jacobean period in which Ferrabosco wrote vocal music, while Thomas Giles and Jeremy Herne looked after the dances. Instead of thinking of a masque being created by a writer, designer, composer, and choreographer, we need a concept which divides the musical components differently. To begin with, vocal music on the one hand and all aspects of dance on the other normally belonged in separate departments. The first of these was likely to be referred to in what now seems a misleadingly comprehensive way as 'the music'.

Even such a division does not give an adequate picture of the way composers' responsibilities were divided. For both vocal music and dance it was normal to have someone other than the person who devised the actual tunes arranging the music for the appropriate ensembles. This was described as 'setting' the music, though 'setter' as a term also overlaps with composer and maker—the earliest reference to Coprario in court records is, in fact, as 'a Setter of Musick'.[60]

Surviving sets of financial records are particularly valuable sources of information about these matters. They not only identify the contribution of particular musicians to a production but also suggest, through the amounts paid, the relative importance (or the investment in time) attached to various aspects of masque creation. Particularly detailed financial records survive from the office of the Exchequer for *Love Freed from Ignorance and Folly* (1611). The section headed 'Rewards to the persons imployed in the Maske' demonstrates very clearly the way in which musical responsibility was dispersed amongst quite a number of people:[61]

Imprimis to m^r Beniamin Iohnson for his invention	40^{li}
It'm to m^r Inigo Iohnes for his paynes and Invention	40^{li}
It'm to m^r Alfonso [Ferrabosco] for making the songes	20^{li}
It'm to m^r [Robert] Iohnson for setting the songes to the lutes	5^{li}
It'm to Thomas Lupo for setting the dances to the violens	5^{li}
It'm to m^r Confesse for teachinge all the dances	50^{li}
It'm to m^r Bochan for teaching the Ladies the footing of 2 danses	20^{li}
To the 12 Musitions that were preestes that songe and played	24^{li}
It'm to the 12 other Lutes that suplied, and wth fluits	12^{li}
It'm to the 10 violens that contynualy practized to the Queene	20^{li}
It'm to 4 more that were added att the Maske	4^{li}
It'm to 15 Musitions that played to the Pages and fooles	20^{li}
It'm to 13 hoboyes and sackbutts	10^{li}

[59] See H&S, vii. 625.

[60] GB-Lbl, Add. MS 27404 (Accounts of the Receiver General to Queen Anne, 1606); quoted Ashbee, *RECM*, iv. 197.

[61] GB-Lpro, E 407/57/1; reproduced in H&S, x. 529 and Ashbee, *RECM*, iv. 30–1.

It'm to 5 boyes that is, 3 graces Sphynkes and Cupid   10[li]
It'm to the 12 fooles that danced   12[li]

How are we to interpret the fact that Ferrabosco was paid £20 while Jonson and Jones were each paid £40? Assuming the masque's courtly sponsors regarded its dramatic, visual, and musical elements as being of broadly equal importance, this suggests that Ferrabosco was responsible for only half of the masque's musical content. And we can see that the musical responsibilities were shared. Two musicians, Ferrabosco and Robert Johnson, had a hand in the vocal music (solo ayres, a dialogue, and 'full' songs or choruses). Johnson arranged the accompaniments for the quite large group of lutes (about which more in Chapter 3). Thomas Lupo was responsible for arranging the dances for the violin band but, on the face of it, nobody appears to have been credited with their composition. Once again, it seems that invention of the tunes and the working out (and teaching) of the steps and figures were seen as a single operation. Certainly Confesse was a composer as well as a dancing-master.[62] The large amounts paid to Confesse and Bochan (compared with, most notably, Inigo Jones's fee) can be explained by the labour-intensive character of their work—a huge amount of time went into coaching dancers for masque performances.

The accounts for Prince Henry's masque *Oberon* (1611) are equally detailed, but more puzzling. Again, however, they make it clear that the music was composed, arranged, and generally worked out by a *group* of people. On 27 April 1611, nearly four months after the performance of *Oberon* and three months after *Love Freed* (the Queen's masque), Sir Thomas Chaloner, Chamberlain to Prince Henry, wrote a memorandum to ensure parity between the payments for both masques: '. . . his Highnes being desirous to reward thoos that tooke peynes in the mask for him, hath giuen order to rase ther rewards according to the last mask of the Queene: After which direction: M[r] Alfonso [Ferrabosco], Monsieur Confess, & M[r] Ieremy Herne, are thought worthy to receiue by your allowance, 20:[l] a peece'.[63] This letter was followed up a few days later by a warrant authorizing the payments. As one would expect, this warrant identifies the three principal creators of music and dance for *Oberon*: Ferrabosco for the songs, and Nicolas Confesse and Jeremy Herne for the dances. It also conveys a picture of the time-consuming nature of preparing music and (especially) dance for performance: 'To Alphonso fferabosco and Monsieur Confesse & Jeremy Herne to eache of them the summe of twentie poundes by waie of reward for their paines having bene imployed in the Princes late Mask by the space almost of six weekes.'[64] But there is a further set of payments to musicians, and while these are predominantly for performers, they include remuneration for composers:[65]

---

[62] The Board Lute manuscript contains an 'Antiq masque by Mr. Confesso set by Mr. Taylor' (fo. 27[v]).

[63] GB-Lbl, Add. MS 24023, fo. 4; quoted H&S, x. 519.

[64] GB-Lpro, E 403/2730, fo. 154; quoted ibid. 520.

[65] GB-Lpro, E 403/2730, fo. 181[v]; quoted ibid. 521.

To M. [Robert] Iohnson for making the Daunces	xx^{li}	
Thomas Lupo for settinge them to the violins	c^s	
Mr Giles for 3 dances	xl^{li}	CCxlvij^{li} viij
Companie of violins	xxxii^{li}	
Thomas Lupo thelder Alex. Chisan & Rowland Rubidge violins	x^{li}	
xiij^n Holt boyes	x^{li}	
x singers & 6 plaiers on the lute provided by Alphonse [Ferrabosco]	xxxij^{li}	
Twoe Cornetts	iii^{li}	
xx lutes provided by Mr Johnson for the Princes Dance	xl^{li}	
xvj other instrumentes for the Satires & faeries	xxj^{li}	
Players imployed in the Barriers	xv^{li}	
for their Spanishe lether bootes bought by themselves	xlviij^s	
Players imployed in the Maske	xv^{li}	
forheades & beards vsed in the maske	xl^s	

Lupo's payment needs no explanation; the amount is exactly what he was paid for his contribution to *Love Freed*. But why, given the involvement of both Confesse and Herne, was Thomas Giles paid 'for 3 dances'? It is even more surprising to see the lutenist Robert Johnson also credited with making dances. There is nothing in what is known of Johnson's life to suggest that his role here could have extended into choreography. Does this mean that in this particular case composition of dance tunes and the devising and teaching of choreography were kept separate? What is certain is that Ferrabosco composed songs, Robert Johnson wrote dance music and co-ordinated an ensemble of twenty lutes to play it, and that Thomas Lupo arranged (other) dance music for the violin band. Presumably, what Lupo arranged was provided by Thomas Giles, Nicolas Confesse, and Jeremy Herne, who must also have choreographed and taught the dances.

The same sort of division of labour can be seen in the records for *The Memorable Masque of the Middle Temple and Lincoln's Inn*, which formed part of the festivities at the wedding of Princess Elizabeth and the Count Palatine in 1613. Robert Johnson received a substantial payment (£45) 'for musicke and songes'. Thomas Ford was paid £5 'for setting songes used at the Maske' (and he received an extra £2.10s. for playing the lute). None of these payments makes any specific reference to dance—and the other payments to performers are all to lutenists and singers:[66]

[66] For the full set of accounts see W. P. Baildon and R. F. Roxburgh (eds.), *The Records of the Honourable Society of Lincoln's Inn: The Black Books*, 2 vols. (London, 1897–8), ii. 154–7; quoted in O&S i. 253–5. Ashbee, *RECM*, iv. 38–9, excerpts the items dealing with music. He identifies Mynars and Jonas [Wrench] as musicians who had been in the service of Prince Henry.

Item, to Mr Rob^{te} Johnson for musicke and songes, 45 li.

. . .

Item, to Thomas Cutting, John Dowland and Phillip Rosseter for playing of Lutes, every one of them 2 li. 10s.

Item, to Mr Thomas Forde for playing of Lute, 2 li. 10s; and more for setting songes used at the Maske, 5 li; and for Mathias Johnson for singing, 2 li

Item, to John Sturte, Robert Taylor, Robert Dowland, and Thomas Davies for playing Lutes, every one of them, 2 li.

Item, to Mr Jonas and Mr Mynars, two of the musicions for the Maske, 6 li. 13s. 8d.

Item to Thomas Daye for . . . 3 li. 6s. 8d.

Item, to 7 singing men, vzt.: John Drue, Willm Godball, John Frost, Davies (one of the Queresters), Marke Thwaites, Walter Porter, and Richard Ball, every one of them, 2 li.; saving Davies, who had bout 1 li. 13s.

Accounts for Campion's *Lords' Masque* (also part of the Palatine wedding celebrations) include a tantalizing list of payments to individuals but do not specify what these payments were for:[67]

Dr Campian	lxvj$^{li.}$ xiij^s. iiij^d.	He that played to y^e boyes	xj$^{li.}$ xiij^s. iiij^d.
Inigo Jones	l$^{li.}$	42 Musitians	xlij$^{li.}$
Jerome Herne	xl$^{li.}$	2 that plaied to y^e Antick Maske	xj$^{li.}$
Bochan	xl$^{li.}$	12 Madfolkes	xij$^{li.}$
Tho: Giles	xxx$^{li.}$	5 speakers	v$^{li.}$
Jo: Coperary	xx$^{li.}$	10 of y^e kinges violins	x$^{li.}$
Mr Confesse	xxx$^{li.}$	3 groomes of y^e Chamber	iij$^{li.}$
Roberte Johnson	x$^{li.}$		
Thomas Lupo	x$^{li.}$		
Steven Thomas	xv$^{li.}$		

Campion, apart from writing the text, composed some of the songs. His dual role may explain why his payment is so much greater than that of Inigo Jones (whose work he praises warmly in this text). It seems likely that Coprario wrote other songs, just as he was to do in Campion's *Somerset Masque*. As in *Love Freed*, Thomas Lupo and Robert Johnson received equal payments—probably again for arranging dances for the violins on the one hand, and songs for the lutes on the other. Steven Thomas, one of the London waits, may have had a role in the provision of loud music in the opening antimasque section.[68] That leaves two French and two English dancing-masters for all the composing of tunes, devising of choreography, and rehearsing of dancers that the production demanded.

All this should alert us to the special difficulties in determining the ways in which the music of court masques fitted into the coherent artistic vision

---

[67] GB-Lpro, E 403/2732, fo. 183^v; reproduced in O&S, i. 241–2, and Ashbee, *RECM*, iv. 234.

[68] W. L. Woodfill, *Musicians in English Society* (Princeton, 1953), 248, lists Stephen Thomas as having been appointed to the Waits in 1597. He died in 1618.

implied by masque texts. It is with Campion most of all that we are forced to abandon any easily made assumption of close co-operation and unity of artistic purpose between poet and musician. Since Campion was proficient in both roles he would seem to have been in an ideal position to retain complete control over the place of music in the imaginative design. In fact, we might have expected him to try to achieve this, given the point of view he expresses in the preface to *Two Bookes of Ayres*: 'In these *English* Ayres, I have chiefly aymed to couple my Words and Notes lovingly together, which will be much for him to doe that hath not power over both'.[69] But, as we have seen, although Campion composed some of his own masque songs, he did not set them all, and—like other song composers—he contributed none of the dance music.

It is not, of course, surprising to find that this parallels the situation in court entertainments elsewhere in Europe. While the overall conception of the 1589 Florentine intermedi was by Count Giovanni de' Bardi, the music was the work of a group of composers: Malvezzi, Archilei, Marenzio, Peri, Cavalieri, Caccini, and Bardi himself.[70] *Il Rapimento di Cefalo*, performed in Florence in 1600, had music by Stefano Venturi del Nibbio, Luca Bati, Piero Strozzi, and Caccini.[71] In Mantua the intermezzi which accompanied the performance of Guarini's *L'Idropica* (given as part of the wedding celebrations of Prince Francesco Gonzaga) had music by Claudio Monteverdi and his brother Giulio Cesare Monteverdi, Salamone Rossi, Gastoldi, Monco, and Paolo Biat.[72] A Neapolitan publication—the *Breve Racconto della Festa a Ballo* of 1620—provides a later example of at least five composers contributing to a court entertainment. In this production, as in the court masque, the composition of some at least of the dance music and the invention of the choreography were in the hands of the same person, Giacomo Spiardo.[73] The complete separation of vocal music and dance was evident in France. Henri Prunières, in his book on the *ballet de cour*, pointed out that it was the dancing-masters who wrote the music for the *entrées*, while the vocal music was the province of a more élite group:

Le soin de composer la musique des entrées était laissé le plus souvent à ceux-là même qui en réglaient les pas et en ordonnaient les figures. Les artistes de réputation qui dirigeaient la Musique de la Chambre du Roi rivalisaient entre eux lorsqu'il s'agissait d'écrire pour les ballets des récits à une ou plusieurs voix, mais ils eussent cru déchoir en se mêlant des danses, cela était bon 'pour Messieurs les Violons'.[74]

[69] *The Works of Thomas Campion*, ed. Davis, 55.

[70] These, in fact, set words supplied by three poets: Bardi again, Rinuccini, and Strozzi. See D. P. Walker (ed.), *Musique des intermèdes de 'La Pellegrina'* (Paris, 1963).

[71] See A. M. Nagler, *Theatre Festivals of the Medici 1539–1637* (New Haven and London, 1964), 97; and Giulio Caccini, *Le nuove musiche*, ed. H. Wiley Hitchcock (Madison, 1970), 101–40.

[72] See Nagler, *Theatre Festivals*, 179.

[73] See R. Jackson (ed.), *A Neapolitan Festa a Ballo* (Madison, 1978).

[74] H. Prunières, *Le Ballet de cour en France avant Benserade et Lully* (Paris, 1914), 208: 'The task of composing the music for the *entrées* was most often left to those same people who devised the steps and

There is a discernible rationale behind the allocation of musical responsibilities to particular people. Firstly, those involved with song composition form a coherent (and distinguished) group. Apart from their vocal works, all are associated with music for the lute or viol. Ferrabosco, Lanier, Coprario, and Campion were gifted song composers. Robert Johnson and Thomas Ford, paid for setting songs to the lutes, also rank highly as composers of vocal music. To this group, on the basis of the masque songs in *A Pilgrim's Solace*, we can add the name of the greatest song writer of the age, John Dowland. With the exception of Campion, who was not a professional musician, all these musicians belonged (eventually at least) to the section of the King's Musick which by the Caroline period was referred to as 'The Lutes, Viols, and Voices'. (Both Lanier and Coprario had begun writing for masques before any permanent court appointment.)[75] Singing and playing the lute (or viol) belonged together even in the administration of the court establishment.

It is equally true that dancing and playing the violin were linked. At first glance, the composers associated with dance music in the Jacobean period may seem to form a more disparate group: Thomas Lupo, Thomas Giles, Jeremy Herne, Nicolas Confesse, Bochan, and again Robert Johnson. As already noted, Robert Johnson—a lutenist and song composer—seems particularly out of place here. His involvement with the theatre may provide something of an explanation for the fact that he alone amongst masque composers seems to have crossed the boundary between vocal music and dance.[76] It was natural that Thomas Lupo should end up arranging dance tunes for the violin band; late in 1621 he was appointed Composer for the Violins.[77] Giles, too, would have seemed an obvious person to be assigned responsibility for dances. A month before the performance of *Hymenaei* he had been appointed as a tutor to Prince Henry and, although the initial warrants describe him as a teacher of music, he is after that more usually referred to as

worked out the figures for them. The celebrated artists who directed the Music of the King's Chamber vied amongst themselves when it came to writing the *récits* for one or several voices for the ballets, but they would have thought it beneath their dignity to get mixed up with the dances—that was for "the gentlemen of the violins".'

[75] Lanier's prestige and influence as a musician and courtier was considerable. From 1626 until the fall of Charles I, and from 1660 until his death in 1666 he was Master of the King's Music, a post which gave him power over other musicians: it was he who authorized the purchase of new instruments for particular players, and so on. In 1634 he used his influence to persuade Whitelocke to back down over the hiring of John Adson's wind musician friends from the public theatres for the procession which preceded *The Triumph of Peace* (see A. Sabol, 'New Documents on Shirley's Masque "The Triumph of Peace"', *ML* 47 (1966), 18–19). John Donne the younger wrote in 1660 that Lanier 'by his great skill gave a life and harmony to all that he set' (quoted by Poulton, *Dowland*, 276).

[76] In 1596 Johnson was apprenticed to Sir George Carey, who was Lord Chamberlain from 1597 until his death in 1603. As such, he was the patron of 'The Lord Chamberlain's Men' (which in 1603 became 'The King's Men'), and it may have been because of this link that Johnson was so prominent as a theatrical composer even after his appointment in 1604 to the court musical establishment (The King's Musick). Johnson's play songs include 'Full fathom five' and 'Where the bee sucks' for *The Tempest*, 'Care-charming sleep' for Fletcher's *Valentinian*, 'Have you seen but a white lily grow' for Jonson's *Devil is an Ass*, and many others.   [77] Ashbee, *RECM*, iv. 53.

the prince's dancing-tutor.[78] From May 1608 (three months after the performance of *The Haddington Masque*) Jeremy Herne appears amongst the violinists in the court music. He became better known, however, as a dancing-master. In July 1616 he was promised the place of the dancing-master Thomas Cardell (although the actual appointment had to wait for the latter's death in 1621). Peter Holman, pointing out that Hearne's name was frequently spelt 'Heron', comments that he may have been French (a surmise which gains some support from the fact that in 1611 he was paid 'for his charges and pains in carrying letters for his Majesty's service to Parys').[79] The appearance of two unequivocally French musicians amongst those involved with dance in the 1611 masques is significant. The impact made by Bochan, Confesse, and their compatriots will be examined in Chapter 6.

To conclude: surveys of the history of English opera invariably begin with the masque. There are good reasons for this, not least that the pre-Commonwealth court masque is recalled in the extended masque sections of Restoration semi-opera. But using an operatic model to think about the use and function of music in the masque will be misleading. One of the crucial elements in the emergence of opera as an art form which has a literal integrity is the fact of a single composer setting the libretto.[80] The result, of course, is a score—potentially at least, a coherent musical dramatization. With the masque the situation is quite different: various kinds of music by several composers relate to a device shaped primarily by writer and designer. This could work well, partly because the structure of the masque was quite different from that of opera. A masque does not involve dramatic conflict in the Aristotelian sense of a single developing action. It is essentially more static—a series of interlocking, animated tableaux, or an unfolding emblem. This was well understood in the early seventeenth century—in two separate letters John Chamberlain criticized Campion's *Lords' Masque* for being 'more like a play than a mask'.[81]

What we have seen, then, is that the composer's role was divided amongst a range of people with different, though often overlapping, responsibilities. Despite Jonson's use of the term 'the music master' (in his 'Expostulation with Inigo Jones'),[82] no one person ever shaped the music for a major masque production. Far from being an early Baroque *Gesamtkunstwerk*, the masque rested upon what must have been a relatively haphazard alliance between music and the other arts. But therein lies much of its interest.

---

[78] Ibid. 12, 28, 36, 127, 211, *et passim*.

[79] Ashbee, *RECM*, iv. 22, 43, 44, 87, 184, *et passim*. In his initial appointment Hearne was described as musician for the bass viol, but thereafter he is consistently described as a violinist. See Holman, *Four and Twenty Fiddlers*, 179.

[80] The *pasticcio* (a late 17th-c. development) is an exception to this.

[81] *The Letters of John Chamberlain*, ed. N. E. McClure, 2 vols. (Philadelphia, 1939), i. 424 and 426. And see below, p. 232, for criticism of masquers being given roles which came too close to 'acting'.

[82] H&S, viii. 402–6, l. 63.

2

Masque Song

Let the *Songs* be *Loud,* and *Cheerful,* and not *Chirpings,* or *Pulings.*

(Francis Bacon, 'Of Masques and Triumphs')[1]

The most frustrating aspect of studying music for the English court masque is that, for so much of the time, it no longer exists. In this respect, masque texts are like fossils—they can give a vivid impression of what was once there, but the substance itself, the music, has often disappeared. Certain types of vocal music (most obviously 'full songs' and almost all the other ensemble pieces) are missing altogether. Occasionally, the texts go as far as indicating the precise scoring of these pieces. The first song in *The Masque of Blackness* ('Sound, sound aloud') is a case in point. A Triton and a pair of sea maids 'began to sing to the others lowd musique, their voyces being a *tenor,* and two *trebles*' (ll. 94–5). The final song in *Pleasure Reconciled to Virtue* was performed 'by 2. *trebles,* 2. *tenors,* a *base,* and yᵉ whole Chorus'.[2] Jonson's poem is both long (twenty-six lines) and metrically irregular; it would be good to know how it was treated musically.

The Lord Hay's Masque is the only Jacobean masque in which details about vocal ensembles can be related to surviving settings (and then only in two songs). 'Now hath Flora robbed her Bowers' was sung 'in a base, Tenor, and treble voyce' (p. 215)—and this scoring is confirmed by the setting printed with the text.[3] 'Move now with measured sound' was sung by two pairs of voices: 'a treble and base were placed neere his Maiestie, and an other treble and base neere the groue, that the words of the song might be heard of all' (p. 220).[4] (Another 'Dialogue of foure voices, two Bases and two trebles' must

---

[1] *Essays* (London, 1625; repr. Menston, 1971), 224. Bacon's first set of essays was published in 1597. An enlarged edition appeared in 1612. The essay 'On Masques and Triumphs' did not appear until the further expanded 1625 edition (which was dedicated to the Duke of Buckingham).

[2] Ferrabosco, for example, used this scoring in a number of motets; see J. Duffy, *The Songs and Motets of Alfonso Ferrabosco, the Younger (1575–1628)* (Ann Arbor, 1980), App. 4, 350–8 ('Libera me, Domine') and 367–78 ('Noli me projicere').

[3] The singers scattered flowers about the stage during the song. Campion is returning to an idea used in one of Elizabeth I's entertainments. In the Entertainment at Elvetham singers scattered flowers as they sang 'With Fragrant Flowers we strew the Way'. See E. Brennecke, 'The Entertainment at Elvetham, 1591', in J. H. Long (ed.), *Music in English Renaissance Drama* (Lexington, Ky., 1968), 38.

[4] The version of this song as 'The peaceful western wind' in *Two Bookes of Ayres* has treble, bass, and altus

have been treated the same way, since the lines are marked, question and answer fashion, '1' and '2'.) It is a pity that the nearest we can get to an actual musical example of the *cori spezzati* effects described in *The Lord Hay's Masque* is a comparatively uninteresting case of voice doubling purely for reasons of audibility.

It is similarly disappointing that none of the apparently ingenious masque echo songs survives with musical settings intact. The echo song is especially interesting since it offered technical challenges to composer and poet alike. There are, of course, some celebrated European antecedents and analogues. The songs in the *Balet Comique de la Royne* evoked a 'réponse de la Voute Dorée' for which Beaujoyeulx gave a rather equivocal explanation—some, he says, regarded it simply as an acoustical phenomenon while others took it as evidence of a heavenly endorsement of the sentiments expressed: 'Laquelle ... aucuns de l'assistance estimerent estre la mesme voix qui fut conuertie en air repercussif, appele depuis Echo: & d'aultres plus instruits en la discipline Platonique, l'estimerent estre la vraye harmonie du ciel de laquelle toutes les choses qui sont en estre, sont conseruees & maintenues.'[5] Echo as a supernatural response to human supplication is an idea that (as Beaujoyeulx, in fact, indicates) fits naturally into the Neoplatonic or Boethian view of music's position in the world order. Divine endorsement provides the basis for pieces like Monteverdi's wonderful 'Salve Regina con dentro un Ecco'.[6] But beyond that, echo songs gave composers an opportunity for a special kind of antiphonal writing. The dramatic context provided an excuse for spatial separation and, of course, hidden responses. The musical techniques involved are ones of particular interest in this period. They formed the basis of, for example, much Venetian polychoral music in the late sixteenth and early seventeenth centuries.[7] The brilliantly asymmetrical echoes in William Lawes's Royal Consort No. 1 in D minor make it clear that English composers were capable of some wonderfully imaginative variations on the echo idea. It is all the more regrettable, therefore, that in relation to the masque we can talk only about the poetic effects.

There is, of course, one masque setting of an echo song which survives but, as we noted earlier, it has been stripped of its echoes in the process of

---

parts (the latter somewhat reluctantly added by Campion). On Campion's reasons for providing inner parts see above, p. 28 and for a discussion of these settings see below, p. 68.

    [5] fo. 5ᵛ. 'Some of the audience thought that it was that voice which was turned into reverberating air and since named Echo, while others, better versed in Platonic philosophy, considered that it was the true celestial harmony by which all things are preserved and maintained.'

    [6] 'Salve Regina con dentro un Ecco: voce sola risposta d'ecco et due violini' from *Selva Morale* (1640); see *Monteverdi: Tutte le opere*, 16 vols., ed. G. F. Malipiero (Asolo, 1926–42), xv. 724. For a discussion of echo in 16th-c. Italian dramatic settings and a list of early operatic uses of the device see F. W. Sternfeld, 'Écho et répétition dans la poésie et la musique', in J.-M. Vaccaro (ed.), *La Chanson à la Renaissance* (Tours, 1981), 242–53 and id., *The Birth of Opera* (Oxford, 1993), ch. 7. The echo scene in John Webster's *Duchess of Malfi* is an instance of an echo as a voice from another world.

    [7] See P. Allsop, *The Italian 'Trio' Sonata* (Oxford, 1992), 87–8 *et passim* for the use of these effects in early 17th–c. instrumental music.

arranging it for 'domestic' use. The echoes in this song, Coprario's 'While Dancing Rests', modify the meaning of the lines they reflect:

> . . . Kind eares with Ioy enchaunting,   chaunting
> . . . To make this Ioy perseuer,   euer
> . . . We leave with charmes enclosing,   closing   (p. 274)

There are echoes in a *Masque of Blackness* song, the second of two calling the lady masquers back to the sea. Here, too, the echo is verbal play, reversing the meaning of the original statement:

> Daughters of the subtle floud,
> Doe not let earth longer intertayne you:
> *1. Ecch.* Let earth longer intertayne you.
> *2. Ecch.* Longer intertayne you   (ll. 306–9)

The echo expresses a general reluctance to allow the masquers to retreat from the dancing area and so bring the festivity to a close. Here we have a double echo. In the next stanza the echo is first supplicating and then voices the despair of the gentlemen with whom the masquers have danced:

> 'Tis to them, inough of good,
> That you giue this little hope, to gayne you.
> *1. Ecch.* Giue this little hope, to gayne you.
> *2. Ecch.* Little hope, to gayne you   (ll. 310–13)

There are two double echo songs in *The Masque of Beauty*—significantly, the only two songs from this masque for which no settings survive. We must conclude that it was their echoes which made them unsuitable for inclusion in Ferrabosco's *Ayres*. In the second of these songs a proposition made by the Chorus is turned into a positive statement by the echo:

> Still turne, and imitate the heauen
> In motion swift and euen . . .
> CHO. { So all that see your *beauties* sphaere,
>   { May know the *'Elysian* fields are here.
> *Ecch.* Th'*Elysian* fields are here.
> *Ecch. Elysian* fields are here.   (ll. 399–409)

The other echo song, the first song in the masque, had no such subtle twists; the ingenuity here lay in the way the echoes were produced; we are told that 'this full *Song* [was] iterated in the closes of two *Eccho*'s, rising out of the Fountaines' (ll. 279–80).[8]

In these last two cases, the staging is designed to represent the echoes as natural pastoral phenomena. In William Browne's *Inner Temple Masque*, the apparently multiple echoes of the Song of the Nymphs in the Wood were

---

[8] Jonson used a variation on this idea in his last masque, *Chloridia*, where Spring sings several songs in which the Fountains 'follow with the close'; what they sing there, however, is not an actual echo of Spring's words.

made to seem similarly part of nature: 'Presently in the wood was heard a full music of lutes which, descending to the stage, had to them sung this following song, the Echoes being placed in several parts of the boscage' (ll. 345–7).

Pastoral echoes are essentially like other forms of echo which suggest divine endorsement. The whole environment, part of a divinely ordered creation, reiterates the sentiments of praise, triumph, or joy which are the subject of all these songs. The other kind of echo are those of Fame and these have a more abstract basis—an allegorical projection of the idea that Fame is built on the repetition of stories about a person's achievements.[9] In the masque, Fame's echoes attest that those present are enjoying a historic era of peace and good government. Often, as in the second echo song of *The Masque of Beauty*, the two suggestions—of Arcadian echoes and Fame's repetitions—are inter-woven. They are similarly combined in *The Lord Hay's Masque* where the choral acclamation 'Long liue *Apollo*, Brittaines glorious eye' and (more particularly) the dance which followed it are described as a 'kind of ecchoing musicke [which] rarely became their *Siluan* attire . . .' (p. 223).[10] An even more obvious example of the mixing of these two strands occurs in *Pan's Anniversary*, where the Arcadians sing

> Of PAN we sing, the best of Singers, *Pan*,
> That taught us swaines, how first to tune our layes . . .
> CHO. Heare, O you groves, and hills, resound his worth.
> And while his powers, and praises thus we sing,
> The Valleys let rebound, and all the rivers ring.   (ll. 172–89)

The next 'hymn' continues this idea with actual echoes.

The Function and Types of Main Masque Songs

Masque musicians were, as we have seen, commonly characterized as priests or poets. In other words, they were portrayed as men of more than ordinary wisdom and authority. Accordingly, their songs elucidate the mysteries of the masque's device and initiate the apparently magical transformations. In *Love Freed from Ignorance and Folly* song is used as the means of bringing insight to the captive Love, restoring order and harmony to a perplexed and confused mind. Music often effects miraculous results (much as it does in *The Winter's Tale*, where it is the agent of Hermione's revival). In *The Masque of Flowers*, the Garden-Gods descended to the stage and sang (to lutes and theorboes) first 'The Song that Induced the Charm', and then the charm itself—which changed flowers back into men. In *The Lord Hay's Masque*, Night, having been persuaded to assist in the festivities, ascended to the grove of trees in which Apollo's knights were trapped and announced:

---

[9] See Ch. 8 for the musical treatment of the iconography of Fame in the masque.
[10] For the description of the elaborate echo pieces see below, p. 155.

> By vertue of this wand, and touch deuine,
> These *Siluan* shadowes back to earth resigne:
> Your natiue formes resume, with habite faire,
> While solemne musick shall enchant the aire.   (p. 221)

Then followed a 'Songe of transformation' during which the masquers were
released from the trees.

There are many such songs. Most use imperative verbs—a way of insisting
that the songs themselves effect the transformations. In *The Memorable Masque*
a mountain opens to reveal the masquers (in a golden mine beneath) while the
six voices and six lutes of the Phoebades sing

> Ope, Earth, thy wombe of golde,
>   Shew, Heauen, thy cope of starres.
> All glad Aspects unfolde,
>   Shine out, and cleere our Cares:
> Kisse, Heauen and Earth, and so combine
> In all mix'd ioy our Nuptiall Twine.   (ll. 238–43)

The musician-priests do not merely describe the action; they appear to
determine it. In the preliminary section of the text outlining the argument of
the masque, Chapman virtually states this; he says that this first full song was
'vsed as an Orphean vertue for the state of the Mines opening' (ll. 156–7).

A very similar transformation takes place in *Pleasure Reconciled*. As Jonson
introduces the transformation song, he too emphasizes its efficacy:

Here yᵉ whole Quire of Musique call yᵉ. 12. Masquers forth from yᵉ Lap of yᵉ
Mountaine: wᶜʰ now opens wᵗʰ this

> Song.
> Ope, aged Atlas, open then thy lap
> and from thy beamy bosom, strike a light,
> yᵗ men may read in thy misterious map
>   all lines
>   and signes
> of roial education, and the righ[t]   (ll. 214–23)

Sixteen years later this transformation was echoed in Carew's *Coelum
Britannicum*; there the three Kingdoms sing:

> Open thy strong entrailes wide
> And breake old *Atlas*, that the pride
> Of three fam'd kingdomes may be spy'd.   (ll. 942–4)

'Appear, appear, you happy Knights!' (*The Mountebanks Masque*), 'Break forth!
thou treasure of our sight' (*Britannia Triumphans*): these sung commands are
typical, and they illustrate how the efficacious transformation song had become a convention.

A related song type banishes disruptive forces and establishes a 'sanctified'
atmosphere in which the happy rites of the masque proper may proceed.

Perhaps the most obvious example of this is the song in *The Somerset Masque* which halts the confused dancing of the antimasque:

> Vanish, vanish hence, confusion;
> Dimme not *Hymens* goulden light
>   With false illusion . . .   (p. 272)

Hymenaei had begun with a similar song which emphasized the masque's ritual and quasi-religious dimension:

> Bid all profane away;
> None here may stay
> To view our *mysteries*,
> But, who themselues haue beene,
> Or will, in time, be seene
> The self-same *sacrifice* . . .   (ll. 67–72)

This, too, finds echoes in the Caroline period. In *The Triumph of Peace*, Irene was to descend and banish the antimasquers with a song beginning, 'Hence, ye profane, far hence away' (ll. 491 ff.).

A less bellicose variant on this idea was sung by Euphemus in *Love's Triumph through Callipolis* at the point of transition between profane antimasque and virtuous masque. The song contains a warning that Love cannot be present until the depraved lovers of the antimasque are thoroughly banished:

> Loue, in perfection, longeth to appeare,
>   But prayes, of fauour, he be not call'd on,
> Till all the suburbes, and the skirts bee cleare
>   Of perturbations, and th'infection gon . . .   (ll. 74–7)

Euphemus' song is followed by a chorus, sung while the place is purified with censers.

All these songs support and give expression to the musician-as-*vates* idea. Moreover, they are typical of main masque songs in having an important structural function. In the case of this latter group, it is to introduce the main masque.

There were other ways in which song was used to articulate the masque's structure. Most obviously, it announced the end of the night's festivities. *The Masque of Blackness* has an aubade of a kind which was to become very familiar: the night being almost over, the revels must cease. This particular song draws on the fact that it was Diana who had initiated the Aethiopians' quest for James I's court; Diana now 'declines' and so the tide must ebb, the masque come to an end:

> Now DIAN, with her burning face,
>   Declines apace:
> By which our Waters know
> To ebbe, that late did flow.

> Back *Seas*, back *Nymphs*; but, with a forward grace,
> Keepe, still, your reuerence to the place:
> And shout with ioy of fauor, you haue wonne,
> In sight of *Albion*, NEPTVNES sonne.   (ll. 354–61)[11]

Oberon, *Love Restored*, and *The Vision of Delight* all have concluding songs which mention the approach of dawn. In *The Vision of Delight*, this was sung by Aurora (as Night and the Moon descended) and answered by a chorus. Aurora's words (for which a very ornate setting survives) express the customary reluctance for the festivities to end:

> I was not wearier where I lay
> By frozen *Tythons* side to night;
> Then I am willing now to stay,
> And be a part of your delight.
> But I am urged by the Day,
> Against my will, to bid you come away.   (ll. 237–42)

The Triumph of Peace has a song associated with Amphiluce ('the forerunner of the morning'), while the concluding song in *Britannia Triumphans* mentions, not the approaching dawn as such, but the prospect of rest that comes with the lateness of the hour:

> Wise Nature, that the Dew of sleepe prepares
> To intermit our joyes and ease our cares,
> Invites you from these Triumphs to your rest.   (p. 208)

In masques associated with wedding celebrations, these aubades have a rather different emphasis: the regret at the passing of the revels is modified by the sense that as time goes on, the courtly celebrations can only hinder nuptial joys. This is given its clearest expression in the brief song which concludes *The Lords' Masque*:

> No longer wrong the night
> Of her *Hymenæan* right;
> A thousand *Cupids* call away,
> Fearing the approching day;
> The Cocks alreadie crow:
> Dance then and goe.   (p. 262)

Such songs—public and ceremonial in form—are like a complementary inversion of the extensive genre of intimate lyrics in which lovers complain about the approaching dawn.[12] Here, the approach of dawn signals, not the

---

[11] This song underlines the decorum in the way the masquers depart, paying their respects to the king until the very end. Similarly, the concluding song in *Love Freed* emphasizes the way in which masquers and musicians leave while paying homage to the king: 'Thus should the *Muses* PRIESTS, and GRACES goe to rest | Bowing to the Sunne, throned in the West' (ll. 377 ff.).

[12] 'Sweet stay a-while' (set three times in the period), or the Donne poem 'Sweetest love I do not goe' (set anonymously in the early 17th c.) are superb examples of this kind of song. On the settings of these

interruption of lovers' intimacies by the demands of public duties, but rather the time for public celebration to give way to private contentment.

Hymenaei ('Thinke, yet, how *night* doth wast'), *The Masque of the Inner Temple and Gray's Inn,* and *The Memorable Masque* all have concluding songs which share this theme. 'Why stays the bridegroom' for *The Haddington Masque* (Ferrabosco's setting is discussed below; see Ex. 2.10) is a particularly fine example. Even Coprario's sailors' song 'Come ashore, come, merry mates' (which concludes *The Somerset Masque*) touches on these themes:

> Hast aboord, hast now away;
> Hymen frownes at your delay:
> Hymen doth long nights affect;
> Yield him then his due respect.   (p. 276)

The final song in *Pleasure Reconciled* fulfils the same structural function but adopts a rather more serious tone. It makes a link between the ideal virtue represented in the masque and the difficulty of living virtuously in the actual world. Almost by virtue of its emphasis on this transition from illusion to reality, this song avoids the conventional suggestion that entertainment should now give way to sleep:

> Theis, theis are howres, by Vertue spar'd
>   hirself, she being hir owne reward,
>   But she will haue you know,
>   that though
> hir sports be soft, hir life is hard.   (ll. 328–32)

Jonson was evidently concerned that the challenging words of this song be heard clearly; it was first declaimed by Mercury and then 'repeated in Song'.

We have seen, then, that these two types of masque song are structurally important; they give emphasis and a sense of triumph to the opening and closing moments of the main masque. These, though, are not the only steps in the masque's ritual pattern which are articulated by song. The largest and most important group of masque songs are those which introduce and inter-pret the set dances and the revels. Structurally and thematically these lie at the very heart of the masque. They will be discussed later in the context of masque dancing.

Masque Song Settings

It is clear that crucial points in the unfolding device and ritual of the main masque were marked by songs, songs which served both to emphasize the importance of these moments and to comment on their significance. Surviv-ing settings indicate that the music which was heard was sufficiently sophis-

poems see my ' "Music and *Sweet* Poetry"? Verse for English Lute Song and Continuo Song', *ML* 65 (1984), 249–50.

ticated to sustain this kind of structural and thematic weight. The fact that the songs which do survive from the Jacobean masque are virtually all solo ayres and are found in sources of a kind normally associated with more intimate forms of musical expression suggests that they have some affinity with other solo vocal music in the period. In order to see what made masque songs distinctive, we need to consider their stylistic context.

Three broadly different types of solo ayre can be distinguished in the early seventeenth century.[13] First there is the essentially polyphonic form in which the vocal line forms one strand of a more complex texture; here the lute part is essentially a reduction to short score of up to four independent lines. (The published volumes provide for, and even encourage, alternative performances using several voices.) It is this style in which Dowland was pre-eminent. In contrast to this, Campion championed an essentially simpler style with accessible, tuneful, vocal lines and relatively uncomplicated chordal accompaniments. He was fond of drawing an analogy between this kind of composition and poetic epigrams—short, pithy statements where a polished technique disguises artifice. (This style of song merges with other forms of light ayres and dance songs.)

The third main type, known as the declamatory ayre, gives priority to preserving the rhythmic characteristics and even the inflections and intonation patterns of real speech. The bass line of the declamatory ayre tends to be much less active than in other types of song. Its defining characteristic is that it leaves the voice unencumbered and capable of imitating the flexibility of the spoken word. Such bass lines—even when written out in tablature with a fixed and sometimes full-sounding harmonization—are essentially continuo lines (and the development of the declamatory ayre goes hand in hand with the growth of continuo song—song written out with only an unrealized bass line). Theoretically, vocal writing which was truly and consistently declamatory would not be self-sufficient as music—it would not respond, for example, to instrumental transcription. In practice, however, no declamatory ayre in this period is quite so uncompromising. By virtue of its being a musical representation of actual speech, the declamatory style is inherently dramatic.

Although these three types of setting coexisted in the early seventeenth century, the first type had its roots in sixteenth-century polyphony and emerged from the consort song. The last variety, the declamatory ayre, is a new development and one which became dominant during the second decade of the century. Its emergence parallels—and was almost certainly influenced by—the development of dramatic monody in Italy.

One of the most interesting aspects of Jacobean masque songs is the way they incorporate declamatory features. For this reason it makes some sense to begin by looking at Lanier's *Somerset Masque* song, 'Bring away this sacred

---

[13] The most helpful survey of English solo song types in this period—one which I have drawn on for this summary—is I. Spink, *English Song, Dowland to Purcell* (London, 1974).

Ex. 2.1. Lanier, 'Bring away this sacred tree', from Campion, *The Description of a Maske* (1614)

Bring a - way, bring a - way this sac – red tree,

The tree of grace and boun – tie, Set it in *Bel- An* – *nœ*'s eye: For shee,

she, one-ly she, one-ly she Can all knot - ted spells un – tie.

Pull'd from this stocke, let her blest hand con-vey To an - y sup-pliant hand_____ a

21: *E* from basso part; tablature has *e*   24: *F♯–G* from basso part; tablature has *f♯–g*

Ex. 2.1. *Continued*

bough, And let that hand ad - vance it now Against a charme, that

charme shall fade a - way.

tree' (Ex. 2.1). This archetypal declamatory ayre can be treated as something of a yardstick for assessing related features in other songs. The voice enters on an unstressed syllable after a single lute chord. This immediately signals a declamatory setting since such openings are a cliché of the style. The line 'Bring away this sacred tree' could, however, be scanned differently: it is Lanier's treatment which determines that it begins with an anapaestic rather than a trochaic foot. In other words, it is—paradoxically—the musical setting which gives a speech-based quality to a line with, potentially, a much more obtrusive rhythm. (The repetition of 'Bring away' at a higher pitch comes across as dramatic emphasis rather than something done for essentially musical reasons.) Musical declamation appears in its most exaggerated form in the next line, 'The tree of grace and bountie'. The singer intones this phrase on a single pitch above a completely static bass line. The repeated C major chords meet the voice only at stressed points; they provide for a delivery in which the notated rhythms may be treated as an approximation of the natural speech-based ones. The chords in the lute tablature need to be read like other realized continuo lines—not as rigidly determined events but as an indication that, for these two bars, the singer needs the support of C major harmonies. (So, for example, a full chord need not be played under 'grace', while the chord on 'bounty' might be spread and filled out beyond the four notes given in the tablature.)

Something starts to change in the next phrase, 'Set it in Bel-Annæ's eye'. Although the intonation on a single pitch is continued, Lanier uses a dotted crotchet for 'in'—not an important word. By the next phrase, as the first half of the song climaxes, musical features move into the foreground. On 'For she, she, onely she' a syncopated vocal line is punctuated by metrically regular chords in the accompaniment (a passage which is strongly reminiscent of Dowland's setting of the line 'She and only she' in 'Say, Love, if ever thou didst find').[14] The declamatory mode is re-established briefly at the beginning of the second half of the song (on 'Pull'd from this stocke'). From then on, however, musical considerations become more important than the representation of (heightened) speech. There is a sequence with a very unspeechlike angular contour on 'let her blest hand convey | to any suppliant hand . . .'. In the next phrase vocal line and bass line move in regular contrary motion while suspensions create quaver movement in the accompaniment. Here, as the song builds to its musical climax, the lute moves out of a purely service role into a much more equal relationship with the voice.

After the double bar, declamatory considerations recede in importance (more rapidly in the second half of the song than in the first). This undoubtedly helps create a musically satisfying structure, but it also indicates something about the function of this style in the masque. The fact that Lanier does not write an unremittingly declamatory setting suggests that what he was seeking to achieve was not primarily clear and natural enunciation in a large space, but rather a dramatic stance: 'Bring away this sacred tree' presents itself to the audience as heroic proclamation. And this seems to hold the key not just to Lanier's approach here, but to Ferrabosco's use of declamatory features—they are dramatic gestures rather than the basis of the composition.

Ferrabosco's 1609 *Ayres* and his songs in GB-Ob, MS Tenbury 1018 together provide a substantial number of settings for the early Jonson masques. (It is unfortunately the case that very much less vocal music survives for the masques performed between 1612 and 1633.) The first masque song in the 1609 *Ayres* is 'Come away', sung by a tenor in *The Masque of Blackness* immediately before the revels (Ex. 2.2). The opening phrase is declamatory; both its scansion and the rise and fall in its melodic contour contribute to the sense of its being speech-based. Rhythmically, this became a stock declamatory phrase; it parallels exactly the opening of 'Bring away this sacred tree' and of one of Campion's songs for *The Lords' Masque* (see Ex. 2.3a). It is repeated (with just one small rhythmic variant) in Ferrabosco's 'Come home my troubled thoughts', printed on the page facing the masque song in the *Ayres*. Here there is an immediate dramatic justification for the use of a declamatory

[14] No. 7 in *The Third and Last Book of Songs or Ayres*. This song seems to have been imitated in the Entertainment at Brougham Castle; see E. H. Fellowes, F. W. Sternfeld, and D. Greer (eds.), *English Madrigal Verse 1588–1632* (Oxford, 1962), 741.

Ex. 2.2. Ferrabosco, 'Come away', from Ferrabosco, *Ayres* (1609)

gesture—the singer apostrophizes his own thoughts on the vanity of human desires:

> Come then obay this summons, come away,
> For here vaine hopes must serue you for your pay.

In this comment on the folly of seeking preferment at court the 'Come away' phrase must operate as an ironic allusion to the masque song.[15] The suggestion

---

[15] The apparent inconsistency in outlook is also evident in Jonson's poetry. Apart from satirical epigrams attacking foppishness ('On Court-Worm', H&S, viii. 31), other more serious poems assert the view that the

Ex. 2.3. (*a*) Campion, 'Come away arm'd with Love's delights', bars 1–2, from *Two Bookes of Ayres* (*c*.1613)

(*b*) Ferrabosco, 'Come home my troubled thoughts', bars 18–23, from *Ayres*

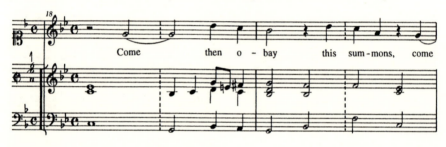

of the spoken voice in 'Come home my troubled thoughts' parallels exactly the tone adopted in so many contemporary metaphysical lyrics. It is, though, a passing moment in a setting which is otherwise more like the 'type 1', contrapuntally conceived, lute song (Ex. 2.3*b*).

The 'Come away' phrase outlines a diminished fourth. This is like an enhanced 'lachrymae' motif, and Ferrabosco uses it a great deal. He seems less interested in its plaintive character than in its inconclusive, suspended quality. At the beginning of a song it often lays the ground, so to speak, of the argument. The proposition 'If all these Cupids now were blind' outlines a

court can be a corrupting environment. See e.g. 'An Epistle answering to one that asked to be sealed of the Tribe of Ben', especially lines 51–3 and 63–6 (H&S, viii. 218–20).

descent from b'' to f'', and the rhetorical question 'Why stays the bridegroom to invade her?' c'' to g''. Interestingly, Dowland uses this same opening to very similar effect in 'Sweet stay awhile', and here, like Ferrabosco, he progresses from an (intimate) speech-based opening to a phrase in which other musical priorities become dominant (see Ex. 2.4, and compare Exx. 2.8 and 2.10 below).

What happens next in the *Masque of Blackness* song is very interesting. The second phrase begins like the first with the voice entering after a chord on a syllable which would be unaccented in normal speech. But now the first word is lightly syncopated and the phrase begins to take on a rhythmic interest which is independent of the words. Here the elements of a declamatory

Ex. 2.4. Dowland, 'Sweet stay awhile', bars 1–5, from *A Pilgrimes Solace* (1612)

Ex. 2.5. Ferrabosco, Alman, bars 1–16 (outer voices only), adapted from *Jacobean Consort Music*, ed. Dart and Coates

rhythm—established in the first phrase—are transmuted into a dance-like feature. From this point on frequent syncopation in the vocal line against regular chords in the accompaniment gives the piece a rhythmic buoyancy which is very much akin to dance. It is interesting to place it alongside one of Ferrabosco's five-part Almans where the outer voices display a very similar kind of rhythmic interest (see Ex. 2.5).

In this short song the declamatory opening is appropriate dramatically; the masquers are being called back to the sea. But once Ferrabosco has made that gesture, he goes on to produce something whose lively rhythms seem designed to support the festive atmosphere of the masque. The accompaniment is chordal (with occasional passing notes), no words are repeated, and there is no use of melisma; but even so, the word setting after the opening phrase is not consistently declamatory. The basic tonality of the piece is G minor, though Ferrabosco plays with sharpened and flattened thirds to the extent that he approaches a continuous ambiguity between major and minor. This is typical. The vocal line extends only over one octave (from *d'* to *d"*) but Ferrabosco gives the piece shape by the way this range is used, expanding outwards towards the middle and contracting again at the end. (The highest note is heard only once, in the middle of the song.) The salient features of 'Come away'—a vocal line which is coloured by expressive intervals, a structural use of vocal range, a fluid harmonic scheme, and an equilibrium

Ex. 2.6. Ferrabosco, 'If all the ages of the earth', bars 9–16, from *Ayres*

Ex. 2.7. Ferrabosco, 'How near to good', bars 1-15, from *Ayres*

How neere to good is what is fayre Which we no soon - er see,

But with the lynes, and out - ward ayer Our sen - ces tak - en bee.

Wee wish it still to ...

between declamatory and dance rhythms—recur in many of Ferrabosco's masque songs.

It is this last feature which I find most interesting. In bars 20–9 of 'Why stays the bridegroom', for example, a chord introduces a declamatory phrase, after which a more broken melody line and dance rhythms take over. Duple and triple groups mingle and, as declamation recedes, the bass line becomes more active (see below, Ex. 2.10). Some songs could even be described as anti-declamatory. In 'If all the ages of the earth' the vocal line is so strongly syncopated that it virtually dislocates the sense of the verse: relatively unimportant words (notably 'of') are thrown into prominence while melisma, sequence, and imitation between voice and bass are all evident (see Ex. 2.6). 'It was no policy of court' presents a similar picture. The opening emphasizes—of all words—'it', and later the accompaniment has a loosely polyphonic texture. The phrase 'were not the men' is sung three times to a sequential pattern.

Ferrabosco's tendency to write angular vocal lines which have an almost fanfare-like quality reaches an extreme in one of the GB-Ob, MS Tenbury 1018 songs, 'How near to good' (from *Love Freed from Ignorance and Folly*). A motif with wide leaps (built initially on the notes of the tonic chord) recurs at the beginning of every phrase in the first half of the piece (see Ex. 2.7). These vocal lines could well be described as heroic—they do have an almost heraldic quality—but not as declamatory (at least, not in the sense that they appear to be moulded on the accents and inflections of natural speech).[16]

Ferrabosco's fluid harmonies are well illustrated by 'If all these cupids' from *The Masque of Beauty*. Bars 3–6 show a rapid movement through four steps in

[16] Ian Spink, in his lucid account of this repertoire (and in particular of 'If all the ages of the earth'), seems to me to place rather too much emphasis on declamation. He sees the acoustic conditions of masquing halls as an important factor in the development of an English declamatory style (and draws attention to the fact that it is stylistically quite distinct from Italian dramatic monody). See *English Song*, 41–2. Spink had originally developed his thesis that the English declamatory style developed as a response to masque conditions in 'English Cavalier Songs 1620–1660'. *PRMA* 86 (1959–60), 61–78.

Ex. 2.8. Ferrabosco, 'If all these cupids', bars 1–6, from *Ayres*

the circle of fifths, together with the characteristic major/minor alternation of the tonic chord and another favourite leap from a dominant chord to the mediant (see Ex. 2.8). A striking example of harmonic mobility occurs in 'Sing the nobless of his race' (one of the three masque songs in the *Ayres* whose context has not been identified). There, dramatizing the words 'breaking all the bounds of place', Ferrabosco leaves a stable C major context and, in the space of a few bars, traverses the circle of fifths from C major to A flat major, moving from there via C minor to G major (Ex. 2.9).[17]

The structural use of the vocal range noticed in 'Come away' can be seen in 'Yes, were the loves', where the highest note in a range extending from *d* to *g'* is saved for the final phrase of the stanza:

> They do not warre with different darts,
> But *strike* a musique of like harts.   (ll. 362–3)

This couplet is the poetic climax of three linked songs in *The Masque of Beauty* and it resolves the speculation with which they had begun. In 'Senses by unjust force banished',[18] Ferrabosco has again organized his pitches carefully so

---

[17] Christopher Field, in a paper entitled 'Jenkins and the Cosmography of Harmony' given at the John Jenkins tercentenary conference at Hitchin in July 1992, demonstrated that in his fantasias on the hexachord, Ferrabosco systematically follows through a widely migrating modulatory scheme.

[18] In GB-Ob, Tenbury MS 1018, this song occurs on fo. 37 between 'O what a fault' and 'How near to good' from *Love Freed from Ignorance and Folly*. Although the words of 'Senses by unjust force banished' do not occur in Jonson's text, the song must have been performed in or intended for this masque.

Ex. 2.9. Ferrabosco, 'Sing the noblesse of his race', bars 8–16, from *Ayres*

that the highest note in the piece has a climactic impact. It is approached from a steadily ascending movement which starts at the beginning of the song; the high *g′* is reserved for the word 'treasure' in the line which contains the central idea of the poem:

> Senses by unjust force banished
> From the object of your pleasure,
> Now of you is all end vanished;
> You who late possessed more treasure,
> When eyes fed on what did shine,
> And ears drank what was divine,
> Than the Earth's broad arms could measure.

The climactic function of 'treasure' is reinforced by the use of melisma. From this point to the end of the piece, the voice gradually descends.

This is only one of the ways in which Ferrabosco gives structure to his songs. The motivic development of 'Why stays the bridegroom', for example, works hand in hand with the pitch organization. The first half of the song has its own internal balance (see Ex. 2.10). The first phrase descends by step (and rises a fourth at the end); this is answered by a short contrasting phrase which contains an octave leap. The juxtaposition of stepwise downward movement and upward movement by leap is carried right through the piece. The two opening phrases are repeated in an abridged form with the second phrase in the repeated version leading to a perfect cadence on to the tonic major (instead of the relative major which is heard the first time). The second half of the song contains its musical and poetic climax:

> To morrow, rise the same
> Your *mother* is, and vse a *nobler* name.   (ll. 419–20)

Jonson's line arrangement creates a momentary ambiguity; not until the second line do we realize that the 'the same' actually means 'different' (no longer the virgin bride). Ferrabosco co-operates with Jonson's wit by making 'same' emphatic through both duration (a dotted minim) and pitch (the highest note in the song). As in 'Come away', this climactic point is free from syncopation and is reached by moving outside the rising octave for the first time to the highest note in the song. The intervallic leaps narrow and the note-values lengthen towards the end of the piece.

Ex. 2.10. Ferrabosco, 'Why stays the bridegroom', from *Ayres*

Ex. 2.10. *Continued*

There is an equally clear motivic organization in 'Had those that dwell in error foul' (see Ex. 2.11). An opening motif built around the interval of a third (*a*) has a tail-piece which moves upward by step (*b*). This is then repeated with a different rhythm (*a*¹), but this time the tail-piece moves downward to the tonic (*c*). After a short section which introduces new material, the first motif (*a*²) with the second tail-piece (*c*) reappears a fifth higher (so that it ends on the dominant); and then, finally, an abridged version of this is repeated at the original pitch.

One of the most finely structured of all these songs is 'So beauty on the waters stood' from *The Masque of Beauty*. It was sung by a 'loud tenor' at the end of a set dance while the masquers were standing still 'in the figure of a *Diamant*'. The song captures perfectly the sense of calm in Jonson's verse:

Ex. 2.11. Ferrabosco, 'Had those that dwell in error foul', bars 1–9 and 17–25, from *Ayres*

So beautie on the waters stood,
When *loue* had seuer'd earth, from flood!
So when he parted ayre, from fire,
He did with concord all inspire!   (ll. 324–7)

Ferrabosco's setting is tonally undisturbed and completely symmetrical. The first section has two (repeated) phrases, one virtually an inversion of the other. Both move predominantly by step. The second section provides a melodic contrast which mirrors a change in the content of the verse. This is most obvious in the way a descriptive use of melisma on the word 'motion' breaks up the stepwise descent of the line. The second phrase in this section ascends to the highest note in the piece (g'') and here the climactic point is made more emphatic through being approached by leap (Ex. 2.12). At one point in this middle section the accompaniment has a diminished and transposed version of the opening phrase, and the final vocal phrase in the song is a further modification of the opening. The symmetry, the smoothness of the melodic transitions, and the undisturbed harmonies suit the Neoplatonic outlook of the poem.

The melisma on 'motion' seen in Ex. 2.12 has an illustrative function. Ferrabosco is fond of this device: 'motion' is given a more melismatic treatment in 'Gentle Knights', like 'error' (wandering) in 'Had those that dwell in error foul'. The effect of the extensive melisma in 'Yes, were the Loves', however, is primarily to give the vocal line a joyous quality. There, sequential patterns are syncopated against a regular chordal accompaniment (see Ex. 2.13).

Ex. 2.12. Ferrabosco, 'So Beauty on the waters stood', bars 9–16, from *Ayres*

Ex. 2.13. Ferrabosco, 'Yes, were the Loves', bars 10–20, from *Ayres*

This combination of features seems quite precisely judged for its context. The declamatory elements project the idea that someone is actually coming forward to *proclaim* the significance of a dance. They often amount to little more than one or two gestures (perhaps just the initial voice entry). Once the song is under way, the balance shifts towards dance. Where Ferrabosco subordinates declamation to other musical techniques it is often to create an exultant atmosphere through fanfare-like contours.

Comparison of Ferrabosco's masque music with his other songs confirms that he must have had a strong sense of the particular demands of the masque. The masque settings stand out as a distinctive achievement from a composer whose works range from motets and esoteric viol fantasias to light songs. Compared with his other solo vocal music, the masque songs show considerable unity of style. (Not surprisingly, the song most like the masque songs is 'Come my Celia' for Jonson's *Volpone*.) A few of the *Ayres* (no. 24, 'Unconstant love', for example) have a lute accompaniment with more sustained interest than that found in any of the masque songs. But there are also a number of lighter Campionesque songs: 'Young and simple though I am' (no. 8), 'I am a lover' (no. 10), and 'Fain I would but O I dare not' (no. 5).

Outside the masque ayres, Ferrabosco's declamatory gestures always have an immediate dramatic justification. We have seen this in 'Come home my troubled thoughts'. In 'Dear, when to thee my sad complaint I make' the singer, addressing his beloved, enters (in a semi-declamatory manner) after an initial lute chord:

> Deere when to thee my sad complaint I make
> And shew how oft Loue doth my death renue . . .

The declamatory opening of Ferrabosco's (strophic) setting of 'The Expiration' is clearly a response to the dramatic quality of Donne's poem:

> So, so, leaue off this last lamenting kisse,
> Which sucks two soules and vapours both away . . .

'Drown not with tears' is another lover's address and, not surprisingly, we find a declamatory suggestion in the phrase 'My dearest love' (see Ex. 2.14).

Ex. 2.14. Ferrabosco, 'Drown not with tears', bars 1–5, from *Ayres*

Ferrabosco's most uncompromisingly declamatory songs are not English at all, but the Italian songs in GB-Ob, MS Tenbury 1019 (discussed below, p. 96).

While it would be limiting to see Ferrabosco's masque song style as founded in heroic declamation, it is nevertheless true that declamatory elements must have been considered especially appropriate in the masque. The clearest evidence for this comes not from the declamatory gestures which inform Ferrabosco's very personal idiom, but from the Dowland masque songs in *A Pilgrimes Solace*. 'Up merry mates' begins as a robust and tuneful ayre which is rhythmically and harmonically uncomplicated. After the first four lines, however, there is an abrupt change in style. A brief dialogue between the first singer and a 'steerman' begins (appropriately enough) in an overtly declamatory manner. The first singer puts his questions in speech rhythms quite unconstricted by the accompaniment. As in other early seventeenth-century dialogues, the bass answers are more rigid, the result of being tied to the functional bass line (see Ex. 2.15). This declamatory passage merges back into a tuneful style, first with a descriptive phrase which descends (in suspensions) across the words 'sink, sink, sink, despair', and then with a short

Ex. 2.15. Dowland, 'Up merry mates', bars 8–15, from *A Pilgrimes Solace*

Ex. 2.16. Campion, 'Now hath Flora', bars 17–21, from Campion, *The Discription of a Maske* (1607)

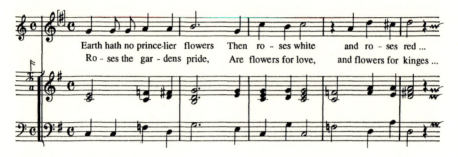

Earth hath no prince-lier flowers   Then ro - ses white   and ro - ses red ...
Ro - ses the gar - dens pride,   Are flowers for love,   and flowers for kinges ...

triple section, a gentle galliard which suggests beautifully the contentment it celebrates ('Come, solace, to the mind'). A mostly homophonic chorus follows (and here the lute essentially doubles the voices).

The opening of 'Welcome black night' is more purely declamatory than any English song by Ferrabosco, but by the end of the second line the vocal line has become shaped by more purely melodic factors, and the lute accompaniment has a linear interest of its own (with short solo passages). The second section of the piece makes a transition from the declamatory style to one which is close to the 'old manner' which Dowland acknowledged as his own in the preface to *A Pilgrimes Solace*. The fact that these three songs stand in such sharp contrast to most of his writing suggests that Dowland considered a style with declamatory elements right for a masque context. Even so, declamation is reserved for the more obviously dramatic passages.

The two Campion songs for *The Lord Hay's Masque* are stylistically very different from those discussed so far. Both accompany rhythmic movement. They conform to—and may have been influential in forming—Bacon's notions of what masque music should be like: '*Dancing to Song*, is a Thing of great State and Pleasure . . . *Acting in Song*, especially in *Dialogues*, hath an extreme Good Grace.'[19]

'Now hath Flora robbed her bowers' is a rather bland song, but Campion's concern with coupling 'words and notes lovingly together'[20] can be seen in his use of a sequence to support an analogous verbal structure (see Ex. 2.16). 'Move now with measured sound' has many of the same features: metrical evenness and melodic grace undisturbed by musical complication of any sort. Except for one central contrasting phrase, the melody line moves almost entirely by step. Like 'Now hath Flora', this song (or at least the opening strain) was played by instruments before the singing began.

---

[19] 'Of Maskes and Triumphs', *Essays* (1625), 223.
[20] Preface to *Two Books of Ayres* (c.1613); *Thomas Campion*, ed. Davis, 115.

The two Campion songs which survive from *The Lords' Masque* (performed six years later in February 1613) show something of a shift in style. Just as Campion's general plan for his masque now took account of Jonsonian models (*The Lords' Masque* has, for example, a clear antimasque section) his 1613 masque songs seem one step closer stylistically to Ferrabosco's. This suggests that Campion's admiration for Ferrabosco—he wrote an epigram for the 1609 *Ayres*—may have extended almost to emulation.

'Come away, bring thy golden theft' makes good use of light syncopation. In the last line of the song Campion underlines the urgency of the words by introducing a stretto effect into a sequential passage (see Ex. 2.17). The other surviving song from *The Lords' Masque*, 'Woo her and win her', lacks the declamatory gestures of 'Come Away', but is similar to Ferrabosco's masque-song style in other ways. There is a pervading counterpoint between verbal and musical rhythms. Much of the song's interest comes from its shifting pulse, the constant ambiguity as to whether the metre is triple or duple. The rhythmic groups are articulated by the changes in harmony, so that each stressed note in the vocal line is accompanied by a significant chord change. This harmonic articulation of synchronous rhythms allows for successive accents on adjacent notes (see 'each woman' in Ex. 2.18). Such rhythmic subtlety makes this the most interesting of Campion's masque songs.

The three Coprario songs from *The Somerset Masque* are all very different from each other. None are declamatory. This is interesting in view of the fact that the final dialogue in *Funeral Teares* (1606) and almost all of the *Songs of Mourning* (1613) give ample evidence of Coprario's fluency (pre-eminence even) in the new style. 'Go happy man' is a concise and graceful ayre accompanying action (a group of Squires take an enchanted bough from the Queen). Some piquancy is given to the first phrase by a prominent augmented second, and duple and triple rhythms are juxtaposed in the second half of the song (Ex. 2.19).

The other two Coprario songs are associated with dancing. Lively triple rhythms in 'While dancing rests' (which lacks its original echo) themselves

Ex. 2.17. Campion, 'Come away, bring thy golden theft', bars 15–18, from *Two Bookes of Ayres*

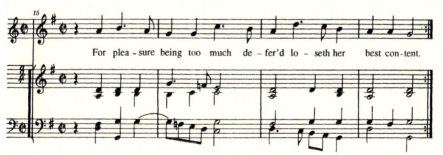

For plea-sure being too much de-fer'd lo-seth her best con-tent.

Ex. 2.18. Campion, 'Woo her and win her', bars 1–6, from Campion, *The Description of a Maske*

Ex. 2.19. Coprario, 'Go happy man', bars 1–3 and 11–17, from Campion, *The Description of a Maske*

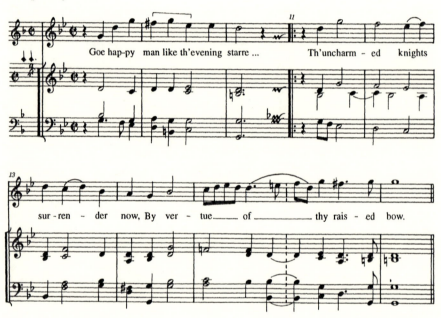

suggest a corant (Ex. 2.20). At the end of each phrase, the basic triple rhythm is varied by a hemiola, and this rhythmic expansion tends to coincide with a slightly more melismatic or florid treatment of the words. This pattern is never predictable, however, since the number of triple bars before the hemiola is varied in each phrase. The structure could be represented schematically as

E x. 2.20. Coprario, 'While dancing rests', bars 1–5, from Campion, *The Description of a Maske*

follows (where 3 stands for a triple bar):

1. 3 + 3 + hemiola–cadence
2. 3 + 3 + 3 + hemiola–cadence
3. 3 + hemiola–cadence [+ cadential echo]
4. ‖: [Chorus] 3 + 3 + C–cadence :‖

The Chorus is robust; there is nothing like the connecting notes and cross-rhythms in the accompaniment of the first half to lighten the movement of the two triple bars. The alla breve bar which replaces the hemiolas of the first half has the effect of a written-out *allargando*. (The other song is a sailor's song, introducing twelve skippers who 'daunced a brave and lively daunce, shouting and tryvmphing after their manner'. Coprario's music changes from the subtlety of 'Go happy man' and 'While dancing rests' to something which is indeed brave and lively.)

Lanier's setting of 'Do not expect to hear' from *The Masque of Augurs* seems rather nondescript. So, too, does 'I was not wearier'—once the basic ayre has been distilled from the extremely florid treble part surviving in GB-Lbl, MS Egerton 2013.[21] This raises quite fascinating questions about performance practice.

An Edmund Waller poem addressed to Henry Lawes ('who had then newly set a Song of mine in the year 1635') suggests that the vogue for elaborate ornamentation was widespread. The musician is praised for not allowing the sense of his songs to become dislocated by fastidious decoration.

> For as a window, thick with paint,
> Lets in a light but dim and faint;

---

[21] A table of contents for the now incomplete US-NYp, MS Drexel 4175 shows that it once contained a version of this song. Transcriptions of the GB-Lbl, MS Egerton 2013 version, together with reconstructions of the 'kernel' ayre may be found in McD. Emslie, 'Nicholas Lanier's Innovations in English Song', *ML* 41 (1960), 23–4, Spink, *English Song*, 47–8 and Sabol, *Four Hundred Songs and Dances*, 87. For a list of similarly ornamented songs see V. Duckles, 'Florid Embellishment in English Song of the late 16th and early 17th Centuries', *AM* 5 (1957), 343–5. See also D. Till, 'Ornamentation in English Song Manuscripts 1620–1660', B.Litt. diss. (Oxford University, 1975).

> So others, with Division hide
> The Light of Sense, the Poet's Pride:
> But you alone may truly boast
> That not a syllable is lost;
> The Writer's and the Setter's skill
> At once the ravish't Eare do fill.
> Let those which only warble long,
> And gargle in their throats a song,
> Content themselves with *Ut, re, mi*:
> Let words, and sense, be set by thee.[22]

Waller's complaints were familiar enough. Dowland had expressed his contempt for 'blind division makers' in the *Pilgrimes Solace* preface (and at least as many seventeenth-century discussions of florid ornamentation deal with its abuse as with its use). Nevertheless, it is clear that singers did use florid ornamentation in masque performances. Orazio Busino, the chaplain to the Venetian ambassador, noted (in his report on *Pleasure Reconciled*) that a musician (Daedalus) sang 'con qualche dispositione di gorga'.[23]

The use of such *gorgie* does not necessarily mean that singers distorted the delivery of the words or obscured the formal characteristics of the songs. 'I was not wearier' is an extreme case; the florid decoration is so elaborate that it all but obscures the underlying structure of the song. Other written–out ornaments for masque songs seem more intelligible. The florid version of Ferrabosco's 'Why stays the bridegroom' in GB-Och, Mus. 439 is a fine example. Here, the intricately decorated vocal line never distorts the basic rhythmic or melodic shape, nor seriously dislocates the words. The ornamentation consists of incidental graces except at cadences, where there are some quite extensive roulades (Ex. 2.21, and compare Ex. 2.10).[24]

Another Ferrabosco masque song appears with some ornaments in this manuscript—'If all these cupids' from *The Masque of Beauty*. Here the tendency for performers to tuck in incidental graces during the course of a piece (indicated in this case only by signs) and to reserve brilliant and extended flourishes for cadential points stands out clearly. At the bottom of the piece, beneath the actual music two roulades have been sketched in; the second and more extensive of them has the last two words of the song written underneath (see Pl. 2). Jotted down at the foot of the page (two attempts at a little cadenza), these flourishes convey a strong visual sense of the improvisatory and unfixed character of such decoration.[25] They point towards a performing

---

[22] The poem prefaces Lawes's *First Booke of Ayres* (London, 1653); lines 17–28 are quoted here. Ironically, seven of the fifty songs in Duckles's list of florid songs ('Florid Embellishment') are by Henry Lawes.

[23] H&S, x. 583.

[24] Robert Toft comments on the ornamented version of this song in *Tune thy Musicke to thy Hart* (Toronto, 1993), 95.

[25] 'Come away' (from *The Masque of Blackness*) also has two cadential trills marked in the GB-Och, Mus. 439 version.

Ex. 2.21. Ferrabosco, 'Why stays the bridegroom', bars 19–28, from GB-Och, Mus. 439

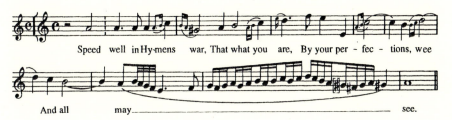

Speed well in Hy-mens war, That what you are, By your per - fec - tions, wee

And all may————————————————— see.

Note-values are unchanged, though type size and (in bar 27) beaming have been used to clarify the rhythmic organization of the ornaments.

tradition in which roulades and graces would be added almost as a matter of course, and they are good enough to show that, in the hands of a gifted musician, this could enhance rather than subvert the composition.

Lanier's 'Weep no more my wearied eyes' (the alternative text for 'Bring away this sacred tree') exists in a very florid version in EIRE-Dtc, MS F. 5. 13. Here the embellishments are extensive, but they do not obliterate the declamatory elements which are such an important feature of this song. As in the GB-Och, Mus. 439 versions of the Ferrabosco songs, most of the ornamentation comes in extended cadential flourishes, although there is enough of it elsewhere to convey an overall impression of a very florid line (Ex. 2.22, and compare Ex. 2.1).[26] In a sense, the existence of ornamented versions of masque songs points to their being regarded as sophisticated vocal writing. Court ayres rather than popular songs were susceptible to such treatment.

The songs by Ferrabosco, Campion, Coprario, and Lanier account for nearly all the surviving songs from the main masque sections of courtly masques in the Jacobean period.[27] Just one other song should be mentioned here. There are two settings of 'Come noble nymphs' from *Neptune's Triumph/The Fortunate Isles*. One occurs in GB-Ob, MS Don. c. 57 and is anonymous; the other, by William Webb, was printed in Playford's *Select Ayres and Dialogues* of 1659. The Webb setting is interesting since it has three changes of metre corresponding exactly to the text's division of the verse amongst three singers in the first stanza. Thus Proteus opens with a call to the Nymphs in a declamatory style, Saron adds a tuneful triple-time couplet, and Portunus concludes with four more lines in common time. It had been thought that this setting could not have been written for the original presentation of the masque; apart from its late publication date, its composer is not

[26] GB-Eu, MS La. III. 483—the bass partbook which originally belonged with EIRE-Dtc, MS F. 5. 13—does not contain this song.

[27] There is a Henry Lawes setting of lines 86–156 of *The Haddington Masque*, but since Lawes was only 12 years old when this masque was performed, his setting could not have been used. See W. M. Evans, *Henry Lawes: Musician and Friend of Poets* (New York, 1941), 27.

Ex. 2.22. Lanier, 'Weep no more', bars 1–15, from EIRE-Dtc, MS F. 5. 13

The values of ornamental notes (all represented as semiquavers in the original) have been altered in order to clarify their relationship to the underlying melody. The notes between square brackets in bars 20–1 are illegible in the manuscript.

known to have been active as a musician until 1634 (when he was mentioned as a tenor in *The Triumph of Peace*). But Ian Spink has shown that other Webb songs are found in manuscript collections which are at least as early as the projected performance of *Neptune's Triumph* (early 1624).[28] Hence it is possible that this setting was intended for that performance or for *The Fortunate Isles* a year later. (When it was reprinted in *The Treasury of Musick*, 'Come noble nymphs' had a heading which read 'At a Masque to invite the Ladies to a Dance'.)

[28] Spink, *English Song*, 60.

The MS Don. c. 57 version is much simpler and gives no hint of the way the lines were divided amongst the three characters. It is, however, more appealing and achieves some sense of nobility in its regular duple movement and restrained cadential ornamentation. The rhythms of the vocal line observe closely the natural accentuation of the spoken words. MS Don. c. 57 is thought to have been copied about 1630 and contains a number of songs from plays performed between 1614 and 1622 (including six songs by William Webb).[29] Hence the anonymous 'Come noble nymphs' could also have been composed about the time of *Neptune's Triumph*. All this makes it difficult to say which, if either, of the two settings belongs to the original performance. It is possible that one was written for the planned performance *Neptune's Triumph* and that the other was a new setting for *The Fortunate Isles*. Neither does complete justice to Jonson's fine poem.

The Place of Vocal Music in the Antimasque

The sophistication of main masque songs is especially obvious when they are viewed in the context of masque performances as a whole. Like all the other elements of the main masque, they make their impact partly by contrast with what has gone before—the antimasque. In the preface to *The Masque of Queens* Jonson describes the antimasque as a 'foil' to the main masque:

And because her Ma.tie (best knowing, that a principall part of life in these *Spectacles* lay in they[r] variety) had commaunded mee to think on some *Daunce*, or shew, that might præcede hers, and haue the place of a foyle, or false-*Masque*; I was carefull to decline not only from others, but mine owne stepps in that kind, since the last yeare I had an *Anti-Masque* of Boyes: and therefore, now, deuis'd that twelue Women, in the habite of *Haggs*, or Witches, sustayning the persons of *Ignorance*, *Suspicion*, *Credulity*, &c. the opposites to good *Fame*, should fill that part; not as a *Masque*, but a spectacle of strangenesse, producing multiplicity of Gesture, and not vnaptly sorting w[t]h the current, and whole fall of the Deuise. (ll. 10–22)

Jonson implied a triple pun in his use of this new term. The 'antimasque' presents a world of misrule which is morally or socially opposed (anti-) to the main masque, it precedes (ante-) the main masque, and it is marked by antic behaviour and especially by antic dancing.[30] (As we shall see, some variants of the term isolate only one element of the word's meaning.) Jonson's antimasques are sometimes, as in *The Masque of Queens*, grotesque representations of an unvirtuous, discordant world which is then obliterated by the virtue and order of the masque proper. Antimasque creatures were not always

---

[29] *The Tempest* (1613), *Valentinian* (c.1610), *The Mad Lover* and *Queen of Corinth* (both 1617), and *Beggars Bush* (1622).

[30] 'Antic' has a long association with revelry. Gaveston in Marlowe's *Edward II* (I. ii. 58–60) describes one of the entertainments he will provide for the king in these terms:

Like *Siluan* Nimphes my pages shall be clad,
My men like Satyres grazing on the lawnes,
Shall with their Goate feete daunce an antick hay.

so threatening, though they invariably existed on a much less elevated plane than the masquers. Cupid and his attendants in *The Haddington Masque* (the previous year's 'antimasque of boys' mentioned above) were not demonic like the witches. Their kind of malevolence in fact appears less frequently as time goes on.

Jonson's later antimasques, and those in non-Jonsonian masques, tend to be scenes of social satire or comedy, either low-life or pastoral. They are, to use an expression from Chapman's *Memorable Masque*, 'low inductions' rather than 'spectacles of strangeness'.[31] Their *dramatis personae* come not from a mythical or supernatural world but from one which is often reminiscent of Jonson's satiric comedies. The discussion between the cook and the poet in *Neptune's Triumph*, for example, anticipates *The Staple of News*.[32]

Antimasques of the first type ('spectacles of strangeness') rarely contain much singing. Jonson, after all, claimed that the Queen had commanded him 'to think on some *dance*, or show'. There is a compelling justification for the absence of singing here. Those represented in spectacles of strangeness are (as Lorenzo puts it in *The Merchant of Venice*) 'fit for treasons, stratagems, and spoils', and so it follows that they must be unmusical. Such ideas, deriving from the notion of *musica humana*, find many other expressions in this period. Henry Peacham shows the potential for using responsiveness to music as a way of establishing a fundamental distinction between antimasque characters and those who grace the main masque: 'I know there are many . . . of such disproportioned spirits, that they avoid her [Music's] company . . . but I am verily persuaded, they are by nature very ill disposed, and of such a brutish stupidity, that scarce anything else that is good and savoreth of virtue, is to be found in them.'[33] It is not surprising that characters from spectacles of strangeness almost never sing (although they invariably express their stunted or perverted natures in antic dance).

It is to the second, or 'low induction', type of antimasque that nearly all antimasque songs belong. Even here, however, the most common pattern is to have a spoken (and usually prose) antimasque, with all the singing confined to the main masque. When song does occur in (low-induction) antimasques, its function is often to supply a model against which the more sophisticated songs of the main masque might be appreciated. Jonson implies this in

[31] 'After this lowe Induction, by these succeeding degrees the chiefe Maskers were aduanc't to their discoverie', *The Memorable Masque*, ll. 190–2.

[32] III. ii. There are even more obvious anticipations of that play in the masque *News from the New World*.

[33] *The Compleat Gentleman* (London, 1622), ed. V. B. Heltzel (Ithaca, 1962), 108 ff. Ronsard expresses similar ideas in a way which also highlights possibilities exploited in various masque devices: 'The ancients used music as a touchstone to distinguish magnanimous souls—such as have not lost their original essence—from those that are bastardized in this mortal body, and have forgotten the celestial harmony, as the companions of Ulysses forgot being men when turned into swine by Circe. The man who, on hearing the sweet accord of instruments or the sweetness of the natural voice, is not delighted and is not moved and does not tremble from head to foot, sweetly ravished and transported, gives proof thereby that he has a crooked, vicious, and depraved soul, and is to be guarded against as one not happily born' (quoted by Hutton, 'Some English Poems in Praise of Music', 4).

Neptune's Triumph. There, a poet—asked why the courtly festivities have been delayed so long—replies:

> It was not time,
> To mixe this Musick with the vulgars chime.
> Stay, till th'abortiue, and extemporall dinne
> Of balladry, were vnderstood a sinne,
> *Minerua* cry'd: that, what tumultuous verse,
> Or prose could make, or steale, they might reherse,
> And euery Songster had sung out his fit . . .
> The *Muses* then might venter, vndeterr'd,
> For they loue, then, to sing, when they are heard.   (ll. 161–74)

In surveying the use or avoidance of vocal music in the antimasque I want to begin with Daniel's *Tethys Festival* (1610) which, though written after Jonson had pronounced on antimasque form and function, is very different in conception. In using the term 'Ante-maske' to describe what is in fact an unthreatening prelude to the main action, Daniel adopted a consciously un-Jonsonian stance: 'From this Scene issued *Zephirus*, with eight Naydes, Nymphs of fountaines, and two *Tritons* sent from *Tethys* to giue notice of intendement, which was the Ante-maske or first shew' (ll. 66–70). It begins with a 'song of foure parts, and a musicke of twelue Lutes' (ll. 89–90). The song was, as far as we can tell from the text, indistinguishable in style and manner of performance from the main masque songs, the first of which was also performed by 'a soft musique of twelue Lutes and twelue voyces' (ll. 303–4). Daniel takes obvious pride in the fact that (unlike Jonson) he did not require the involvement of professional actors or dancers for his 'antemaske'. He announces that 'the Duke of Yorke presented *Zephirus*' (l. 70) and—at the end of the text—that

. . . in all these shewes, this is to be noted, that there were none of inferiour sort, mixed amongst these great Personages of State and Honour (as vsually there haue beene) but all was performed by themselues with a due reseruation of their dignity. And for those two which did Personate the Tritons, they were Gentlemen knowne of good worth and respect.   (ll. 416–22)

While Daniel was clearly distancing himself from Jonson's methods here, he was also returning to the concept of a non-comic prologue like that in his first masque, *The Vision of the Twelve Goddesses*. There Night wakes Sleep to help her present the masque: '*Night* and *Sleepe* were to produce a Vision, an effect proper to their power, & fit to shadow our purpose, for that these apparitions and shewes are but as imaginations, and dreames that portend our affections' (ll. 124–7). This first Jacobean 'ante-maske' is like the framework of a medieval dream vision; spoken throughout, it establishes that the singing of the main masque is visionary.

Like *The Vision of the Twelve Goddesses*, Campion's *Lord Hay's Masque* (1607) predates the development of the antimasque proper. Nevertheless, it had a section in which Night—outraged at the offence being done to Cynthia (goddess of chastity) by the wedding celebrations—interrupts the entertainment. She is placated by Hesperus (who reassures her that Cynthia is 'well content her Nymph is made a Bride') and becomes a presenter of the 'princely revelling and timely sport'. Night initially interrupts a sung dialogue, and once she has been calmed down and her co-operation secured, the festivities resume in song. Once again, the absence of song makes this episode stand outside the main part of the masque.

The musical contrasts, not surprisingly, became stronger and clearer once the full-blown antimasque had evolved. In *The Masque of Queens* eleven witches plot to prevent the arrival of the masquers—twelve queens who are paragons of honour and virtue. The witches' chanted charms are, in effect, unmusical songs, a sinister antimasque equivalent of those main masque songs which initiate the magical scenic transformations:

> Dame, *Dame*, the watch is set:
> Quickly come, we all are met.
> From the lakes, and from the fennes,
> From the rockes, and from the dennes,
> From the woods, and from the caues,
> From the Church-yards, from the graues,
> From the dungeon, from the tree,
> That they die on, here are wee.   (ll. 53–60)

The same four-stress/seven-syllable lines are used for the witches' unholy chants in *Macbeth* ('For a charm of powerful trouble, | Like a hell-broth boil and bubble'.) Short lines, strong rhythms, and bald rhymes are the essence of this kind of incantation and they are calculated to produce a sinister effect. It is a demonic parody of religious ritual. The rest of the time the witches communicate in relatively free iambic pentameter:

> DAME: Well done, my *Hagges*. And come We, fraught wᵗh spight,
>   To ouerthrow the glory of this night?
>   Holds our great purpose. HAG. yes. DAM. But wants there none
>   Of our iust number? HAG. Call vs one, by one,
>   And then oʳ *Dame* shall see   (ll. 112–16)

The main masque has long passages of explanatory iambic pentameter from Heroic Virtue and Fame, but the presence of the twelve virtuous queens who displace the witches on the stage is celebrated in three songs, the first of which, we are pointedly told, was performed by 'a full triumphant *Musique*' (l. 720). The words explain why Jonson has reserved true singing until this moment; song is the proper way to proclaim the presence of virtue and true reputation:

> Helpe, helpe all Tongues, to celebrate this wonder:
> The voyce of FAME should be as loud as Thonder.
>   Her House is all of *echo* made,

> Where neuer dies the sound;
> And, as her browes the cloudes invade,
> Her feete do strike the ground.
> Sing then *good Fame*, that's out of *Vertue* borne,
> For, Who doth fame neglect, doth vertue scorne.   (ll. 723–30)

The main masque songs stand out in sharp contrast to the witches' chants. Ferrabosco's setting of 'If all the ages of the earth', with its angular vocal line and lively, varied rhythms, is most strikingly distinct from the insistent regularity of the antimasque's incantation.

The antimasque in *Mercury Vindicated* is one of the few 'spectacles of strangeness' to contain any singing. Vulcan, the arch-alchemist, tries to harness and control Mercury for his own ends; but his perverted art withers away when Nature and Prometheus are revealed in the main masque. The antimasque is set in a laboratory or alchemists' workshop where Vulcan tends the registers. Like the witches' incantations, the Cyclope's song is a charm used to elicit Mercury from the furnace. It is accompanied by cornets (appropriate to the underworld), in definite contrast to the lutes of the main masque songs.

The words of the antimasque and main masque songs here merit close comparison. The Cyclope's song depicts alchemy as an art that prides itself in overcoming Nature:

> Soft, subtile fire, thou soule of art,
>   Now doe thy part
> On weaker Nature, that through age is lamed.
>   Take but thy time, now she is old,
>   And the Sunne her friend growne cold,
> She will no more, in strife with thee be named . . .   (ll. 6–11)

The antimasque makes the point that base unnatural art undermines the function of true art. Mercury protests about the alchemists' outrages:

Howsoeuer they may pretend vnder the specious names of *Geber, Arnold, Lully, Bombast of Hohenhein*, to commit miracles in art, and treason again' nature . . . Art thou not asham'd, *Vulcan*, to offer in defence of thy fire and Art, against the excellence of the Sunne and Nature, creatures more imperfect, then the very flies and insects, that are her trespasses and scapes?   (ll. 45–8 and 186–9)[34]

Ultimately, as in *The Alchemist*, this must function as a comment on the prostitution of art which arises from the evil or misguided application of an artist's skills. While the antimasque song is preoccupied with the strength of Vulcan's presumptuous and mechanistic art, the songs in the main masque

---

[34] It seems that Jonson may have included some of his rival masque writers amongst these false artists since he includes a reference to making statues dance: 'Sir, would you beleeue, it should be come to that height of impudence . . . that such a nest of fire-wormes, as they are (because their Patron *Mulciber* heretofore has made stooles stirre, and statues dance, a dog of brasse to barke . . .) professe to outworke the *Sunne* in vertue, and contend to the great act of generation, nay, almost creation?' (ll. 126–34).

assert the true place and value of an art which co-operates with Nature. Nature is revealed in a glorious bower with the artist Prometheus at her feet (as a subject). She descends and sings the first song, which asks the artist's assistance in showing that the masquers are children of Nature:

> How yong and fresh am I to night,
>   To see't kept day, by so much light,
> And twelue my sonnes stand in their Makers sight?
> Helpe, wise *Prometheus*, something must be done,
> To shew they are the creatures of the Sunne,
>   That each to other
>   Is a brother,
> And *Nature* here no stepdame, but a mother.   (ll. 202–9)

The antimasque song in *Mercury Vindicated* reflects Jonson's preoccupation with the uses and abuses of art. It deliberately parallels the masque songs in subject—and it is a pity that we have no more than Jonson's single reference to cornets to suggest how the contrasts between these songs might have been projected in performance.

The other spectacle of strangeness to include singing occurs in *Pleasure Reconciled to Virtue*. This opened with a bacchic 'hymn' (as the Folio text describes it) sung by one of Comus's retinue:

> Roome, roome, make roome for yᵉ bouncing belly,
> first father of Sauce, & deuiser of gelly,
> Prime master of arts, & yᵉ giuer of wit,
> yᵗ found out yᵉ excellent ingine, yᵉ spit . . .   (ll. 13–16)

The first line echoes the conventional opening of a mummers' play, here intended to establish its basis in ignorance or barbarism. Comus, as 'prime master of arts', is a grotesque inversion of the learning and wit shortly to be demonstrated in the main masque. As in *Mercury Vindicated*, the antimasque song could be seen as a kind of anti-art.

The antimasque *For the Honour of Wales*, which Jonson added for the second performance of *Pleasure Reconciled*, was of the 'low induction' type. Here there were seven songs which were not so much anti-art as sub-art. There is nothing malevolent about this antimasque, and the loyalty of the king's Welsh subjects seems as far beyond dispute as their stupidity and ignorance. Their songs deal with Welsh produce, fabrics, food and drink, and, finally, music and dancing:

> And yet, is nothing now aull this,
>   if of our Musiques we doe misse;
> Both Harpes, and Pipes too, and the Crowd,
>   must aull come in and tauke alowd,
> As lowd as Bangu, Davies bell,
>   of which is no doubt yow have heare tell,
> As well as our lowder Wrexham Organ,
>   and rumbling Rocks in S'eere Glamorgan . . .   (ll. 273–80)

The Irish Masque (performed four years earlier) has a similar antimasque. Interestingly, it had a mixed reception. Chamberlain reported to Dudley Carleton that some members of the court had been worried that it was perhaps damagingly provocative: 'The loftie maskers were so well liked at court the last weeke that they were appointed to performe y^t againe on monday, yet theyre deuice (wch was a mimicall imitation of the Irish) was not so pleasing to many, wch thincke yt no time (as the case stands) to exasperat that nation by making yt ridiculous'.[35] The contrast between antimasque and masque in *The Irish Masque* is achieved basically through the juxtaposition of two types of Irish music, rough folk music and something which is supposed to relate to a dignified bardic tradition. Two songs in the (very short) main masque were sung by 'the Bard . . . to two harpes'.[36] In the antimasque six footmen and six boys danced 'to the bag-pipe, and other rude musique, after which they had a song' (ll. 136–7). 'Rude music', in fact, sums up very well the intended impact of most low-induction song.

Two days after the second performance of *The Irish Masque* and as part of the same wedding celebrations, *The Masque of Flowers* was performed. The quarto edition of this masque included the four-part antimasque song 'Kawasha comes in majesty'. John Wilson published a three-part version of this in *Cheerful Ayres* (1660), and it is possible that this is one of his earliest forays into dramatic composition (since he would have been only 19 when the masque was performed).[37] 'Kawasha comes' is indeed a 'cheerful ayre' (Ex. 2.23). It forms the climax of the antimasque contest between Silenus, the champion of wine, and Kawasha, the champion of tobacco. The whole episode is called 'The Antic-Masque of the Song' and it precedes an 'Antic-masque of the Dance'. The contesting vocalists (four to each team, and hence one to a part) are accompanied by a very odd mixture of instruments:

Before *Silenus* marched foure Singers, and behind him fiue Fidlers; Before and behinde *Kawasha* as many of each kinde. The Singers on *Silenus* part were a Miller, a Wine Cooper, a Vintners boy, a Brewer. His musicke, a Taber and a Pipe, a base Violin, a trebble Violin, a sagbut, a Mandora. *Kawashaes* Singers, a Skipper, a Fencer, a Pedler, a Barber. His musicke, a Bobtaile, a blind Harper and his boy, a base Violin, a tenor-Cornet, a sagbut. (ll. 184–90)

The instrumental groups are both distorted mixed consorts. The tabor and pipe mark out Silenus' group as uncourtly. It is not known what a bobtail is, but its name suggests an unsophisticated origin.[38] The contrast with main

[35] Letter dated 5 Jan. 1614; cited in H&S, x. 541.

[36] Peter Holman, 'The Harp in Stuart England: New Light on William Lawes's Harp Consovts', *EM* 15 (1987), 194, points out that one of the harpists must have been Cormack MacDermott, a highly esteemed Irish-born harpist who held a place in the King's Musick from 1605 until his death in 1618.

[37] The *Cheerful Ayres* version of the song also occurs in the pair of manuscript songbooks GB-Eu, MS Dc. 1. 69, and GB-Ob, MS Mus. d. 238.

[38] H. A. Evans suggested that this instrument must be a kit. See *English Masques* (London, 1897), 106 n. 6.

Ex. 2.23. 'Antic Masque of the Song', bars 87–102, from *The Masque of Flowers* (1614)

masque lutes and theorbos was heavily underlined by the manner of performance: both groups 'frumpled over' their music (ll. 215 and 227). 'Kawasha
comes' is appealingly straightforward and robust. Its main point of interest is
that it alternates between duple and triple strains. Clearly there is a world of
difference between this and any of the settings of main masque songs considered earlier in this chapter.

Like *The Masque of Flowers*, *The Mountebanks' Masque* has two antimasques,
the first dominated by a song and the second by a dance. These antimasques
have little to do with the device as a whole. Paradox recites a long list of his
inventions (many of them obscene) and the mountebanks distribute 'witty'
remedies for various ills. While they do so, they advertise their wares by
singing a series of verses which are preserved as a single very extended song.[39]
This song, 'What is't you lack', is a metrically crude and harmonically static
ballad, a street-cry advertising the singer's wares.[40] It has an opening section
(marked as a chorus in the text) in common time, and the rest of the song is
in triple time.

The main masque songs presuppose a more cultivated musical style:

> Lightly rise, and lightly fall you
>   In the motion of your feete;
> Move not till our noats doe call you;
>   Musicke maks the action sweet.
> Musicke breathinge blowes the fyer,
>   Which Cupid feeds with fuell,
> Kindlinge honour and desire,
>   And taming hearts most cruell.   (p. 104)

We are told that 'The pages sing this song to lutes whereunto the masquers
dance their first measure.' The song is self-referential—the words point to
music and dance as the essential sources of meaning.

The ballad sung by John Urson, the bear ward, in the low-induction
antimasque of *The Masque of Augurs* is, like the mountebanks' song, a plain and
inconspicuous vehicle for the words.[41] The antimasque enterainingly demonstrates the claims made by Van-goose (the voice of popular taste): 'O Sir, all
de better, vor an Antick-maske, de more absurd it be, and vrom de purpose,
it be ever all de better. If it goe from de *Nature* of de ting, it is de more *Art*:
for deare is *Art*, and deare is *Nature* . . .' (ll. 265–8).[42] The vocal music in the
main masque, on the other hand, must have been sufficiently dignified and

---

[39] In GB-Lbl Add. MS 29481, fos. 17ᵛ–19. The first part of the song is also found in US-Nyp, MS Drexel
4175, no. 29; see Sabol, *Four Hundred Songs and Dances*, 89–94 and 555–6.

[40] For more sophisticated pieces based on street-cries by Gibbons, Weelkes, Dering, and others see
P. Brett (ed.), *Consort Songs*, MB 22 (London, 1967).

[41] A tune is found in T. D'Urfey, *Pills to Purge Melancholy*, iv (London, 1719), 38. It is headed 'A Ballad
called *The Jovial Bear Ward*' with a note saying that it is to be sung to the tune on the preceding page entitled
'The Catholick Ballad'.

[42] Both the 1622 Quarto and the 1640 Folio print Van Goose's speeches in black letter.

sophisticated to substantiate the claims made by Apollo in his sung proclamation to the King:

> Prince of thy Peace, see what it is to love
> The Powers above!
> *Jove* hath commanded me
> To visit thee;
> And in thine honour with my Musique reare
> a Colledge here,
> Of tunefull *Augures*, whose divining skill
> shall waite thee still,
> And be the *Heralds* of his highest will.   (ll. 322–30)

The Masque of Augurs (1622) is the last court masque to contain any antimasque
singing.

As we have said, most antimasque songs come from 'low inductions' where
they distinguish themselves from main masque songs by being popular rather
than courtly. This stylistic distinction takes its place in the wider context of
differences in mode (prose, verse, song) which masque writers used to establish different levels of solemnity within their productions. Many antimasques,
especially those of the low-induction type, were dominated by 'tumultuous
prose', and even spoken verse was reserved for the main masque. Linguistic
stratification is so fundamental to the way the masque establishes levels of
dignity (and consequently levels of credibility or authority for those singing or
speaking) that we must pursue this further.

Jonson developed a differentiation in types of speech and song most
obviously in the masques written after 1611. *Love Restored* has an antimasque
completely in prose, and a main masque consisting of a mixture of spoken
verse and song. The *Irish Masque*, one year later, continued the trend with
prose for all of the antimasque except for the (textless) song and a main
masque which was entirely sung. *Mercury Vindicated* (1616), *Pleasure Reconciled*
(1618), *News from the New World* (1620), *The Masque of Augurs* (1622), *Time
Vindicated* (1623), *Neptune's Triumph* (1624, and, of course, *The Fortunate Isles*
with its new antimasque, 1625), and *Chloridia* (1631) all follow the same
pattern. In most of those cases, the main masque would appear to have been
sung throughout.

Other masque writers made similar distinctions in register. Campion uses
prose for rustic characters and verse for the pastoral deity Silvanus in his
Entertainment at Caversham (1613), but this is not carried through into his three
full masques. Chapman has a prose antimasque and verse main masque in *The
Memorable Masque of the Middle Temple and Lincoln's Inn* (1613). Middleton uses
verse for the main masque in his *Masque of Heroes* (1619), and a mixture of
verse and prose for his antimasque. Carew, in *Coelum Britannicum* (1634),
carries this kind of differentiation in speech to the point where he has
conversations in which Mercury speaks in verse while Momus (the
antimasque presenter) speaks in prose. Again, the main masque is sung

throughout. Townshend's masque *Albion's Triumph* (1632) follows the Jonsonian practice exactly.

Jonson's use of different modes to establish levels of human perfection is best illustrated in *Pleasure Reconciled to Virtue*. The prose of the antimasque is so disordered that it is itself an image of the moral degeneration of Comus and his retinue:

Now yo^u sing of god *Comus* here, the *Belly-god*. I say it is well, & I say it is not well: it is well, as it is a Ballad, and ye Belly worthie of it I must needs say, and 'twer forty yards of ballad, more: as much ballad as tripe: But when ye Belly is not edified by it, it is not well: for where did yo^u ever read, or heare, that the Belly had any eares? . . . I would haue a *Tun* now, brought in to daunce, and so many *Bottles* about it: Ha? yo^u looke as if yo^u would make a probleme of this: do yo^u see? a probleme? why *Bottles*? and why a *Tun*? and why a *Tun*? and why *Bottles*? to daunce? I say, that men that drink hard, and serve the belly in any place of quality (as the *Jouiall Tinkers*, or a *lusty kindred*) are living measures of drinck: and can transforme themselues, & doe every daie, to *Bottles* or *Tuns* when they please: and when they ha' don all they can, they are, as I say agen, (for I thinck I said somewhat like it afore) but moving measures of drinck . . . (ll. 44–50, 68–79)

This rambling and seemingly extempore prose with its clumsy puns on 'ballad' and 'measure' could hardly present a stronger contrast with the beautifully shaped songs of Daedalus describing the delightful order of the masque dances:

> And when they see ye Graces meet,
>   admire ye wisdom of your feet.
> For Dauncing is an exercise
>   not only shews ye mouers wit,
> but maketh ye beholder wise,
>   as he hath powre to rise to it.   (ll. 267–72)

Jonson mused upon the significance of different forms of speech (or language) in his *Discoveries*:

Language most shewes a man: speake that I may see thee. It springs out of the most retired, and inmost parts of us, and is the Image of the Parent of it, the mind. No glasse renders a mans forme, or likenesse, so true as his speeche. Nay, it is likened to a man; and as we consider feature and composition in a man; so words in Language: in the greatnesse, aptnesse, sound, structure and harmony of it.[43]

It follows that harmonious speech (like a responsiveness to music) is an indication of mental integrity. Jonson goes on to comment on fragmented and disjointed speech in a way which seems directly relevant to the Bowl Bearer in *Pleasure Reconciled*: 'Neither can his mind be thought to be in tune, whose words doe jarre; nor his reason in frame whose sentence is preposterous; nor his Elocution cleare and perfect, whose utterance breakes it selfe into fragments and uncertainties.'[44] Jonson's belief that '*Speech* is the only benefit man

---

[43] H&S, viii. 625, ll. 2031 ff.   [44] Ibid. 628, ll. 2142–6.

hath to express his excellence of mind above other creatures', that it is 'the instrument of *Society*',[45] accounts for the consistent pattern of distinctions in mode that can be seen in his masques—a hierarchy ascending from prose, through spoken verse, to song.

A strong sense that verse (even unsung) is a kind of music (and as such, superior to ordinary speech) is endorsed by other writers in the period. George Puttenham habitually writes about poetry as an intermediate step between prose and song. In dealing with poetic technique he stresses the identification between poetry and music: 'Poesie is a skill to speake & write harmonically: and verses or rime be a kind of Musicall vtterance, by reason of a certaine congruitie in sounds pleasing the eare, though not perchance so exquisitely as the harmonicall concents of the artificiall Musicke . . .'.[46] Sidney, too, insists on the dignity of poetry over ordinary speech, and notes in passing that music can bestow even greater nobility: 'For if . . . Speech next to Reason bee the greatest gyft bestowed vpon mortalitie, that cannot be praiselesse which doth most pollish that blessing of speech . . . But lay a side the iust prayse it hath, by beeing the onely fit speech for Musick (Musick, I say, the most diuine striker of the sences) . . .'.[47]

The contrast between popular song in the antimasque and sophisticated song in the main masque, or between a songless antimasque and the full songs of the main masque, is only part of a differentiation between quite wide-ranging modes of expression. It was through the use of rambling prose, doggerel verse, popular song, spoken poetry, and sophisticated song that the masques established various levels of courtly enjoyment and dignity. The most interesting manifestation of this preoccupation with linguistic register comes with the claim that recitative was introduced to England through the court masque.

The Origins of English Recitative

While masque texts tell us a great deal about some aspects of musical perform-ance, on other issues they are reticent and equivocal. Textual information is at its most frustratingly perplexed when it comes to the question of the extent to which the new Italian monody (and in particular the recitative style) influenced the music for the Jacobean masque. When was recitative first introduced to England? The answer depends on the reliability of two refer-ences in the 1640 Folio of Ben Jonson's *Works*. According to this edition *The Vision of Delight*, performed twice in January 1617, began as Delight 'spake in song (*stylo recitativo*)' (l. 8). In the following month, *Lovers Made Men* was presented at Essex House with, apparently, a more extensive use of this novel musical style. The 1640 Folio reports: '*And the whole Maske was sung (after the*

---

[45] H&S, viii. 620–1, ll. 1881–3.

[46] *The Arte of English Poesie* (1589), in Smith (ed.), *Elizabethan Critical Essays*, ii. 67–8.

[47] *An Apology for Poetry*, ibid., i. 182

Italian manner) Stylo recitativo, *by Master* Nicholas Lanier; *who ordered and made both the Scene, and the Musicke*' (ll. 26–8). For many years both these statements were taken at face value and the conclusion drawn that recitative was known and being written in England by 1617. In 1960, however, McDonald Emslie drew attention to the fact that the vital sentence about Lanier's innovations was missing from the 1617 Quarto of *Lovers Made Men*, and that there was no known edition of *The Vision of Delight* earlier than the 1640 Folio. In other words, the assertion that recitative was used in both these masques is first found some twenty years after the event. Emslie argued that it was unlikely that Lanier would have written recitative before what was thought to be his first visit to Italy in 1625. He argued that Lanier's dramatic monody *Hero and Leander* (written no earlier than 1628—and possibly much later) was probably the first example of real English recitative. Emslie based his case on Roger North's account of Lanier performing this work for Charles I. North called it 'the first Recitative kind that ever graced ye English lang[uage]'.

Emslie, pointing to Lanier's setting of 'Bring away this sacred tree' from Campion's *Somerset Masque* of 1613, and 'Do not expect to hear' from *The Masque of Augurs* (1622), asserted that it was very likely that what Lanier had written in 1617 for *The Vision of Delight* and *Lovers Made Men* was not full recitative, but at the most declamatory ayres. He concluded:

Jonson could well have added the references to *recitativo* after 1628, when Lanier had become known as the composer of the first English recitative; the new Italian expression was doubtless associated with his name. 'Declamatory ayre' is not a seventeenth-century classification, and that song-form more than any other, resembles recitative—it is sometimes difficult to distinguish between them—so that Jonson, relying on his memory, could easily have confused the two.[48]

In 1967 Vincent Duckles published a paper which accepted Emslie's conclusions and went on to examine *Hero and Leander* as the first example of English recitative.[49]

While these articles justify their suspicion of the 1640 Folio's claims, I am uneasy about some aspects of the argument which seeks to extend that into outright disbelief. In the first place, we need to be cautious about using a Roger North anecdote written down some sixty-odd years after the event to discredit an authorial statement, even one made up to twenty years after the performance.[50] It must also be said that even if Jonson's references to recitative were inserted only in the mid-1630s when he was preparing these texts for the Folio, it would not therefore follow that the information was wrong. As Ian Spink has noted, North's account is not entirely credible:

[48] 'Nicholas Lanier's Innovations in English Song', 23. For the North quotation see 15–16.

[49] 'English Song and the Challenge of Italian Monody', in V. Duckles and F. B. Zimmerman, *Words to Music* (Los Angeles, 1967), 3–42.

[50] I say 'up to' twenty years because the copy for the second Folio was obviously complete at the time of Jonson's death in 1637. A bill to the Court of Chancery makes it clear that a few months before he died Jonson handed over his writings to Sir Kenelme Digby 'to whose care & trust the said Beniamin left the publishing and printing of them and delivered him true & perfect Copies . . .'; H&S, ix. 98.

Even North's description of Charles I causing Lanier to sing it 'to a consort attendance while he stood next with his hand upon his shoulder' would have more of a ring of truth about it if Charles II had not stood likewise with his hand on Tom Durfey's shoulder. And why was a consort necessary to accompany Lanier in this recitative?[51]

He points out that there are no sources for *Hero and Leander* earlier than the Restoration period and questions whether the work was, in fact, written as early as North claimed.

The use of the expression 'stylo recitativo' is itself interesting. Even by 1640 this was by no means the standard way of describing the style. F. W. Sternfeld notes that 'if any term predominates in the scores before 1610, it is "stile rappresentativo"'. It is nevertheless true that '*stylo recitativo*' was, as it were, available by 1617. Sternfeld cites Sigismondo d'India referring in 1609 to 'stile recitativo' and Bonini describing compositions as being 'in istile recitativo' (1613) and 'in istile di Firenze o recitativo' (1615). A letter from Jacopo Cicognini about a mascherata held in 1611 at the Pitti Palace in Florence described Jacopo Peri (as Neptune) singing 'nel suo nobilissimo stile recitativo'.[52] *Stilo*, the less common (and now archaic) form of the noun, was used by Schütz in 1619 in the preface to *Psalmen Davids* (though he must be referring here to choral declamation): 'Weil ich auch gegenwertige meine Psalmen in *stylo recitativo* (welcher biß Dato in Teutschland fast vnbekandt) gestellet . . .'.[53] It is thus not impossible that the term '*stylo recitativo*' had reached England as early as *The Vision of Delight*.

What may once have seemed like a matter of fact has been turned into an open question: was recitative heard in two English masques in 1617? And that question generates another equally problematic one: if Lanier was writing recitative for Jonson's masques, what was it like? Neither question can be given a definitive answer, but despite their intractability, they are worth considering if only because they invite us to confront some basic issues about attitudes to word-setting in seventeenth-century England. But there is another question which may allow us to get closer to a satisfactory answer: *why* did Jonson state that recitative had been used? For anyone interested in Jonson's literary aims, this is an important question and would be even if it could be established that Lanier definitely did not set those texts in *stylo recitativo*. Of course, this third question cannot be answered in isolation since it is really two alternative questions: (i) if recitative was used, why does Jonson choose to tell us that, when he ignores so many other aspects of the musical treatment of his masque texts? or (ii) if recitative was not used, what led him

---

[51] 'English Cavalier Songs 1620–1660', 71.

[52] See F. W. Sternfeld, 'A Note on Stile Recitativo', *PRMA* 110 (1984), 41–4. Cicognini letter quoted by Nagler, *Theatre Festivals*, 117.

[53] Heinrich Schütz, *Psalmen Davids* (Dresden, 1619), preface, p. iii (§6). 'Because I have set some of my psalms in *stylo recitativo* (which until now has been virtually unknown in Germany) . . .'. John Caldwell has pointed out that 'it is possible that Schütz's form *stylo recitativo* is actually a Latin dative/ablative following the German "in" here' (private communication).

to claim that it had been? In other words, one cannot really answer the question about the literary significance of the references to recitative without first forming some notion of what probably was heard in those masques of 1617.

If we are to readmit the possibility that *Lovers Made Men* was given a continuous setting in a style that Jonson recognized as new and Italian, we must first try to find an explanation for the fact that the sentence about Lanier's contribution is missing from the 1617 Quarto of the masque. This may have been due to the special nature of that edition. As we saw in Chapter 1, the Quarto of *Lovers Made Men* is one of a group of masque texts printed before the performance for the use of members of the audience—their format and function were rather like souvenir programmes. Whereas the title-page in the 1640 Folio is haphazardly arranged, the 1617 Quarto's title-page highlights the names of Lord Hay and the Baron de la Tour, sponsor and guest of honour respectively. It is not at all surprising that Lanier's part in composing the music and designing the scene is not mentioned here since it is normal for these 'presentation' editions not to acknowledge the work of poets, designers, or musicians. Ben Jonson's own name appears nowhere in this edition. Beaumont's name was actualy removed from the quarto of *The Masque of the Inner Temple and Gray's Inn*.[54] One is reminded of George Chapman's statement in *The Memorable Masque* that 'all these courtly and honoring inuentions . . . should expressiuely-arise out of the places, and persons for and by whome they are presented' (see above, pp. 14–15). We cannot afford to dismiss out of hand the references to recitative in the 1640 Folio. The different nature of the two editions could explain the disparity between the early quartos and the collected masques in the 1640 Folio.

If we examine the lines sung in Jacobean masques, *Lovers Made Men* stands out, with a small group of others like it, as a special case. This group must have departed from the conventional use of song within the masque, and, whatever the vocal technique was, it must have been something more malleable than we find, for example, in Lanier's archetypal declamatory ayre, 'Bring away this sacred tree'.

Just about the time *Lovers Made Men* was staged, there seems to have been a definite change in the use of singing in Jonson's masques. With masques up until *The Golden Age Restored* (1616) it is not difficult to distinguish between spoken verse and song. Each masque contained a number of discrete songs. These might be sung as solos, choruses, or simple dialogues, in which whole lines were not normally subdivided between voices. In the text, the stanzaic pattern of such songs is generally very apparent, and usually a clear indication is given that the verses were sung. This is often done simply by the heading 'Song', sometimes by a more elaborate statement, such as (in *Hymenaei*) 'this song importun'd them to a fit remembrance of the time' (ll. 342–3).

---

[54] See *The Dramatic Works in the Beaumont and Fletcher Canon*, ed. F. Bowers (Cambridge, 1966), i. 113.

By and large, Jonson has his main masque speakers using rhyming octosyllabic couplets or heroic couplets. For the songs he uses more varied and intricate stanzaic patterns. He is so consistent about this that where he happens to leave out his usual heading, 'Song', we can still be quite certain that a particular group of lines are to be sung. In *Love Freed from Ignorance and Folly* there is an extended passage in rhyming tetrameters which is eventually interrupted by the Muses' Priests' song, which Jonson says was 'to a measure' (l. 270) or, in other words, danced to. This song has a stanza form of three four-stress lines plus one three-stress line rhyming *abab*. After three stanzas Love speaks again and then the Muses' Priests have more lines in the same stanza form as their song. It seems clear that, although Jonson has omitted the heading, these lines too must have been sung.

With *The Golden Age Restored*, it becomes impossible to distinguish between the parts of the masque that were spoken and those that were sung.[55] The whole masque is in verse and no discrete songs are indicated at all, although a number of passages, which fit in as part of a continuous text, are marked for 'Quire'. Moreover, the masque opens with the directions 'Lowd musique | *Pallas* in her chariot descending. | To a softer musique . . .'. Then follow seven four-line stanzas. One wonders whether these were spoken above the soft music, or whether they were sung. With this masque as a whole, it seems impossible to say with any certainty which parts were sung and which spoken (that is, assuming that the mixture of song and speech that had characterized previous productions was carried forward into this one). Moreover, in the main masque line lengths vary from two syllables to alexandrines. The quick exchanges in verse, interspersed with short two- or four-line passages for choir, suggest the possibility of a continuous musical setting for much of the masque anyway.

A masque like *Mercury Vindicated from the Alchemists at Court* presents us with intriguing metrical problems. At first Jonson specifies, in his usual manner, exactly what was sung. At the end of the antimasque (which contains the Cyclope's song and an extended prose dialogue), Nature and a Chorus have a song with a complex but clear metrical pattern and rhyme scheme which is repeated over two stanzas. But later we are given an extended dialogue sung by Prometheus, Nature, and a Chorus. This is nineteen lines long and has an unusually complicated rhyme scheme (ll. 226–44). But what is so extraordinary about it is the very irregular metrical arrangement. (In the following

---

[55] In the manuscript of *The Masque of Blackness*, the songs are copied in roman script while the rest of the text is in an English hand. It was not until after 1616 that this was paralleled in printed masques by the convention of alternating italic and roman type for sung and spoken verse. After that date, such typographical distinctions were made—but only inconsistently. Masque texts had to accommodate so many different sets of words (spoken dialogue, songs, stage directions, and descriptions of scenes or costumes) that it would have been almost impossible to reflect these different verbal functions typographically. The Folio text of *Pleasure Reconciled to Virtue* adopts the convention of printing songs in italic for the second half only. Despite this inconsistency, there is no real problem in knowing what was sung and what was spoken in masques up until 1616.

quotation the number of syllables per line and the rhyme scheme are indicated in the columns on the right.)

PROMETHEUS. NATURE

PRO.	How many, 'mongst these Ladies here,	8	a
	Wish now they such a mother were!	8	a
NA.	Not one, I feare,	4	a
	And read it in their laughters.	7	b
	Ther[e]'s more, I guesse, would wish to be my daughters.	11	b
PRO.	You thinke they would not be so old,	8	c
	For so much glory.	5	d
NA.	I thinke that thought so told	6	c
	Is no false piece of story.	7	d
	'Tis yet with them, but Beauties noone,	8	e
	They would not Grandames be too soone.	8	e
PRO.	Is that your Sexes humor?	7	f
	'Tis then since *Niobe* was chang'd, that they haue left that tumor.	15	f
CHO.	Moue, moue againe, in formes as heretofore.	10	g
NA.	'Tis forme allures.	4	h
	Then moue, the Ladies here are store.	8	g
PRO.	*Nature* is motions mother, as she is your's.	11	h
CHO.	The spring, whence order flowes, that all directs,	10	i
	And knits the causes with th'effects.	8	i

Here there is no recurring stanzaic pattern nor any semblance of metrical regularity. It is tempting to imagine Jonson offering another writer's justification for this sort of thing:

You may inquire, being a Reader, why in an heroick Argument my numbers are so often diversify'd and fall into short fractions; considering that a continuation of the usual length of *English* verse would appear more Heroical in reading. But when you are an Auditor you will finde that in this, I rather deserve approbation then need excuse; for frequent alterations of measure (which cannot be so unpleasant to him that reads as troublesome to him that writes) are necessary to *Recitative Musick* for variation of *Ayres*.[56]

But that writer is, of course, Davenant in his preface to *The Siege of Rhodes* (1656), and he can scarcely be called to account for Jonson's unusually irregular verse forms in the much earlier *Mercury Vindicated*. Whatever kind of musical setting this passage received it was clearly not at all like any other surviving Jacobean masque songs.

The verse found in *Lovers Made Men*, produced the following year, is actually more regular. Once again there is no separation in the text between song and speech, and here too, we find passages marked out for Chorus. Most of the masque is in blocks of ten- or eight-syllable lines—only one section

---

[56] Davenant, *The Siege of Rhodes*, ed. A.-M. Hedback, Acta Universitatis Upsaliensis, 14 (Uppsala, 1973), 4.

marked for Chorus has a more varied structure. But in the dialogue sections
the change from one participant to another often happens mid-line:

LETHE.

Stay, who, or what phantastique shades are these
That HERMES leades?

MERCURY.

They are the gentle formes,
Of *Lovers*, tost upon those frantique seas,
Whence VENUS sprung.

LETHE.

And have rid out her storms?

MERCURY.

No.

LETHE.

Did they perish?

MERCURY.

Yes.

LETHE.

How?

MERCURY.

Drown'd by love,
That drew them forth with hopes as smooth as were
Th'unfaithfull waters he desir'd 'hem prove.   (ll. 38–58)

It is hard to see how a series of ayres, each having a significant musical
structure, could cope with this type of verse.

With *The Vision of Delight* the situation is slightly different, for there are a
number of places in the text where singing is specified and the verse is
arranged in separate stanzas as in earlier masques. Nevertheless, at times the
text is ambiguous; after the initial direction 'Delight spake in song (*stylo
recitativo*)' we read before the next passage 'Delight spoke againe' (l. 24), and
one wonders if 'again' also implies *stylo recitativo*. The situation is possibly
clarified by a later direction which implies the more usual dichotomy between
song and speech: 'The Song ended, *Wonder* spake' (l. 140). (Dr Burney, in
discussing this masque, made the assumption that this meant 'in recitative'.[57])
The one surviving fragment of vocal music from *The Vision of Delight* cannot
tell us how these problematic sections were set. 'I was not wearier where I lay'
is the solo section of a short, self-contained, and metrically regular 'Epilogue'
(as Jonson calls it) following the revels.[58]

Where we do find irregular verse of the kind met in these masque texts is,

---

[57] C. Burney, *A General History of Music* (London, 1776–89), ed. F. Mercer (London, 1935; repr. 1957),
ii. 278.

[58] This setting can be found in Spink, *English Song*, 47–8, or Sabol, *Four Hundred Songs and Dances*,
87–8.

significantly, in some of the declamatory dialogues written by Lanier and others as the century progressed. Lanier's 'Tell me, shepherd, dost thou love?' has an erratic rhyme scheme and lines which are quite irregular in length:

Nymph:	Tell me, shepherd, dost thou love?	7	a
Shepherd:	Tell me, nymph, why woulds't thou know?	7	b
Nymph:	Thy wand'ring flock that without guide doth rove,	10	a
	Thy blubber'd eyes that still with tears o'erflow,	10	b
	Makes me to ask.		
Shepherd:	I do.	6	c
Nymph:	Dear shepherd, tell me who.	6	c
Shepherd:	I love a nymph from whose fair eyes	8	d
	Phoebus did his brightness borrow,	8	e
	Where love did first my heart surprise,	8	d
	Which since hath caus'd my sorrow.	7	e
Nymph:	Love sits enthron'd within the circle of bright eyes,	12	d
	But say (good shepherd) do her virtues beauties equalize?	14	d
Shepherd:	As she in beauty doth all else excel,	10	f
	So are her virtues without parallel.	10	f
Nymph:	Doth she disdain thee?		
Shepherd:	No.		
Nymph:	Why griev'st thou then?	10	g
Shepherd:	Because her love is only worthy of the gods, not men.	14	g
Chorus:	Love's chiefest joy is but a pleasing anguish,	11	h
	Who lives in love doth dying live, and living languish.[59]	13	h

Other dialogues have more regular line lengths but have the change-over from one singer to another taking place mid-line as a way of disguising the formal verse structure and creating some (limited) sense of dramatic naturalness. Thomas Carew's 'As Celia rested in the shade' (set by Henry Lawes) is a readily accessible example of this type. It has a stanza pattern of alternating four- and three-stress lines with an *abab* rhyme scheme. But the irregularity in the changes from one voice to the other helps sustain—as far as that is necessary anyway—the illusion that this is natural dialogue.

> Cl[eon]: I dote not on thy snow-white skin.
> Ce[lia]: What then? CL: Thy purer mind.
> CE: It lov'd too soone. CL: Thou hadst not bin
> So faire, if not so kind. (ll. 21–4)[60]

On the basis of verse forms, then, it would seem that the lost music for *The Golden Age Restored*, *Mercury Vindicated*, *Lovers Made Men*, and *The Vision of Delight* may have resembled extended declamatory dialogues of the kind that were to become fashionable within a few years. If so, we need to clarify the relationship between the various English declamatory forms: simple airs ('Bring away this sacred tree'), more extended dialogue airs ('Tell me,

---

[59] Setting by Lanier in *English Songs 1625–1660*, ed. Spink, 22–4.
[60] *Poems of Thomas Carew*, ed. Dunlap, 43; and see *English Songs 1625–1660*, ed. Spink, 93–8.

shepherd'), and extended recitatives (Lanier's *Hero and Leander* or Lawes's 'Ariadne' lament). Are these types characterized by any essential *musical* features, or are the distinctions entirely a matter of the length and character of the verse set? It is interesting that Hawkins saw Henry Lawes's 'Ariadne' (published 1653) not as straightforward recitative, but as 'neither recitative nor air, but in so precise a medium between both, that a name is wanting for it'.[61]

Whether or not it was his first essay in that style, *Hero and Leander* does provide us with an example of Lanier's English recitative. It seems no less melodic than 'Bring away this sacred tree', although there is a closer relationship between music and text. The vocal line often has an independent musical significance—a feature which Emslie considered marked out the declamatory ayre from the recitative. This is perhaps most obvious in bars 110 to 123, which form a coherent musical section (see Ex. 2.24). The third phrase in this picks up the opening of the second phrase in a diminished form and then ascends, balancing nicely the second phrase's descending line. The next phrase ('For pity's sake . . .') uses a sequence, and here the rhythm seems determined by musical considerations rather than by the natural rhythm of the lines. The next section, in which Hero addresses the elements, begins in a way which links it to the earlier apostrophe to the winds. What really marks this out as being different from Lanier's declamatory ayres is mostly determined by the length and nature of the verse. *Hero and Leander* is a continuous setting of eighty lines and the verse is of the most malleable kind. It consists of loose heroic couplets, characterized by a great deal of enjambment and quite short phrases; these enable Lanier to avoid musical phrases which coincide with rhyming lines so that the piece has considerable fluidity. Rhyme scheme and scansion show that the original line arrangement of the verse in the excerpt discussed must have been as follows:

> You gentle, peaceful winds, if ever Love
> Had pow'r in you, if ever you did prove
> Least spark of Cupid's flame, for pity's sake
> With softest gales more smooth and easy make
> The troubled floods unto my soul's delight.

But Lanier set it in the following phrases:

> You gentle, peaceful winds,
> If ever Love had pow'r in you,
> if ever you did prove Least spark of Cupid's flame,
> for pity's sake,
> with softest gales
> more smooth and easy make
> the troubled floods
> unto my soul's delight.

[61] Sir John Hawkins, *A General History of the Science and Practice of Music* (London, 1776), ed. C. Cudworth (New York, 1963), ii. 579.

Ex. 2.24. Lanier, 'Hero and Leander', bars 110–23, adapted from *English Songs 1625–1660*, ed. Spink

You gen - tle, peace - ful winds; if ev - er love Had pow'r in you,

if ev-er you did prove Least spark of Cu - pid's flame, for pi - ty's

sake, With soft - est gales more smooth and eas - y make The trou-bled floods un -

-to my soul's de - light.

Again, this kind of verse agrees well with Davenant's criteria for verse to be set in *stylo recitativo*.

It seems arguable that the essential difference between English melodious recitative and what we now call declamatory ayre is largely one of continuousness, and that it should be possible to determine from the formal structure and length of the verse set whether it was treated as a self-contained declamatory ayre or a fluid recitative. Declamatory ayres do have regular verse forms; dramatic dialogues do not. The distinction is already there, of course, in the Italian prototypes and can be seen by comparing a monodic madrigal such as Caccini's 'Amarilli' with the same composer's use of pure *stile rappresentativo* in *Euridice*.

There is a great deal of seventeenth-century English declamatory monody, but whether in fact it owes anything to Italian models has been a matter of some discussion. Indeed, Ian Spink has argued that it does not, but that it is instead an indigenous development encouraged by the dramatic requirements

Ex. 2.25. Ferrabosco, 'Udite lagrimosi Spir'ti d'Averno', bars 1–12, from GB-Ob, MS Tenbury 1018

and acoustic conditions of the courtly masque. A comparison of Ferrabosco's English masque songs with his four Italian monodies preserved in MS Tenbury 1018 makes it clear that the declamatory elements in his English songs cannot be accounted for by a simple application of the *stile rappresentativo* to English texts. Certainly, a song like 'Udite lagrimose spir'ti d'Averno' could conceivably have been written by one of Caccini's circle: it is uncompromising dramatic declamation. The bass line has a purely harmonic function and leaves the voice entirely free to retain the rhythmic elasticity of ordinary speech (see Ex. 2.25). No English song by Ferrabosco is quite like this; his English declamation is always a matter of dramatic gestures kept in balance with other more purely musical features. Even when his bass lines are most static, a dance-like dimension to his songs is never entirely absent. The basis of Ferrabosco's English ayres is always, so to speak, more obtrusively musical than any Caccini monody.

Obviously songs like Dowland's 'Welcome black night' or Lanier's 'Bring away this sacred tree' involved something more than a simple transposition of the new Italian style to English-language texts; yet the underlying principles— if not the actual musical language—are similar. In both there is a commitment to allowing the natural verbal rhythms to come into the foreground of the musical structure. English declamatory writing may well have been influenced by the new Italian monody, but if so, the composers who adapted the Italian style did so with an obvious sensitivity to the different characteristics of English as a language. In a speech-based style like this, it is clear that the intelligent application of the same basic principles to two different languages would produce two different musical contours.

English musicians must have been very aware of the different characteristics of Italian and English since it was a standard topic in contemporary criticism.

Sidney, in his *Apology for Poetry*, discusses both the frequency of monosyllabic words in English and the different kinds of rhyme which are possible:

the Italian is so full of Vowels that it must euer be cumbred with *Elisions*; the Dutch so, of the other side, with Consonants, that they cannot yeeld the sweet slyding fit for a Verse . . . The English is subiect to none of these defects . . . Lastly, euen the very ryme it selfe the Italian cannot put it in the last silable, by the French named the Masculine ryme, but still in the next to last, which the French call the Female, or in the next before that, which the Italians terme *Sdrucciola* . . . The English hath all three [types of rhyme], as *Due, True, Father, Rather, Motion, Potion.*[62]

Both these topics are picked up—though not always as a pair—by numerous other late sixteenth- and seventeenth-century writers. Even Sidney's placing of English half-way between Italian and Dutch on a vowel-dominated to consonant-dominated scale is echoed by others. In George Chapman's *Preface to Homer* (written just at the time that English composers were developing the declamatory ayre) we find a mixture of linguistic observation and national chauvinism:

> Our Monosyllables so kindly fall,
> And meete, opposde in rime, as they did kisse:
> French and Italian most immetricall,
> Their many syllables in harsh Collision
> Fall as they brake their necks; their bastard Rimes
> Saluting as they iustl'd in transition,
> And set our teeth on edge . . .[63]

Campion's preface to *Two Books of Ayres* shows a similar awareness of the prevalence of both monosyllables and consonants in English: 'The light of this will best appeare to him who hath pays'd our Monosyllables and Syllables combined, both which are so loaded with Consonants, as they will hardly keepe company with swift Notes or give the Vowell convenient liberty . . .'.[64] Henry Lawes, in the preface to the 1653 *Ayres and Dialogues*, repeats these notions and makes a direct comparison with Italian: 'I confesse the Italian language may have some advantage by being better smooth'd and *vowell'd* for Musick . . . and our English seems a little over-clogg'd with *Consonants*'.[65] It was this volume which contained 'Ariadne', Lawes's ex-

---

[62] *An Apology for Poetry* in Smith (ed.), *Elizabethan Critical Essays*, i. 205.

[63] J. E. Spingarn (ed.), *Critical Essays of the Seventeenth Century* (London, 1908–9), i. 79.

[64] *Thomas Campion*, ed. Davis, 55–6.

[65] H. Lawes, *Ayres and Dialogues* (London, 1653), sig b. Lawes returned to this theme in the preface to his *Second Book of Ayres and Dialogues* (London, 1655): '[There is] a Beleefe among our selves, that *English words will not run well in Musick:* this I have sayd and must ever avow, is one of the Errors of this Generation. I confesse I could wish that some of our words could spare a *Consonant* . . . but those are few, and seldome occur; and when they do, are manageable enough by giving each Syllable its particular humour; provided the breath of the *sense* bee observed. And I speak it freely once for all that if *English* words which are fitted for Song do not run smooth enough, 'tis the fault either of the *Composer* or *Singer*. Our *English* is so stor'd with plenty of *Monosyllables* (which like small stones fill up the chinks) that it hath great priviledge over divers of its Neighbours, and in some particulars (with reverence be it spoken) above the very *Latin*, which Language we find overcharg'd with the letter s, especially in *bus* and such hissing *Terminations* . . .'.

tended dramatic recitative. One year later *Ariadne deserted by Theseus* was published by Richard Flecknoe—the poet immortalized by Dryden as the father of Macflecknoe, the supreme dunce. Flecknoe described his *Ariadne* as a 'Dramatick Piece apted for Recitative Musick' and his preface makes it clear that he was intending to set it himself. After praising the wonderful union of music and poetry forged 'in our Fathers days' by Claudio Montanendo [*sic*] he embarks on the familiar theme of Italian's greater number of vowels. He then moves very directly to acknowledge that the differences between English and Italian will mean that English-language recitative will involve more than the simple setting of English words to Italian-style music:

Where I cannot but note their want of judgement, who have endevoured to imitate at all parts in our language the Italian Recitative Musick, not considering, that the Musick of all Nations is cast in the mould of their language, whence there being great difference betwixt their verbosity, and our concised speech, it consequently follows, that that difference should also be betwixt their Musick and Poetry, and ours.[66]

When Dryden came to write about the difficulties of writing recitative in English he too was to pick up issues which had been thoroughly discussed in our period:

'Tis almost needless to speak any thing of that noble Language, in which the Musical *Drama* was first invented and perform'd. All who are conversant in the *Italian*, cannot but observe, that it is the softest, the sweetest, the most harmonious, not only of any modern Tongue, but even beyond any of the Learned. . . . The *English* has yet more natural disadvantages than the *French*; our original *Teutonique* consisting most in Monosyllables, and those incumber'd with Consonants, cannot possibly be freed from those Inconveniences.[67]

(The same issues were still being discussed by Addison in his *Spectator* essays on opera.[68])

Composers who were at all aware of this discussion in English criticism of the seventeenth century would surely have acknowledged the impossibility of too direct a transference of the musical language of Italian recitative to English settings of free dramatic verse. Lully's success in adapting the principles of Italian recitative to the morphology of the French language has been acclaimed since his own time. Perhaps we should be prepared to allow the composers of English dramatic dialogues (and, therefore, masque recitative) credit for an analogous development.

Much depends on the degree of exposure English musicians had to Italian influences, and in particular on how well acquainted they were with the new

[66] R. Flecknoe, *Ariadne deserted by Thesus, and found courted by Bacchus* (London, 1654), sig. [A6ᵛ]–[A7].

[67] Preface to *Albion and Albanius* (1685), in *The Works of John Dryden*, ed. E. Miner, G. R. Guffey, and F. B. Zimmerman (Berkeley and Los Angeles, 1976), xv. 6–7. In their notes, the editors have a useful discussion of the comparison of vernaculars in English Renaissance criticism in which they mention the Sidney and Chapman passages cited above; see p. 326.

[68] Especially No. 29, dated 3 Apr. 1711. See J. Addison, *The Spectator*, ed. D. F. Bond, 5 vols. (Oxford, 1965), i. 119–23.

monody. Some felt that English musicians were all too susceptible to con-
tamination from Europe. In commending the solidly English compositions
of Byrd, Bull, and Gibbons printed in *Parthenia* (*c.*1613), George Chapman
complained of the way composers were entertaining foreign styles:

> By theis choice lessons of theise Musique Mast[rs]:
>   Ancient, and heightn'd wth y[e] Arts full Bowles,
> Let all ou[r] moderne, mere Phantastique Tasters,
>   (Whose Art but foreigne Noveltie extolls)
> Rule and confine theyr fancies . . .[69]

Campion, in his preface to *Two Bookes of Ayres*, asserted that his ayres were
truly English, unlike the works of those 'who admit onely of *French* or *Italian
Ayres*'.[70]

English musicians associated with the courtly masque certainly could have
been acquainted with the Italian monodic style. It is even possible that some
of the key musicians involved in this issue encountered the new monody at
first hand in Italy. Diana Poulton points out that Dowland would almost
certainly have met Caccini during his visit to Florence in 1595.[71] Lanier
himself planned to go to Italy in about 1610. We know at least that William
Cecil got permission from his father, Robert Cecil (Lanier's employer), to
have the musician accompany him as a companion and viol tutor on an Italian
trip which he was planning in 1610.[72] It seems that Lanier may have visited
Venice as a courier for the Privy Council early in 1611.[73] (A year earlier he had
made a similar trip to Paris.) What would he have heard there? If he was
treated to the kind of experiences Edward Herbert so enjoyed on his visit
there three years later, he might well have been inspired.[74] (Lanier did, of
course, make several extended visits to Italy at the beginning of Charles I's
reign in order to buy paintings for the king, but these travels are too late to
have any bearing on what happened in the masques of 1617.)

Obviously though, visits to Italy were not the only way in which English
musicians could have become familar with the innovations of the Florentine
Camerata. Examples of the new monody (though not full-blown recitative)

---

[69] *Parthenia* (London, *c.*1613), ed. R. T. Dart (London, 1962), 3.

[70] *Thomas Campion*, ed. Davis, 55.   [71] Poulton, *John Dowland*, 36.

[72] See R. Charteris, 'Jacobean Musicians at Hatfield House, 1605–13', *RMARC* 12 (1974), 116.

[73] Ashbee, *RECM*, iv. 87. Nicholas Lanier remained in the service of the Earl of Salisbury until April
1614. It is possible that this could have been the elder Nicholas Lanier.

[74] See E. Herbert, *The Life of Edward, First Lord Herbert of Cherbury, Written by Himself* (*c.*1642), ed. J. M.
Shuttleworth (London, 1976), 73: 'I was received by the English Ambassador, Sir Dudley Carlton, with
much Honor; among other favors shewed mee I was brought to see a Nunne in Murano who being an
Admirable beauty and together singing extreamly well, who was thought one of the Rarityes not onely of
that Place but of the Tyme; we came to a Roome opposite unto the Cloyster when she coming on the
other side of the Grate betwixt vs sung soe extreamly well That when shee departed . . . I sayd in Italian,
Muoia pur quando vuol non bisogna mutar ni voce ni faccia per esser un Angelo, Dye whensoeuer you will you
neither neede to Change voice nor face to bee an Angell. These words it seemed were Fatall For going then
to Rome and returning shortly afterwards I heard shee was dead in the meane tyme.' Carleton took Herbert
to hear another remarkable singing nun in Milan (see *Life*, 76).

are found in early seventeenth-century English collections, and a number of these sources have some connection with the courtly masque. Robert Dowland printed four Italian monodic songs in his *Musical Banquet* (1610), and although that has no obvious connection with the masque, its companion volume, *Varietie of Lute Lessons* (also 1610) contains four dances for the *Masque of Queens* (1609). One of the songs Dowland prints, 'Amarilli mia bella', crops up in various other English sources, notably GB-Lbl, Add. MS 15117 (which contains some songs for the theatre)[75] and GB-Ob, MS Tenbury 1018. This last manuscript is especially interesting as it contains Ferrabosco's four Italian monodies and several of his masque songs. Lanier and other English composers at court would have been acquainted with at least two influential Italian musicians. In 1607 the lutenist John Maria Lugario was appointed by Queen Anne as a groom of her privy chamber at the exceptionally high salary of £100 'in regard of his skill and verie speciall quality in Musicke'. Lugario had previously been employed at the court of Mantua where Monteverdi was *maestro di cappella* and shortly before his arrival in England and again in 1616 he exchanged letters with Ottavio Rinuccini (the librettist for Peri's and Caccini's *Euridice*).[76] Possibly even more important was the composer Angelo Notari, a lutenist in Prince Henry's retinue whose *Prime musiche nuove* (London, 1613) contained some Italian monody.[77]

It is particularly interesting that (after Castiglione's *Il Cortegiano*) one of the most widely read Italian books in England in the early seventeenth century was Vincenzo Galilei's *Dialogo della musica antica e della moderna*. (The only other musical theorist read quite so widely was Zarlino.) The Bodleian library had the *Dialogo* before 1605 when Thomas James catalogued its holdings. Lord Herbert of Cherbury owned a copy (which he bequeathed—together with copies of Zarlino's and Mersenne's treatises—to Jesus College, Oxford). The occurrence of Galilei's treatise at least indicates that Englishmen had some opportunity to acquaint themselves with the ideals and rationale which lay behind the new Italian style. In his Gresham College lectures of 1611, John Taverner cites Galilei's treatise when arguing that the ancients paid more attention to setting words appropriately than modern composers. The latter, he said, often indulge in 'a kind of fruitlesse curiosity in making divers parts answerable one to the other, whereas indeede none of them answere the Argument wch should bee their chiefe ground . . .'.[78]

---

[75] See M. Joiner, 'British Museum Add. MS 15117: An Index, Commentary, and Bibliography', *RMARC* 7 (1969), 51–109.

[76] See Ashbee, *RECM*, iv. 16. On the Rinuccini correspondence, see A. Bertolotti, *Musici alla Corte dei Gonzaga in Mantova* (1890; repr. Bologna, 1969), 80–1, and Spink, *English Song*, 42.

[77] By the 1630s numerous collections of Italian monody were apparently on sale in London. Robert Martin lists a considerable number amongst the 'Libri Musici' in his various editions of *Catalogus Librorum* (London, 1633, 1635, 1639, 1640). See D. W. Krummel, 'Venetian Baroque Music in a London Book-shop', in O. Neighbour (ed.), *Music and Bibliography* (London, 1980), 1–27.

[78] GB-Lbl MS Sloane 2329, fo. 75^v. I am grateful to Dr Penelope Gouk for drawing my attention to the Galilei references here.

Any attempts made to write recitative in English in the seventeenth century remained sufficiently isolated for each new endeavour to be described as if it were the first. Most obviously, Davenant in the preface to *The Siege of Rhodes* wrote of recitative as being 'unpractis'd here' and 'though of great reputation amongst other Nations, the very attempt of it is an obligation to our own'. Henry Lawes, Flecknoe, Dryden, and even Congreve and Addison in the early eighteenth century all imply that there was no tradition of recitative in England.

In the absence of any surviving music, the literary implications of this are really more interesting than the musical ones.[79] The relatively frequent appearance of Galilei's *Dialogo* in English libraries of the period possibly indicates an interest in the ideals of the Florentine Camerata from which the *stile rappresentativo* emerged. Galilei's insistence that 'è impossibile di trovare vn huomo che sia Musico veramente, & che sia vitioso'[80] shows the same attitude to the artist's role that we find emphasized again and again in the *Discoveries* and throughout Jonson's poems and plays: 'For, if men will impartially, and not asquint, looke toward the offices and function of a Poet, they will easily conclude to themselves the impossibility of any man's being the good Poet, without first being a good man.'[81] The consonance of Jonson's views with Galilei's is not in itself remarkable—these attitudes were Renaissance commonplaces—but the parallels do, I think, suggest that Jonson would have been very receptive to the ideals of the Camerata. The notion that the *stile recitativo* was founded on the practice of the ancients would clearly have appealed to Jonson: he claimed that his masques were 'grounded vpon *antiquitie* and solide *learnings*'[82] and sought to demonstrate that in his marginal glosses for the masques of *Blackness*, *Beauty*, *Hymenaei*, *Queens*, and *Oberon*. Above all, he would have been enthusiastic about the recitative style as a heightened form of speech, or, in Caccini's words, 'una sorte di musica, per cui altri potesse quasi che in armonia fauellare vsando in essa . . . vna certa nobile sprezzatura di canto'.[83] The phrase 'in armonia fauellare' is virtually the same as that used by Jonson in *The Vision of Delight* where Delight 'spake in song *(stylo recitativo)*' (l. 8).

Besides this and *Lovers Made Men*, the only other mention of recitative before the Commonwealth is also in a masque text. In *Albion's Triumph* (1632), Mercury descends and '*In voce Recitativa*, he declares the substance of his commission' (p. 77). In each case, the use of recitative (or the assertion that

---

[79] Professor Stoddart Lincoln has drawn my attention to an example from a Davenant play which illustrates the caution with which such references must be treated. In *The Man's the Master* (1668), one of the characters calls for a song, and the stage direction reads, 'The SONG in recitative and in parts'. GB-Lbl Add. MS 33234 contains a setting of this song by John Bannister, which may well have been used in the play, yet it gives no hint of either recitative or parts.

[80] *Dialogo della musica antica e della moderna* (1581); the translation in O. Strunk, *Source Readings in Music History* (New York, 1950), 378 reads 'it is impossible to find a man who is truly a musician and is vicious'.

[81] Preface to *Volpone*; H&S, v. 17. [82] *Hymenaei*, l. 16.

[83] *Le Nuove Musiche* (Florence, 1601).

it was used) seems designed to give the words declaimed a certain weight and dignity. The fitness of recitative for subjects which are not trivial was later articulated in England by Davenant, who in *The Playhouse to Let* has a musician say in answer to the objection that recitative is not natural:

> Recitative Musick is not compos'd
> Of matter so familiar, as may serve
> For every low occasion of discourse.[84]

The concept of recitative as elevated speech would obviously have appealed to Jonson for the possibility it offered of giving an added sense of portent to the utterance of the demigods and allegorical figures who are the spokesmen in the masque for a vision of social perfection. There can be no doubt of the literary significance of the references to recitative in *The Vision of Delight* and *Lovers Made Men*: the use of recitative formed part of a differentiation between various modes of speech and singing which always corresponded to the dignity and importance of the communication. Recitative would have been perceived as an appropriately noble vehicle for main masque verse which in earlier Jacobean masques was spoken.

It is not necessarily very significant that the reference to recitative is missing from the quarto of *Lovers Made Men*; given the nature of that edition, it was to be expected that Lanier's contribution would not be acknowledged. I am convinced that recitative was used in the masques of 1615–17. The character of the verse for *Lovers Made Men* and for a group of other masques written at about the same time makes it clear that the discrete ayres heard in earlier masques could not have been used. The structure of this verse seems similar to that of the extended declamatory dialogues and the two famous recitatives found in the song manuscripts of the 1620s and later. But the musical language of English declamation—whether short ayres, more extended dialogues, or cantata-length recitatives—is quite distinct from that of the Italian *stile rappresentativo*. The kind of relationship that exists between the two musical styles cannot be established definitively. English musicians clearly did have some access to Italian monody, but they seem not to have imitated it directly. If their declamation was inspired by Italian *stile rappresentativo*, composers must nevertheless have taken account of a strong critical tradition which emphasized the markedly different character of the two languages and the consequent need for a distinct musical idiom. Perhaps the relationship between the two styles goes no further than a perceived analogy—that composers and poets in England saw that, like their Italian counterparts, they were forging a musical style which preserved and heightened the metrical subtleties and patterns of natural speech. The principles underlying the *stile rappresentativo* were not lost on Jonson, as his echoing of the Camerata's phraseology makes clear. Recitative offered him one more level in the linguistic hierarchy which

---

[84] Quoted by J. Westrup, 'The Nature of Recitative', *Proceedings of the British Academy*, 42 (1956), 28.

is essential to masque texts, a hierarchy which runs from the disordered, rambling prose given to base antimasque characters to the lyricism of the noble characters in the main masque. To speak in song is to give evidence of an ordered mind and a benevolent disposition. As we have seen, Jonson says as much in the *Discoveries* (see above, p. 85).

In 'Love's Alchymie' John Donne places 'rude hoarse minstrelsy' and the music of the spheres at opposite ends of the musical spectrum. Main masques were obviously intended to come as near as possible to the heavenly end of this spectrum, while the antimasque tended—if it incorporated any music at all—to draw on rude minstrelsy. This was not so much a simple opposition of styles as part of a much broader and significant differentiation between various modes of speech and singing which always corresponded to the dignity and importance of the communication. Recitative would have been an appropriately noble vehicle for main masque verse which in earlier Jacobean masques was spoken.

3

Dance and Instrumental Music

Interpreting Masque Dances

Aurelia: We have forgot the brawle.
Guerino: Why? 'Tis but two singles on the left, two on the right, three doubles
forward, a traverse of six round: do this twice, three singles side, galliard trick of
twentie, curranto pace: a figure of eight, three singles broken down, come up,
meete, two doubles fall backe, and then honour.
Aurelia: O Dedalus! thy maze, I have quite forgot it.

(John Marston, The Malcontent, IV. i. 65)

Guerino's complicated directions and Aurelia's bemused reaction suggest that
an onlooker might have had great difficulty in seeing this particular dance as
a model of celestial order. Yet in the songs of *Pleasure Reconciled to Virtue*
Jonson takes up the very image used by the bewildered Aurelia to communicate a sense of the beautiful orderliness of set masque dances and the revels.
Daedalus describes the the intricate choreography of the dance as being like
his maze, an artefact with the potential to instruct and delight:

> Then, as all actions of mankind
> are but a Laborinth, or maze,
> so let your Daunces be entwin'd,
> yet not perplex men, vnto gaze.
> But measur'd, and so numerous too,
> as men may read each act you doo.
> And when they see yᵉ Graces meet,
> admire yᵉ wisdom of your feet.
> For Dauncing is an exercise
> not only shews yᵉ mouers wit,
> but maketh yᵉ beholder wise,
> as he hath powre to rise to it.   (ll. 261–72)

We may interpret—or 'read'—the complex and subtle figures of the dance as
emblems of alert and virtuous social action. Regrettably, the setting is lost, but
the accomplishment of the verse itself gives a kind of authority to the singer's
statements about intelligent artifice. This fine poem is typical of the largest and
most important group of masque songs—songs which introduce the dances.

We have already encountered some of these. 'Move now with measured sound' (*The Lord Hay's Masque*) is a commentary on the dance it accompanies. Another song is danced to in *The Lords' Masque* where stars move 'in an exceeding strange and delightful manner' according to the 'humour' of the song, 'Advance your Chorall motions now, You musick-loving lights' (p. 253).

Daniel's 'If joy had other figure' in *Tethys' Festival* claims that the music, verse, and dancing of this masque are the best means of expressing devotion to the crown:

> . . . Our motions, soundes, and wordes,
> Tun'd to accordes;
> Must shew the well-set partes,
> Of our affections and our harts.   (ll. 329–36)

This song encapsulates the idea—implicit in almost every masque device—that the visible and audible concord of the masque externalizes or provides a model of less tangible social contentment. Jonson enlarges on this notion in the second song of *News from the New World*. There the masquers are invited to look at James I as sun king and (again) to 'read' his significance. Thus inspired they will be able to produce a dance of 'pure harmony':

> Now looke and see in yonder throne,
> How all those beames are cast from one.
> This is that Orbe so bright,
> Has kept your wonder so awake;
> Whence you as from a mirrour take
> The Suns reflected light.
> Read him as you would doe the booke
> Of all perfection, and but looke
> What his proportions be;
> No measure that is thence contriv'd,
> Or any motion thence deriv'd,
> But is pure harmonie.   (ll. 334–45)

Songs often assert a connection between the movements of the dance and the masque's central device. The relationship between the two is necessarily of a rather general kind. Nothing that is known about the process of 'making' and rehearsing these dances suggests that there can often have been very much scope for a choreographic realization of a specific image central to a particular device. It seems likely, in fact, that rehearsals for the dances may have been under way before the masque device was fully worked out. Nevertheless, the words of the songs repeatedly claim for the choreography a relevance to the main themes of the masque. In *Love Restored*, for example, love is said to be responsible for the positive qualities of the dancing:

> This motion was of loue begot,
> It was so ayrie, light, and good,

> His wings into their feet he shot,
>   Or else himselfe into their bloud . . .   (ll. 273–6)

The songs in *Mercury Vindicated* present the dances as being created by Prometheus at the request of Nature, or in other words, as the result of a fruitful co-operation between art and nature. One of Nature's songs in this masque describes the dance as a form of courtship, and courtship as a microcosmic reflection of the workings of the universe:

> But shew thy winding wayes and artes,
>   Thy risings, and thy timely startes
> Of stealing fire, from Ladies eyes and hearts.
>   Those softer circles are the yong mans heauen,
>   And there more orbes and Planets are then seuen,
>   To know whose motion
>   Were a Notion
>   As worthy of youthes study, as deuotion.   (ll. 213–20)

Similarly, in *The Vision of Delight* one of the songs interpolated between the dances (performed by 'the Glories of the Spring') presents them as analogous to the delicacy of nature:

> In curious knots and mazes so
>   The Spring at first was taught to go;
> And *Zephire*, when he came to wooe
> His *Flora*, had their motions too,
>   And thence did *Venus* learne to lead
>   Th'*Idalian* Braules, and so [to] tread
> As if the wind, not she did walke;
>   Nor prest a flower, nor bow'd a stalke.   (ll. 224–31)

The audience are invited to see the realization of a humanist ideal in the dances—'an art which shares with great creating nature'.[1]

Harmony's exhortations to the dancers in *The Masque of Heroes* impose on the intricate movements of the dance a positive significance, doing so in terms of the masque's central device:

> Moue on, Moue on, be still the same,
>   You Beauteous Sonnes of Brightnesse,
> You adde to Honour Spirit and Flame,
>   To Vertue, Grace and Whitenesse;
>   You, whose euery little motion

---

[1] H&S, x. 573 explain that Idalium was a grove in Cyprus dedicated to Venus. Jonson associates the word Idalian with Venus' beautiful dancing in *Time Vindicated* (l. 425) and in his epigram To Lady Mary Wroth: 'If dancing, all would cry th'Idalian Queene, | Were leading forth the Graces on the greene.' Graham Parry, *The Golden Age Restor'd* (Manchester, 1981), 168, comments that in this epigram Jonson 'casts an appreciative glance at her intelligent realisation of classical deities in her masquing roles'. Lady Mary Wroth danced in *The Masque of Blackness*.

> May learne Strictnesse more Deuotion,
> Euery Pace of that high worth
> It treades a faire Example forth,
> Quickens a vertue, makes a Storie,
> To make your owne Heroick Glorie,
> May your three times thrice Blest Number
> Raise Merit from his Ancient Slumber   (ll. 342–53)

These lines exemplify another conventional trait. Many of the songs which follow the first dance begin, like Harmony's song, by encouraging the dancers to continue. Even the sense of urgency created by the repeated words in the opening line is thoroughly typical; we see it, for example, in *Hymenaei* ('Now, now, beginne to set | Your spirits in actiue heate'), *Oberon* ('Nay, nay | You must not stay, Nor be weary, yet' and 'Nor yet, nor yet, O you in this night blest, Must you haue will, or hope to rest'), and *The Vision of Delight* ('Againe, againe; you cannot be | Of such a true delight too free'). While adopting this urgent tone, most of these songs serve the practical function of allowing the dancers a few minutes' rest ('While dancing rests, fit place to musicke graunting', as Campion puts it in *The Somerset Masque*).

The songs which introduce the revels are calculated to ensure that the pleasures of social dancing are seen in the context of the masque's social vision. Often these songs point to the revels as the most crucial section of the masque, since there a model of joyful and intelligent social integration might be established. In *Lovers Made Men* the lovers, transformed from an entranced state into alert men, are invited to fulfil their intelligent humanity in the revels:

> Goe, take the Ladies forth, and talke,
>   And touch, and taste too: Ghosts can walke.
> 'Twixt eyes, tongues, hands, the mutuall strife
>   Is bred, that tries the truth of life.
> They doe, indeed, like dead men move,
> That thinke they live, and not in love!   (ll. 175–80)

Daedalus' third song in *Pleasure Reconciled* exhorts the masquers to take out the ladies for the dances of the revels, and his advice to them evokes the sensitivity, wit, and sociability of true courtliness:

> Goe choose among—But wth a mind
>   as gentle as ye stroaking wind
>   runs ore the gentler flowres.
> And so let all your actions smile,
>   as if they meant not to beguile
>   the Ladies, but ye howres.
> Grace, Laughter, & discourse, may meet,
>   and yet, the beautie not goe les:
> for what is noble, should be sweet,
>   but not dissolu'd in wantonnes.   (ll. 303–12)

'Come noble nymphs' in *Neptune's Triumph* (ll. 472–503) is another rather beautiful variation on this type.[2]

Choreography

While it is true that the masque dances and revels were endowed with significance by the songs which introduced them, it would be wrong to infer that the dances themselves had no intrinsically expressive properties. Quite the contrary. Writers on dance from the Renaissance through to the eighteenth century argued for the expressiveness of their art by drawing analogies with oratory. Arbeau (writing in 1588) stresses the interdependence of movement and music and calls dance 'a kind of mute rhetoric':

Ie vous ay ia dit, quelle [la danse] depend de la musique & modulations d'icelle: car sans la vertu rithmique, la dance seroit obscure & confuse: daultant qu'il fault que les gestes des membres accompaignent les cadances des instruments musicaulx, & ne fault pas que le pied parle d'un, & l'instrument daultre. Mais principallement tous les doctes tiennent que la dance est vne espece de Rhetorique muette, par laquelle l'Orateur peult par ses mouements, sans parler vn seul mot, se faire entendre, & persuader aux spectateurs, quil est gaillard digne d'estre loué, aymé, & chery . . .[3]

Thanks largely to expectations about courtly accomplishment and a strong sense of the boundaries of acceptable movement defined by notions of decorum, dancing could indeed be understood as displaying ignorance or cultivation, as revealing a lewd or a moral ('upright') disposition. But where do we find the conventions which lie beneath such interpretations articulated and elaborated in a way that might allow us to visualize masque dancing?

While no single treatise focuses directly on the kind of choreography seen in early seventeenth-century English masques, a range of late Renaissance dance books help us towards some idea of the appropriate dancing styles and of the expressive potential of specific steps or dance forms. These sources deal primarily with social dances for couples or small mixed groups, and not with elaborately choreographed measures for, say, twelve masquers (of the same sex). From the point of view of both their orientation and the circumstances of their compilation they hover around our present concerns. If we discount Morley's few remarks in *A Plain and Easy Introduction to Practical Music* (which were directed at composers rather than dancers), there are no published contemporary English-language books of instructions. None were printed between Copland's 'Maner of Dauncynge of Bace Daunces after the Use of

---

[2] The two extant settings of this song discussed above (pp. 73–5).

[3] *Orchésographie* (Langres, 1588), fo. 5ʳ⁻ᵛ. 'I have said to you already that dance depends on music and its modulations; for without rhythmic strength, dance would be obscure and confused. Thus it is essential that the movements of limbs agree with the phrasing of musical instruments, and it must not happen that the foot speaks of one thing while the instrument speaks of another. But first and foremost, all the authorities hold that dance is a type of mute rhetoric in which the orator, without speaking a single word, can make himself understood through his movements and can persuade the audience that he is gay, and worthy of being praised, loved, and held dear . . .'.

Fraunce' (1521) and Playford's *English Dancing Master* (1651). The latter deals anyway with country dancing (which, though popular at court and embraced as part of the revels, has only a limited bearing on set masque dances).[4]

There was, however, one dancing-manual published in the late Jacobean period which has a strong (albeit circumstantial) link with the Stuart masque. F. de Lauze dedicated his *Apologie de la Danse et la Parfaicte Methode de l'enseigner tant aux Cavaliers quaux Dames* (1623) to the Duke of Buckingham. He complained in his dedicatory letter that a pirated version of this treatise had been put into circulation about three years earlier by a Mr Montague. This, it seems, was B. de Montagut's 'Louange de la Danse' (GB-Lbl, MS Royal 16 E. 37–39) which, interestingly, is also dedicated to Buckingham. It is not impossible that these treatises originated in England. Nothing seems to be known of either de Lauze or Montagut (though there was a Berthelmy Montegu in Henrietta Maria's household in 1625).[5]

While the 'Louange' and the *Apologie* are closely enough related to be regarded as two versions of one treatise, there are substantial differences. Both, however, have extended sections proclaiming the nobility of dance. Both work their way through the main social dances and are in some respects quite painstaking in their attempts to build up a refined technique. They contain, for example, preparatory exercises for the steps of the courante. Both pre-suppose a courtly milieu. De Lauze writes about occasions when one might dance 'deuant vn Roy, où [*sic*] en la presence de quelques personnes qualifiees . . .'.[6]

In acknowledging his own indebtedness to Arbeau, de Lauze suggests the continuing relevance of *Orchésographie* in the early seventeenth century. Despite Arbeau's interest in dances which by the Jacobean period were obsolete (the *basse danse* being the most obvious case) there does seem to have been a measure of continuity between the principles outlined in that important late sixteenth-century French treatise and the practice of dancing in the early seventeenth-century English court.

There are, too, a number of late sixteenth- or early seventeenth-century English manuscript sources—all, it seems, originating with members of the Inns of Court—which give shorthand choreographic instructions for a re-markably circumscribed group of dances (basically the sequence of dances which make up the framework of the revels at the Inns).[7] These instructions

---

[4] Robert Copland's 'The maner of dauncynge of bace daunces after the use of fraunce and other places translated out of frenche in englyshe' was published with *The Introductory to Wryte and to Pronounce Frenche compyled by Alexander Barcley* (London, 1521).

[5] It is not certain where the *Apologie* was published. The British Library Catalogue gives the place of publication as '[Paris?]'. For Montegu see GB-Lpro, SP 16 3 173.

[6] 'In front of a king, or in the presence of high-ranking persons'. F. de Lauze, *Apologie de la Danse*, 1623, translated & ed. J. Wildeblood (London, 1952), 102.

[7] On the Inns of Court revels see below, pp. 114–15 and 261–2. The manuscripts containing dance instructions are as follows: GB-Ob, MS Rawl. Poet. 108 (*c.*1570), MS Rawl. d. 864 (*c.*1630), MS Douce 280 (*c.*1610), GB-Lbl, MS Harl. 367, GB-Lcm, MS 1119, and Inner Temple Library Misc. Vol. 27 (Buggins MS No. 1). The manuscript containing the greatest number of dance instructions, GB-Ob, MS Douce 280,

Ex. 3.1. Essex Measures, from GB-Lcm, MS 1119

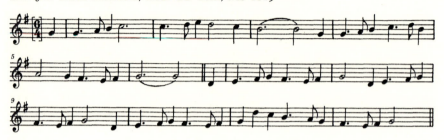

all take the form which was to be parodied in Guerino's speech (quoted at the beginning of this chapter). One manuscript (GB-Lcm, MS 1119) is described on its back cover as 'The old Measures of the Inner Temple London as they were first begun and taught by Robert Holeman a Dancing-Master before 1640 and continued ever since in the Inner Temple Hall'. This has instructions for eight dances and music for five. The 'Earle of Essex Measure'—the shortest of these dances—will suffice to show that the description parodied in *The Malcontent* took a fairly standard form (and see Ex. 3.1): 'A Double forwards and a Single back four times, then two Singles sides & a Double forwards and a Double back once, then all this measure once over and so end.'[8] The fact that theatre audiences were expected to recognize the technical vocabulary of dancing instruction suggests that the fundamentals of courtly dancing enjoyed quite a wide currency.

The affinity between English and French dancing seems clear. The eventual domination of French dancing-masters at the English court is described in Chapter 6, and there is ample musical evidence that Englishmen took an interest in French dance music of the period. Robert Dowland's *Varietie of Lute Lessons* contains two of Robert Ballard's dances and Lord Herbert of Cherbury (who recommended learning dancing from 'the more accurate Dancing Masters in France') included five in his Lute Book.[9]

Italian dancing-manuals also found their way to England. There are several important publications. Marco Fabritio Caroso published *Il Ballarino* in Venice in 1581. It appeared in a revised and expanded edition as *Nobiltà di dame* in 1600 and 1605. Cesare Negri acknowledged Caroso's influence in his *Gratie d'Amore* (Milan, 1600), which likewise appeared in a revised version with a new title, *Nuove Inventioni di Balli* (1604). One of the British Library's copies

is transcribed by Sabol, *Four Hundred Songs and Dances*, 546–8. All are transcribed in the appendices of J. P. Cunningham, *Dancing in the Inns of Court* (London, 1965).

[8] See Cunningham, *Dancing at the Inns of Court*, 35. J. M. Ward, 'The English Measure', *EM* 14 (1986), 18, discusses this dance in some detail in relation to both its choreographic and musical sources. Ward argues convincingly that 'the term "measure" . . . was applied to dances with individual choreographies . . . to distinguish them from dances whose steps were typical' (p. 17).

[9] See Herbert, *Life of Edward, First Lord Herbert of Cherbury*, 31. There are more French dances in Tobias Hume's *The First Part of Ayres, French, Polish and Others* (London, 1605).

of Caroso's *Nobiltà di Dame* has on its binding a coat of arms which indicates that it was originally in the Prince of Wales's library during the reign of James I.[10] The Bodleian Library listed in its 1605 catalogue 'Fabrito Caraso del Ballarino. Ven. 1581', and by 1620 it had added another copy and had acquired Negri's *Nuove Inventioni di Balli*. When Robert Martin began selling Italian books in England in the 1630s, he included both Negri and Caroso in his catalogues.[11] All this suggests that these works may have been reasonably well known in courtly circles. As Julia Sutton has pointed out, some idea of the influence of Italian dancing-masters throughout Europe can be gauged from Negri's list of 'tutti i più famosi ballarini, che fiorirono nel secolo dell'Autore'.[12] Several on this list served at the French court.

The two Italian manuals arise from a milieu not unlike that of the court masque. Both Caroso and Negri devote an entire section of their treatises to general etiquette. They present a norm of a socially desirable level of proficiency in dancing and of controlling standards of polite behaviour. Though most of their dances are for one or two couples and designed with participants rather than with an audience in mind, they do include some specifically choreographed *balli*, often detailing (apparently for the sake of the reflected prestige) when, where, and by whom these were danced. The final section of Negri's treatise is of most interest here. Having referred throughout the volume to various court entertainments—*mascherate, entrate,* and *intermedi*—Negri rounds off the third book with a detailed account of intermedi performed in 1599 before the Infanta Donna Isabella, the Archduke of Austria, the papal legate Cardinal Diattristano, and all the nobility of Milan. The intermedi themselves deal with episodes from the Orpheus and Jason legends. They ended with a spectacular pastoral epilogue:

Nel fine della rappresentatione della pastorale si vidde vna grandissima nugola, nella quale discendeua la felicità con molti musici apportatrice essendo di molte gratie alla Serenissima Infante, & al Serenissimo Arciduca, andaua spiegandole con vn gratiosissimo madrigale, & di nuovo più che prima bello vedeuasi il cielo aperto, dou'era concerto di musici eccellenti in persona delli dei d'esso, quali fecero diletteuole rispondenza à i musici discesi nella nugola, & finito'l canto della felicità vscirono quattro pastori, & quattro ninfe, da quali si fece vn bellissimo brando, nel fine de gl'Intermedij della detta Comedia Armenia pastorale, il quale brando fu fatto dall'Auttore di quest'opera . . .[13]

[10] The shelf-mark of this volume is C. 77. d. 12. The College of Arms informs me that it is impossible to tell from the coat of arms whether the book was acquired for Prince Henry's library or for the future Charles I. See also J. Smith and I. Gratiss, 'What did Prince Henry do with his Feet on Sunday 19 August 1604?', *EM* 14 (1986), 198–207.

[11] See Krummel, 'Venetian Baroque Music'.

[12] C. Negri, *Le Gratie d'Amore* (Milan, 1600), 2. See Julia Sutton, 'Cesare Negri', in *Grove 6*.

[13] *Le Gratie d'Amore*, 290. 'At the end of the presentation of the pastoral a huge cloud was seen in which Happiness descended with many musicians, bearing many gifts to the most Serene Princess and to the most Serene Archduke. They came presenting a most graceful madrigal. And once again, even more beautiful than at the beginning, the heavens were seen to open, where there was a consort of the most excellent musicians in the persons of gods, who produced a delightful response to the musicians who had descended

Negri's description of the concluding *brando* allows us a rare glimpse of a choreographed theatrical dance from a courtly entertainment. The ninth of its eleven sections involves all eight dancers:

Tutti pigliano la man della sua ninfa, e fanno sedici .S. in passeggio attorno alla sala volgendosi alla sinistra, fatti li due primi .S. innanzi, i Pastori girano attorno alla sinistra, e pigliano con la man sinistra quella della sua ninfa sempre passeggiando, e fanno altri due .S. poi pigliano la mano, e fanno altri due .S. innanzi, e due .S. girando vna volta attorno ad essa mano con le sue ninfe. questo si fà quattro volte, due girando attorno, li Pastori, & due fanno girare le ninfe si fermano tutti in fila nel mezo del ballo, & il primo che guida si troua in capo del ballo con la sua ninfa.[14]

Quite typically this culminates in a pleasing tableau of all the dancers. (At the conclusion of the eleventh part, all the dancers make a reverence together, finishing the *brando* 'con grazia & decoro'.)

All these treatises allow us to see how certain kinds of gesture and movement could make (for want of a better term) a rhetorical point. All insist that dancing is a mark of cultivation. Titles like *Nobiltà di Dame* or *Gratie d'Amore* speak for themselves; they point directly to a Renaissance courtly ideal. Caroso's preface deals with the nobility and physical benefits of dancing; dance, he concludes, unites grace, beauty, and decorum. Arbeau's *Orchésographie* is written as a dialogue between the dancing-master and a pupil who has found that education for a profession is not in itself sufficient for someone wishing to mix in good society.[15] De Lauze, too, insists on the social prestige of dancing:

le seul exercice de la danse peut non seulement arracher les mauuaises actions qu'vne negligente nourriture auroit enracinee, mais donner encore vn maintien & une grace que nous disons entregent, & que ie peux appeler proprement *le bel estre*, chose tout à faict necessaire à quiconque veut rendre son port & son abort agreable dans le monde.[16]

in the cloud; and at the end of the song of Happiness four shepherds and four nymphs came out and danced a most beautiful *brando* concluding the Intermedi of the said pastoral comedy *Armenia*. That *brando* was devised by the author of this work.'

[14] *Le Gratie d'Amore*, 293. 'Each shepherd takes the hand of his nymph, and makes sixteen .S. [*Li siguiti ordinarij*] while progressing around the room turning towards the left; the shepherds, having completed the first two .S. forward, turn around to the left, and each takes with his left hand that of his nymph while still moving forward; and they do two more .S. then taking her hand, and do two more .S. forward, and two .S. going around once in this direction with the nymphs. This is done four times, twice with the shepherds going around the nymphs, and twice when the nymphs are made to revolve around the shepherds, ending with everyone in a file the middle of the dancing area, and the leader is at the head of the figure with his nymph.'

[15] Arbeau's Capriol is like Morley's Philomathes who—for similar reasons—seeks instruction from a music master; see Thomas Morley, *A Plain and Easy Introduction to Practical Music* (London, 1597), ed. R. A. Harman (London, 1952).

[16] De Lauze, *Apologie*, 68. Wildeblood's translation reads 'For the sole exercise of the dance is able, not only to eradicate the bad actions which a negligent upbringing has ingrained, but gives also a decorum and a grace which we call Civility, and which I am able to call properly *le bel estre* (elegant presence), a thing absolutely necessary to whosoever wishes to render his deportment and his approach agreeable to society.'

In emphasizing that dancing was an important social accomplishment for anyone wishing to mix in elegant society, these dancing-masters echoed Castiglione's influential *Il Cortegiano*. Sir Thomas Hoby's translation (first published in 1561) concluded with 'A Breef Rehersall of the Chiefe Conditions and Qualities in a Courtier', and amongst these dancing and musical skills are given a prominent place. By the seventeenth century these ideas had become commonplace in courtesy books and treatises on education.

More than a merely social gentility was claimed for this. Just as speculative music provided a context in which the suggestion could be made that the music of the main masque participated in a cosmic harmony, so parallel Renaissance ideas about dance tended to transform an urbane Castiglione-like decorum into a model of the 'exquisite chorus of the stars and of the heavens, and the interweaving of the planets with the fixed stars, and the elegant and harmonious organization and wonderful order'.[17] One stanza spoken by Love in Sir John Davies's *Orchestra, or a Poem of Dancing* makes the link between de Lauze's concept of *bel estre* and the idea of the cosmic dance:

> If sence hath not yet taught you, learne of me
> A comly moderation and discreet,
> That your assemblies may well ordered be
> When my uniting power shall make you meet;
> With heav'nly tunes it shall be tempered sweet:
> And be the modell of the worlds great frame,
> And you Earths children, *Dauncing* shall it name.   (Stanza 33)

That such images were still current in the Jacobean period can be nicely demonstrated from Antimo Galli's poetic evocation of *The Masque of Beauty*. This describes the first of the masquers' dances, led by the queen, as follows:

> Quando sorger la vede, e in vaghi giri
> Menar Celeste, e gloriosa danza.
> Amor, che fai? che pensi? ò che rimiri?
> Han forse i Dei nel Ciel simile usanza?
> Non più febo [*sic*], ò Diana intorno giri,
> Che questa i moti de bei Cieli auanza;
> Ceda pur Giove, e ogni stellata sfera
> Al moto di costei, che l'alme impera.[18]

---

[17] Caelius Rhodiginus, *Lectionum Antiquarum Libri XXX* (Lyons, 1560), Bk. 5, ch. 3; quoted by Meagher, *Method and Meaning in Jonson's Masques*, 83.

[18] 'Stanze fatte con l'occasione d'un balletto guidato da la Real M^ta de la Regina de la gran Brettagna &c. Li 6 di Genaro del 1608' from *Rime di Antimo Galli all'Illustrissima Signora Elizabetta Talbot-Grey* (London, 1609). See J. Orrell, 'Antimo Galli's Description of the Masque of Beauty,' *Huntington Library Quarterly*, 43 (1979), 13–23. Orrell translates Stanza 17 'When he sees her rise and lead a celestial and glorious dance in graceful turns, Cupid says to himself, "What are you doing? thinking? gazing at? Do even the gods in heaven have such ways? Not Phoebus, not Diana in their orbits can set forth the motions of the heavens better than this lady; even Jove and every starry sphere yield to her motions, who rules over souls".'

Caroso claimed that his instruction is based on the laws of symmetry and perfect theory.[19]

It is fairly easy to see what courtly dancing did *not* involve. Hoby's list of courtly qualities is as much concerned with defining limits as it is with setting goals. The courtier is urged 'To daunce well without over nimble footinges or to busie trickes' while the waiting gentlewoman is warned 'Not to come on loft nor use to swift measures in her daunsinge'.[20] His injunction against ostentation was a very familiar warning. De Lauze elaborates upon it in a way which can be seen as a specific application of Castiglione's *sprezzatura*:

on danse auiourd'huy, d'vne certaine negligence nullement affectee; & n'aymerois point qu'ils meslassent parmy leurs compositions des pas qui sentissent son baladin, comme fleurets frisoteries, ou branslemens de pieds, pirouetes (i'entens a plusieurs tours violens & forcez,) caprioles, pas mesmes des demy caprioles, si ce n'est en tournant ou finissant, & tout plain d'autres petites actions ennemies du vray air qu'on y doit obseruer, mais seulement des pas coupez, & entrecoupez, d'autres graues, ensemble des liaisons, & des beaux temps, parce que les mouuemens qui on procedent, peuuent avec assez d'air & de grace accompagner tels pas sans force . . .[21]

The idea that certain kinds of energetic movement might be frowned upon in courtly dancing found other expressions in England. In 1633 Justinian Pagitt, a student at the Middle Temple, noted four precepts about dancing in his journal:[22]

De arte Saltandi

1. ffollow yr daucing hard till you have gott a habit of dauncing neately
2. Care not to daunce loftily, as to carry yr body sweetly & smoothly away with a graceful comportment
3. In some places hanging steps are very gracefull & whill give you much ease & time to breath
4. Write the marks for the stepps in every daunce under the notes of the tune, as the words are in songs.

We can only regret that Pagitt's fourth point does not ever seem to have been put into practice. The first three combine to present a picture of dancing

[19] See F. Caroso, *Nobiltà di Dame* (Venice, 1600), trans. by J. Sutton with music ed. F. M. Walker (Oxford, 1986), 87–8.

[20] Sir Thomas Hoby, *The Book of the Courtier*, ed. W. Raleigh (London, 1900), 370 and 375. See also R. Ascham, *The Scholemaster* (London, 1570), ed. L. V. Ryan (New York, 1967), 52–3; R. Braithwait, *The English Gentleman* (London, 1630), 204; Barnabe Riche, *Riche his Farewell to the Militarie Profession* (London, 1581), sig. aiij.

[21] De Lauze, *Apologie*, 98 and 100. 'People today dance with a certain unaffected nonchalance, and they would not want to include in their choreography steps which smack of the comedian, such as *fleurets*, *frisoteries*, or *branlements de pieds*, *pirouettes* (by which I mean those which make several vigorous and energetic turns), capers, not even half-capers (unless in turning or finishing), and all the other little actions which are inimical to the true bearing that should be maintained; instead only *pas coupez* and *entrecoupez*, and other serious steps, together with *liaisons*, and *beaux temps* should be admitted, because these movements have sufficient air and grace to accompany such steps without violence . . .'.

[22] GB-Lbl, MS Harleian 1026, fos. 70ʳ–71ᵛ; quoted by R. W. Wienpahl, *Music at the Inns of Court during the Reigns of Elizabeth, James, and Charles* (Ann Arbor, 1979), 180.

which was interesting, quite sophisticated, and yet avoided tasteless flamboyance. It is more than likely that some of what was inappropriate for the courtier would furnish excellent material for an antimasque.

Orchésographie provides some support for this idea. Arbeau's description of the 'Branle du Haut Barrois' suggests a style of dancing which would fit well into certain types of antimasque: 'Ce branle se dance par les vallets & chamberieres, & quelquesfois par les ieusnes hommes & damoiselles quand ils font quelques mascarades, desguisez en paysans & bergiers ou qu'ils se veullent esgayer priueement . . .'.[23] Specific steps have similar connotations. Arbeau explains three which involve kicking one foot up into the air: the *grève* in which the foot is raised in front, the *ruade* behind, and the *ru de vache* when it is thrown out to the side. Capriole, the pupil in the dialogue, is scandalized by these unbecoming steps and won't believe that the *ru de vache* is often used, while he says of the *grève*, 'Cette mode ne me semble belle ny honneste, si ce n'est pour dancer avec quelque bonne galoise de chambeliere' (see Pl. 3).[24] Needless to say, characters from the servants' hall (and a style of dancing appropriate to them) were not out of place in low-induction antimasques.

Inigo Jones repeatedly depicted antimasque figures in postures which suggest the kind of ungainly movement so frowned upon by dance manuals and courtesy books. Plate 4 shows antimasque figures for *Britannia Triumphans* in positions which correspond to the vigorous *ruade*, *grève*, and *ru de vache*. Drawings of masquers, on the other hand, invariably depict them in elegant and dignified poses. Plates 5 to 8 juxtapose some of Inigo Jones's drawings for masque costumes with illustrations from Negri. The stance of the noble Persian youth (a design for Davenant's *Temple of Love*) is like that of the youth who illustrates Negri's section on general deportment.[25] The similarity in pose between Jones's 'Influences of the Stars' (for *Albion's Triumph*) and the Negri engraving of a gentleman leading a lady out to dance (which appears six times in the course of the treatise) is striking.[26] The graceful, elegant, and yet alert bearing seen here is represented as an ideal in much contemporary painting and sculpture.

[23] *Orchésographie*, fo. 73ʳ. 'This branle is danced by valets and chambermaids, and sometimes by young men and gentlewomen when they act in mascarades, disguised as peasants and shepherds, or when they want to have fun privately.'

[24] *Orchésographie* (Langres, 1588), fo. 45ᵛ. 'This type seems to me to be neither beautiful nor virtuous—unless it is for dancing with some fine wench who is a chambermaid.'

[25] Cesare Negri, *Nuove Inventioni di Balli* (Milan, 1604), 37. The relevant section is entitled 'Del modo, col quale s'insegna la regola d'andare su la vita con bella gratia, come dimostra il presente disegno, si nel ballare, come ancora dell'andare per le strade' ('Of the manner in which one learns the rule for conducting onself in life with a good grace, as the present drawing shows, whether in dancing or simply in walking down the street').

[26] The Jones drawings reproduced in Pl. 4, 5, and 7 are all from Caroline masques, but the particular selection was made only on the grounds of clarity; the same points could have been made from numerous other drawings, including a number of Jacobean masques. For other drawings of antimasque figures depicted making vigorous movements see O&S, Pl. 65, 95, 150, 151, 152 (all Jacobean examples), and 171, 194, 196, 198. Masquers (who are, after all, courtiers) are always depicted in elegant poses.

The lines between acceptable and unacceptable behaviour are not quite so boldly drawn as I have indicated so far. Caroso and Negri are, on the face of it, less anxious about ostentation—even though the overriding impression of their writings is that they are addressing a class of people whose personal dignity must never be violated. Both masters include instructions for a range of *salti*, *capriole*, and such like. The *brando* from the 1599 *intermedi* cited earlier includes quite intricate steps. These apparently could be accommodated decorously within an entertainment of this kind. Negri and Caroso approve of energetic movement provided it is deft and elegant; the only sin is ungainly, coarse movement. Even here, however, we are provided with an obvious basis for distinguishing between styles of dancing appropriate to the main masque on the one hand and the antimasque on the other.

Main-masque dances involved an impressive demonstration of tastefully exercised skill and technical control. The admiration which they elicited from many observers points to their having been both beautiful and interesting. Above all, the concept of *sprezzatura* invoked in the dance manuals suggests that audiences would have been able to delight in a non-exhibitionist display of graceful and alert movement. These dances were vibrant, not staid. Conversely, it must be recognized that antimasque choreography (like the dance music) gained its expressiveness by a kind of expansion—but not a removal— of boundaries. Its eccentric gesture operated within an aesthetic of order, symmetry, and musicality.

Many masque texts insist that movement and music in antimasque and main-masque dances co-operated in a non-verbal expression of the masque's themes. The antic dance in *Hymenaei* is an early example: 'Here out of a Microcosme, or Globe, (figuring Man) with a kind of contentious Musique, issued forth the first *Masque*, of eight men. These represented the foure Humors, and foure Affections . . . and, dauncing out on the Stage . . . offered to encompasse the Altar, and disturbe the Ceremonies' (ll. 109–16). Shortly after this, Reason descended from the top of the Globe ('as in the braine, or highest part of *Man*') and subdued these unruly beings; they fit naturally into 'the whole fall of the device' by making the point that Reason masters the Humours and Affections in marriage (Hymen's union). Like so many antimasque descriptions, this communicates the effect only through rather general expressions like 'with a kind of contentious music' and 'offered to disturb the ceremonies'; unfortunately, it gives no more specific indication of what was so strange and threatening about the music and dancing.

The text of *The Haddington Masque* is a little more informative. Although it still describes the music merely as 'odd', it highlights the place of exaggerated gesture in antimasque dancing:

CVPID discouered himselfe, and came forth armed; attended with twelue *boyes*, most antickly attyr'd, that represented the sports, and prettie lightnesses, that accompanie *Loue* . . . they fell into a subtle *capricious Daunce*, to as odde a *Musique*, each of them bearing two torches, and nodding with their antique faces, with other varietie of ridiculous gesture, which gaue much occasion of mirth, and delight, to the *spectators*. (ll. 157–75)

In a letter to Dudley Carleton written two days after the masque, Chamberlain compared masque and antimasque dances (the latter involving the vigorous *matachina*, a sword dance):

Venus wth her chariot drawne by swannes [came] in a cloude to seeke her sonne, who wth his companions *Lusus risus* and *Jocus*, and foure or fiue waggs more, were dauncing a matachina and acted y^t very antiquely, before the twelue signes (who were the master-maskers) descended from the zodiake, and plaide theyre parts more grauely beeing very gracefully attired.[27]

Chamberlain's expression '*acted* that very anticly' gets at the histrionic quality of the antimasque dancing.

The antimasque of witches in *The Masque of Queens* is much more fully developed than the antic sequence in either *Hymenaei* or *The Haddington Masque*, and there is correspondingly more information about its methods. Once again, sudden changes and exaggerated gestures are central:

wth a strange and sodayne Musique, they fell into a *magicall Daunce*, full of præposterous change, and gesticulation, but most applying to they^r property: who, at they^r meetings, do all thinges contrary to the custome of Men, dauncing, back to back, hip to hip, they^r handes ioyn'd, and making they^r *circles* backward, to the left hand, wth strange phantastique motions of they^r heads, and bodyes. (ll. 344–50)

Clearly, Jeremy Herne's extraordinary choreography gave the dance detailed applicability to the demonic theme of the antimasque.

The same kind of energetic choreography is mentioned in Campion's *Lords' Masque* where twelve Frantics enter 'at the sound of a strange musicke': 'in middest of whom *Entheus* (or Poeticke furie) was hurried forth, and tost up and downe, till by vertue of a new change in the musicke, the Lunatickes fell into a madde measure, fitted to a loud phantasticke tune' (pp. 250–1). This must have been exciting to watch. The accounts for this masque serve as reminders that these Lunatickes were professionals (each paid one pound for his efforts).[28] This meant two things: the dancers were free to go beyond the boundaries of courtly modesty and decorum, and they must have been very skilled—superb mime artists who were also first-rate gymnasts. *The Mountebanks' Masque* makes an explicit link between energetic, virtuoso steps and antimasque dancing. Paradox, introducing each of his disciples, indicates

---

[27] H&S, x. 482. There are two other mentions of the matachina in a masque context. In a letter written to Chamberlain on 15 Jan. 1604 Carleton reported that on Twelfth Night there was 'a masquerade of certain Scotchmen, who came in with a sword dance, not unlike a matachin, and performed it cleanly'; quoted by M. S. Steele, *Plays and Masques at Court during the Reigns of Elizabeth, James, and Charles* (New Haven, 1926), 136. In the *Masque at Knowsley* a group of hags representing fasting days 'dance an Antemasque in a way of a Matachine, wth postures of strugling and wrestlinge . . .' (p. 9). Arbeau describes the mattachins (which he also calls the 'buffens') as one in which a sword fight is mimed in dance; the terminology used for the gestures in this dance overlaps with that of actual fencing (*feincte, estocade*, etc.).

[28] See above, p. 39.

that they will perform with just the kind of ostentatious effort so frowned upon in some of the manuals: 'This second master of the science of footmanshipe . . . was famed at the Feast of Pallas, when in dauncinge he came off with such lofty tricks, turnes above grownd, capers, crosse-capers, horse-capers, soe high and soe lofty performed, that he for prize bore away the helmet of Pallas' (p. 106). None of these steps in fact lies outside the scope of court dancing; it is the exhibitionism rather than the actual vocabulary which would be unacceptable in a main masque.

Beaumont's *Masque of the Inner Temple and Gray's Inn* contained two antimasques. In the first (described in Howes's *Chronicle* as 'an Anti-Maske of a strange and different fashion from others, both in habit and manners') Naiads, Hyades, Cupids, and statues from the altar of Jove dance in succession.[29] The style (and instrumentation) of the dance music changed dramatically as the dancing of various groups of nymphs gave way to the more ponderous movements of animated statues:

At their comming, the Musicke changed from Violins to Hoboyes, Cornets, &c. And the ayre of the Musicke was utterly turned into a soft time, with drawing notes, excellently expressing their natures, and the Measure likewise was fitted unto the same, and the *Statuaes* placed in such severall postures, sometimes all together in the Center of the daunce, and sometimes in the foure utmost Angles, as was very gracefull besides the noveltie.   (ll. 173–9)

This is a far cry from, say, the frenzied character of the witches' dance in *The Masque of Queens*, but what it has in common with that and other antimasque choreographies is a combination of eccentricity and a histrionic quality—a commitment to dramatic projection.

Beaumont's other antimasque is called by Howes 'a rurall countrey maske consisting of many persons, men and women, being all in sundry habits and manners'. Although the text does not describe it in the same degree of detail as the first, we are nevertheless given a clear impression of a style of antimasque dance paralleling the singing of ballads and catches in low inductions. This second antimasque (similar to the danced antimasque of *The Masque of Flowers*) is of comic figures from the natural world—a pedant, May Lord, Servingman, a country clown or shepherd, a host, a he-baboon, a he-fool, and the female counterparts of all these. They 'rush in, daunce their Measure, and as rudely depart'. The suggestion of 'rudeness' here could be taken as the most typical element in dancing of low inductions. Beaumont says of this antimasque that 'the Musicke was extremely well fitted, having such a spirit of Country jollitie as can hardly be imagined' (l. 238). He adds that the dancing complemented the music: 'The dance likewise was of the same strain, and the Dancers, or rather Actors, expressed every one their part so naturally, and aptly, as when a Mans eye was caught with the one, and then past on to the other, hee could not satisfie himselfe which did best' (ll. 208–10).

[29] E. Howes, *The Annales or Generall Chronicle of England, begun first by maister John Stow* (London, 1614), 917.

As we have just seen, Chamberlain referred to antimasque dancers in *The Haddington Masque* as having 'acted' their parts; Beaumont's suggestion that these dancers could more properly be considered actors than dancers not only highlights the distinctive expressiveness of antimasque dancing, but also points to a difference between antimasque and main masque roles. Those courtiers who danced in the main masque did not act, at least not in the same sense. The expression Jonson favoured was that they 'personated' their roles,[30] and this was more a matter of fitting into a part which corresponded in dignity to their real standing in the court. In fact, when the balance between masque role and reality shifted too far in the direction of acting, it tended to bring sharp criticism. Carleton wrote to Chamberlain after *The Masque of Blackness* describing the lady masquers' rich apparel as 'too light and curtisan-like; They^r black faces, and hands wch were painted and bare vp to the elbowes, was a very lothsome sight, and I am sory that strangers should see owr court so strangely disguised'.[31] Acting, on the other hand, was exactly what was needed in antimasque roles, and it was an essential element in antimasque dancing. Paradox in *The Mountebanks' Masque* suggests the strong association of antimasque dancing and acting in introducing one of the antimasque dancers as an Amoroso who 'did exprese such passion with his eyes, such casts, such winks, such glaunces, and with his whole body such delightfull gestures, such cringes, such pretty wanton mimicks, that he wonne the applause of all . . .' (p. 107).

There is more rustic dancing in *Love Restored*. Masquerado announces that, since the musicians for the main masque have not arrived, there can be no masque: 'Vnlesse wee should come in like a Morrice-dance, and whistle our ballat [i.e. ballet] our selues, I know not what we should doe: we ha' no other Musician to play our tunes, but the wild musique here . . .' (ll. 13–16). (It is interesting to see antimasque musicians referred to as 'the wild music' in an offhand way, almost as if that were a normal term.) The morris dance is unmistakably antimasque material. Edward Waterhouse, defending the ancient traditions of the Inns of Court in 1663, gives a vivid sense of social stratification in dancing. Morris dancing seems particularly base:

With us we have onely *French* dancing and Country dancing used by the best rank of people. *Morris-dancing* is an exercise that the loose and vile sort onely use, and that onely in faires and meetings of lewdness: but the *tripudare* [*recte* tripudiare] in our Text [Fortescue] is that decent, harmless, and graceful carriage of the body in all the motions of it, which answers the exactness of perfect Majesty of gate and grace of comportment, for which men are said to be well-bred and well-fashioned, or of good behaviour, *de bonne meane*. This in these places is expressed in part by Revellings.[32]

Several antimasques give a lower-class comic perspective on behind-the-scenes preparations for a masque. One such antimasque has some relevance to

[30] See *Hymenaei*, l. 11.

[31] GB-Lpro, SP. 14. 12. 6, letter of 7 Jan. 1605; quoted in H&S, x. 449.

[32] E. Waterhouse, *Fortescutus Illustratus, or a Commentary on the Nervous Treatise De Laudibus Legum Angliae* (London, 1663), 534; quoted in Wienpahl, *Music at the Inns of Court*, 172.

the question of masque choreography. In *Pan's Anniversary*, an arrogant Fencer attempts to outdo the celebrations which the Arcadians have prepared for Pan. Learning that dancing is to form 'the better part of the solemnity', he calls his own dancers and musicians together. His description of their preparations parodies the concern with precise movement which must have characterized masque rehearsals, furnishes satirical comment on the opportunities for social insinuation in the revels, and gives a humorous (but nevertheless interesting) picture of someone attempting to record the dance movements in shorthand (brachygraphy):

Nay, we have made our provisions beyond example, I hope. For to these there is annexed a Clock-keeper, a grave person, as *Time* himselfe, who is to see that they all keepe time to a nick, and move every elbow in order, every knee in compasse . . . Then is there a subtile shrewd-bearded Sir, that hath beene a Politician, but is now a maker of Mouse-traps, a great Inginer yet; and he is to catch the Ladyes favours in the Daunce with certaine cringes he is to make; and to baite their benevolence ⹁. . a great Clerke, who (they say) can write . . . is to take the whole Daunces from the foot by Brachygraphie, and so make a memoriall, if not a map of the businesse. (ll. 122–45)[33]

It is possible to differentiate between spectacle of strangeness and low-induction antimasque dances: the first set out to express the idea of the antimasque device through 'wild' music and movement, while the second tended towards simple rustic dances, often made ridiculous by the comic characters who performed them. Low inductions contained elements of mild satire rather than emblematic distortion or vicious caricature. Exaggerated gesture, used to make the dancers seem unnatural, vulgar, or ridiculous, had its place in both types.[34]

These classifications may serve to bring into focus a broad distinction between two quite different types of antimasque contrivance. It will, though, be obvious that some antimasques do not belong in either group, while others combine elements of both types. The antimasque of good, bad, and indifferent days in *The Masque of Heroes* offers comedy as its only justification; the dancers, according to the text, 'purchasde a Smile from the Cheekes of many a Beautie, by their Ridiculous Figures . . .' (l. 291). In the antimasque to *The Masque of Augurs* various characters from the area of St Katharine's bring along antimasques which might win them admission to the Twelfth Night festiv-

---

[33] For other similar antimasques see *The Masque of Augurs* and *The Triumph of Peace*.

[34] A parallel can be drawn here with the *ballets burlesques* which become popular in France after 1620. Margaret McGowan, *L'Art du ballet de cour en France 1581–1643* (Paris, 1963), 138–9, writes of burlesque *entrées* that 'Le danseur fait comprendre son personnage . . . par sa musique et quelquefois par des acrobaties. Dans ce dernier cas on fait appel à un baladin professionel, qui devient de plus en plus indispensable au ballet où l'on cherche avant tout à étonner; il se charge des sauts et des pas périlleux qu'un danseur noble . . . ne pourrait faire.' ('The dancer made his character understood through music and sometimes through acrobatics. In the latter case, recourse was made to a professional dancer who became more and more essential to the ballet, where the aim was above all to astonish; he would take on leaps and daring steps that a noble dancer would not be able to do.')

ities. One of these antimasques-within-an-antimasque is performed by bears while John Urson sings his ballad; the other, presented by Van Goose, was 'a perplex'd Dance of straying, and deform'd Pilgrims, taking seuerall pathes' (ll. 271–2). This was, in effect, a grotesquely expressive dance of the spectacle-of-strangeness type within a low induction. Similarly, the antimasque of Volatees (bird-like creatures from the moon) in *News from the New World* is a spectacle of strangeness presented for the entertainment of the court by the characters of a low induction.

Overall there is less actual description of main-masque dances than of antimasque dances, doubtless because they were less extraordinary. A general comment to the effect that they were 'full of elegancy, and curious device' was often thought more than enough to evoke their dignity and grace. A few Jacobean masque texts are, fortunately, more forthcoming. We are very largely dependent on these for what we can know about the choreography of set masque dances, especially since (as noted earlier) dancing instructions are almost exclusively concerned with social dancing rather than with the choreographed movement of a group intended to be viewed by an audience. Those masque descriptions which do go beyond a rather general expression of enthusiasm for what was seen indicate that the formation of geometrical groupings played a prominent part in set-dance choreography.

The Goddesses in Daniel's first masque performed 'with great maiesty & Art' a dance 'consisting of diuers strains, fram'd vnto motions circular, square, and triangular, with other proportions exceeding rare and full of variety' (ll. 173–5).[35] After the revels they performed 'another short dance, with some few pleasant changes' (l. 180). This emphasis on pleasing variety and change is typical of the more general descriptions of main-masque dances. It is clear that Daniel's other court masque, *Tethys Festival*, also had intricately worked-out figures. We learn about these not from the text, but from Sir John Finnett's report of the event: '. . . *the little Ladies* performed their Dance to the Amazement of all the Beholders, considering the Tenderness of their Years and the many intricate Changes of the Dance which was so disposed that which way soever the Changes went the *little Duke* was still found to be in the midst of these little Dancers'.[36]

In *The Masque of Beauty*, the lady masquers performed 'a most curious *Daunce*, full of excellent deuice, and change, [and] ended it in the figure of a *Diamant*, and so, standing still, were by the *Musicians*, with a second *Song* (sung by a loud *Tenor*) celebrated' (ll. 320–3). The song, 'So beauty on the waters stood', interprets the orderly geometrical stance taken up by the dancers in terms of a platonic view of the creation; as we have seen,

[35] Spenser's arithmetical stanza (*Faerie Queene* II. ix. 22) has a circle, triangle, and square representing the human body; it suggests that early 17th-c. masque audiences might have been ready to associate an aura of esoteric significance to these figures.

[36] In R. Winwood, *Memorials of Affairs of State in the Reign of Queen Elizabeth and King James I*, 3 vols. (London, 1725), iii. 180–1; quoted in O&S, i. 192.

Ferrabosco's setting is beautifully suited to this moment of stillness in the masque (see above, p. 63).

The first set dance of *Hymenaei* had the dancers forming significant patterns and letters:

Here, they daunced forth a most neate and curious measure, full of *Subtilty* and *Deuice*; which was so excellently performed, as it seemed to take away that *Spirit* from the *Inuention*, which the *Inuention* gaue to it: and left it doubtfull, whether the *Formes* flow'd more perfectly from the *Authors* braine, or their feete. The straines were all notably different, some of them formed into *Letters*, very signifying to the name of the *Bridegrome*, and ended in manner of a chaine, linking hands . . .   (ll. 310–18)

The chain is described by Reason as an image of quintessential social harmony and a correlative of the *harmonia mundi*:

> Such was the *Golden Chaine* let downe from *Heauen*;
>   And not those linkes more euen,
> Then these: so sweetly temper'd, so combin'd
>   By VNION, and refin'd.
> Here no *contention, enuy, griefe, deceit*,
>   *Feare, iealousie* haue weight;
> But all is *peace*, and *loue*, and *faith*, and *blisse*:
>   What *harmony* like this?   (ll. 320–7)

After the revels the masquers again performed set dances. We are told that these were 'full of excellent delight and change' and that in the last strain the masquers 'fell into a faire *orbe*, or *circle*' (ll. 399 ff.). This time Reason, standing in the middle, explains 'Here stay, and let your sports be crown'd: | The perfect'st *figure* is the *round*' (ll. 403–4).

The Masque of Queens also contained a dance with geometric and alphabetic figures:

a more *numerous* composition could not be seene: *graphically* dispos'd into *letters*, and honoring the Name of the most sweete, and ingenious *Prince, Charles, Duke of Yorke* Wherin, beside that principall grace of perspicuity, the motions were so euen, & apt, and they' expression so iust; as if *Mathematicians* had lost *proportion*, they might there haue found it.   (ll. 749–56)

Alphabetic figures were left to speak for themselves, but whenever a dance with other sorts of geometric patterns is described in a text, there are songs or speeches interpreting them. This may mean that we have the songs or speeches to thank for the inclusion of the description—and that other geometrically figured dances went without comment because the text did not have such a dependent relationship on the choreography. Apart from making a very general demonstration of the grace, intelligence, and social harmony of the court, no main-masque dance was ever expected in itself to convey any more specific meaning; for this, one must go to the speeches or the songs which introduced them.

The most detailed dance descriptions occur early in the period. In the *Hymenaei* and *Masque of Queens* texts there is a sense of strain about the way Jonson tries to communicate something of the dances' sophistication and their conformity with the masques' vision. Although masque texts began to provide much less detail about the form of set dances, geometric patterns and intricate figures obviously did not disappear after *The Masque of Queens*. Ingenious choreographies continue to be mentioned from time to time in observers' reports. Orazio Busino wrote of the set dances for *Pleasure Reconciled* that

Tutti questi discessero uniti dalla scene à modo di piramide, con spuntar sempre primo il solo Principe. fermati à terra, subito si sentì la Musica de' Violini, con le sue parti sonore, al numero certo di più di 25. ò trenta, tutti in un palco, fatta la riuerenza à S. M^{ta}. cominciorno à ballare con quel me$_{j}$d^{mo} ordine per un pezzo molto à tempo et con varieta di cose, et poi s'andauano muttando in diuerse forme fra di loro, sempre concludendo il salto uniti.[37]

As we have seen in the Negri *brando*, geometrically patterned dances were not unique to the English masque, and doubtless occurred in virtually all related European forms of court entertainments. Most famously the patterns formed in the *Ballet de M. de Vendôme* (1610) were illustrated in the *livret* together with a brief description of their significance.[38] A notebook compiled between 1614 and 1619 by a French dancing-master working in Brussels contains—amongst recipes for making fireworks, instructions for fumigating houses against the plague, and receipts for dancing-lessons—outline descriptions of ballets (presumably devised by the dancing-master) together with numerous diagrams illustrating the disposition of groups of dancers in geometrical and alphabetical figures.[39] Geometrically patterned dances were the most obvious examples of the orderliness which was such an essential element of all main-masque dances.

The Musical Structure of Masque Dances

It will have been clear from Chapter 1 that there is no shortage of dance music from the Jacobean period. Given the abundance of evidence, we might expect to have very little difficulty in establishing how these dances related to court productions. Yet there are problems. Some—like the fact that every source is at one or more removes from what might be called a production score—have been dealt with already.

[37] The original Italian is printed in H&S, x. 583. The translation from *CVSP*, xv (1909), 114 reads as follows: 'All these [The masquers] descended together from above the scene in the figure of a pyramid, of which the prince formed the apex. When they reached the ground the violins, to the number of twenty-five or thirty, began to play their airs. After they had made an obeisance to his Majesty, they began to dance in a very good time, preserving for a while the same pyramidical figure, and with a variety of steps. Afterwards they changed places with each other in various ways, but ever ending the jump together.'

[38] See McGowan, *L'Art du ballet de cour*, Pl. 6 and 7.

[39] S-Sk, Cod. Holm. S 253; See Ward, 'Newly Devis'd Measures', 115–16.

The first and most obvious step in determining how appropriate the musical structures were to their context would seem to be to establish what that context actually was. And therein lies a problem which has led scholars astray for over a century. GB-Lbl, Add. MS 10444, in particular, provides us with a very sizeable body of tunes (138 altogether), nearly all with titles which seem to point towards an origin in a specific masque. Trying to use those titles to establish contexts, however, is a bit like having a bad dream: an apparently quite precise designation becomes very misty as soon as it is scrutinized. This is most obviously the case with dances attached by their titles to lords, ladies, the prince, or the temple.

Almost ever since the British Museum purchased it, Add. MS 10444 has attracted considerable attention. In the nineteenth century it was responsible for begetting a whole range of specious plays which were first listed in J. O. Halliwell-Phillipps's *Dictionary of Old English Plays* (1860), then in W. C. Hazlitt's *Manual for the Collector of Old English Plays* (1892), and even in Gertrude Sibley's *Lost Plays and Masques 1500–1642*, published in 1933, long after the real significance of the titles had been established. The most curious part of all this is not that the titles of individual dances in Add. MS 10444 were elevated to the status of independent masques, but that these phantom productions were assigned dates. Thus *The Essex Antic Masque* was supposed to have been performed about 1620, *The Furies' Masque* about 1624, and *The Cuckolds' Masque* during the reign of Charles I.

Most commentators this century have recognized that the significance of the titles in the manuscript varies. Sometimes they do indeed refer to the name of a masque, but sometimes they allude to a patron, performer, or composer, sometimes to the venue of the masque, and sometimes to a device within the masque. With a few titles it is impossible to work out what connection they might have with a masque. (Perhaps there was none—we cannot rule out the possibility that there are non-masque tunes in the manuscript's main sequence of dances.)

The chief preoccupation of those studying the manuscript has, until recently at least, been with attempting to ascribe the tunes to known masques and plays. The effort has often been misguided. In 1922 W. J. Lawrence offered tentative suggestions about the original context of some items, but prefaced his remarks with this warning:

It is not within the province of the average, well-equipped musicologist readily to identify (so far as identification is possible) the court entertainments for which these tunes were composed . . . [In the Hughes-Hughes *Catalogue of Manuscript Music in the British Museum* (London, 1909)] the feebleness of the conjecturing demonstrates that the task is one purely for the dramatico–literary historian, some investigator who has long been concerning himself with the origin, development, *modus operandi* of the masque.[40]

_____

[40] Lawrence, 'Notes on a Collection of Masque Music', *ML* 3 (1922), 49.

Regrettably, a number of scholars apparently read this as a challenge and applied themselves to identifying the original context of as many of the tunes as possible. The results are very wayward. In 1954 J. P. Cutts followed up Lawrence's article with another in which he used his obviously extensive knowledge of masque texts to offer suggestions about the context of 112 tunes. He relied mainly on the titles and sometimes missed musical clues. He did not offer a location for no. 28, 'A Masque' (S 79), but it is the dance by Thomas Lupo published with the text of *The Lord Hay's Masque* (as 'Time that leads the fatal round'). In other words, this dance is one of the very few that *can* be confidently assigned to a particular masque.

This process of ascription has been carried further—by J. E. Knowlton in her thesis on the manuscript, by David Fuller in a 1973 article, and most influentially by Andrew Sabol in his *Four Hundred Songs and Dances from the Stuart Masque*. Taking a single dance and looking at various ascriptions highlights the precarious nature of the exercise. No. 66, 'The Shepherds Dance' (S 118), was ascribed by Lawrence to *Coelum Britannicum* (impossible if we accept that the manuscript was compiled at least ten years earlier than the performance of that masque; he was obviously led astray by a later marginal date reading 1635). Cutts rejected Lawrence's ascription, and after considering *Pan's Anniversary* and Beaumont and Fletcher's *Prophetess* (1622) concluded, 'if choice had to be made I should favour *The Winter's Tale*'. Knowlton opted for Beaumont's *Masque of the Inner Temple and Gray's Inn* and Fuller gave *Pan's Anniversary* as a first choice and mentioned *Coelum Britannicum* and *Salmacida Spolia* as other possibilities (both later than the probable date of the manuscript). Sabol settles for *Pan's Anniversary*.[41]

The practice of ascribing some of these tunes to plays (especially those without the words 'masque' or 'anti/antic masque' in their titles) should also be regarded warily. There is positive evidence that the manuscript is a source of masque tunes, but only these tantalizing titles to suggest that it might also be a source of other theatrical tunes. Even no. 62, 'The Tempest' (S 114), which has so often been linked with Shakespeare's play—because, of course, it would be nice to know that this was the music used there—could just as easily have fitted into an antimasque with a storm like *The Somerset Masque*. A number of the tunes without masque titles in Add. MS 10444 are elsewhere described as masque tunes. No. 55, 'The Nobleman' (S 106), is called 'The noblemens mask tune' in GB-Cu, MS Dd. 4. 22 (fos. 8ᵛ–9ʳ). In two other cases, titles which give no hint of a masque origin—no. 64, 'Van-weelly' (S 116), and the beautiful no. 110, 'Williams his Love' (S 59)—are included in Adson's *Courtly Masquing Ayres*. While this is not an absolute guarantee that they are in fact masque tunes, it certainly makes it seem likely.

---

[41] Lawrence, 'Notes on a Collection of Masque Music,' 55; J. P. Cutts, 'Jacobean Masque and Stage Music', *ML* 35 (1954), 197; J. E. Knowlton, 'Some Dances of the Stuart Masque Identified and Analyzed' (Ph.D. diss., Indiana University, 1966), 352–3; D. Fuller, 'The Jonsonian Masque and its Music', *ML* 14 (1973), 450; Sabol, *Four Hundred Songs and Dances*, 576.

Concordances in other sources often complicate rather than clarify the picture. The titles in Brade's *Newe ausserlesene liebliche Branden*, especially, diverge wildly from those in Add. 10444. The same dance is associated in Add. 10444 with baboons and in Brade with princesses.[42] No simple explanation presents itself here. A title like 'Auffzug vor Grienwitsch' ('Procession in front of Greenwich'), for example, applied to the same dance as Add. 10444, no. 41, 'The Third of the Temple' (S 92), argues against the suggestion that Brade's titles might refer to new uses of these tunes in Germany (though, of course, the titles' derivations could differ from case to case).[43] The situation should alert us to the futility of attempting to establish precise contexts for these tunes.

The best reason for wanting to establish the original context of a particular dance tune would be in order to see how appropriate it was dramatically. I am convinced that there are very few tunes which can be assigned with any certainty to a particular production, but it is also true that there is little about the actual structure of most masque dances to give them any intrinsic applicability to the device of a specific masque or antimasque; as we have seen, it was the function of the songs and speeches to endow the visual spectacle of the dance with this kind of significance. No given antimasque dance seems more obviously suited to baboons than to fools. John Ward has demonstrated that many of these dances share melodic patterns to such an extent that the tunes seem to be created through a process like centonization in plainchant— the combination and recombination of rather featureless melodic fragments. Although there are a few really distinctive and memorable dances in Add. MS 10444 they are exceptional, and Ward is obviously right:

The first thing that strikes one on reading through a sheaf of the 'newly devis'd measures' in Add. MS 10444 is how little they resemble other dance music of the period, corantos, voltes, moriscos and the like. Few of the tunes are memorable; most of them are more cobbled than composed and of a remarkable sameness of style. . . . This brief bit of dance music [no. 38 (S 89)] is put together out of commonplace motifs that appear with some frequency in many of the measures of Add. MS 10444. They are easily recognized, difficult to define, can best be described as brief tonal configurations that take a new form with each realization. Like a tune family, but on a much smaller scale, each has a recognizable outline or contour, stresses the same scale degrees, and exploits a stereotypical motif. . . . The recycling of shared motifs was almost certainly not a conscious compositional act on the part of the composers. The motifs appear to have been an integral part of the musical language of the measures of the court masque, their variation a matter of composition habit, choice of motif determined as much by the key chosen as by the accidents of choice, the composer dipping into a common fund of musical ideas, much as the choreographers appear to have drawn on a shared figural vocabulary for their dances.[44]

[42] Add. 10444, no. 27, 'The Babboons Dance' (S 78); Brade, no. 9, 'Intrada der Jungen Princessinnen'.
[43] See Holman, *Four and Twenty Fiddlers*, 188.
[44] Ward, 'Newly Devis'd Measures', 121, 123, and 127.

What Ward describes was obviously common enough in the composition of dance music throughout Europe (and not just, as Ward implies, in France).[45] Such a process does not hold out the promise of being able to find in an individual dance tune features which relate in a particularly apt way to the device of any one masque. For this reason, the question of ascription is not just elusive; it is for the most part not very interesting. There are, of course, many places where the title (and sometimes other circumstantial evidence as well) points to a particular tune's having been associated with a specific production. It would be as silly to ignore these connections as it is to force them in other instances. By and large, however, it is more fruitful to concentrate on the broader stylistic differences between antimasque and main-masque dances and to accept that the affects attributed to particular dances in the texts might have been realized through any number of tunes.

The titles in Add. MS 10444 can help to unlock some of the basic distinctions between antimasque and masque dances. Table 3.1 (developing an approach taken by J. E. Knowlton) summarizes the structure of those dances in the manuscript whose titles allow us to sort them with reasonable confidence into antimasque and main-masque categories.[46] The antimasque dances chosen are quite simply all those which contain the words 'antimasque' or 'antic masque' in their titles. In addition to these, the two witches' dances (nos. 25 and 26) and 'The Satyres Masque' (no. 56) have been included since we may be reasonably certain of their antimasque context. 'The Cuckolds Masque' also finds a place in the list since it is clear from the sequence of dances formed by nos. 73–7 (S 126–30) that this, too, must have been an antimasque tune. The main-masque dances in the second part of Table 3.1 all belong in linked series of dances (of the type entitled 'The Prince's first/ second/third masque').

Alongside the title of each dance I have indicated schematically the metrical structure of the tune. In this, a time signature is given for each strain and—as a very rough indication of length and balance—this is followed by the number of metrical groups within the strain. In duple strains this is always equal to the number of (editorial) bars, but in triple strains it means the number of the simplest possible triple groupings. (In other words hemiolas or ambiguous 3/2 or 6/4 bars are all treated as if they contained two triple groups.) Finally, as a way of sketching in the tonal schemes of each dance, the table states the key in which each piece begins and the chord at the end of each strain.

---

[45] Julia Sutton and F. Marian Walker write of Caroso's *Nobiltà di Dame*, 'In keeping with its purpose, the style of the music is in general simple, homophonic, and formulaic. Each piece is normally made up of one to three strains of four-bar (or multiples of four bar) phrases in the same key. Many of the pieces, in fact, seem merely to be assembled through a pasticcio technique, out of reusable units chosen for their durations rather than for any aesthetic qualities . . .'; *Nobiltà di Dame*, 49.

[46] Knowlton, 'Some Dances of the Stuart Masque', 142–50 provides a table organizing all the dances in Add. MS 10444 by number of strains and by metre. She observes from this that any list which departs from the regular duple, or duple-plus-triple organization 'tends to turn into a catalogue of antimasque dances' (183).

TABLE 3.1. *Structure of antimasque and main-masque dances in Add. MS 10444*

Changes of time signature enclosed by brackets take place within a strain. An oblique stroke separating two groups of bar numbers indicates that a *petite reprise* occurs at that point in the strain, i.e. 8/4 indicates a twelve-bar strain (repeatable as a whole) with a four-bar *petite reprise*.

Approximate time signature equivalents: $3_1 = \frac{3}{4}$ $6_1 = \frac{6}{4}$ $\odot = \frac{3}{2}$ ₵ $= \frac{2}{2}$ ₵ $= \frac{2}{2}$ fast   ♭ $= \frac{2}{2}$ fast

No.	Title	Strains	First Chord	Cadences
Antimasque dances				
6	The Temple Anticke	₵6 $3_1$10 ₵4 ♭8 ♭15 $3_1$12	G	G e G G G G
7	The Temple Anticke 2	₵6 $3_1$8 ₵8 ♭8 $3_1$16 $3_1$12	G	G a e D D G G
25	The First Witches Dance	$3_1$12 $3_1$14 $6_1$8	C	C C C C
26	The Second Witches Dance	₵8 (₵2+$3_1$3+♭2) $6_1$8	F	F F F F
33	The Old Anticke Masque	₵4 ₵2 ₵4 ♭8	F	C F F F
56	The Satyres Masque	₵8 ₵12 ($3_1$10+₵5) ⊙8 ♭8 $3_1$6	G	G D G D G
73	The Cuckolds Masque	$3_1$17 $3_1$18 ₵5 ₵8	G	e e g g b
91	Graysin Anticke Masque	₵4 ₵4 $3_1$16 ₵4 ₵2 $3_1$16	C	e C e C b G C
92	Essex Anticke Masque	♭6 (₵4+♭4) $3_1$12 D	D	d D d D
98	The Anticke Masque at Court	♭14 ₵6 $3_1$8 ₵8 $3_1$17	G	G G G g
122	The First of the Temple Anticke	♭8 (♭5+$3_1$4) $3_1$10 ♭8	D	D d D d
123	The Second	₵8 ♭4 ₵7 $3_1$16	G	G e G G G
Main-masque dance sequences				
1	The Queenes Masque, the first	₵5 ₵6 ₵15 $3_1$14 $3_1$8	D	D D D D D
2	The Queenes Maske, the second	₵9/8 ₵16 $3_1$12 $3_1$8 (⊙5+₵5)	D	D D D D a
3	The Queenes third Masque	₵4 ₵5 ₵3 ₵5 (₵8+$3_1$9)	D	D D D A D
4	Broxborn berry Maske	₵6 ₵6 $3_1$11	C	C C
5	Broxborn berry Maske	₵4 ₵7	G	G G

No.	Title									
10	The Prince's Masque	¢7	¢7	3ı8	3ı8		D	A	D	D
11	The Princes 2 Masque	¢6	¢6	3ı8			D	A	D	
12	The Princes third Masque	¢7	¢7				d	F	d	
14	The Ladies masque. I	¢8	¢8	3ı12			a	a	a	
15	The Ladyes second Masque	¢8	¢9				a	a	a	
16	The Ladyes third Masque	¢4	¢8	3ı8			A	A	A	
22	The First of the Lords	3ı5	3ı11				D	D	D	
23	The Second of the Lordes	¢8	¢12	3ı9			G	D	D	
24	The Third of the Lords	¢8	¢10				G	D	D	
39	The First of the Temple	¢4	¢7	3ı8			G	D	G	
40	The Second of the Temple	¢8	¢8	3ı8			g	g	g	
41	The Third of the Temple	¢8	(¢4+3ı5)	3ı8			G	(d+G)G	G	
42	The First of the Lords	¢6	¢6				C	e	a	
43	The Second of the Lords	¢6	¢7				d	F	d	
44	The Third of the Temple	¢6	¢7	3ı8/8			D	A	A	D
48	Sr Francis Bacons Masque. I	¢8	¢8	3ı14			G	G	G	
49	Sr Francis Bacons Second Masque	¢6	¢8	¢6			G	G	G	
50	Cuperaree or Graysin	¢8	¢10				g	g	g	
51	The Second	¢6	¢9	3ı8			D	D	D	D
68	The Lord Hayes his first Masque	¢6	¢7				G	D	D	
69	The Second	¢6	¢7				g	D	g	
74	The first of the Ladyes; after the Cuckolds	¢6	¢6				G	D	G	
75	The Second	¢7	¢9				g	B♭	g	
76	The Third	¢8	¢6	3ı7			G	D	G	G
77	The Fourth	¢5	¢6	3ı17			D	A	D	
83	Mr Adsons Masque	¢6	¢8	3ı8			d	d	d	
84	Adsons Masque	¢8	¢8	3ı8			D	D	D	
87	The First of the Temple	¢6	¢8	3ı8			G	G	G	

TABLE 3.1. *Continued*

Changes of time signature enclosed by brackets take place within a strain. An oblique stroke separating two groups of bar numbers indicates that a *petite reprise* occurs at that point in the strain, i.e. 8/4 indicates a twelve-bar strain (repeatable as a whole) with a four-bar *petite reprise*.

Approximate time signature equivalents: 3₁ = 3/4   6₁ = 6/4   ⊙ = 3/2   ¢ = 2/2   ₵ = 2/2 fast

No.	Title	Strains	First Chord	Cadences
88	The Second of the Temple	₵8 ₵6 3₁8	D	D D D
89	The Third of the Temple	₵8 ₵9 3₁8	g	g g g
93	The first of my Lord of Essex	₵6 ₵6	D	D D
94	The Second	₵8 ₵8	d	d d
95	The Third	₵6 ₵6 3₁16	D	D D D
105	The First of the Princes Masques	₵6 ₵6	d	F d
106	The Second	₵6 ₵6	D	D D
107	The Third	₵7 ₵7	D	A D
116	The First of the Temple	₵7 ₵6 ₵6	d	d F d
117	The Second	₵6 ₵8 3₁15	d	F d d
118	The Third	₵6 ₵6 3₁6 3₁6	D	D A D A D
119	The First of Sr John Paggintons	₵8 ₵8 3₁8	D	D D
120	The Second	₵8 ₵9	d	d d
121	The Third	₵8 3₁15	d	d d
124	The First of the Temple Masques	₵4 ₵6 3₁7	C	C G C
125	The Second	₵4 ₵4	d	F d
126	The Third	₵6 ₵6 3₁8	C	C G C
127	The First of the Prince his Masque	₵6 ₵7	d	F d
128	The Second	₵6 ₵6	d	a
129	The Third	₵7 ♩13 3₁16	A	A D D
135	The First of the Prince his	₵8 ₵8	C	C C
136	The Second	₵8 ₵8	C	C C
137	[The third]	₵8 ₵8 3₁8 3₁8	C	C C C C

Marked structural differences between the antimasque and main-masque dances immediately become apparent. Antimasque dances tend to be longer and, more importantly, they have a greater number of metrical changes than masque dances. With only two exceptions (no. 2, 'The Queenes Maske, the second' (S 53), and no. 129, 'The third [of the Prince's]' (S 182)), the only metrical change which takes place within a main-masque dance is the change from the common alla breve metre to a concluding triple section. Approximately half the main-masque dances have this triple section, while the other half have no change in metre at all. It is more likely than not that the final dance in a group will have a ¢–¢–3 metrical structure, and there is a tendency, although less marked, for the intermediate dance or dances to keep to the alla breve metre throughout. There is a roughly equal distribution of ¢–¢–3 and ¢–¢ structures in the initial dances of these groups.

The tendency for final dances to have the slightly more elaborate ¢–¢–3 structure is perhaps surprising in view of a tendency (evident in texts from about 1615 on) to designate the second of the set dances as a 'main dance'.[47] (This may be a further argument for settling on quite an early date for the compilation of Add. MS 10444.)

There are two dances in the sample which remain in triple time for the whole of the piece: no. 22, 'The first of the Lords' (S 73), and no. 24, 'The third of the Lords' (S 75). Both come from the same group and both were tacked on to alla breve dances in Brade versions, thus becoming part of a 'normal' ¢–¢–3 structure. We can only speculate whether Brade preserves the original dances in a more complete form, or whether he reformatted the tunes to assimilate them into a more regular masque-dance form.

Table 3.1 shows that the occurrence of a triple-time section in any position other than as the concluding strain is an antimasque dance characteristic. Similarly, only antimasque dances ever use the ₵ fast duple time signature. There is just one exception to this: no. 129, 'The third [of the Prince's]' (S 182). The table also suggests that antimasque dances tend to have less balanced strains: both no. 91, 'Graysin Anticke Masque' (S 144) and no. 92, 'Essex Anticke Masque' (S 145) have strains which are only two bars long combined with strains of sixteen triple groups. The nearest any main-masque dance comes to such lopsidedness is no. 3, 'The Queenes third Masque' (S 54), which has a four-bar strain combined with a concluding triple strain of sixteen triple groups (and we have already noted that the dances in this group do not conform to the standard pattern). The tonal indications in Table 3.1 show first and foremost that we should not expect much in the way of harmonic adventure here. But only antimasque dances ever contain a

[47] Intermediate main dances occur in *Lovers Made Men* (l. 169), *Mercury Vindicated* (l. 245), *The Vision of Delight* (l. 223), *News from the New World* (l. 346), *The Masque of Augurs* (l. 392), and *Neptune's Triumph* (l. 462). In the revision of *Neptune's Triumph* as *The Fortunate Isles* Jonson reverts to the term 'measures' for the second set dance (l. 576). The term 'main dance' is also used for the second dance in *The Golden Age Restored* (l. 176), and *Time Vindicated* (l. 355); in neither of these cases, however, do the texts give any indication that the masquers performed a third set dance.

change of key within a piece. (Again, the exception to this is no. 2, 'The Queenes Maske. the second' (S 53).)

In summary, we may conclude that main-masque dance tunes were metrically undisturbed and made up of two balanced duple strains with or without a concluding triple strain. Antimasque dances, on the other hand, often have more than three strains, are less balanced rhythmically, and are characterized by sudden and unexpected changes in metre or tempo. A few were harmonically more disturbed than main-masque dances. Francis Bacon gave a cryptic summary of what these dances should be like: 'Let *Antimasques* not be long . . . But chiefly, let the *Musicke* of them be Recreative, and with some strange Changes'.[48]

Table 3.2 takes all the Add. MS 10444 dances not already accounted for and distributes them, not by title, but by the characteristics isolated in Table 3.1. The results for the most part are exactly as we would expect—dances with titles suggesting antimasque contexts dominate the first section, while main-masque dances fill the second section. There are, however, a few misfits. Three tunes in the first section (nos. 8, 35, and 99) apparently have main-masque titles. The second section of the table has many more surprises. There we find 'The Hay-makers Masque', 'The Beares Dance', 'The Birds Dance', 'The Babboons Dance', 'The Saylers Masque', 'The Pages Masque', 'The May-pole', and 'The French Morris', to name only the most obvious of those dances which we would not expect to be performed by courtly masquers.

In view of the very consistent way in which the dances in Table 3.1 with the prefix 'anti-' or 'antic-' in their titles shared recurrent structural features, some explanation must be sought for these maverick tunes which end up in the 'wrong' part of Table 3.2. Most seem to belong in the low-induction type of antimasque rather than in a spectacle of strangeness. Indeed, no. 13, 'The Hay-makers Masque' (S 64, Ex. 3.2) does seem to have 'a spirit of country jollity' about it, with its tonic pedal in the opening, its robust rhythms, and its melodic figures which play around the notes of D major and A major chords. There is no way of telling from the schematic structures outlined in Tables 3.1 and 3.2 whether the balanced phrase-lengths of a particular dance derive from the orderliness of main-masque dancing or whether they have more to do with the naïve unadventurousness of a popular style. It would be misleading, however, to suggest that the other six dances in question could be separated from definite main-masque dances on the basis of popular rather than courtly traits. For the most part, these low-induction dances (if that is what they are) are indistinguishable from a lot of main-masque dances, and any distinctively antimasque elements must have been confined to choreography and instrumentation.

Individual dances can give a more satisfying impression of the distinctive character of antimasque and main-masque dances. The best-known main-

----

[48] Bacon, *Essays* (1625), 225.

TABLE 3.2. *Antimasque and main-masque dances in Add. MS 10444 selected by metrical structure*

No.	Title	Strains						

Dances containing ɸ signature, 3ı except as the final change of metre, or some other structural irregularity

No.	Title							
8	A Re Masque	¢12	(¢4+[3ı]6+¢3)			3ı16		
18	The Turkes Dances	¢8	¢2	3ı10	ɸ8			
19	The Beares Dance	¢12						
27	The Babboons Dance	¢8	¢4	¢4	¢6	3ı16		
31	Hampton Court masque	¢8	¢8	⊙9	⊙8			
35	A Masque	¢6	3ı8	[¢]10				
45	A Masque	¢7	3ı15	3ı8				
46	A Masque	¢4/4	¢13	¢8				
52	The Fooles Masque	¢6	¢6	¢3	ɸ6	ɸ4	ɸ4	ɸ8
53	The Nymphes Dance	¢8	3ı8	¢4	¢9			
55	The Nobleman	¢4	¢4	ɸ4	ɸ8	ɸ4	ɸ10	
57	The Fairey Masque	¢4	(¢4+ɸ4)	3ı15	(¢4+ɸ10+¢2)	3ı16		
58	The Pages Masque	¢5	¢5	¢10	¢8	3ı9		
60	The Gypsies masque	¢5	¢4	3ı8	ɸ8	3ı8		
62	The Tempest	¢8	3ı20	ɸ6				
63	A Masque	¢4	¢4	¢4				
66	The Sheapheards Masque	¢8.5	¢8.5	ɸ8				
70	The May-pole	¢4	¢7	¢8	¢4/4	3ı16		
72	The Furies	(¢2+[3/2]1+¢3+[3/2]1+¢6)	¢4	¢8				
79	Good Words for your Mony	¢6	(¢7 + 3ı9)	3ı16				
85	The Divells Dance	¢8	ɸ8	¢2.5	3ı13			
90	The French Morris	¢4	¢8	¢4	¢8			
99	Graysinne Masque	¢8	ɸ4	ɸ4	¢4	ɸ4	3ı15	
101	The Mountebanks Dance at Grayes Inn	¢8	ɸ10	¢15				
103	The May-pole Dance at Grayes Inne	¢7.5/4.5	3ı15	ɸ8	3ı8			
104	The Goates Masque	¢6	¢4	3ı19	¢8			
108	The Kings Mistress	¢7	¢8	¢8				
132	The Apes Dance at the Temple	¢5/2	3ı15	¢6	3ı17			
133	Grayes Inne Masque	3ı12	3ı12	3ı8				
138	[no title]	¢6	ɸ6					

Dances with ¢-¢ or ¢-¢-3 structure

No.	Title			
9	Adsonns Maske	¢8	¢8	3ı16
13	The Hay-makers Masque	¢8	¢6	
17	Batemans Masque	¢8	¢8	
20	The Birds Dance	¢4	¢6	3ı16
21	A Masque at Fryers	¢8	¢8	3ı17
28	A Masque	¢6	¢7	
29	Pearce his Maske	¢10	¢9	
30	Sr Jerome Pooles Masque	¢6	¢10	
32	The Cadua	¢4	¢4	
34	A Masque	¢6	¢8	3ı11
36	A Masque in Flowers	¢8	¢8	
37	Johnsons Flatt Masque	¢6	¢8	3ı10
38	A Masque	¢6	¢6	3ı15
47	The Saylers Masque	¢4	¢8	
54	The Lord Hays his Masque	¢9	¢9	
59	A Masque	¢4	¢4	
61	Blacke Fryars Masque	¢7	¢6	3ı14
64	Van-weelly	¢8	¢8	3ı16
65	A Masque	ɸ4	ɸ9	
67	Durance Masque	¢4	¢4	
71	The Amazonians Masque	¢8	¢8	
78	A Masque	¢6	¢6	3ı12

TABLE 3.2. *Continued*

No.	Title	Strains		
80	The Second	¢6	¢6	3'12
81	The Bull Masque	¢8	¢4	3'12
82	The Lady Lucies masque	¢8	¢8	
86	Mary Maudling Masque	¢4	¢4	
96	Fly Foul Soul	¢8	¢8	
97	A Masque	¢7	¢7	3'10
100	York House Masque	¢7	¢7	
102	The Standing Masque	¢8	¢10	
109	Wilsons Love	¢8	¢8	3'8
110	Williams his Love	¢8	¢8	3'16
111	Waters his Love	¢6	¢8	3'18
112	Broxboorn Berry Masque	¢8	¢8	3'12
113	The New Yeares Gift	¢8	¢8	3'14
114	Batemans Masque	¢8	¢8	3'14
115	Squiers Masque	¢6	¢4	
130	Lincolnes Inne Masque	¢8	¢8	3'16
131	The Prince his Masque	¢6	¢6	3'16
132	Grayes Inne Masque	¢4	¢8	3'15

Ex. 3.2. 'The Hay-makers Masque', from GB-Lbl, Add. MS 10444, no. 13 (S 64)

Ex. 3.3. 'Cuperaree or Graysin', from GB-Lbl, Add. MS 10444, no. 50 (S 101)

masque tune in Table 3.1 is no. 50, 'Cuperaree or Graysin' (S 101), which in its evenness, balance, and general sense of dignity conforms exactly to expectations for this kind of dance (see Ex. 3.3). Admittedly, its rather beautiful, melancholy melodic line has a subtlety and eloquence which is not so characteristic, though no. 102, 'The Standing Masque' (S 155)—another tune well represented in lute, keyboard, and consort sources—is similarly expressive.[49] The dance which follows 'Cuperaree' in Add. MS 10444, 'The second [of Grays Inn?]', is perhaps more typical. It has a bright D major tonality, and an uncomplicated melody which, in its use of repeated notes and notes from common chords, reinforces both the tonality and the piece's robust rhythms.

[49] It appears in GB-Och, Mus. 437 (fo. 5) as 'Greiseind: Maske', and Mus. 531–2 (no. 31); GB-Lbl, Add. MS 10337 ('Elizabeth Roger's Virginal Book'), no. 4, 'The Fairest Nimphes the Valleys . . .', Add. MS 36661, fo. 60ᵛ, 'A Maske By Orlando Gibbons', Add. MS 24665 ('Giles Earle's Song Book') Add. MS 38539, fo. 30, 'Graysin Maske'; F-Pn, Rés. 1186, fos. 36 and 39, 'Ye Fairest Nymphes Ye Valleyes'; J. Starter, *Friesche Lust-Hof* (1625), 'The fairest Nymph those Valleis, or Mountaines ever bred, &c.'; Van Eyck, *Der Fluyten Lust-Hof*, i. 32, 'Ballette Gravesand', and iii. 137, 'Laura'; Priscilla Bunbury's Virginal Book (MS in private ownership—see J. L. Boston, 'Priscilla Bunbury's Virginal Book', *ML* 36 (1955), 365–73), fo. 13ᵛ, Grayes Inn Maske'.

Nos. 135–7 (S 188–90), the final complete set of dances in the manuscript, are fine examples of main-masque dances (Ex. 3.4). All three are in C major, and all are quite uncomplicated harmonically. The first two each have a pair of perfectly balanced strains, and the third repeats this structure but with a triple section added at the end. These cheerful dances avoid eccentricity of any kind. Ex. 3.4 presents them in Brade's five-part versions (where in a few places the bass line departs from that in Add. MS 10444 to accommodate rather more suave harmonic progressions).

The antimasque dances have a less predictable structure. No. 25, 'The First Witches Dance' (S 76), is well known from other sources (principally Robert Dowland's *Varietie of Lute Lessons*). It has some obvious antimasque features (Ex. 3.5). The constant shift between long notes (dotted minims) and short notes (crotchets) creates a sense of repeated disruption; any choreography to fit this dance would have to take account of the 'stop–go' character of the piece. Some versions (Brade and GB-Lbl, Add. MSS 17786–9 and 91) have fermata marks over the dotted minims.[50] In Add. MS 10444 (although in none of the other sources), the time signature for the last strain changes from 3 1 to 6 1, suggesting a quickening in tempo. 'The Second Witches Dance' (no. 26, S 77) is even more extraordinary. It is one of the few examples where it seems that choreographic/dramatic ideas may have affected the structure of the piece to the extent that purely musical logic has been set aside. The second strain has three abrupt changes of metre (Ex. 3.6). It is interesting that in the keyboard version of this piece which survives in GB-Och, Mus. 92 (fo. 15),[51] the rhythmic irregularities have largely been ironed out—the second strain, for example, remains in an even metre throughout. For once, we are dealing with a dance whose original context can be established with a reasonable degree of certainty. It is easy to see a relationship between the idiosyncratic structures of this antimasque dance and the bizarre choreography described in the text of *The Masque of Queens*. No. 98, 'The Antick-Masque at Court' (S 151), has the usual rhythmic features of antimasque dances and some harmonic eccentricities besides (Ex. 3.7). It changes from major to minor halfway through and virtually the whole of the first strain takes place over a tonic pedal.

There are three sequences of dances listed in Table 3.1 which include both antimasque and main-masque dances. The relationship between the two types of dance within each is worth considering briefly. Dances 73–7, 'The Cuckolds Masque' and 'The first/second/third/fourth of the Ladyes after the Cuckolds' (S 126–30), form the first group. 'The Cuckolds Masque' has a definite antimasque profile (Ex. 3.8). It begins with two triple strains; after the final cadence in each of these strains, there is a short tail-piece which shifts the tonality from G major to E minor, and at the same time interrupts the strong

---

[50] These fermata marks may indicate some kind of expressive accent rather than an actual pause. Add. MS 10444 has a rest after the first set of dotted minims in the last strain of the piece.

[51] This version is published in J. Cutts (ed.), *La Musique de scène de la troupe de Shakespeare* (Paris, 1972), 16.

triple rhythms with sustained notes in a duple pattern. It is unusually mobile
harmonically. At the duple time signature, the piece moves into G minor; the
next strain begins in F major and moves—via an intermediate cadence in D
minor—back to G minor at the end. The three main-masque dances in G
major which follow are all quite unremarkable examples of their kind.

The Essex 'anticke' and main-masque dances (nos. 92–5) also conform to
type. All four dances are harmonically related. The first and third main-
masque dances are in D major while the intervening dance is in D minor. The
antimasque dance begins and ends in D major but has a central section in D

Ex. 3.4. (*a*) 'Der Erste Mascharada der Pfaltzgraffen'

3A: final two quavers emended from: $f^\sharp$–e
4A: $f^\sharp$ minim in original

Ex. 3.4(*a*). *Continued*

(*b*) 'Der Ander Mascharada'

Ex. 3.4(*b*). Continued

(c) 'Der Dritte Mascharada', from Brade, *Newe ausserlesene liebliche Branden* (1617), nos. 31–3

Ex. 3.4(c). *Continued*

Ex. 3.5. 'The First Witches Dance', bars 1–6, from GB-Lbl, Add. MS 10444, no. 25 (S 76)

Ex. 3.6. 'The Second Witches Dance', bars 8–15, from GB-Lbl, Add. MS 10444, no. 26 (S 77)

minor. This antimasque dance has the characteristic mixture of fast and normal duple metres, while its concluding triple section hovers between a 3/2 and a 6/4 metre for quite some time. The main-masque dances are perfectly balanced rhythmically. The first two each consist of two strains which are exactly equal in length, while the third repeats this structure and adds a triple section which, complete with cadential hemiolas, is itself made up of two balanced phrases.

Nos. 122–6 (S 175–9), the third group of dances, does not show the key relationships evident in the Essex dances. The first two dances in this set are superb examples of the expressive eccentricities of antimasque dances, and the other three are all unremarkable examples of the main-masque type. No. 122, 'The First of the Temple Anticke', is in D major but it has a central D minor section, and the return to D major takes place across a short and very angular few bars in triple time which interrupt the second duple strain. The most remarkable feature of no. 123, 'The Second [of the Temple Anticke]', is its first strain, which begins with a flourish of G major chords (more impressive in Adson's semiquaver version than in Add. MS 10444's quavers), and then continues with a more sustained E minor passage; the opening two bars suggest a sudden entry of antimasque characters before the actual dance begins. The short (four-bar) second strain is in the fast duple metre, the third in the normal alla breve metre. The final triple strain has frequent hemiola-based cross rhythms (Ex. 3.9).

The length and sense of balance within these antimasque and main-masque dances must have been affected by the way repeats were treated. If we regard any strain as repeatable only once, then clearly all that has been said about the normal proportions of each dance type needs no qualification. Instrumental sources which give decorated versions of a section initially stated in a simple

Ex. 3.7. 'The Antick-Masque at Court', from GB-Lbl, Add. MS 10444, no. 98 (S 151)

20: 3rd crotchet is a minim in the original
33B: *F* emended from *B*♭

Ex. 3.8. 'The Cuckolds Masque', from GB-Lbl, Add. MS 10444, no. 73 (S 126)

31–2B: *F–G* originally *B–c*

Ex. 3.9. Adson, *Courtly Masquing Ayres* (1621), no. 8 of 5 Parts

Ex. 3.9. *Continued*

form seem to presuppose a single repeat—but whether such a tidy arrangement was abandoned when dances were used for dancing (rather than as instrumental 'lessons') is another question.[52] It may be worth noting that Brade—amongst the group of masque sources which come closest to suggesting a production context—introduces a few divisions in a repeat which is written out in the top part but indicated only by the usual double bars in the others (see above, Ex. 3.4*b*).

Brade has other repeat instructions besides double bars. The final strain in his no. 18, 'Der Satyrn Tanz', is marked '2 mal' in most parts. At the end of the final strain of his no. 10, 'Mascharad der Edelfrawen' (a version of Add.

---

[52] The three pieces from *The Lord Hay's Masque* which were published in Philip Rosseter's *Lessons for Consort* (1609) are a case in point. See W. Edwards (ed.), *Music for Mixed Consort*, MB 40 (London, 1975), 146–51.

MS 10444's no. 43, 'The Nymphes Dance'), the direction 'Ein Mal' appears, suppressing the expected repeat.

Needless to say, the situation is not simple. At the opposite end from a single-repeat practice in the range of possibilities there is the sort of thing we find in Negri. The sonata for the *brando* described earlier (see p. 112) has nine strains in the staff-notation melody line but only eight in the intabulated lute part (where the final two strains run together as one). All this is to cope with a *brando* divided into eleven sections. The instructions preceding the music read as follows:

La Musica della sonata con l'intauolatura di liuto del Brando, fatto da quattro pastori, e quatro ninfe, la prima parte si fa tre volte, la seconda tre volte, la terza due volte, la quarta due volte, la quinta due volte, la sesta che è la gagliarda, si fa due volte, poi si torna à fare la prima parte due volte, e la seconda due volte, e la terza una volta sola, la quarta due volte, e la quinta due volte, la sesta due volte, l'ultima parte si fa una volta sola, e poi si finisce il brando.[53]

Negri's arithmetic is hard to follow since he seems here to be describing a piece of seven (not eight or nine) strains which, with the repeat scheme described, would provide for a dance choreographed in thirteen (not eleven) sections. The seventh strain (the penultimate in the lute part) *is* in a galliard rhythm, so half the problem is solved, but only if two strains earlier in the piece are regarded as a single unit. What is interesting here, however, is the very flexible attitude to repeats—some sections are played only once while others are heard three times. The overall structure of this sonata, however, is (regardless of repeats) rather different from any masque dances.

One reference in a masque text suggests that repeating a strain more than once may have seemed quite a normal thing to do. In *The Inner Temple Masque*, William Browne casually mentions that 'With this the triplex of their tune [i.e. the concluding triple strain] was played twice or thrice over and by turns brought them from the stage' (ll. 278–80). There is one other very interesting piece of evidence here. Nicholas Le Strange (thought to be the compiler of Add. MS 10444) made some notes on the score of pieces which he had copied by John Jenkins, mostly in 1644. Several of these annotations deal with repeats and these presuppose that the number of times a particular strain will be played is not necessarily predetermined by the notation. Three of Le Strange's repeat schemes relate to the characteristic masque-dance arrangement of two duple strains followed by a concluding triple section. In each of these instances he writes, 'the I and 2d straine: twice apiece then the Tripl: thrice'.[54]

---

[53] Negri, *Nuove Inventioni di Balli*, 294. 'The music of the sonata with lute intabulation for the *brando* danced by four shepherds and four nymphs: the first part is played three times, the second three times, the third two times, the fourth two times, the fifth two times, the sixth—which is the galliard—is played two times; then go back and play the first part two times, the second two times, and the third once only, the fourth two times, and the fifth two times, the sixth two times; the last part is played once only, and then the *brando* is finished.'

[54] J. T. Johnson, 'How to "Humour" John Jenkins' Three-part Dances: Performance Directions in

This obviously has implications for the way the dances were choreographed. None of the repeat schemes envisaged here (except perhaps Negri's) would disrupt the sense of order and balance in individual dances. A flexible attitude to repeats may even have helped bring out the eccentricity of antimasque dances—if, for example, some of the very short and strongly characterized strains were not repeated at all. (Before leaving this subject, I should perhaps give notice that we shall see in Chapter 6 that in the *ballet de cour* it does not seem to have been usual to repeat a strain more than once.)

Instrumentation in the Jacobean Masque

As we have seen, choreography and musical structure worked hand in hand to polarize masque and antimasque dances. This must have been achieved reasonably easily since, as we have seen, it was normal for one person both to compose the tunes and to devise the dancers' figures. The opposition between the two types of dance was further reinforced by instrumentation. Broadly speaking, the picture is clear: the masquers danced to violins or lutes while the antimasquers performed to all manner of 'wild music'. In exploring this, we are inevitably drawn beyond a consideration of dance alone and into the richly varied palette of instrumental colours to which masque audiences were treated. This is a vitally important element in masque music generally. The masque, like the intermedi and *ballet de cour*, is remarkable for what (anachronistically) we might call its spectacular orchestration. Not only were great numbers of musicians involved but the different groups offered an extraordinarily diverse range of colours and spatial effects—possibilities which were exploited to the full.

This can hardly be stressed enough since anyone interested in masque performance has an imaginative gap to fill between the rather skeletal versions of the surviving musical scores and their realization by, usually, the largest and most proficient group of professional musicians in England. In attempting to flesh out the scores, we are thrown back on what are by now a familiar group of sources: the texts, observers' reports, and miscellaneous documentation (of which the most important here are the records of payments to musicians referred to in Chapter 1). On their own, all these are frustratingly limited, but together they begin to produce a picture of something which might appropriately be described as 'rich and strange'.

Predictably, instrumentation for antimasque dances is the most diverse. The deployment of instruments which had no part in regular consorts went hand in hand with eccentric choreography in projecting a sense of the bizarre and grotesque. In trying to pin this down beyond a general impression that the instruments contributed to creating a spectacle of strangeness, we come up against the usual problem that—particularly in the case of Jonson masques—

a Newberry Library MS', *JAMS* 20 (1967), 202. The markings are found in US-Cn, Case MS VM 1.A. 18 J (a score which relates to the partbooks which make up GB-Och, Mus. 1005).

the texts are more concerned with, as it were, a free-standing literary integrity than with documentation of the historical event. Other forms of documentation do not offer very much help here either: the accounts for *Love Freed* and the *Lords' Masque* show antimasque musicians being paid separately from other instrumentalists but throw no light on who they were or what they played.

The witches in *The Masque of Queens* emerge from an ugly, smoking Hell to 'a kind of hollow and infernall musique' (ll. 29–30).[55] The impression Jonson wants to create here is clear enough, but what did this mean in performance (sackbuts and cornetti?). The witches themselves come forth 'all w^{t}h spindells, timbrells, rattles, or other *veneficall* instruments, making a confused noyse, w^{t}h strange gestures' (ll. 34–6).[56] Jonson's marginal glosses indicate that the choice of instruments (noise-producers, rather) was determined by an iconographic tradition. He cites occult authorities as sources for the music of the witches' antic dance: 'Nor do they want *Musique* and in strange manner giuen y^{em} by the *Deuill*, if we credite they^r confessions in *Remig. Dæm. lib. j. cap. xjx . . .*' (gloss on l. 340).

Percussive instruments like those used in the witches' antimasque were prominent in other antimasques. For the bacchic attributes of Silenus and the satyrs in *Oberon*, Jonson refers to an emblem in Isaac Casaubon's *De Satyrica Graecorum Poesi & Romanorum Satira* (1605) showing Bacchus' retinue playing pipes and cymbals (Pl. 9). The Casaubon emblem seems equally relevant to the opening of *Pleasure Reconciled*, where Comus is brought out on a triumphal chariot 'to a wild Musique of *Cimbals, Flutes, & Tabers*' (ll. 4–5). The 'wild Musique' would make its impact not just aurally but visually (Pl. 10). Here and in *Oberon* emblem is animated *and* made audible. The links through the seventeenth-century emblematic tradition to classical precedent were meant to be perceived (as the glosses for *Oberon*, at least, make clear).

Eccentric instruments, particularly what might be called informal percussion, seem to have been fairly consistently used in the spectacle-of-strangeness type of antimasque. We noted earlier the use of the phrase 'wild music' in *Love Restored* (see p. 119). It reappears in *Love Freed from Ignorance and Folly*. There the Sphynx danced in at the beginning of the masque leading the captive, Love, to 'a strange Musique of wilde Instruments' (l. 2). In the antimasque of *The Golden Age Restored*, Iron Age, Ignorance, Folly, Ambition, Pride, and other evils wage a war against the promised reinstatement of the Golden Age. The cryptic description of the antimasque dance shows that the instrumentation was threateningly military and disordered: 'The Antimasque, and their dance, two drummes, trumpets, and a confusion of martiall musique' (ll. 66–7).

Low-induction antimasques abound in very uncourtly instruments. Again, percussion features prominently. (The instruments depicted in Pl. 4 indicate

---

[55] H&S, x. 300 point out the similarity here to *The Tempest*, iv. i. 138, where the masquers 'to a strange, hollow, and confused noise . . . heavily vanish'.

[56] 'Veneficall' means 'used in malignant sorcery' (see H&S, x. 500, note to l. 35).

that makeshift percussion intruments continued to be associated with
antimasque figures in the Caroline period.) The fencer in *Pan's Anniversary*
describes the musicians who are to play for the dances he has prepared: 'Then
comes my learned *Theban*, the Tinker I told you of, with his kettle Drum
(before and after) a Master of Musique, and a man of mettall; He beates the
march to the tune of Tickle-foot, *Pam, pam, pam*, brave *Epam* with a *nondas*.
That's the straine' (ll. 96–100). A kettledrum accompaniment in itself would
set the antimasque dance in quite a different world from the set dances of the
main masque. Tabor and bagpipes were used in *The Gypsies Metamorphosed*.[57]
As we have seen (above, p. 81), bagpipes with 'other rude musique' accompanied a footmen's antimasque dance in *The Irish Masque*; moments later,
the masquers themselves danced forth 'in their Irish mantles, to a solemne
musique of harpes' (l. 140). The contrast between uncouth and courtly could
be made aurally here in the terms of the masque's (ethnic) device. (Harps
receive relatively little mention in masque literature. Various observers' accounts, though not the text itself, indicate that the part of Orpheus in
Campion's *Lords' Masque* was taken by an excellent harpist who also sang—
presumably Cormack McDermott, the harpist in the Jacobean court music. In
the Caroline period a Mr Bedoes performed in *The Triumph of Peace*, and La
Flelle, the harpist in the King's Music, took a starring role as Orpheus in
Davenant's *Temple of Love*.[58])

The arrangements made for dance composition (examined in Ch. 1) suggest
that the standard ensemble for accompanying the dances was the violin band
from the King's Musick. The violin group was balanced by a lute ensemble.
We saw that in the accounts for *Love Freed* Thomas Lupo and Robert Johnson
were each paid £5, one for setting the dances to the violins and the other for
setting the songs to the lutes. Those accounts reimburse fourteen violinists
altogether—a number which corresponds exactly to a 1631 memorandum
outlining the composition of the five-part violin band at court.[59] There appear
to have been up to twenty-four lutenists—twelve who sang and played as the
Muses's Priests and twelve others who simply played. This can be regarded as
the norm for main-masque instrumentation: a violin consort for the dances
and a very sizeable group of lutes for vocal pieces. In practice, the two groups
were not kept entirely separate and the lines of demarcation between their
functions were not rigidly drawn. The only masque *text* to indicate a straightforward division is *The Masque of the Inner Temple* (1615), which—as an Inns
of Court entertainment—cannot be taken as reflecting court practice (particularly in an area where the employment of outside professionals was involved).
That masque, however, has at one point: 'Presently in the wood was heard a
full music of lutes which, descending to the stage, had to them sung this

---

[57] See H&S, x. 613.

[58] See A. Sabol (ed.), *A Score for 'The Lords' Masque' by Thomas Campion* (Hanover and London, 1993),
24; and Holman, 'The Harp in Stuart England', 196–8.

[59] See Ashbee, *RECM*, iii. 59; and below, p. 174.

following song' (ll. 345–7), while later we read, 'Then [the Knights] to the violins danced their first measure' (ll. 434–5).

In Jacobean England, the violin was regarded first and foremost as an instrument to be played in consorts; only as the century went on did it develop a solo role (at least, one which was distinct from its function as the dancing-master's tool of trade). The lute, on the other hand, is primarily a solo instrument. It did have an important function in mixed consorts, but never—outside court entertainments—as part of a massed plucked-string ensemble. The lute ensembles of the masque must have seemed wonderfully rich and exotic even to seventeenth-century audiences. (Even the most privileged could not expect to hear it more than twice in one year.) Caliban's uncomprehending impression of there being 'a thousand twangling instruments' on his island communicates something of the magical quality of such a grouping. *Hymenaei*'s 'rare and full musique of twelue Lutes' suggests this ensemble's novel and entrancing character. Twelve lutes seems to have been a virtually standard number (though, as we have seen, the *Love Freed* accounts indicate that two groups of twelve lutenists were involved there, and Robert Johnson organized a group of twenty for *Oberon*). *Tethys Festival* has a 'song of foure parts' accompanied by 'a musicke of twelue Lutes' (ll. 90–1), and twelve lutenists are again mentioned in *The Masque of the Inner Temple and Gray's Inn* and *The Masque of Flowers*.

The lute ensemble was primarily associated with vocal music, but it did also accompany dancing. In *Hymenaei*, the masquers 'daunced forth in paires, and each paire with a varied and noble grace; to a rare and full musique of twelue Lutes: led on by ORDER, the seruant of REASON . . .' (ll. 270–2). The *Oberon* and *Love Freed* accounts suggest a similar function for the lutes there. Other instruments too occasionally accompanied main-masque dances. In *The Masque of Queens* the change from cornetti to violins illustrates an enjoyment of varied instrumental colours: 'Here, they [the masquers] alighted from they^r Chariots, and daunc'd forth they^r first *Daunce*; then a second, immediately following it: both right curious, and full of subtile, and excellent Changes, and seem'd performed wth no lesse spirits, then those they personated. The first was to the *Cornets*, the second to the *Violins*' (ll. 731–6).

The cornett occupied a rather ambiguous position. It was played by satyrs and used as an antimasque instrument in *Oberon*. It was used (with oboes) in Beaumont's *Masque of the Inner Temple and Gray's Inn* for the antimasque dance of statues (where it was contrasted with the lightness of the violins heard in the dance of nymphs). Cornetts accompanied Vulcan's antimasque song in *Mercury Vindicated*, and (according to the financial records) a cornett was used somewhere in *The Gypsies Metamorphosed*. Yet they were also used to provide some of the 'singular variety' which, according to Jonson, characterized the main-masque dances in *The Masque of Queens*. Three cornetts played when the fleet was discovered at the end of the main masque in *The Fortunate Isles*, and an entry in the text of *Neptune's Triumph* tells us that the final song was to have been performed by 'the whole *Musique*, fiue lutes, three Cornets, and ten voyces' (ll. 533–4). Presumably, as noble wind instruments they seemed particularly appropriate for a main-masque maritime theme. Hence this instrument took on very different guises: a rustic horn, Vulcan's hollow music, or a companion for the lutes and violins of the main masque.

Wind instruments in the masque mostly form part of the 'loud music'. (It is helpful in this context to remember that 'hautbois'—anglicized as 'hautboy' or 'oboe'—means 'loud wood'; in this period, it is synonymous with 'shawm'.) 'Loud music' as a term needs to be understood less as a comment about volume than as an indication that wind instruments made up the ensemble. (Conversely, 'soft music' need not necessarily be quiet; the adjective in 'a soft musique of twelue Lutes and twelue voyces'—*Tethys Festival*, l. 303—is probably intended to indicate something about sophistication and quality rather than volume.) It is not easy to say exactly how the 'loud music' would have been constituted on a particular occasion, though the general pattern is clear enough. In the early Jacobean period the royal wind music included a consort of nine oboes and sackbuts. In addition to these there were six recorder-players and six flautists, some of whom also doubled as cornettists. By the end of James I's reign, two regular consorts of five sackbuts, one double sackbut, and four treble instruments (flutes, oboes, or cornetts) could—separately or combined—have provided the loud music.[60]

Loud music had several functions. It was used to announce the arrival of the king and/or the beginning of the masque. Campion mentions in *The Lord Hay's Masque* that 'as soone as the King was entred the great Hall, the Hoboyes . . . entertained the time till his Majestie and his trayne were placed' (p. 64, ll. 23–5). Oboes (shawms) played when the royal party entered for the performance of *Oberon*. Busino's description of *Pleasure Reconciled* suggests the way in which loud music would have both honoured the king's arrival and created an expectant air: 'Nell'entrar della stanza cominciorno a sonar le Piffari et i Tromboni, al numero di quindeci, o uenti, molto bene, a modo di recercate di contrapunto musicale'.[61] Again, these instruments provide some continuity with those used in the opening antimasque scene.

Loud music was especially important at transformation scenes, where it could contribute to the sense of wonder while at the same time covering the noise of the machinery. This clearly was something of a problem: soap for pulleys and engines appears regularly in the works accounts for masque performances.[62] The agent of Savoy's criticisms of *The Somerset Masque* in-

---

[60] See Dart, 'The Repertory of the Royal Wind Music', 75.

[61] H&S, x. 582. 'On [the king's] entering the room, the oboes and sackbuts, numbering fifteen to twenty, began to play a contrapuntal ricercar'. I have translated 'piffari' as oboes, but it is a generic word applicable to almost any treble wind instruments. The English translation from *CVSP* 15 (1909), 111–14 (reproduced in *A Book of Masques* and in O&S) mistranslates all the musical terms in this sentence. The number of players—fifteen to twenty—approximately matches the royal wind music's strength in 1618.

[62] See R. F. Hill (ed.), 'Dramatic Records in the Declared Accounts of the Office of Works 1560–1640', *MSC* 10 (1977), 36, 44, 47, and 54.

cluded the complaint that De Servi's badly conceived machines operated without any music to cover their noise: 'Finita questa musica, l'ingegnero fiorentino calò la serazinesca, discesero i Cav^{ri} senza musica, senz'altro suono, solo il strepito delle ruote . . .'.[63]

The first mention of loud music for transformation scenes occurs in *The Masque of Beauty* where Jonson says at the end of his description of the freshly revealed masque scene, 'Here the loud *Musique* ceas'd' (l. 277)—implying that it must have been playing during the transformation. *The Haddington Masque* is more explicit; there 'with a lowd and full musique, the Cliffe parted in the midst, and discouered an illustrious *Concaue* . . .' (ll. 264–5). In *The Masque of Queens* the loud music assumes for the first time the dual role of banishing the antimasque and heralding the appearance of the main-masque scene:

In the heate of they^r *Daunce*, on the sodayne, was heard a sound of loud Musique, as if many Instruments had giuen one blast. Wth w^{ch}, not only the *Hagges* themselues, but they^r Hell, into wch they ranne, quite vanishd; and the whole face of the *Scene* alterd: scarse suffring the memory of any such thing: But, in the place of it appear'd a glorious and magnificent Building, figuring the *House of Fame*. (ll. 354–60)

The twelve masquers were discovered in the House of Fame sitting upon a triumphal throne which later rotated to reveal the figure of Fama Bona; at this new change the music 'wayted on the turning of the *Machine*' (ll. 455–6).

Three changes of scene in *Tethys Festival* utilized loud music: first, for the appearance of the Naydes (l. 34) and then at the moment of change from 'ante-maske' to the scene in which the masquers are revealed: 'the Naydes daunce about *Zephirus* and then withdraw them aside; when suddenly, at the sound of a loud and fuller musique, *Tethys* with her Nymphes appeares, with another Scene' (ll. 182–5). Finally, at the very end of the masque, 'the lowde Musique soundes, and sodainely appeares the Queenes Maiesty in a most pleasant and artificiall Groue . . .' (ll. 410–12).

Examples like this occur in almost every court masque in the Jacobean period. Jonson mentions loud music at transformation scenes in *Oberon* (the song, l. 295), *The Vision of Delight* (l. 170), *Pan's Anniversary* (l. 46), *Time Vindicated* (l. 271), and *Neptunes Triumph* (ll. 455 and 464). The change from antimasque to masque in Chapman's *Memorable Masque* is prepared by the arrival of Honour, who appears to loud music (p. 542). In *The Masque of Flowers*, loud music sounds when a garden of 'a glorious and strange beauty' displaces the antimasque scene (ll. 260–1). Middleton has loud music dividing antimasque from main masque in *The Masque of Heroes* (ll. 305–6).

Loud music had other uses. It sometimes, for example, accompanied the masquers' descent from the scene to the dancing-area (in Browne's *Inner Temple Masque* and in Jonson's *Time Vindicated*, for example). It belonged

---

[63] See J. Orrel, 'The Agent of Savoy at *The Somerset Masque*', *RES* 28 (1977), 303. Orrel translates, 'The music done, the Florentine engineer let drop his portcullis and the lords came down without any music, with no other sound but the screeching of the wheels'.

primarily to the world of magical transformation in the main masque—but it also crossed the boundary into the antimasque world as an aural symbol of the power which could sweep away profane misrule. It constitutes a further group of musicians regularly deployed in masque performances. The total stands at four: antimasque musicians, the wind band (loud music), a violin band for the dances, and a lute-based ensemble (in the Caroline period referred to as the symphony) for vocal music. A small subgroup of lutenists used for accompanying solos or small vocal ensembles constitute a fifth regularly used combination. Since masque dances were invariably introduced by song, there must always have been (at least in a limited sense) a polychoral dimension to masque performances, with one ensemble giving way to the other. This merits further exploration—and the obvious place to start is with Campion's description of the musical arrangements for *The Lord Hay's Masque*.

Campion's Masques: A Special Case?

Campion's *The Lord Hay's Masque* provides far more information about instrumental music than any other masque text. Five groups of musicians are described: a consort of ten which, roughly speaking, was an extended mixed consort (bass and mean lutes, bandora, double sackbut, harpsichord, and two treble violins), a consort of twelve (nine violins and three lutes), a group of six cornetts and six chapel voices, a group of oboes, and finally an ensemble of three lutenists (one playing bass lute) and a bandora-player dressed as silvans. The four silvans (later referred to as 'the first Musique') moved about the performing area as participants in the drama to accompany various vocal pieces. The other groups all occupied fixed positions in the hall.

The oboists were placed on a mountain shaded by many trees at the back of the set; as we have just seen, these 'entertained the time till his Majestie and his trayne were placed', but are not mentioned again. They do not appear to have been used, like the loud music in other masques, for transformation scenes—but it is perhaps worth noting that the only actual scene changes in *The Lord Hay's Masque* involved the drawing of a painted 'double vale' to reveal the tableau behind and so would have been relatively noiseless. (Machinery was used for trees which sank down and then opened to reveal the masquers—but it was the smallest group, the silvans, who played and sang the 'Songe of transformation' while this took place.)

The consort of ten was placed on stage left of the dancing-area.[64] They were perhaps primarily associated with the vocal music (although the mobile silvan group are more closely identified with this role). The consort of twelve were on the opposite side of the dancing-area and slightly nearer to the raised stage. Their main responsibility was for the dances; in the later part of the masque Campion refers to them simply as 'the violins' and says that they

---

[64] Some aspects of Campion's description of how the musicians were placed are quite ambiguous. O&S, i. 120, give a diagrammatic reconstruction of the layout for *The Lord Hay's Masque*.

played for the third and fourth 'new' dances. (We should be alert to the possibility of a plucked-string presence in other ensembles described in this way.) In fact, the roles of these two consorts were so inextricably mixed that the associations I have described here amount to no more than tendencies. The group of cornetts and chapel voices ('raised higher in respect of the pearcing sound of those Instruments') seem primarily to have been involved in three great choruses, one of which is described as 'a solemne motet of sixe parts'.

The most striking thing about these various groups of musicians is not their separate functions, but the fact that they were used to build up a polychoral texture. As soon as the king was seated and the oboes finished playing, the consort of ten 'began to play an Ayre'—an instrumental version of the opening dance song 'Now hath *Flora* rob'd her bowers' (p. 215). The climax of the masque, when the last three masquers had been transformed from trees, was given an extravagant musical celebration in which the dazzling spatial treatment of instruments and voices must have done a great deal to create a sense of triumph:

This *Chorus* ['Againe this song reuiue'] was in manner of an Eccho seconded by the Cornets, then by the consort of ten, then by the consort of twelue, and by a double *Chorus* of voices standing on either side, the one against the other bearing fiue voices a peece, and sometime euery *Chorus* was heard seuerally, sometime mixt, but in the end all together: which kinde of harmony so distinguisht by the place, and by the seuerall nature of instruments, and changeable conveyance of the song, and performed by so many excellent masters, as were actors in that musicke, (their number in all amounting to fortie two voyces and instruments) could not but yeeld great satisfaction to the hearers.   (p. 223)

Immediately after this the second masque dance was performed, and once again the music was passed from one group to another: 'the violins, or consorte of twelue began to play the second new daunce, which was taken in forme of an Eccho by the cornetts, and then cat'cht in like manner by the consort of ten, sometime they mingled two musickes together; sometime plaid all at once . . .' (p. 223). The concluding chorus in the masque was also 'performed with seuerall Ecchoes of musicke and voices, in manner as the great *Chorus* before' (p. 227).

The Lord Hay's Masque is justly famous for its musical effects. No other masque text describes anything quite as magnificent as these, so how typical were they? Campion is unique in being the only musician ever to write up a description of a masque for publication. Undoubtedly his personal involvement in music was a factor here, but the problem is knowing how much this affected Campion as inventor rather than Campion as reporter. As poet and musician, he may have seized the opportunity for musical effects more lavish than, say, Jonson would be interested in or competent to provide for. There is certainly no evidence of anyone else attempting truly polychoral effects (as against the alternation of separate groups from number to number). On the other hand, Campion himself became more reticent about musical resources with each production. In *The Lords' Masque* he mentions only 'a double consort, exprest by seuerall instruments, plac't on either side of the roome' (p. 249), while the text of *The Somerset Masque* reveals nothing at all about the use of instruments, let alone their spatial disposition. So how much can we extrapolate from *The Lord Hay's Masque* about the ways in which the opulent musical resources of the Jacobean masque were managed?

First, we should remember that Campion's masque comes very early in the Jacobean period—after Jonson's first two masques, admittedly, but before conventions about overall structure became too fixed. *The Lord Hay's Masque* predates the antimasque/masque axis, and—as we have already noted—the scenic transformations are less ambitious than in many later productions. The fact that it does not conform structurally to the classical model makes it a little difficult to see exactly how Campion's musical effects relate to those in other masques; to some extent we are not comparing like with like. For all that, my view is that *The Lord Hay's Masque* was not untypical in its disposition of musical resources.

Samuel Daniel's *Vision of the Twelve Goddesses* illustrates that Campion was not an innovator in having different instrumental groups spacially separate from each other and used in alternation. This masque is, not surprisingly, more old-fashioned in using a dispersed set. A mountain stood at the lower end of the hall and the Temple of Peace at the other; during the course of the masque the goddesses progressed to the temple. Daniel tells us that cornett-players dressed as satyrs sat in the concaves of the mountain and played 'stately' and 'delightful' marches while the goddesses were approaching the temple and again when they were returning to the mountain at the end of the masque. In the central part of the masque, three Graces (Desert, Reward, and Gratitude) sang to the music of a consort which was hidden in the cupola of the temple, and the masquers danced to the music of lutes and viols placed on one side of the hall. Here, in the earliest Jacobean masque (as in its sixteenth-century precursors), the musicians were incorporated into the imaginative device. Daniel shows some awareness of the appeal of having instruments of different timbres sounding in different parts of the room and taking over from each other with each new stage in the masque's unfolding device. The summary description of the action he gives in the preface (actually framed as a dedicatory letter to Lucy, Countess of Bedford) is so concentrated in musical detail that it is worth quoting at some length:

. . . And betweene euery ranke of Goddesses marched three Torch-bearers in the like seuerall colours, their heads and Robes all decked with Starres and in their descending, the Cornets sitting in the Concaues of the Mountaine and seene but to their brests, in the habit of *Satyres*, sounded a stately March, which continued vntil the Goddesses were approached iust before the Temple, & then ceased, when the Consort Musicke (placed in the Cupola thereof, out of sight) began: whereunto the 3. *Graces*, retyring themselues aside, sang, whiles the Goddesses one after an other with solemne pace ascended vp into the Temple, and deliuering their presents to the *Sybilla* . . . returned downe into the midst of the Hall, preparing themselues to their dance, which (as soon as the *Graces* had ended their song) they began to the Musicke of the Violls and Lutes, placed on one side of the Hal. Which Dance being performed with great Maiesty & Art, consisting of diuers strains fram'd vnto motions circular, square, triangular, with other proportions exceeding rare & full of variety; the Goddesses made a pawse, casting themselues into a circle, whilst the *Graces* againe sang to the Musicke of the Temple, and prepared to take out the Lords to dance. With Whom after they had performed certain Measures, Galliards, and Curranto's, *Iris* againe comes and giues notice of their pleasure to depart: whose speech ended, they drew themselues againe into another short dance with some few pleasant changes, still retyring them toward the foote of the Mountaine, which they ascended in yᵉ same manner as they came downe, whilst the Cornets taking their Notes from the ceasing of the Musick below, sounded another delightfull Marche. (ll. 160–83)

It is not hard to see what Campion was doing as, in some ways, a modest development from this point.[65]

On one level, the musical arrangements for *The Lord Hay's Masque* are *inevitably* typical of the early seventeenth-century court masque. The resources available—the members of the royal musical establishment—were effectively a fixed quantity. In the description of the great Chorus quoted earlier, Campion says with evident pride that there were 'fortie two voyces and instruments'. Exactly the same number—'42 Musitians'—crops up in the accounts for Campion's *Lords' Masque*—a text which provides considerably less musical detail than the 1607 text. Antonio Foscarini's dispatch to the Venetian Doge and Senate after the masques for Princess Elizabeth's wedding noted 'nine choruses of voices and instruments' in Campion's masque, but music is only one of several elements (including costume and scenery) which he found 'remarkable'.[66] Excluding antimasque musicians and members of the loud music, the accounts for *Oberon* and *Love Freed* show payments to thirty-nine and thirty-eight performers respectively (see above, pp. 36–8). The arithmetic remains remarkably constant in the Caroline period. *Tempe Restored* has a 'great *Chorus* consisting of five and thirty Musitions' who, in the final section of the masque, responded to Cupid, Jupiter, Circe, Pallas, and four Nymphs as soloists; in other words the total number of musicians involved here was forty-two. As we shall see, the main group of musicians (the 'Symphony') in *The Triumph of Peace* also numbered forty-two (though the

---

[65] Specifically on the question of polychoral effects in *The Lord Hay's Masque* it is interesting that the masque-like entertainment presented to James I by the Company of Merchant Taylors at their hall on 16 July 1607 featured spatial alternation of a similar kind. Howes's *Chronicle* records that 'The musique consisted of 12 lutes, equally divided, six and six, in a window on either side the Hall, and in the ayre betweene them were a gallant shippe triumphant, wherein were three rare menne like saylors, being eminent for voice and skill, who in their several ways were assisted and seconded by the cunning lutenist.' Nichols, *Progresses*, ii. 141–2.

[66] The figure of nine choruses seems to refer to the number of separate compositions (rather than to the number of groups of musicians).

total number of those who played and sang in the main masque reached sixty-eight). All this suggests that the resources deployed in court masques were determined first and foremost by the size of the court establishment, and that (at least on the level of head-counting) the spectacular arrangements for *Lord Hay's Masque* were matched in other years.

4

The William Lawes Masques

The Triumph of Peace: *A Case Study in Job Demarcation*

The published text of *The Triumph of Peace* is one of the relatively few to mention the contribution of specific musicians. Its author, James Shirley, signs off by paying tribute, first to Inigo Jones as designer, and then—in particularly generous terms—to the musicians: 'The composition of the music was performed by Mr. William Lawes and Mr. Simon Ives, whose art gave an harmonious soul to the otherwise languishing numbers' (ll. 787–9). This picture of the music's genesis is corroborated by the best-known account of *The Triumph of Peace*, that in Bulstrode Whitelocke's *Memorials of English Affairs* (1682). Whitelocke seems in a position to speak with authority; he describes himself as the person primarily responsible for the organization of the musical side of the entertainment and takes credit for the choice of such fine composers.

All of this makes it look as if Ives and Lawes shared the composition. Yet since the 1960s, when Murray Lefkowitz and Andrew Sabol investigated Whitelocke's surviving records at Longleat, it has been clear that the picture presented by the masque text and the *Memorials* was not complete.[1] The Longleat papers do include payments to Lawes and Ives, 'for Composition of songes and symphonyes', but they also reveal that, amongst other duties, Davis Mell composed music for the antimasque. His payment is described as 'the reward of the Inns of Courte for service performed in attending the grand masquers practise playing to them on the treble violin & making some of the tunes for the antimasques'.[2]

Even then, the picture is not complete. Not one, but two sets of financial records dealing with music for *The Triumph of Peace* survive. In addition to the Longleat receipts and memoranda, there are a further set of accounts in the

---

[1] See M. Lefkowitz, 'The Longleat Papers of Bulstrode Whitelocke; New Light on Shirley's *Triumph of Peace*', *JAMS* 18 (1965), 42–60; and Sabol, 'New Documents on Shirley's Masque'.

[2] Longleat House, Whitelocke papers, Parcel II, Item 9 (6), fo. 3ᵛ. Mell was, in fact, a fine violinist—'accounted hitherto the best for the violin in England' (Anthony à Wood)—and an interesting composer. For a discussion of Mell's music in relation to the development of 17th-c. violin-playing in England see my 'Influence of the Italian Violin School in Seventeenth-Century England', *EM* 18 (1990), 575–87.

Middle Temple Library.[3] To some extent the Middle Temple documents help
to verify Whitelocke's figures since they consist partly of authorizations for
paying that Inn's quarter-share in various aspects of the entertainment, including, of course, the music. But what is more intriguing is that they contain
payments for musical items which do not appear in the Whitelocke records.
Of most interest is a warrant dated 25 February 1633 (i.e. 1634 NS) authorizing payment of the Middle Temple's share of a very substantial fee for two
musicians who composed and choreographed dances:

ffyftie poundes beinge the fourth parte of Twoe hundred poundes to bee forthw[th]
paide equallie to M[r] De Noe and M[r] Sebastian for Composinge the tunes and settinge
the figures for the graund Masque and Anti=Masques and for their seruices performed
in their attendance on the graund Masquers in their practise and in their directions to
the Anti=Masquers[4]

Hence at least five people were involved in the composition of the music:
William Lawes and Simon Ives (both mentioned in all sources), Davis Mell
(mentioned in the Longleat papers), and now De Noe and Sebastian (referred
to in the Middle Temple records). It is interesting to note that these last two
each received £100—as much as Lawes and Ives, and five times as much as
Mell—though it must be borne in mind that (like Mell's) their payments were
partly to cover the time spent rehearsing with the dancers.[5]

As the recipients of such large fees, Mr De Noe and Mr Sebastian could
hardly have been unknown as dancing-masters or musicians. Sebastian, as we
shall see, can be positively identified as Sebastian La Pierre, and De Noe must
surely have been Étienne Nau (whose name is variously spelt in court records
as Nant, Nawe, and Nawse and elsewhere as Naw, Nawes, Noa, Noe, and
Noë).[6] These two would have been eminently suited to the task outlined in
the warrant. Étienne Nau had succeeded Thomas Lupo as 'composer of music
for his Majesty's violins' in April 1628 (just fourteen months after he had first
joined the violins at court).[7] La Pierre had begun his career in England in 1611
as dancing-master to Prince Charles, then Duke of York; typically for a

---

[3] These are published in T. Orbison and R. F. Hill (eds.), 'The Middle Temple Documents Relating
to James Shirley's *The Triumph of Peace*', *MSC* 12 (1983), 31–84. Because of the collaboration of the four
principal Inns of Court, financial information is, in fact, distributed in various archives, but much of this
material has no direct bearing on the music for the masque; see J. Limon, 'Neglected Evidence for James
Shirley's *The Triumph of Peace* (1634)', *REED Newsletter*, 13 (1988), 2–9; and C. E. McGee, '"Strangest
consequence from remotest cause": The Second Performance of *The Triumph of Peace*', *Medieval and
Renaissance Drama in England*, 5 (1991), 309–42.

[4] Orbison and Hill (eds.), 'The Middle Temple Documents', 58, § 51.

[5] The figure of £100 is taken from Whitelocke's 'Annales', GB-Lbl, Add. MS 53726, fo. 95[r]: 'For the
Musicke, which was particularly committed to my charge, I gave to Mr. Ives, and to Mr. Lawes £100 a
piece, for their rewards'. In fact, the full amount cannot be traced through the Longleat receipts though the
figure is mentioned in a deleted reference to 'threescore & five pounds in pt of the somme of one hundred
pounds' (item 6, fo. 5[v]); payments of £35 and £20 to both composers are recorded (fo. 7[r], 7[v]).

[6] See Ashbee, *RECM*, iii, *passim*; J. J. S. Mráček (ed.), *Seventeenth-Century Instrumental Dance Music in
Uppsala University Library Inst. mus. hs 409* (Stockholm, 1976), 16, and below, p. 258.

[7] See Ashbee, *RECM*, iii. 23, 24, 31, *et passim*.

dancing-master, he also played the violin.[8] The combination of dancing-master/violinist and composer for the violins—one which we have already seen in relation to the Jacobean masque—would have been ideal for 'Composinge the tunes and settinge the figures for the graund Masque and Anti=Masques'.

Nau and La Pierre were to work together on dances for William Cartwright's *Royal Slave* when it was performed at Hampton Court in 1637. The division of musical responsibility for this occasion has illuminating parallels with *The Triumph of Peace*. Cartwright's play—which has many masque-like features[9]—had been presented in the hall of Christ Church, Oxford the previous August during the visit of Charles and Henrietta Maria to the city. Inigo Jones designed sets and costumes and Henry Lawes wrote settings of the songs. It is not known who composed the dance music for this Oxford performance. Archbishop Laud (Chancellor of the University) wrote in his autobiography that the Queen had so enjoyed *The Royal Slave* that she asked for the materials to be sent to Hampton Court so that she could have her own players present it. Laud relates with some pride how he arranged for Inigo Jones's 'Cloaths and Perspectives of the Stage' to be sent in a wagon to Hampton Court.[10] Amongst the Lord Chamberlain's records for this occasion are warrants covering 'alterations and additions made in the scene, apparel, and properties . . . together with the charge of dancers and composers of music'. A payment of £54 is authorized in favour of 'Etienne Nau & Sebastian la Pierre for themselues and twelue Dancers'.[11] It is unlikely that for the Hampton Court performance vocal music by a highly respected song composer like Henry Lawes would be discarded in favour of completely new settings by musicians who appear to have had no involvement with song-writing at all. (In fact, the state of the sources for the text of *The Royal Slave* opens up the possibility that some of Lawes's songs were written for the Hampton Court performance.[12]) Nau and La Pierre must, therefore, have been engaged to write dance music.

---

[8] He is listed among the 'Musitians for ye violins' in a 1641 list of the Royal Household; see Ashbee, *RECM*, iii. 109. I. Spink, 'The Musicians of Queen Henrietta-Maria: Some Notes and References in the English State Papers', *AM* 36 (1964), 179, suggests that the 'Mounsier Sebastian, the dancing master' who received a month's wages from the Earl of Rutland in 1643 was Sebastian de La Pierre. For the excerpts from the Earl of Rutland's accounts see Woodfill, *Musicians in English Society*, 268.

[9] G. B. Evans writes 'In many respects *The Royal Slave* may be looked upon as an extension of the masque into the field of drama, a collaboration which left the drama very much on the defensive. Scenery, singing, and dancing are all brought over in a body, while the tempo of the play must be radically altered to adapt itself to a new environment. Signs of this invasion by the masque may be seen in many plays, but *The Royal Slave* is perhaps the best example of the finished product . . .'; W. Cartwright, *The Plays and Poems of William Cartwright*, ed. G. B. Evans (Madison, 1951), 173.

[10] Quoted by G. E. Bentley, *The Jacobean and Caroline Stage*, 7 vols. (Oxford, 1941–68), iii. 136–7.

[11] E. Boswell and E. K. Chambers (eds.), 'Dramatic Records: The Lord Chamberlain's Office', *MSC* 2 (1931), ii. 383.

[12] The four manuscript copies of *The Royal Slave* all omit the Prologue and Epilogue for the Hampton Court presentation and they lack a large section of Act V, Scene vii, including the song 'Thou O bright Sun'. G. B. Evans describes these manuscripts as representing 'some state of the text before the London

But why was the dance music used in Oxford not also reused at Hampton Court? Nau and La Pierre were needed as choreographers and dancing-masters to teach the new cast their 'figures'. It seems that composing dance patterns and music for them were thought of as two inextricably linked parts of a single process. Everything in masque documentation points to this. So, it seems that the De Noe and Sebastian who contributed to *The Triumph of Peace* were Étienne Nau and Sebastian La Pierre—two well-established figures whose complementary talents were to be utilized for at least one other major royal entertainment.

La Pierre is, in fact, mentioned once in the Longleat papers. One of the orders dealing with arrangements for the procession reads 'Mr Herne to take care about all ye Antique Masquers and Sebastian Warned to attend Mr Herne'.[13] The idea that he had a particular responsibility for the antimasques is confirmed by several entries in the Middle Temple documents. One in particular authorized payment of 'one fourth [the Middle Temple's share] of twelue poundes tenn shillinges . . . vnto Mr Sebastian for monies by him laid out vpon the Antemaskers'.[14] This payment, interesting in itself, helps to establish beyond any shadow of doubt that Mr Sebastian was, in fact, Sebastian La Pierre. Four years after *The Triumph of Peace* the Council of Lincoln's Inn moved to clear up a bad debt: 'Upon the peticion of Sebastian La Peer to the foure Innes of Court, who was about foure yeares sithence imployed for making the great Maske, and hath disbursed, as hee doth alleadge, xij li. xs. therein, which hee is not yet satisfied . . .'.[15] Twelve pounds, ten shillings is, of course, exactly the sum which the Middle Temple had noted as La Pierre's expenditure on the antimasques. He was, it seems, doomed to be overlooked.

Although the Middle Temple accounts refer to him only as Mr Sebastian, it is interesting to note that they do several times mention a 'Monsieur la Pierre', but he is William or Guillaume La Pierre. The payments to this person are always unspecific, so it is not clear what services he provided. In 1638, however, a warrant issued from the Lord Chamberlain's office authorized generous payment of arrears to Guillaume La Pierre, who had been instructing Prince Charles and Princess Mary in the art of dancing since Michaelmas 1636.[16] The careers of these two La Pierres seem to mirror each other (though twenty-five years apart); both were dancing-masters to royal children. Was Guillaume perhaps a son of Sebastian?

To summarize so far, Nau and La Pierre created dances for the main masque and Mell assisted them with antimasque dances. That leaves Lawes and Ives responsible for the main masque's vocal music and its associated

performance' (Cartwright, *Plays and Poems*, 169–70). Willa McClung Evans, however, points out that the changes could equally well have arisen at Henry Lawes's suggestion and in Oxford before the first performance; see 'Cartwright's Debt to Lawes', in Long (ed.), *Music in English Renaissance Drama*, 103–16.

[13] Whitelocke papers, Parcel II, Item 9 (1), fo. 1^v, § 15.
[14] Orbison and Hill, 'The Middle Temple Documents Relating to *The Triumph of Peace*', 61, § 62.
[15] Quoted in Wienpahl, *Music at the Inns of Court*, 144.
[16] Warrant dated 7 June 1638; Ashbee, *RECM*, iii. 97–8.

'symphonies'. It will be clear from Chapter 1 that the distribution of compositional tasks here follows a well-established pattern. Ives and Lawes, like their Jacobean predecessors, came from a background of lutes, viols, and voices (in Ives's case associated with the London Waits rather than the King's Musick),[17] while those connected with dance were all violinists.

How do we reconcile this picture of the music's composition with the fact that Shirley and Whitelocke acknowledge Lawes and Ives alone, and that, as far as we can tell from the Longleat papers, Whitelocke seems not to have dealt with Nau and La Pierre despite his claim that he was in overall charge of the music? These are interesting questions and they lead us to a better understanding of the way those involved with masque performances thought about its musical components. In order to see why Nau and La Pierre escaped Whitelocke's attention we need to look first at the character and content of his memoirs and then at what we can deduce about the management of this ambitious Inns of Court venture. It seems only fair to warn readers that we are left with some unresolved puzzles here, but the lack of ultimate clarity is, I hope, offset by the inherent interest of the evidence.

The *Memorials* contains the last of three surviving accounts by Whitelocke. The earliest occurs in the manuscript now published as *The Diary of Bulstrode Whitelocke*, though the title is misleading in respect of its pre-Restoration sections. Whitelocke copied his summary memoirs of these years some time after 1663 from an earlier diary which is now lost. The 'Diary' is written in the third person, but its character as a personal record is nevertheless obvious. The second and fuller account occurs in Whitelocke's 'Annales of his own Life Dedicated to his Children'. Ruth Spalding has demonstrated that these manuscripts, like the Diary, must also date from after 1663.[18] The 'Annales' are a different kind of reminiscence; in fact, the use of a first-person narrative (and the many moralizing asides to the children) make them seem more intimate than the 'Diary'. They are not, however, pure recollection since they draw on other written accounts to fill out the picture. Whitelocke's outline of the sequence of events leading from Prynne's publication of *Histrio-Mastix* (1633) to his imprisonment (a story represented as treachery on the part of Archbishop Laud and his cohorts) is taken directly from Prynne's own account published in 1641 in *A New Discovery of the Prelates Tyranny*.[19]

Finally, the 1682 *Memorials of English Affairs*, edited for publication seven years after Whitelocke's death, is an abridged version of the 'Annales' converted to a third-person narrative (like the 'Diary'). The new title points to a

---

[17] Ives was appointed to the Waits in 1637. See Woodfill, *Musicians in English Society*, 36 n.

[18] See *The Diary of Bulstrode Whitelocke 1605–1675*, ed. R. Spalding (Oxford, 1990), 29. The 'Annales' are preserved in a series of GB-Lbl manuscripts: Add. MS 4992 (Preface), Add. MS 53726 (the volume containing *The Triumph of Peace* account), and Add. MSS 37343–5. Charles Burney printed a wildly inaccurate and (silently) cut version of *The Triumph of Peace* section in *A General History of Music*, ed. Mercer, ii. 293–300.

[19] See K. Walker, 'New Prison: Representing the Female Actor in Shirley's *The Bird in a Cage*', *ELR* 21 (1991), 385–6.

change in focus here—the element of personal reminiscence is drastically reduced (and William Penn was to complain in 1709 that Whitelocke's original had been 'castrated of many excellent passages').[20]

Given the history of these various memoirs, it is interesting to compare what each has to say about the music for *The Triumph of Peace*. First, the *Diary*:

Wh[itelocke] chose the Masters & others for the musicke the best he could meet with in London, of all Nations, & had 4 of the Queens Chappell the more to please her M[ajest]^ty, he caused them all to meet in practise att his house in Salisbury Court, where he might be with them, & had sometimes 40 lutes, besides other instruments & voyces, in consort togither . . .   (p. 74)

There is no mention here of Ives or Lawes—in fact the passage is not about composition at all. Foremost in Whitelocke's mind was the opportunity that the masque gave him to win favour with Henrietta Maria. Whitelocke's personal enthusiasms—especially his fondness for mingling with musicians—come through strongly.

The 'Annales' introduce the names, not just of Ives and Lawes, but of the four French musicians. Whitelocke's motivation in engaging the Frenchmen is no longer mentioned, though later in the 'Annales' account he develops this theme at considerable length.[21] The excitement of having all these able musicians rehearsing at his house is still there:

I made choyce of Mr. Symon Ive, an honest & able Musitian, of excellent skill in his Art, and of Mr. Lawes to compose the aiers, lessons, and songs for the masque, & to be masters of all the Musicke under me.

I also made choice of 4 of the most excellent Musitians of the Queens Chappell, M^nr La Mare, M^nr Du Vale, M^nr Robert, and M^nr Mari, and of divers others of forrein nations, who were most eminent in their Art, not in the least neglecting any of my own Countrymen, whose Knowledge in Musicke rendered them usefull in this action, to beare their parts in the Musicke, which I resolved if I could to have so performed, as might excell any musicke, that ever before this time had bin in England.

Herein I kept my purpose, & for the better preparation & practise of the Musicke, & that I myselfe might take the better care, & be present with them, I caused the meetings of all the Musitians to be frequent att my house in Salisbury Court; and there I have had togither att one time, of English, French, Italian, Germans, and other Masters of Musicke, fourty lutes, besides other instruments, and voyces of the most excellent kind in consort.   (fo. 90^r)

We should note that this account is not accurate in all its details. To begin with, Whitelocke seems to have become carried away somewhat in its

---

[20] See Whitelocke, *Diary*, 35. The *Memorials* were edited by Arthur Annesly, 1st Earl of Anglesey, Lord Privy Seal. The section dealing with *The Triumph of Peace* from the *Memorials* is reprinted in M. Lefkowitz (ed.), *Trois Masques à la cour de Charles 1er d'Angleterre* (Paris, 1970), 29–36.

[21] 'for the 4 French gentlemen, the queen's servants, I thought that a handsome and liberall gratifying of them would be made known to the queen, their mistris, and well taken by her. I therefore invited them one morning to a collation, att St. Dunstan's taverne, in the great room, the oracle of Apollo, where each of them had his plate lay'd for him, covered, and the napkin by it, and when they opened their plates they found in each of them forty pices of gould, of their masters' coyne, for the first dish, and they had cause to be much pleased with this surprisall.' GB-Lbl, Add. MS 53726, fo. 96^r.

recounting: the only German amongst the musicians for *The Triumph of Peace* was Dietrich Steffkin, and there do not appear to have been any Italians. More interestingly, Whitelocke names Pierre de La Mare as one of the four Frenchmen, but this musician did not, in fact, take part in *The Triumph of Peace*. His name is absent from both the Longleat papers and the Middle Temple accounts, and his place seems to have been filled by the illustrious (and notorious) lutenist, Jacques Gaultier.[22] La Mare must have been engaged to play but then pulled out. When writing the 'Annales' Whitelocke doubtless referred to notes relating to an earlier stage of the planning when de La Mare was still expected to take part. The shorter and less personal *Memorials* account no longer mentions that rehearsals took place at Whitelocke's house.[23]

Two points need emphasizing here in relation to *The Triumph of Peace*. First, none of the surviving Whitelocke memoirs originates in the Caroline period, though the original diary may have done so. Secondly, the first specific mention of Ives and Lawes as composers, or for that matter of the four French musicians, comes in the 'Annales', a source which clearly drew on more than Whitelocke's own memory and which the La Mare case shows to be not as comprehensive or reliable as it might at first seem. Whatever Whitelocke was referring to as an *aide-mémoire* when writing up the 'Annales', it cannot have been the papers now at Longleat. The points at which Whitelocke's narratives and the Longleat papers do not correspond present a number of questions which have intriguing ramifications for the musical aspects of this masque.

For an explanation of the fact that the Longleat papers and the Middle Temple accounts do not completely match we must look at the way the masque was administered. Whitelocke outlines the basic organizational structures. A committee was set up with two representatives from each of the Inns. The grand committee then established four subcommittees. Exactly how responsibilities were shared amongst these subcommittees is not completely clear, however. Whitelocke's proud description of his own place in this structure is famous:

---

[22] Nicholas Duval was a lutenist and bass singer who was appointed to the King's Musick as one of the musicians for the lutes and voices in the place of Robert Johnson in Nov. 1633. Duval seems to have taken over Johnson's role as a selector of instruments and provider of strings (see Ashbee, *RECM*, iii. 73–5 *et passim*). Duval and his family were given a pass to travel to France in 1641 (ibid. 107). The third musician mentioned, Antoine Robert, was a theorbo-player and is grouped with the countertenors in the Longleat list of musicians for *The Triumph of Peace*. In Dec. 1638 he was engaged as a singing-tutor to the Princess Mary (ibid., 66, 100). Mathurin Mari was one of the eleven original musicians to have come from France with Henrietta Maria; he is listed as a soprano in the Longleat documents.

[23] '*Whitelocke* made choice of Mr. *Simon Ivy*, an honest and able Musician, of excellent skill in his Art, and of Mr. *Laws* to compose the Airs, Lessons, and Songs for the Masque, and to be Master of all the Musick under him. He also made choice of Four of the most excellent Musicians of the Queen's Chappel, *Monsieur la Mare, Monsieur du Vall, Monsieur Robert,* and *Monsieur Mari,* and of divers others of foreign Nations, who were most eminent in their Art not in the least neglecting his owne Country-men, whose knowledge in Musick rendered them usefull in this Action, to bear their parts in the Musick; and for the better preparation and practice of the Musick, they had Meetings together of *English, French, Italians, Germans,* and other Masters of Musick: Fourty Lutes at one time, besides other instruments and Voices of the most excellent Musicians in Consort . . .': Whitelocke, *Memorials,* 19.

This committee being impowered by the benchers of each society, mett togither, & out of their own number made severall subcommittees, one subcommittee to take care, of the poeticall part of the busines; another for the severall properties of the masquers, and antimasquers, and other actors; another was for the dauncing, and to me in particular was committed the whole care & charge of all the Musicke for this great Masque.[24]

This account implies that Whitelocke was a one-person subcommittee in charge of the music while three larger subcommittees dealt with the text, props, and dancing. The papers at Longleat, however, give quite a different breakdown: one subcommittee for the 'Graund Masque' (seven members), one for 'Antimasques' (eight members), one for the 'Procession' (eight members), and one for 'Musique' (four members).[25] A number of people served on several of these committes and Whitelocke himself had links with three: he was a member of the Procession committee (though 'Mr Herne to assist' is written alongside his name), he was listed in the Antimasques committee as a deputy for Edward Hyde in his absences, and he was a full member of the Music committee. It is not easy to see how to match up the information in the Longleat papers with Whitelocke's narratives.

The musicians not mentioned by Whitelocke could conceivably have escaped his view if they had been engaged by any of the committees of which he was not a member. In Whitelocke's account of the committee structure the missing musicians could have been responsible to the dance subcommittee. But we can see that his memoirs are fallible: the identity of the Queen's four French musicians is evidence of that. Moreover, the committee membership list in the Longleat papers seems incontrovertible evidence for a rather different division of responsibilities. Nau and La Pierre must then have worked under the aegis of the 'Grand Masque' subcommittee and/or the 'Antimasque' subcommittee, on which Whitelocke deputized only occasionally. (As we shall see shortly, there were other antimasque musicians who also go without mention in the Longleat papers.) Nau and La Pierre's omission from Whitelocke's records suggests that we need to think of matters relating to dancing as being distinct from those affecting 'the music'.

One of the Middle Temple warrants is particularly interesting in this regard: '. . . two hundred & eleuen poundes fiue shilllinges beinge one fourth of eight hundred fforty fiue poundes to bee forthw[th] paid for rewardes for the musicke in Composeinge the tunes & attendance vpon the Masques both dayes'.[26] It has been pointed out that the total sum of £845 corresponds almost exactly to the combined total given in the Longleat papers for the payments made to

[24] GB-Lbl, Add. MS 53726, fos. 89ᵛ–90ʳ.

[25] Whitelocke papers, Parcel II, Item 9 (3). The members of the subcommittee were Thomas Gardiner (Gray's Inn), Robert Caesar (Inner Temple), Bulstrode Whitelocke (Middle Temple), and Peter Brereton (also Gray's Inn).

[26] Orbison and Hill, 'The Middle Temple Documents relating to *The Triumph of Peace*', 57, § 47. The warrant is dated 21 Feb. 1633 (i.e. 1634 NS).

Lawes, Ives, and the performing musicians.[27] Since this figure does not include the payments made to Nau and La Pierre, it might be inferred that the composition and choreographing of dances were thought of as being separate from the 'music' (though admittedly that does not explain why the payments to Davis Mell and to the fourteen violinists who played for the dances did pass through the same set of accounts).

The Longleat papers support the idea that Whitelocke's responsibilities for the music excluded dance. Most revealing in this respect are the group of items dealing with production: the various lists and diagrams showing the placement of musicians in the performing area are exclusively concerned with the thirty-five adults and seven boys who performed the songs and symphonies.[28] This group was made up of singers, lutenists, viol-players, a stringer, and one violinist (John Woodington). Item four in the Longleat papers is a list—in a more formal hand—giving 'The names of ye Kinges Musitions for ye violins' who took part in *The Triumph of Peace*. Woodington is there, of course, but the remaining fourteen are otherwise referred to only as a group in the financial records.[29] Shirley's masque text confirms that, as usual, the violins played for the masque dances, and as it does so, it mentions another group which are ignored in the production documents (as distinct from the financial records) in the Longleat papers: 'Here with loud Musicke the Masquers descend and dance their entry to the Violins, which ended, they retire to the Scene, and then the Howers and Chori againe move toward the State and sing' (ll. 648–50). Here, three distinct groups of musicians perform in succession: the loud music, the violins, and 'the Hours and Chori', who are, of course, the group of musicians associated with the songs. It is with this last group that Whitelocke was most involved and whose disposition within the performance area is so fascinatingly documented in his papers. The text refers to them as 'the Musicians' and even 'the whole Train of Musicians', sharing Whitelocke's usage of a language which to modern readers might suggest something more comprehensive than was meant in 1634.

Whitelocke's estimate in the 'Diary' and the 'Annales' that sometimes he had forty musicians at Salisbury Court corresponds roughly to the total membership of this central group. It would be wrong to make too much of this (since 'forty' might be read simply as 'a great many' and since we might expect rehearsals not to involve all sections simultaneously), but had the violins, loud music, and antimasque musicians also resorted to Whitelocke's

[27] Ibid., introduction, 43: 'According to Sabol's list (20–1), the total disbursed to musicians, singers, and messengers was £735.13s., and later payments to the composers, William Lawes and Simon Ives, bring the total to £845.13s., a figure that corresponds almost exactly with that on warrant § 47: £845.'

[28] Sabol suggested that the diagram reproduced here as Pl. 11 showed the disposition of the entire musical forces (since he counted sixty-nine dots); see 'New Documents', 17. It is, I think, easier to see it as several attempts at different configurations. (The middle of the diagram—beneath the semicircular line—might even show the movement of seven musicians from a straight line, through a semicircle to a rectangular cluster; but this is an area where speculation does not seem very fruitful.)

[29] 'Paid to the fowerteene violins 120 0 0' (Item 6, fo. 1^r). Thomas Warren, John Haydon, and John Hopper signed the receipt for this amount (fo. 2^r).

house the number might have risen even higher. What all this does seem to indicate, however, is that for Whitelocke and his contemporaries, 'the Music' in a masque referred to the ensemble of voices and their accompanying instruments. In this sense, we can see that Shirley and Whitelocke were quite right in claiming that the composition of the music was left in the capable hands of Simon Ives and William Lawes.

The only real evidence of Whitelocke having a wider responsibility for other musicians comes through his having acted as paymaster to virtually the whole group (though not, of course, to Nau and La Pierre). Even here, however, there is a sense of a two-tier responsibility: every member of the vocally oriented ensemble is represented by an individually signed receipt for payment while the other musicians are simply paid through representatives in three groups: 'fowerteene violins the kings servants', 'twelve of the kings servants for the loud musique', and 'the waites who were disappointed'.[30]

The other way in which Whitelocke was involved with musicians outside this central ensemble was through his membership of the procession subcommittee. His claim that he was entrusted with the 'whole care and charge of the Musick' does find an echo in the Longleat papers—but in the context of the arrangements made for the procession (and it might still be read to mean 'the members of the Music'). The seventeenth of eighteen resolutions dealing with its organization reads 'Mr Whitlocke to take care for all the musique & all all [sic] thinges belonging to them and for any alteration shall be fitt'. The resolutions immediately preceding this imply that 'all the musique' did not include the trumpeters and drummers or the antimasque musicians.[31] But here, in the procession at least, his papers show a general concern with where all kinds of musicians fitted into the overall plan. The listings showing which musicians were allocated to particular chariots in the procession extends, for example, to the theatre musicians from the Cockpit and Blackfriars (a group also referred to—no doubt because of widespread pluralism—as 'the waits').

The disappointed waits, in fact, illustrate best that Whitelocke had a managerial role in relation to musicians who took part in the procession. The Longleat papers include an exchange of letters between Whitelocke and Nicholas Lanier about the involvement of the waits. Lanier complained that John Adson ('an unworthy fellow') had used his influence to have the waits engaged for the procession before the second performance in preference to

---

[30] Whitelocke papers, Parcel II, Item 9 (6), fo. 2 (for the references to violins and loud music); fo. 1ʳ (Whitelocke's summary) for the reference to the waites. The actual receipt has the ungrammatical phrasing 'eleven of the waites of the Citty given them by the fower Innes of Court for their attendance one day when the maske was disappointed'.

[31] Ibid., Item 9 (1), fos. 1ʳ and 1ᵛ. Resolution 12 reads 'Mr Stiles to take care the Antique Musique provide their horses and habitts' and resolution 14 'Mr Whitfield to take care for the Trumpetters and all belonges to them'.

court wind-players.[32] Whitelocke's reply (and his payment of compensation to the waits) may be seen as a diplomatic retreat:[33]

Noble Sir. I perceive by your letters some apprehension of discontent by the kinges servantes from the Committees for the Masque bicause they were not ingaged to the imployment of playing in the charriotts, I acknowledge my selfe being a servant to the Committees in this perticular, to have bespoken others uppon this ground only, bicause I thought the service too meane for these you write for, butt since themselves guided by your advise esteeme it not so, and very earnestly request the undertaking of it, to give your selfe and them contentment, and to take of all shew of the least neglect to any of the kinges servants I have resolved to dismisse the others, and to give entertainment for the present to those whose assistance we have already had. To your selfe I shall ever really expresse my selfe

    Whitehall, febr: 12 1633

Your affectionate friend and servant,
Bulstrode Whitelocke.

I pray take no dislike to Mr Adson upon this occat.

The Staging of The Triumph of Peace

The 'production' documents in the Longleat papers contain a cue sheet for songs 1–5, and seven diagrams showing the disposition of musicians.[34] (An additional diagram with 'My Lord Chamberlaine' at its head is for the procession rather than the masque itself.) The way in which these relate to music and text is set out in Table 4.1. The cue sheet incorporates William Lawes's modifications to Shirley's text, such as the reallocation of the chorus at the end of Song 2 to, first a solo bass (John Drew) and then, as the Lawes autograph puts it, '3 Voc from yᵉ Cho:' (Drew, Henry Lawes, and William Webb). Presumably the departures from the text in the cue sheet's outline of Song 4 also reflect the treatment of the words in the (now lost) setting. We learn, too, that Song 5 was a solo performed by Mathurin Mari, one of the four French musicians Whitelocke had felt so pleased to enlist.

Attempting to relate the diagrams to particular moments in the masque is necessarily a bit more speculative (and Table 4.1 makes suggestions only for two of those reproduced in this book). For one thing, they have the appearance of working sketches (especially the two that consist of patterns of dots) and it is possible that several may represent different attempts at solving the same problem (see Pl. 11–13). Transitions between any two of these figures

[32] Adson, a former wait, had been assigned the late Henry Lanier's place as a musician for the flute and cornett only late in 1633, a few months before *The Triumph of Peace*. See Ashbee, *RECM*, iii. 73. In the Longleat papers, Adson's name appears both amongst the musicians from Blackfriars and in the 'Loud Musique' list.

[33] Whitelocke papers, Parcel II, Item 9 (18), fo. 1ʳ. Lanier's letter to Whitelocke is transcribed by Sabol, 'New Documents', 18–19.

[34] The cue sheet is Parcel II, Item 9 (11), fo. 1 in the Whitelocke papers. The production diagrams comprise fo. 1ᵛ and Item 9 (12).

TBALE 4.1. *Music in the main masque of* The Triumph of Peace

Line	Musical event	Musical source [tonality]	Whitelocke Papers, cue sheet [line numbers; plate reference]	
491	[Song 1] 'Hence ye profane'	GB-Ob, Mus. Sch. b. 2: Simfony & Song [C]	Symphony. twice Mr. Jo: Laniere Hence [l. 491]	q. King and Queene [l. 500]^a
504	Song 2, 'Wherefore do my sisters stay?'	GB-Ob, Mus. Sch. b. 2: Simfony & Song [C–a]	Symph: once Mr. J. Laniere. Why doe &c: [l. 504]^b Mr. Drue. See where &c: [l. 512] Mr. H. L. Mr. Webb. Mr. Drue. In her &c: [l. 513]	q. to order me [l. 511] q. oh see [l. 512] q. in her brow [l. 515]
523	Song 3, 'Think not I could absent myself this night'	GB-Ob, Mus. Sch. b. 2: Simfony & Song [a–C]	Mr. Porter's boy. Thinke not. [l. 523] both. q. flourish but together. [l. 540] Chor. q. his oune sheaves [l. 544]^c	
552	Song 4, 'Swiftly, O swiftly, I do move too slow!'		Symphony once Mnr. Mari: Swiftly &c: [l. 552] Mr. J. L. Mr. P. boy Wee &c: [l. 561] Mr. Porters boy Descend [not in text] both descend &c: [ll. 565–7]^f Mr. J. Lan: Now gaze. &c: [l. 572] Mnr. Mari Never till &c: [l. 574] Mr. P. Boy What throne &c: [l. 578] Mnr. Mari My eies &c: [l. 580] Chos twice. Tis Jove &c: [l. 582] [Pl. 12?] the second time thei discend to the stage singing.	q. chast Eunomia [l. 559] descend [l. 565]^d q^e q. dietyes translated [l. 571]^g q. hast beheld [l. 573]^h q. earth or heaven [l. 577] q. doe waite [l. 579]^i q. of us three [l. 581]
587	Song 5, 'To you great King and Queen'		Symphony [Pl. 13: 'The figure for the first going up to the state']	

648	Here with loud music the Masquers descend and dance their entry to the violins ...	Mnr. Mari. To you great &c: [l. 587] q. wᵗʰin your sight. [l. 603]ᵏ Symphony.—wᶜʰ retire to the roome wᵗʰin the scene
652	Song 6, 'They that were never happy Hours'	
667	The song ended, and the Musicians returned, the Masquers dance their main dance ...	
712	[Anti-masque of tradespeople] The violins play ... They dance	
719	Song 7, 'Why do you dwell so long in clouds'	GB-Eu, MS Dc. I. 69/GB-Ob, MS Mus. d. 238: Song [g]
731	The Revels	
747	Song 8, 'In envy to the night'	GB-Lbl, Add. MS 31432: [Song] 'In envye of the night' [g]
760	Song 9, 'Come away, away, away'	GB-Ob, Mus. Sch. b. 2: cancelled fragment [g]

ᵃ 'King and Queene' is in a different hand written over a cancelled 'while you stay' (l. 502—the correct cue for the Song 2 Symphony).
ᵇ L. 504 begins 'Wherefore do ...' in the text.
ᶜ The words in italics have been extracted from a cancelled section at the top of the cue sheet.
ᵈ Followed by a cancelled '[deil]ryes translated' (l. 568).
ᵉ Cancelled 'expecting thee' (l. 561)
ᶠ 'Both' here means Eunomia and Irene (Mr. Porter's boy and John Lanier); according to the text, they alternate with 'decend'.
ᵍ Ll. 567–9 are assigned to Eunomia in the text; they are followed by a two-line chorus not accounted for in the cue sheet.
ʰ These lines are assigned to Eunomia (Mr. Porter's boy) in the text.
ⁱ These lines are assigned to Irene (John Lanier) in the text.
ʲ In the text ll. 582–3 are still assigned to Dice (M. Mari).
ᵏ The text does not indicate that Song 5 was sung by Dice (M. Mari).

always seem straightforward in relation to the key musicians nearest the State (Mari, Lanier, Mr Porter's boy, etc.) but invariably involve some rather awkward regrouping further back in the ensemble. All this reinforces the impression that these diagrams represent not a record of final decisions about blocking so much as sketches made in the course of discussions with the music committee. Nevertheless, put together with the information given in the text about the disposition of the performing-area itself, they provide a unique insight into the management of large numbers of people in the production.

Shirley's text gives a clear description of the way the Banqueting House was set up. At one end of the room a stage enclosed by a proscenium arch was erected. At the back of this stage, but concealed for the first part of the masque by other scenes, were steps 'like the degrees of a theatre' on which the sixteen masquers would be revealed. Leading down from the front of the stage to the floor were stairs, 'in two branches'. (It would help greatly in interpreting the diagrams if we knew whether this meant a set of stairs that had a single entrance at the top dividing into two at the bottom, or whether it simply means two staircases, leading down from each side of the stage. What appears to be the stage sketched at the foot of the diagram representing 'The figure for the first going up to the state' does not help in clarifying this puzzle—see Pl. 12.) At the far end of the room was the State, the royal seat. 'Degrees' (stepped platforms) had been erected for the audience, along the sides of the dancing-area at right angles to the State and the proscenium arch, leaving a rectangular space on the floor bounded by the stage at one end and the State at the other. It is here that the set dances, the revels, and some of the vocal music and associated 'symphonies' were performed.

A cloud bearing Irene's chariot descended into view—but not down to stage level—during the first symphony (which the cue sheet notes was to be played twice). The text makes it clear that Irene's chariot was downstage (immediately behind the proscenium) and we can work out from the diagrams that it must have appeared on stage right. At the end of Song 2, Eunomia's chariot was lowered on the opposite side of the stage, and finally—during the Symphony which precedes Song 4—Dice's chariot 'begins to descend toward the middle of the Scene with somewhat swifter motion'. The cue sheet then informs us that during the repeat of the chorus which concludes Song 4 (music missing) 'thei descend to the stage singing'. (Aerial music of this kind is discussed more fully in Chapter 5.)

During these first four songs, the musicians of the 'Symphony' must have been grouped on the stage area. A diagram with two groups on each side of the stage probably shows their positions immediately before Song 5 as the musicians (divided because of the branched stairs) descend from the stage with Irene, Eunomia, and Dice at their head and 'move in a comely figure toward the King and Queen'. As they reached the floor, they moved into the configuration depicted in Pl. 12 which has a heading 'The figure for the first going up to the state'. Their movement to floor level was essential in allowing

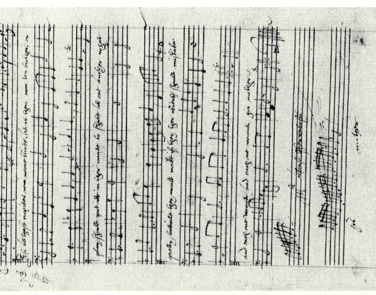

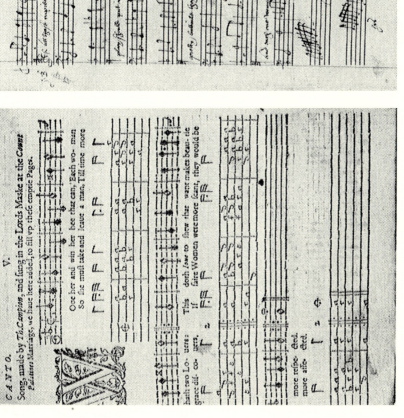

1. 'Woo her and win her' from Campion, *The Description of a Masque presented at the Marriage of the Right Honourable the Earle of Somerset* (London, 1614). GB-Ob, Mal. 221 (6). Courtesy of the Bodleian Library, Oxford

2. Ferrabosco, 'If all these Cupids', from GB-Och, MS 439, p. 93. Courtesy of the Library of Christ Church, Oxford

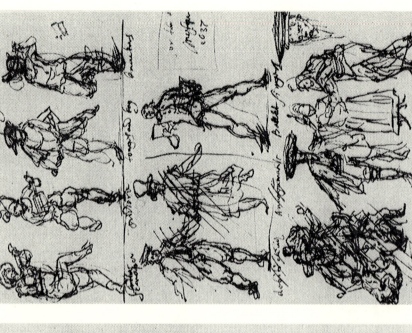

ORCHESOGRAPHIE

.elles monstrent au dl les genoulx, si elles ne mettent la main à leurs habits pour y obuier.

Capriol.

Ceste mode ne me semble belle ny honneste, si ce n'est pour dancer auec quelque bonne galoise de chambediere.

Arbeau.

Ie ne laisseray de vous donner cy aprez la tabulature pour la dancer : Ce pendant voiez cy les figures des mouuemens de greue & de pied en l'air.

Greue droicte,   Greue gaulche,
ov   ov
Pied en l'air droict.   Pied en l'air gaulche.

Ledit mouuement de greue est faict & causé aulcunesfois, quand le danceur gette & met l'vn de ses pieds en la place de l'aultre pied, & cependant ledit autre pied est esleué en l'air deuant : Et tel mouuemens s'appelle entretaille , & en est aussi de deux sortes, comme il y a deux sortes de greue : Sçauoir entretaille du gaulche, causant greue droicte, & entretaille du droict, causant greue gaulche.

Capriol.

4. Inigo Jones, antimasque characters for *Britannia Triumphans*. Courtesy of the Duke of Devonshire

3. Arbeau, *Orchésographie*, fo. 45ᵛ. BG-Ob, Douce A 224. Courtesy of the Bodleian Library, Oxford

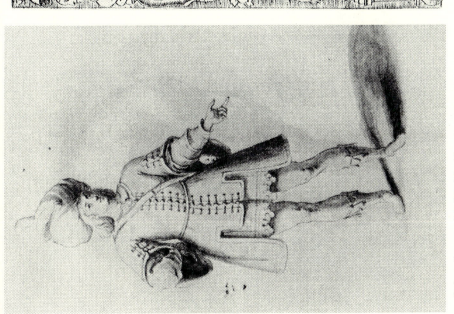

6. Negri, *Nuove Inventioni di Balli*, p. 36. Courtesy of the Bodleian Library, Oxford

5. Inigo Jones, 'A Noble Persian Youth'; design for *The Temple of Love*. Courtesy of the Duke of Devonshire

8. Negri, *Nuove Inventioni di Balli*, p. 131. Courtesy of the Bodleian Library, Oxford

7. Inigo Jones, 'Influences of the Stars'; design for *Albion's Triumph*. Courtesy of the Duke of Devonshire

9. Isaac Casaubon, *De Satyrica Græcorum Romanorum Satira* (1605), p. 67

10. Inigo Jones, 'Comus and his retinue'; design for *Pleasure Reconciled to Virtue*. Courtesy of the Duke of Devonshire

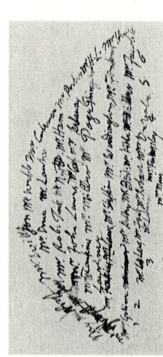

12. Longleat House, Whitelocke papers, Parcel II, Item 9 (II), fo. 1ᵛ. Courtesy of the Marquess of Bath

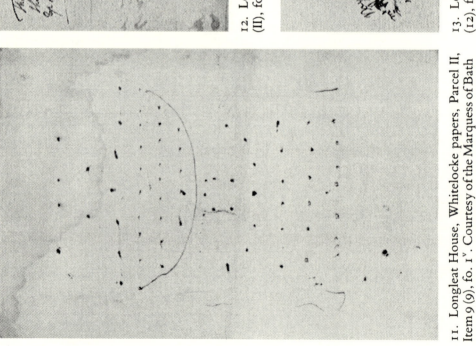

13. Longleat House, Whitelocke papers, Parcel II, Item 9 (12), fo. 1ᵛ. Courtesy of the Marquess of Bath

11. Longleat House, Whitelocke papers, Parcel II, Item 9 (9), fo. 1ᵛ. Courtesy of the Marquess of Bath

14. Inigo Jones, 'The suburbs of a great city'; design by *Salmacida Spolia*. Courtesy of the Duke of Devonshire

15. From the 'Ballet de M. le Prince de Condé dansé l'an 1620';
F- Pn, MS Rés. F. 497, p. 156

the masquers to be revealed 'sitting on the ascent of an hill' at the back of the stage. Two diagrams with six boys missing are probably, as Sabol suggests, for later in the masque when the young singers were being given a spell.[35] It is clear from the text that, from Song 5 on, the musicians of the Symphony must have moved several times, coming forward to perform and then clearing space for the dancers.

Item 12, fo. 2ᵛ (the page with the diagram for what I take to be the descent from the stage) also has on it (in a different hand) what appears to be a list for a smaller instrumental ensemble:

Mʳ
Bedoes. Harpe/
Coleman. Treble violl./
Jinkins Treble violl./
Page ~~Theorbo~~ /base violl
Will Tomkins. base violl
Willson Theorbo/
Caesar Theorbo
Lawrence ~~3 treble lutes~~
Kelley
Kithe

Did this group, rather than the larger 'Symphony', accompany one of the songs (Amphiluce's solo, perhaps)?

There is no indication of where the violin ensemble, who played the dances, or the loud music was positioned. Despite the wealth of documentation associated with this masque, we still have to return to Campion's *Lord Hay's Masque* description to form any idea of how these groups might have been accommodated within the performing-area.

The Musicians

It is, however, possible to form a good idea of how the various instrumental ensembles in *The Triumph of Peace* were constituted. The list of the 'twelve of the kings servants for the loud musique' in the Longleat papers appears—from comparison with other lists in the court records—to be organized by instrument. In fact, if we add to the Longleat memorandum the headings from a 1628 subsidy exemption list, we get the following result:[36]

Jerome Lanier	For the recorders
Clement Lanier	For the recorders
Anthony Bassano	For the recorders
Henry Bassano	For the hoboies and sackbutts
Richard Blagrave	For the hoboies and sackbutts

[35] Sabol, 'New Documents', 16.
[36] Whitelocke papers, Parcel II, Item 9 (18), fo. 2ʳ. For the 1628 subsidy list see Ashbee, *RECM*, iii. 32–3.

John Mason	For the hoboies and sackbutts
Christopher Bell	For the hoboies and sackbutts
Henry Ferrabosco	For the flutes
Alfonso Ferrabosco III	For the flutes
Thomas Mell	[not appointed to the royal wind music until 1631]
Robert Baker [jun.]?	For the hoboies and sackbutts
John Adson	[not appointed to the royal wind music until 1633]

Baker's is the only name which appears out of sequence here, and interestingly he—like Adson—has associations with the cornett.[37] Thomas Mell's name appears on numerous court lists but his role in the wind music is always unspecified. It seems possible that the last three players on the Longleat list were all there as cornettists, giving a Loud Music which could have consisted of, say, three recorders, two flutes, two oboes, three cornets, and two sackbuts (or—putting Baker back in the oboe and sackbut section—three recorders, two flutes, two oboes, two cornets, and three sackbuts). The waits/theatre musicians who had hoped to displace this loud music ensemble in the procession preceding the second performance also numbered twelve.

The masquers, we are told, 'descend and dance their entry to the violins' (ll. 648–9) and everything in the Longleat papers points to this group providing the music for set masque dances and, one would assume, for the revels. Fifteen violinists are listed in item 4. In April 1631 the Lord Chamberlain's office issued a memorandum directed to Nau concerning the musicians for the violins which lists the fourteen violinists in the King's Musick and indicates their place in the ensemble.[38] This list is identical to that in the Longleat papers, except that the latter has an extra name, Simon Hopper, a musician associated with the household of the Prince of Wales at Richmond. Woodington, we know, was drafted out of the violins to play in the 'Symphony', so Hopper must have taken his place in an ensemble which would then have been constituted as follows:

Treble violins
Étienne Nau
Davis Mell
Nicholas Picart

Contratenor violins
Simon Hopper (replacing John Woodington)
Theophilus Lupo

Tenor violins
James Johnson
Leonard Mell
John Heydon

Low tenor violins
Thomas Lupo
Robert Parker

Bass violins
John Hopper
Thomas Warren
Richard Dorney
Robert Kindersley

[37] The Longleat list does not specify whether it was Robert Baker jun. or his father (a recorder-player) who performed in *The Triumph of Peace*. There is a warrant from the Lord Chamberlain's office dated 4 Mar. 1633 made out in favour of Andrea Lanier, Jerome Lanier, Clement Lanier, Alfonso Ferrabosco (III), Henry Ferrabosco, and Robert Baker for six cornetts and a set of books.

[38] Ashbee, *RECM*, iii. 59.

There is ample evidence that violinists did not necessarily stick to the same size of instrument. Woodington, for example, despite his designation in the Lord Chamberlain's order as a contratenor-player, presumably played treble violin in the Symphony—as the only violinist in this group he would not have been assigned an inner part.[39] Nevertheless, the coincidence of that order with the list of violinists in the Longleat papers helps greatly in clarifying the character of the ensemble which played for the masque dances: a five-part string group in which the weight of numbers slightly favoured treble and bass.

Amongst those who played in the 'Symphony', some are identified with several instruments (and ten instrumentalists also sang). On one side of the sheet listing musicians' roles, John Jenkins is designated as playing 'Base Viole', while on its verso he is described as a 'theorbo & m. lute'; elsewhere in the papers he is noted (by a different hand) as a treble-viol player.[40] It is possible (though not, I think, likely) that he played all four instruments in the course of the masque. The overall composition of the ensemble for the songs and symphonies must have been something like this: one violin, six mean lutes, eleven theorbos, one harp, and three bass viols.[41] The ensemble is effectively a lute band with a small number of bowed strings included to give more definition to the outer lines. Amongst the bowed strings, a single violin and three bass viols might seem rather bottom-heavy, yet something like this balance was to be countenanced slightly later in the seventeenth century. Thomas Mace (giving advice on building up a chest of instruments for consort-playing) emphasized the need to offset violins with a sufficiently strong bass line:

After all *This*, you may add to your *Press*, a *Pair* of *Violins*, to be in Readiness for any *Extraordinary Jolly* or *Jocund Consort-Occasion*; But never use Them, but with *This Proviso*, viz. Be sure you make an *Equal Provision* for Them, by the *Addition*, and *Strength* of *Basses*; so that They may not *Out-cry* the *Rest* of the *Musick*, (the *Basses* especially) to which end, It will be *Requisite*, you *Store* your *Press* with a *Pair* of *Lusty Full-Sciz'd Theorboes*, always to strike in with your *Consorts*, or *Vocal-Musick*; to which, *That Instrument* is most *Naturally* Proper.[42]

The Longleat papers give no information about antimasque musicians. Here, again, the Middle Temple documents come to the rescue. They include a warrant to cover the Inn's share of a £10 payment to 'Thomas Bassett the Bagge pipe Iohn Seywell the Shalme, Thomas Rudstone the Iewes harpe

---

[39] Simon Hopper, too, must have played treble violin in accompanying dances at Richmond (see below, p. 279). Since he replaced Woodington in the *Triumph of Peace*, it looks as if he was expected to play the contratenor part there; in 1642 he was assigned a place in the King's Music in place of the late Robert Dorney, who is listed as a 'basso' player in the 1631 document.

[40] Whitelocke papers, Parcel II, Item 9 (8), fos. 1ʳ and 1ᵛ, and item 9 (12), fo. 2ᵛ.

[41] Robert Keith, who is listed as 'theorbo and mean lute', has been counted here as a mean lute (i.e. the standard treble instrument); William Page, listed as playing a 'bass lute', is here counted amongst the theorboists; and Jenkins has been counted as a bass viol. (Steffkins and William Tomkins are described only as playing the viol; I have assumed here that this means bass viol.) Obviously, the net result of changing any or all of these choices within the ensemble would be to reduce the number of bass viols to two while increasing the number of lutes or theorbos by one.

[42] *Musick's Monument* (London, 1676), 192.

Iohn ffulher the tonges Robert Davis the bird and Iohn Morton the bird as gratuities for attendinge the Masq's'.[43] The unsophisticated character of the sounds evoked here is, of course, very much in keeping with what we have seen about antimasque instrumentation in Chapter 3. The warrant is partly corroborated by what the masque text tells us about the procession: 'The Anti-masques were ushered by a Hornpipe [bagpipe?] and a Shawm' (l. 25) and there were musicians 'conterfeiting the voices of birds' (l. 61). These last would have given those lining the streets a taste of what went on in the seventh antimasque entry—a dance of an owl, crow, kite, jay, and magpie.

Trumpeters were also involved in the procession. Interestingly, in listing their names the Longleat papers suggest that their presence was a more or less regular feature of Inns of Court entertainments: 'The Noblemens Trumpett:ors, who have Always heretofore bin Imployed in all the services wherein these honourable howses, of the Inns of Courte have had occasion to use the quallity of a trumpett eyther in Courtly maskes or revells'.[44]

Finally, a word should be said about the singers. Here the Longleat papers provide fascinating information about the balance of different voice types. The four principal singing roles in the main masque of *The Triumph of Peace* are all female roles: Irene (Peace), Eunomia (Law), Dice (Justice), and—at the end of the masque—Amphiluce (the forerunner of the morning). Eunomia and Amphiluce were both sung by boys (and we know that the singing of the unbroken voices of apprentice musicians was much valued in the period).[45] English audiences expected to see and hear boys taking female roles—the norm in the public theatres, of course—and the link between acting and singing amongst these children was both close and traditional. Dice was sung by Mathurin Mari. Mari was a male soprano, presumably a falsettist; unfortunately, none of the music he sang survives. Irene (whose solos have a range of d–f') was sung by the tenor, John Lanier. On the face of it, the masque audiences accepted not just a male in this role (standard practice), but one who sang in a normal adult male range. (As we have seen, Nicholas Lanier singing Eternity in *The Somerset Masque* is a parallel case.)

The Longleat papers reveal that five singers—Thomas Holmes, John Frost, Henry Lawes, Thomas Day, and one of his apprentices—were characterized as Constellations. It is easy enough to identify these people in the description of the procession: in the chariot following the one containing 'Musicians like priest and Sybills, sonnes and daughters of Harmony', Genius and Amphiluce

[43] Orbison and Hill (eds.), 'The Middle Temple Documents', 53, § 28.

[44] Whitelocke papers, Parcel II, Item 9 (14). Eleven names are given on this list, though the description of the procession published with the masque text mentions fourteen trumpeters.

[45] The part of Eunomia was taken by 'Mr Porter's boy' and that of Amphiluce by the Lord Chamberlain's boy. In the first case, Walter Porter is the boy's tutor; in the second, the Lord Chamberlain was the principal in the apprenticeship agreement, and the boy's actual tuition would be in the hands of a professional musician. In both cases the boys were on a path leading to a professional career as a musician. See Lynn Hulse, 'The Musical Patronage of Robert Cecil, First Earl of Salisbury (1563–1612),' *JRMA* 116 (1991), 27–8.

sat with 'foure in skie-coloured taffata Robes seeded with Starres, Mantles ashe-coloured, adorn'd with Fringe and Silver lace, Coronets with Starres upon their heads'. The four adult Constellations, all members of the Chapel Royal, were obviously fine singers. They are not mentioned in the text and none of the diagrams position them together as a group. Presumably they retained the role implied by their place in the procession as attendants on Amphiluce. If so, they may have changed into their Constellation costumes during the revels and then taken solo roles in the missing sections of the final song.

In summary, we should note that *The Triumph of Peace* involved five groups of musicians: Whitelocke's music (singers and instrumentalists), the violins, the loud music, antimasque musicians, and—for the procession—eleven trumpeters.

Musical Sources for the Caroline Masque

Obviously central to any discussion on this subject is the William Lawes autograph in GB-Ob, MS Mus. Sch. b. 2, a source unique in preserving music for masques in a form which lets us see how it fitted into the production. Here for once we are not confronted with excerpts selected and adapted for use outside the original masquing context. What we know of the composition of the 'Symphony' for *The Triumph of Peace* suggests that, if the bass line in Mus. Sch. b. 2 is regarded as an unfigured basso continuo, then this score is essentially complete—it clearly does not represent something awaiting a five-part arrangement for violins (a stage through which virtually all masque dance music passed).[46] Mus. Sch. b. 2 might seem less self-sufficient in the Choruses where no separate bass line is provided. In some (but not all) instances where there are rests in all the vocal lines, musical logic might lead us to expect a sounding bass line—though in fact the music does always work without it (see Ex. 4.1, bar 59).[47]

For *The Triumph of Peace* Mus. Sch. b. 2 contains settings of the first three songs. This is not, in itself, particularly remarkable—there are, after all, Ferrabosco settings for a sequence of four consecutive songs in *The Masque of Beauty* (1608). Lawes himself, however, clearly thought of this in rather different terms. His *Triumph of Peace* excerpt in Mus. Sch. b. 2 concludes with the inscription 'the first part of the Inns of Court Masque: W Lawes'. This

[46] Sabol, *Four Hundred Songs and Dances*, adds the alto viol part from GB-Lbl, Add. MS 18940 in his edition of the three *Triumph of Peace* symphonies. The versions of these pieces in Add. MSS 18940–4 were, I suspect, arrangements by Charles Coleman (hence their attribution to him). It is difficult to see from the information in the Longleat papers who could have played any inner linear part (and Sabol's designation of the top line as 'treble viol' runs counter to what we know of the ensemble's make-up). On the other hand, GB-Ob, Mus. Sch. b. 2 does have an alto line (very much in the style of the inner lines in Add. 18940) for the two *Britannia Triumphans* symphonies. We do not know how the instrumental ensemble for *Britannia Triumphans* was constituted.

[47] Lefkowitz, *Trois masques*, and—to a lesser extent—Sabol, *Four Hundred Songs and Dances* tend to provide bass notes in such cases.

opening section of *The Triumph of Peace* (Songs 1–3) is in C major. The sense
of its being conceived as a whole is very clear from the way the ending of
Song 2 and the beginning of Song 3 are in A minor; the third of the
symphonies consequently functions, not as a fresh beginning for a new
musical number, but as a kind of instrumental ritornello in the middle of a
much larger structure. (Like the other symphonies, this has a dramatic function—it is music for the descent of Eunomia.) This evidence of tonal planning

Ex. 4.1. W. Lawes, 'Britanocles the great and good' (*Britannia Triumphans*), from
GB–Ob, MS Mus. Sch. b. 2

41B: extra semibreve tied to dotted semibreve in original
65: final note a breve in all parts

spir-it cheers,] His vir-tue [ev' – ry droop – ing spir-it cheers

spir-it cheers, His vir-tue ev' – ry droop – ing spir-it cheers

spir-it cheers, His vir-tue ev' – ry droop-ing spir-it cheers

spir – it cheers, His vir-tue ev' – ry droop – ing spir-it cheers

spir-it cheers, His vir-tue ev' – ry droop – ing spir-it cheers

21 Song of Fame

Why move these princes [of his train so slow? As, tak-ing root, they would to stat-ues

25

grow, But that their won-der of his vir-tue turns them so. Ciacona

29 Fame againe

'Tis fitt you mixe [that won-der with de-light, As you were warm'd to mo-tion with his

35

sight. So pay the ex – pec-ta – tion of this night.]

Ex. 4.1. *Continued*

has some importance, as we shall see, when trying to find missing pieces in this jigsaw.

There is one other song setting by William Lawes for *The Triumph of Peace* which survives in autograph; this is Song 8, Amphiluce's 'In Envy of the night'. This is found, not in the same volume as the larger masque sections, but in GB-Lbl, Add. MS 31432. Murray Lefkowitz concluded from his study

Ex. 4.1. *Continued*

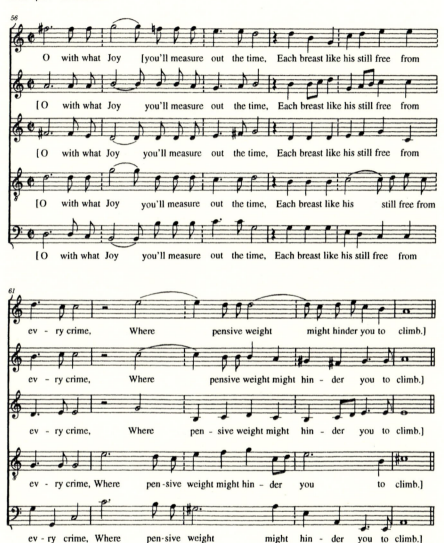

of the six uniformly bound Lawes autograph volumes in the Bodleian and the British Library that Lawes had prepared them as a set in the early 1640s while the court was at Oxford. As Lefkowitz notes, there is a strong sense of organization running through these manuscripts with music grouped according to genre and the resources needed for performance. This reinforces the impression that Lawes wished the context of the masque music presented in score in Mus. Sch. b. 2 to be recognized. This is not music which lends itself easily to domestic adaptation. On the other hand, Amphiluce's song—the only song identified in the text as a vocal solo[48]—keeps company in Add. MS 31432 with other discrete songs and dialogues. The character of this manuscript anthology makes it seem that Lawes (like others before him) was interested in selecting—and possibly adapting for domestic performance— songs which could survive outside the original masque context. Amphiluce's song is headed up in Add. 31432 'In a masque at court'.

There is one more source for masque vocal music by William Lawes which needs describing here. GB-Eu, MS Dc. 1. 69 and GB-Ob, MS Mus. d. 238 together make up the first and second cantus parts of what was once a three-part set of vocal music copied by Edward Lowe, who succeeded John Wilson as Professor of Music at Oxford.[49] Since both cantus parts include a continuo bass line, together they give a reasonably complete picture of many of the three-part songs in the collection. This is particularly true for the central section of the manuscripts, which may have been used as copy for the publication of John Wilson's *Cheerful Ayres* (Oxford, 1660). At the end of the manuscripts there is a group of nine William Lawes songs. (The volumes have been reversed and the new group of songs copied into the last ten or so folios, working back in towards the centre of each volume.) Amongst these are three masque songs: 'Why do you dwell' from *The Triumph of Peace*, 'Cease warring Thoughts' (from Shirley's private masque, *The Triumph of Beauty*), and 'Behold how this Conjunction thrives' (from Davenant's *The Triumphs of the Prince D'Amour*).

'Cease warring Thoughts' and 'Behold how this Conjunction thrives' also occur in Mus. Sch. b. 2 (although 'Cease warring Thoughts' is crossed out). A comparison of the two versions of both these songs reveals numerous substantial differences. In both, the overall harmonic plan of the manuscript partbook versions is quite different from the autograph versions, although the basic key of each piece is the same. For the most part, the manuscript partbook versions preserve the motivic ideas of the autograph, but their contrapuntal continuation of these is often so different as to make the two versions scarcely recognizable as the same song.

'Cease warring Thoughts' (Ex. 4.2) falls into four sections. In the first of these, both settings are essentially identical for the first nine bars, manipulate the same ideas quite differently for the next ten bars, and then return to a virtually identical treatment of the final six bars (with their chromatically descending bass line). Except for the first nine bars, however, the version in the autograph has no first treble part. In the second section of the song (beginning 'Ye warbling nightingales') not even the motivic ideas are shared. Where the autograph version has a melodic line which descends by step, the

---

[48] The cue sheet makes it clear that Song 5, which the text implies was performed by 'the whole train of musicians', was in fact sung as a solo by M. Mari (Dice).

[49] See P. Walls, 'New Light on Songs by William Lawes and John Wilson', *ML* 57 (1976), 55–64.

(*b*) from GB-Eu, MS Dc. 1. 69, and GB-Ob, MS Mus. d. 238

Cease war - ring thoughts, and let his braine Noe more discord ent- er-
taine, But be smooth and calme a - gaine. Ye chris - tall riv-ers that are nigh
As the streames are pass-inge by, Teach your mur - murs
har - mon-y. Ye winds that waite up-on the spring And

Cease warring thoughts, and let his braine Noe more discord ent - er-
taine, But be smooth and calme a - gaine. Ye chris - tall riv-ers that are nigh
As the streames are pass-inge by, Teach your mur - murs
har - mon-y. And per-fumes to the

Ex. 4.2(*b*). *Continued*

Ex. 4.2(*b*). *Continued*

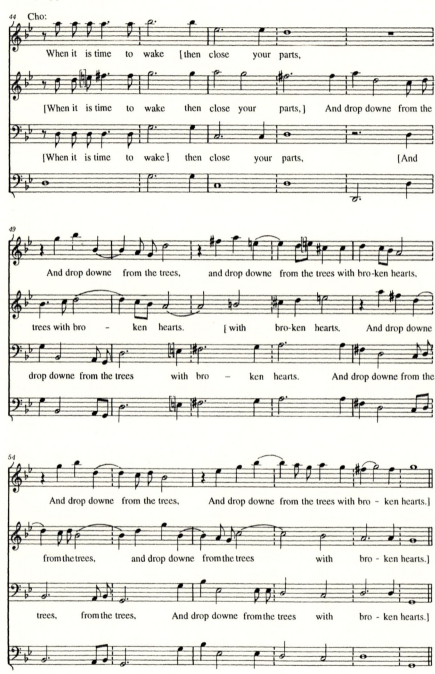

Ex. 4.2(*b*). *Continued*

7 semibreve added in instrumental bass part; minim in second tenor line is a semibreve in
original

10–11 minim added in instrumental bass line

54: *d'* in Tenor 1 part is dotted minim in original

partbooks have a canonic phrase which begins with rising two-note slurs. This new motif can, however, be found at the beginning of another Lawes masque song in the autograph—Fame's 'Ciacona' in Davenant's masque, *Britannia Triumphans* (see Ex. 4.1, bars 29 ff.). In the final two sections of the song there are resemblances between the two versions, but the partbooks must be regarded as recomposition rather than revision. Both, for example, indulge in word-painting at 'then drop down', but each uses quite different figures.

It is not at all clear how one accounts for these differences.[50] While the deletion of 'Cease warring Thoughts' (and the state of the part-writing) in the autograph score suggests that the manuscript partbooks contain Lawes's revised version, this can hardly be the case with 'Behold how this Conjunction thrives' (with which Lawes apparently was happy); yet this song is almost equally different in the two sources. It is not easy to see what circumstances produced these, let alone how they relate to what was actually heard in the masque performances.

With the vocal sources other than Mus. Sch. b. 2 we cannot be sure exactly what relationship their contents bear to the versions actually used in masque performance. There is, for example, no hint in the autograph Add. MS 31432 that Amphiluce's song was preceded (or followed) by an instrumental symphony like the earlier songs in this masque. Yet the dramatic context of this song and the one which follows it suggests that both must originally have had symphonies. The expansive action of scene and participants here needs instrumental music rather more than the entrance of Irene and Eunomia at the beginning of the masque. At the end of the Revels and immediately before Song 8

the Scene is changed into a plaine Champion Country, which terminates with the Horizon, and above a darkish skie, with duskie clouds, through which appeared the new Moone, but with a faint light by the approach of the morning; from the furthest part of this ground, arose by little and little a great vapour which being come about the middle of the Seene, it slackens its motion, and begins to fall downward to the earth from whence it came: and out of this rose another cloud of a strange shape, and colour, on which sate a young Maide, with a dim Torch in her hand . . . (ll. 731–9)

Amphiluce sings her song, and then—during the performance of the final song—she ascends on her cloud while the masquers move back. The use of symphonies not just at the beginning of this masque but in *The Triumphs of the Prince d'Amour* and *Britannia Triumphans* suggests that similar instrumental movements must have been deployed here.

[50] It seems possible that these are John Wilson's adaptations of Lawes's songs. The central section of the manuscript partbooks provides examples of Wilson's adapting other composers' songs (especially songs by Robert Johnson). There is even a rather tenuous link between *The Triumph of Beauty* song in the manuscript partbooks and John Wilson since 'Cease warring Thoughts' was also set by John Gamble, who seems to have made a habit of setting songs which had previously received Wilson's attention.

Many of the identifiable instrumental pieces from Caroline masques are introductory symphonies, not masque dances. These symphonies have a different function from dances—although they accompany movement, it is the movement of musicians and singer/actors (positioning themselves for the next song) rather than the dancing of courtly masquers. Cues in the Lawes autograph often indicate what is taking place during the symphony. At the head of the first Simfony for *The Triumph of Peace* Lawes has written 'The howers descending'; Whitelocke's cue sheet specifies that this movement is to be played twice, whereas the second symphony (during which no stage movement is indicated either by the text or the score) is to be played only once (see Table 4.1). Similarly, cues written above the music for *The Triumphs of the Prince d'Amour* show that groups of musicians positioned themselves during the symphonies ('Last part of the Simphony playes and the Priests of Venus descend'). Despite their different function, however, symphonies often have a similar structure to established dance forms. This is illustrated by a number of instances in which a piece is labelled 'symphony' in one source and 'almain' in another (or sometimes in a different part of the same source).[51]

Song 8, Amphiluce's song, is in G minor, and so too is the fragment of Song 9 which survives in Mus. Sch. b. 2.[52] Consequently, we can see the same kind of tonal planning at the end of the masque that was evident at the beginning. (Song 7, 'Why do you dwell', is also in G minor, but the Revels intervened between it and Song 8.) As we shall see, it is quite possible that symphonies for these songs have become detached from them and survive in instrumental sources.

A considerable amount of instrumental music composed for Caroline masques is extant. But since collections of English instrumental music dating from the 1630s and later preserve music from earlier masques as well, it can be difficult to assign even a rough date to particular pieces. Nevertheless, there are ways of making these sources give up their secrets.

Anne Cromwell's Virginal Book (London Museum, MS 46.78/748), which carries a date of 1638, is a case in point. A number of the pieces in the book have early seventeenth-century origins and two masque dances—'The Princes Masque' and 'The Queenes Masque'—are certainly Jacobean.[53] But the book has circumstantial links with the Caroline masque and, in particular, with *The Triumph of Peace*. 'Mr. Whitelocke's Coranto' is there, and, more importantly, so is a whole group of pieces by Simon Ives.[54] There are five pieces called

---

[51] M. Lefkowitz, 'New Facts Concerning William Lawes and the Caroline Masque', *ML* 40 (1959), 329, speaks of the 'identical function of the "symfony" and dance tune of the period'; it would be more accurate to describe these as having similar forms but distinct functions.

[52] Lefkowitz, *Trois masques*, 108–9 transcribes this without its key signature.

[53] See H. Ferguson (ed.), *Anne Cromwell's Virginal Book* (London, 1974); 'The Princes Masque' (no. 14) occurs in Add. 10444; 'The Queenes Masque' (no. 16) has a concordance in F-Pn, MS Rés. 1185 (336), a manuscript which was indexed by Benjamin Cosyn in 1625.

[54] No. 34, 'The choyce by Mr Ives', no. 42, 'Simphony by Mr Ives', no. 45, 'An Almon [sic] by Mr Ive', nos. 46 and 47, both called 'A Coranto by Mr Ive', and no. 49, 'A Simphony by Mr Ive'. No. 24,

Symphony, two attributed to Ives and two which are keyboard arrangements of Lawes symphonies for *The Triumph of Peace*.

Elizabeth Rogers's Virginal Book (GB-Lbl, Add. MS 10337) presents a similar picture. The volume bears a date of 1656 but contains a number of pieces by Orlando Gibbons, including several masque tunes, all obviously composed before 1625.[55] There are, though, arrangements of the same two symphonies from *The Triumph of Peace* that are found in Anne Cromwell's Book. The first of these in Elizabeth Rogers's Book is called 'One of ye Symphonies', and it is preceded by another piece with the same title.

Sources like these which have concordances with the Lawes masque music in Mus. Sch. b. 2 may lead us to other music used in the same masques. The most valuable in this respect is the set of three- and four-part pieces for violins and/or viols found in GB-Lbl, Add. MSS 18940–4.[56] These manuscripts are a particularly rich source of music by Simon Ives since they contain a group of twenty-four of his pieces (plus, again, 'Whitelocke's Coranto'). About fifteen pieces in this collection look likely to have been composed as instrumental symphonies for Caroline masques. Of most interest are a 'Symphonie' (in G minor) by William Lawes and a group of six Symphonies which have been erroneously attributed to Charles Coleman.[57] The G minor Lawes Symphony could well belong in the closing section of *The Triumph of Peace*.

The six 'Coleman' pieces may all have their origins in the music for *The Triumph of Peace*. The introductory symphonies for songs 1–3 are all there, although the last of them is transposed down a tone to G minor. The other three could also be connected with the masque. The first in the group occurs (without its two final triple strains) in Playford's *Court Ayres* (1655), where it is called 'Simphony' and is moreover attributed to Simon Ives. Surely this must have been one of his contributions to *The Triumph of Peace*? Amongst the large number of Ives pieces in the four-part section of this collection is 'The Fancy', which occurs in other sources with titles and circumstantial links connecting it with the Caroline masque.

'Symphony', is not ascribed to Ives here, but in another source—GB-Lbl, Add. MSS 18940–4 (see Table 4.2). Sabol, *Four Hundred Songs and Dances*, 31 n., suggests that Anne Cromwell acquired *The Triumph of Peace* material through her husband, John Neale, who was admitted to the Middle Temple in 1632.

[55] The Gibbons pieces are—using the numbering from G. Sargent (ed.), *Elizabeth Rogers' Virginal Book* ([American Institute of Musicology], 1971)—no. 2, 'Nann's Maske', no. 4, 'The Fairest Nimphes', and no. 46, 'Almaygne Mr Johnson'; see *Orlando Gibbons: Keyboard Music*, ed. G. Hendrie, MB 20 (2nd edn., London, 1967), 79, 80, and 56. 'The Fairest Nimphes' occurs in Add. MS 10444; see above, p. 135n.

[56] Dr Robert Thompson has concluded, on the basis of paper type and a study of the hands found in the collection, that Add. MSS 18940–4 could have been begun c.1640, with a few pieces (notably the Ground in D by John Banister) copied some years after the rest. He notes that, if this hypothesis is correct, Add. MSS 18940–4 'could be one of the earliest secondary sources of *The Triumph of Peace* instrumental music' (private communication).

[57] The Lawes Symphonie is on fo. 7 in all parts. The group of Simon Ives pieces occupy fos. 28ʳ–35ᵛ in the Superius and Altus parts, fos. 8ʳ–15ᵛ in the Medius, and fos. 27ʳ–34ᵛ in the Bassus part; the part marked Bassus Continuus has only the first eleven of these pieces (beginning on fo. 27ʳ). The group of pieces attributed to Coleman occupies fos. 9ᵛ–10ᵛ in the Superius, Altus, and Bassus parts, and fos. 8ᵛ–9ᵛ in the Bassus Continuus. Only the first of these pieces has the title 'Symphony'; the rest are untitled.

Table 4.2 lists the instrumental introductions (the 'symphonies') to the songs in *The Triumph of Peace* and *Britannia Triumphans* and then arranges concordances with these tunes alongside them. The lower section of the table shows pieces from the concordant sources which have titles or attributions indicating some connection with the masque tunes in the top half. This facilitates identification of other instrumental pieces which may have been used in these masques. (The table incidentally illustrates the extraordinary range of titles and ascriptions that masque tunes acquired as they passed out into 'secular' sources.[58]) An optimistic reading of the table suggests that it enables recognition of possibly all the remaining *Triumph of Peace* symphonies and of some additional pieces for *Britannia Triumphans*. Using for the moment the titles and numbers from *Anne Cromwell's Book* as a reference point, we could hypothesize that in addition to the definite Lawes symphonies (nos. 23 and 33), the other pieces entitled 'Symphony' (nos. 21, 24, 42, and 49) were also composed for *The Triumph of Peace*, the last three at least by Simon Ives.

Another series of symphonies can be identified through the concordance between Mus. Sch. b. 2 and van Eyck, *Der Fluyten Lust-Hof* (1646). Since 'Derde Carileen' matches the Valediction symphony from *Britannia Triumphans*, it would seem reasonable to assume that the whole series comes from that masque. This is complicated, however, by further concordances in another Dutch publication, Paulus Matthysz's *'t Uitnement Kabinet* (1646 and 1649). There, the piece called 'Eerste Carileen' is a version of the Symphony for Song 1 in *The Triumph of Peace*, while 'Tweede Carileen', 'Derde Carileen', and 'Vierde Carileen' are identical with the pieces with the same titles in van Eyck's publication. In each source, a single concordance points in a different direction for the series. Furthermore, 'Vierde Carileen' is apparently not a piece borrowed from the English masque repertoire, but a new melody in the same style composed by Cornelis Kist.[59]

If these deductions are correct, they allow a better sense at least of what music Simon Ives contributed to *The Triumph of Peace*. Ives must have composed the vocal music for the central section, where each of the songs was preceded by movement on stage for which instrumental symphonies would have been needed. Song 4 follows the descent of Dice in a cloud. At its end, the musicians move forward towards the State before singing the next 'ode'. This is followed by the transformation scene in which the masquers are revealed sitting on a hill (see above, pp. 172–3). During (or perhaps just before) the opening of the scene, the musicians move back. Song 6 is preceded and followed by the masquers' set dances and during these the 'symphony' remained behind the dancing-area. They move forward again for

---

[58] e.g. William Lawes's final Simfony for *Britannia Triumphans* is attributed to Charles Coleman in one source and called an Ayre and Derde Carileen in two others.

[59] See Matthysz, *'t Uitnement Kabinet*, iv, ed. R. A. Rasch (Amsterdam, 1973), introduction. Rasch points out that 'The name "Carileen" is the first word of a Dutch text set to the *Eerste Carileen* ("Carileen, ay wilt u niet verschuilen")'.

TABLE 4.2. 'Symphonies' for The Triumph of Peace and Britannia Triumphans

	GB-Ob, Mus. Sch b. 2	Elizabeth Rogers's Virginal Book	Anne Cromwell's Virginal Book	GB-Lbl, Add. MSS 18940–4	Playford, Court Ayres (1655)	Van Eyck, Der Fluyten lust-Hof (1646)	Matthysz, 't Uitmement Kabinet (1649)
MASQUE TUNES							
Triumph of Peace—Simfony to Song 1		8. One of ye Symphonies [C]	23. Symphony fo. 16ᵛ [C]	fo. 10 Mr. C. Coleman [C]			Eerste Carileen
Triumph of Peace—Simfony to Song 2 [C]		31. A Maske [C]ᵃ	33. Symphony fo. 24 [C]	fo. 10ᵛ Mr. C. Coleman [C]			
Triumph of Peace—Simfony to Song 3 [a]				fo. 10 Mr. C. Coleman [g]			
Britannia Triumphans—Simfony to Song of Galatea [c]					No. 135 Almaine [c]ᵇ		
Britannia Triumphans—Simfony to Valediction [C]					No. 143 Ayre [C]ᶜ	Derde Carileen	Derde Carileen

TABLE 4.2. *Continued*

GB-Ob, Mus. Sch b. 2	Elizabeth Rogers's Virginal Book	Anne Cromwell's Virginal Book	GB-Lbl, Add. MSS 18940–4	Playford, *Court Ayres* (1655)	Van Eyck, *Der Fluyten lust-Hof* (1646)	Matthysz, *'t Uitnement Kabinet* (1649)
RELATED MUSIC						
	7. One of ye Symphonies[d]	21. Symphony [C]			Tweede Carileen	Tweede Carileen
		24. Symphony [C][e]	The Fancy Simon Ives [C]			
		42. Symphhony by Mr. Ives [F]				
			fo. 9^v Symphony Mr. C. Coleman [F]	188. Simphony Mr. Simon Ives [F]		
		49. A Simphony by Mr. Ive [G]	fo. 10^v Mr. C. Coleman [C]			
			fo. 10^v Mr. C. Coleman [c]			
			fo. 7 Symphonie W. Lawes [g]	No. 12 Simphony Mr William Lawes [g][f]		
					Erste Carileen	

[a] Has a second duple strain in place of the triple strain found in the Lawes autograph.
[b] Has a concluding triple strain which is an arrangement of the 'On ever moving waves' section of the Song.
[c] Has a concluding triple strain.
[d] Also in US-NYp, MS Drexel 5612, p. 27, 'A Maske'.
[e] Also in GB-Och, MS 431, fo. 5, 'Anne Piff's Maske'.
[f] Also in *Courtly Masquing Ayres* (1666), No. 1, Symphony, Mr. Will Lawes.

Ex. 4.3. W. Lawes, 'Hence, hence, ye profane' (*The Triumph of Peace*), bars 1–9, from GB-Ob, MS Mus. Sch. b. 2

Song 6, retiring to make room for the next set dance ('the main dance'). Clearly, Ives had plenty of scope for composing 'aiers and lessons' for these transitions between dance, song, and stage movement—and I suspect that we have these in Add. 18940–4.

None of this gets us any further towards identifying *dance* music for both main masque and antimasque. That question will be taken up again in Chapter 6, but for the moment, we should look more closely at William Lawes's main-masque composition.

William Lawes's Music

The opening music for the main masque of *The Triumph of Peace* (Songs 1–3 in the text) is uncomplicated and extrovert. The three instrumental symphonies are simple, sprightly, binary pieces. The solos given to Irene (in Songs 1 and 2) are consistently declamatory: they are sung over a fairly still bass, and the vocal line—typically moulded around the notes of common chords—has a fanfare-like quality appropriate to her imperious calls ('Hence ye profane', 'Appear Eunomia'). There is one short division on the word 'delight' which helps convey a sense of exhilaration (see Ex. 4.3).

The two brief choruses are predominantly homophonic, and the first of them picks up the declamatory rhythms from Irene's preceding recitative-like opening. The last of the choruses ('Irene enters like a perfumed spring') is graceful and—except for a single scrunch produced by conflicting passing notes at the end of the second bar—uniformly consonant. The trio sung by three voices from the chorus (introduced by a few bars of baldly declamatory writing) begins in a galliard rhythm ('In her celestial gaiety') and then changes to the only piece of imitative writing in this section (and even here Lawes always has a pair of voices moving in thirds). Smoothness is the overriding

Ex. 4.4. W. Lawes 'Crown'd with a wreath' (from Song 2 of *The Triumph of Peace*),
bars 45–54, from GB-Ob, MS Mus. Sch. b. 2

characteristic of this trio: the basic motif on which it is built has a triadic
outline ameliorated by passing notes. The three vocal parts are placed close
together: the two upper voices often cross. Although the cue sheet reveals that
the upper parts here were sung by Henry Lawes (a countertenor) and William
Webb (tenor), they are both written in the alto clef and have an identical
range (Ex. 4.4).

Mr Drew's five bars of declamation draw attention to the most interesting aspect of this whole section. They form the first line of a quatrain which Shirley allocates to a chorus:

> See where she shines, O see,
> In her cellestiall gayety,
> Crownd with a wreath of Starres to shew
> The Evening glory in her brow.   (ll. 512–15)

Lawes could easily have followed Shirley's stanza form and set these half-dozen words as part of the attractive trio which follows. (As it is, the second line has to be repeated to fill out Lawes's balanced phrases in this section.) It is dramatically appropriate that the first line should be declaimed and that the second should be accommodated within a graceful and more lyrical triple metre. As we have seen, Song 2 is the central block in a larger continuous structure which can be represented schematically as follows:

Description	Key strain	Time signature and Length in bars for each	
[Song 2] Symphony	C	¢8	¢8
declamatory solo (Irene)	C	¢19	
Chorus	C	¢7	
[Song 2] Symphony	C	¢7	3₁11
declamatory solo (Irene)	C	¢13	
declamatory solo (Mr Drew)	a–C	¢4	
Trio (voices from the chorus)	C–a	38	¢10
[Song 3] Symphony	a–C	¢5	¢5
dialogue (Eunomia/Irene)	a–	¢45 (final 8 bars duet)	
Chorus	C	¢9	

This continuous section takes a good seven minutes to perform (following the repeat instructions on the cue sheet). Taken as a whole it presents an extended structure, remarkable for its balance and integration. Its main subdivisions (the individual 'Songs' of Shirley's text) are punctuated by ritornelli (the Symphonies) at their beginning, and by concerted music at the end. Appropriately, the middle song has a trio rather than the full Choruses of the other two. This central section—Song 2—resembles some of the structures being explored in Italy just at this time, particularly in the way it has a brief section of recitative interrupting the flow before a final more lyrical section. John Whenham's comments on this kind of mixed style in Italian dialogues helps throw the avant-garde character of Lawes's procedures in 1634 into relief: 'The use of both declamatory and arioso styles within a single setting occasionally leads to an incipient recitative–aria relationship . . . And relationships of this kind are particularly striking when the passage of arioso is in triple meter. Prior to the late 1620s, extended passages of triple-meter ariosos are rare . . .'.[60]

---

[60] J. Whenham, *Duet and Dialogue in the Age of Monteverdi*, 2 vols. (Ann Arbor, 1982), i. 198–9.

Altogether, the Lawes autograph shows that larger, more continuous musical structures were composed for the main masques in the Caroline period—though we must bear in mind that the paucity of vocal music for the later Jacobean masque may make this development seem more sudden than it really was. (As we have seen, Jonson's later masques do provide for a more continuous musical setting than his earlier ones.)

The predominantly transparent harmonies and homophonic character of the ensemble writing would not, in itself, seem particularly noteworthy were it not that William Lawes's music has become a byword for contrapuntal inventiveness and harmonic daring. Anthony à Wood was to note that Lawes had been 'an excellent composer for instrumentall musick—but to indulge the ear he broke sometimes ye rules of mathematicall composition'.[61] What the music for *The Triumph of Peace* demonstrates is a strong sense of contextual decorum. A parallel might be drawn in the contrast between, say, Marenzio's madrigal style and the rather less complicated music he wrote for the Florentine intermedi of 1589. With Lawes's masque music, more than in Ferrabosco's masque songs, the declamatory rhythms, simple harmonies, and even vocal lines moulded around common chords seem to have been shaped by dramatic considerations. They are arresting and immediately accessible. In Lawes's *œuvre* a connection can be seen between musical function and contrapuntal/harmonic complexity. The consort fantasias—music written primarily for the performers—stand at one end of a continuum, the masque compositions (particularly *The Triumph of Peace*) at the other, while pieces like the Royal Consorts (which have, as it were, a semi-public function) occupy the middle ground.

Consonant and predominantly homophonic textures as a vehicle for extrovert and direct 'public' communication characterize all Lawes's masque music, though never quite as strongly as in *The Triumph of Peace*. Contrapuntal writing is more in evidence in the music for *The Triumphs of the Prince d'Amour*, for example. 'Behold how this conjunction thrives' opens with an imitative gesture and its second, triple, section takes this further: two out of its three phrases are strictly canonic (Ex. 4.5). (The intervening non-imitative phrase allows Lawes to move the voices apart—the bass descends to *D*, two octaves beneath the tenor's highest note.) More noteworthy, however, is the way Lawes has allowed his interest in dissonant textures (so firmly repressed in *The Triumph of Peace*) to show through occasionally in the ensembles.

Britannia Triumphans has similar instances of passing dissonance. Often these arise in sections where the harmonic implications of the outer parts seem both clear and unremarkable but where inner voices complicate the picture. In Ex. 4.1 the expected dominant-seventh harmonies on the third beat of bar 7 are obscured by passing notes in the second treble and alto lines. (What is most puzzling about this kind of part-writing is the frequent obscuring of the upper

---

[61] Notes on English musicians in GB-Ob, MS Wood D. 19 (4), no. 106, fo. 83^r; quoted by M. Lefkowitz, *William Lawes* (London, 1960), 6.

Ex. 4.5. W. Lawes, 'Behold how this conjunction thrives' (*The Triumphs of the Prince d'Amour*), bars 37–51, from GB-Ob, MS Mus. Sch. b. 2

line's contour by crossing inner parts.) Similarly-generated random dissonance can be seen in the four-part section of the same song.

For all that, the music for *Britannia Triumphans*—like that for *The Triumph of Peace*—seems well judged for a festive public occasion. Homophonic full choruses and dance-like metres abound. Mus. Sch. b. 2 contains settings of three songs (though the word seems rather inadequate to describe these architecturally conceived sections). Each song builds up to a climax through an expansion of forces to the end of the song. Both Galatea's song and the Valediction begin with a symphony, then move to solo sections, a trio, and finally a five-part chorus (labelled 'Grand Chorus' in the final song). Although the first of the settings does not have a symphony, it begins with a five-part 'Full Song' before moving through sections for one voice, two voices, and four voices, to the final 'full chorus'. The solo section begins as declamatory writing, then gives way to a dance-like ayre which Lawes labels 'Ciacona'. This is an early use of this term anywhere, and certainly its first application to English music.[62] Lawes does not write a chaconne in the sense of a dance-like

---

[62] Lanier's setting of Thomas Carew's poem 'No more shall meads be deck'd with flowers' is built on a ground bass and is labelled 'Ciacono' in GB-Lbl, Add. MS 25707. All the sources for this song, however, are later than 1638, the year of *Britannia Triumphans*. See Spink (ed.), *English Songs 1625–1660*, 192–3.

movement on an ostinato bass, though this has related characteristics—a confident triple metre and a bass line which, while not treated as a ground, nevertheless involves an element of repetition since it is drawn from the opening of the preceding chorus (see Ex. 4.1 above). Such a procedure—just as with the alternation of declamatory and more lyrical solo sections—parallels contemporary Italian models.[63]

Lawes redistributes Davenant's text with, it seems, both dramatic and musical considerations in mind. Davenant's words are arranged in five triplets made up of iambic pentameter lines; the text indicates that the first is to be sung by a chorus, the next two by Fame, and the final two by the chorus again. In the Lawes autograph, the first triplet is given to a five-part chorus (as the text prescribes). It is grandly homophonic and set in a triple metre, but the most interesting feature is that Lawes repeats the final line of Davenant's triplet to make four balanced five-bar phrases. Following this chorus, Fame sings; her first triplet is recitative-like declamation while the second is the 'Ciacona'. Again, the final line of the triplet is repeated, this time by two boys characterized as the Arts and Science; Lawes clearly felt that whereas the three-line stanza was satisfactory for declamatory passages, it was musically awkward when it came to writing confident-sounding music for Fame or her chorus. The mixture of declamatory and tuneful writing in Fame's solo triplets projects a basic distinction which is already there in Davenant's verse. Fame's declamation interprets the masquers' solemn procession to the dancing-place as the movements of men filled with awe by the presence of Britanocles:

> Why move these Princes of his traine so slow,
> As taking root, they would to Statues grow,
> But that their wonder of his vertue turnes them so!

The lighter tuneful section sets out the pattern for the dancing which is to follow:

> 'Tis fit you mix that wonder with delight,
> As you were warm'd to motion with his sight,
> So pay the expectation of this night.   (pp. 205–6)

For the two final triplets, Lawes switches to a duple metre. Both these sections (the first for four voices, the second for a five-part chorus) have some contrapuntal interest which at one point assumes an illustrative function: Lawes has the first treble voice preceding the other voices on the words 'And he mov'd first', a musical pun on Charles I's leadership.[64]

---

[63] John Whenham writes: 'The appearance of the designation *ciaccona* does not necessarily indicate the use of an ostinato. It can simply indicate a particular type of dance-song. Frescobaldi's "Deh vien da me pastorella" (*Second Libro d'Arie*, 1630), for example, consists of three sections of duet writing separated by two passages of solo recitative. The bass for the first of the duet sections begins with the same pattern as Falconieri's duet ["Aria sopra la Ciaccona", 1616], but is then developed into a longer, more diffuse line lacking any regular repetition pattern'; *Duet and Dialogue in the Age of Monteverdi*, i. 175.

[64] It should be noted, however, that in the printed text of the masque the line reads 'And they move first'. Lawes uses a very similar image in Galatea's song where 'When he shall lead with Harmony' is treated

Galatea's song is also interesting for the way in which Lawes treats Davenant's verse. The text prints this song in four quatrains with alternate lines of ten and eight syllables. The first two quatrains are sung by Galatea alone, and Lawes sets them as a continuous declamatory section. Just as the 'unbalanced' triplet in Fame's song was retained only for natural-sounding declamatory passages, here the alternating ten- and eight-syllable lines are kept only for Galatea's declamation. Appropriately, Lawes turns the third stanza into a lilting, galliard-like song for three voices and the lines are adapted to make an even eight syllables each. 'On ever moving waves they us'd to dance', for example, becomes 'On ever moving waves they dance'.

Of the three stanzas which are given a declamatory setting, no two are alike. In the first quatrain the musical phrases match the lines of the verse, but in the second quatrain Lawes follows the enjambment in Davenant's lines and gives no hint in his setting of where the first and third lines of the stanza end; the result is very natural-sounding declamation. The final two lines of Galatea's declamatory fourth quatrain are repeated in a modified form by a five-part chorus. Once again, the ten-syllable line is reduced to eight syllables so that what Lawes actually sets for the chorus is a metrically balanced couplet. (Like the last two triplets of Fame's song, this chorus has some contrapuntal interest.) Lawes's adaptations of Davenant's text reveal a strong sense of the kind of verse appropriate to different types of dramatic expression. When writing in a declamatory style, he makes the most of the slightest irregularity to produce a setting which makes its impact as real declamation, while he smooths out Davenant's verse for the choruses. The overall result is very much more varied, both musically and dramatically, than Davenant envisaged.

The text of *The Triumphs of the Prince d'Amour* concludes with an acknowledgement not just to William Lawes but to his brother Henry as well:

The Music of the songs and Symphonies were excellently composed by Mr HENRY, and Mr WILLIAM LAWES, His Majesty's servants.

The only vocal music for this masque by Henry Lawes now extant is Cupid's song, 'Whither so gladly and so fast'.[65] It is a beautifully judged setting—appropriate in its fluent lightness to the characterization of Cupid. It has Henry Lawes's characteristic virtues of clarity of form and a sensitivity to the rhythmic qualities of English as a language which, as Ian Spink has demonstrated, is without equal before Purcell.[66] It is, in fact, a modified strophic setting with each stanza occupying two musical sentences: the first (five bars long) cadences on the dominant while the second (six bars) returns to the tonic; the whole has an A–B–A¹–B structure. The third stanza of Davenant's

---

imitatively, with two voices preceding the other three. (Davenant's text has 'When you shall lead them by such harmony | As can direct their ears and feet'.)

[65] Included in the Henry Lawes autograph songbook GB-Lbl, Add. MS 53723, p. 78 and published in Playford's *Select Ayres and Dialogues* (1667).

[66] See Spink, *English Song, Dowland to Purcell*, 75–99.

Ex. 4.6. H. Lawes, 'Whither so gladly and so fast' (*The Triumphs of the Prince d'Amour*), from GB-Lbl, Add. MS 53723

text is omitted in the Lawes setting. This kind of strophic variation is typical of Lawes and shows his commitment to developing the appropriate declamatory features for each set of words (Ex. 4.6).

According to the text, Cupid's song was the only vocal solo in the masque; all the other sung sections were performed either by choruses (the Priests of Venus, Apollo, and Mars) or by solo voices alternating with choruses. There is no way of knowing how the lost vocal music was distributed between the composer brothers, but it would be reasonable to assume that Henry set some of the larger concerted numbers. How would he have approached this? Amongst Henry Lawes's extant vocal music, that which most resembles the task he must have faced in *The Triumphs of the Prince d'Amour* are his songs for Cartwright's *The Royal Slave*, the play about fidelity, loyalty, and the uses and abuses of power performed for Charles and Henrietta Maria just six months after the masque.[67] The first of the songs in that play has a structure which is similar to the second song in *The Triumphs of the Prince d'Amour* (sung by the Priests of Mars) with (apparently) solo quatrains separated by two-line choruses. *The Royal Slave* is set in Persia, where a chosen Ephesian captive is to be crowned king for three days before being sacrificed to the gods. 'The Priest's song whiles he puts on the Robes' has two stanzas of uneven length and a repeated chorus:

> Come from the Dungeon to the Throne
> To be a King, and streight be none.
> Reigne then a while, that thou mayst be
> Fitter to fall by Majesty
> *Cho.*   So Beasts for sacrifice we feed;
> First they are crown'd, and then they bleed.
>
> Wash with thy Bloud what wars have done
> Offensive to our God the Sun:
> That as thou fallest we may see
> Him pleas'd, and set as red as thee.
> Enjoy the Gloryes then of state,
> Whiles pleasures ripen thee for fate.
> *Cho.*   So Beasts: &c.   (I. ii. 168–78)

Lawes balances the poem by having the words of the chorus incorporated into the first stanza (making it six lines like the second) before they are repeated as a chorus in five parts. As might be expected, the solo sections are declamatory. The first stanza is set as a tenor solo, and the second a dialogue between soprano and bass, who join in a brief imitative duet for the final couplet. These sections illustrate well the way in which the preservation of spoken rhythmic patterns in the musical setting belongs with free solo declamation and not to a less flexible choral style. 'So beasts for sacrifice we feed' is given a much more straightforward rhythmic treatment in its five-part version even though the top line has essentially the same melody as that sung by the solo tenor (Ex. 4.7). The chorus itself is quite similar to, say, William Lawes's *Britannia Triumphans* ensembles; it makes some use of imitative entries, and its most adventurous harmonic feature is a false relation (appropriately in the phrase 'and then they bleed').

---

[67] See above, p. 161.

Ex. 4.7. H. Lawes, 'Come from the Dungeon to the Throne' (*The Royal Slave*), bars 12–25, from US-NYp, MS Drexel 4041

Ex. 4.8. Henry Lawes, 'Thou, O bright Sun, who seest all' (*The Royal Slave*), bars 45–9, from US-NYp, MS Drexel 4041

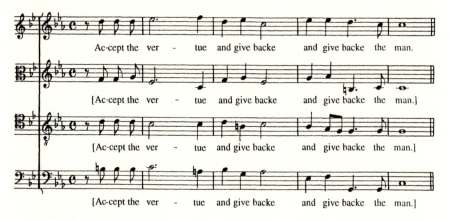

The other *Royal Slave* song which allows us to see how Henry Lawes must have approached the grander vocal sections of *The Triumphs of the Prince d'Amour* is the final song in the play, sung by priests as they prepare to sacrifice the virtuous Ephesian slave-king (a sacrifice prevented by an eclipse of the sun, a sign from the gods). This, also in C minor, is similar in style to 'Come from the Dungeon'. In the choral sections, Lawes shows a particular fondness, not just for false relations (of which there are several) but for augmented triads, particularly a first-inversion mediant triad with a sharpened leading-note (functioning either as a preliminary dominant chord in cadences or moving to the submediant (see Ex. 4.8)).

Putting the music for *The Royal Slave* alongside the William Lawes 'songs' in Mus. Sch. b. 2 suggests that, musically speaking, the Caroline masque was dominated by large-scale structures.

5

Music for the Eyes

Oh, to make Boardes to speake! There is a taske
Painting & Carpentry are yᵉ Soule of Masque.
Pack wᵗh your pedling Poetry to the Stage,
This is yᵉ money-gett, Mechanick Age!
To plant yᵉ Musick where noe eare can reach!
Attyre yᵉ persons as noe thought can teach
Sense, what they are! which by a specious fyne
Terme of yᵉ Architects is called Designe!
Ben Jonson, 'Expostulation with Inigo Jones' (ll. 49–56)

Jonson's 'Expostulation' marks the final parting of the ways in a partnership which—despite very evident difficulties—had given the Jacobean masque a consistency of structure and an artistic integrity which no other form of courtly entertainment in Europe could rival. The occasion of the quarrel was said to have been Jones's annoyance at having had his name placed alongside (rather than above) Jonson's on the title-page of *Love's Triumph through Callipolis*.[1] The battle between these two men was not simply a matter of either's feeling that their particular sphere should take precedence in the masque device. Jonson's attacks consistently claimed that Jones wanted all the arts—including music—subsumed under his control. As the 'Expostulation' has it 'but he now is come | To be yᵉ Musick Master! Fabler too! | He is, or would be yᵉ mayne Dominus doe | All in yᵉ Worke!' Whatever the cause of the argument, Jonson's friends felt he was unwise to rail against as influential a person at court as Inigo Jones. James Howell wrote 'you shall do well to represse any more copies of the Satyre, for to deale plainly with you, you have

---

[1] Letter from John Pory to Sir Thomas Puckering, 12 Jan. 1632: 'The last Sunday at night the Kinges masque was acted in the banquetting house, the Queens being suspended till another time, by reason of a sorenes which fell into one of her delicate eyes. The Inventor or Poet of this masque was Mr. Aurelian Townshend sometimes towards the lord Treasurer Salisbury, Ben Jonson being for this time discarded, by reason of the predominant power of his Antagonist, Innigo Jones, who this time tweluemoneth was angry with him for putting his owne name before his in the title-page, which Ben Jonson made the subject of a bitter Satyr or twoe agains Innigo.' GB-Lbl, MS Harl. 7000, fo. 318ᵛ; quoted in Bentley, *Jacobean and Caroline Stage*, v. 1228. It is interesting, in this context, to note the form of words which had been used on the title-page of *The Memorable Masque* in 1613: 'Inuented, and fashioned, with the ground, and speciall structure of the whole worke, By our Kingdomes most Artfull and Ingenious *Architect* INNIGO IONES. *Supplied, Aplied, Digested, and written, by* GEO: CHAPMAN.'

lost some ground at Court by it'.[2] That advice came too late (and was unheeded anyway).[3] Apart from *Chloridia*, which excludes both their names (but does have very full descriptions of the scenes), Jonson was never to write another full court masque. Within a year he was sending abject letters to the Earl of Newcastle from whom, in 1633–4, he was to receive his last commissions for masque-like entertainments.

We are left in no doubt that Jones was the major contributor in the invention of subsequent court masques. Aurelian Townshend began his text of *Albion's Triumph* with a statement that suggested an equal partnership ('Master *Inigo Jones* and I were employed in the Invention. And we agreed the subject of it should be a Triumphe in ALBIPOLIS the chiefe City of ALBION . . .'). At the end of the text he adds a further comment in which, despite his wittily modest stance, he did make some claim to 'invention' as well as 'writing':

Those that will prayse the structure and changes of the Scene, the sweetnesse and variety of the Musicke, or the Beauty of the Figures, and Paces, I thinke may doe it with cause enough.

But for the Invention and writing of the Maske, I was as loath to be brought upon the Stage as an unhansom Man is to see himselfe in a great Glasse. But my excuse, and Glory is, The King commanded, and I obeyed.   (p. 90)

A month later, with *Tempe Restored*, a pecking-order had been clearly established: 'All the Verses were written by M^r. *Aurelian Townesend*. The subject and Allegory of the Masque, with the descriptions, and Apparatus of the Sceanes, were invented by *Inigo Iones*, Surveyor of his Maiesties worke' (pp. 104–5). This formula for producing the text—Jones working out the basic device and writing up the description while someone else wrote the verses—became the norm for court masques in the 1630s. Thomas Carew does seem to have been solely responsible for the text of *Coelum Britannicum* (the most verbose of all masque texts), but Davenant, engaged for all the texts thereafter, never claimed credit for more than their poetic content. Davenant's name appears nowhere in the published texts of either the *Temple of Love* or *Luminalia*, and the opening of *Luminalia* makes it plain that Jones was the dominant intelligence:

The Kings Majesties Masque being performed, the Queene commanded *Inigo Iones* Surveyor of her Majesties works, to make a new subject of a Masque for her selfe, that with high and hearty invention, might give occasion for variety of Scenes, strange apparitions, Songs, Musick and dancing of several kinds: from whence doth result the true pleasure peculiar to our English Masques, which by strangers and travellers of judgement, are held to be as noble and ingenious, as those of any other nations . . .

---

[2] Quoted in H&S, xi. 152.

[3] Jonson's portrait of Vitruvius Hoop in *A Tale of a Tub* (1633) had to be struck out—apparently at Jones's insistence—before the play could be licensed. Jonson's revised version substituted another arrogant cooper-turned-masque-inventor called In-and-In Medlay, and Vitruvius resurfaced as the Surveyor-Supervisor-Overseer of a dance of mechanicals in *Love's Welcome at Bolsover*.

This little preface has a highly charged subtext. Even with his erstwhile rival six months in the grave, Jones still felt the need to assert an aggressively un-Jonsonian view of the masque's character and function. (And the comparison made with the entertainments of 'any other nations' makes it obvious—if it were not already—that the English masques of the 1630s were devised in a context of heightened awareness about court entertainments on the other side of the Channel.) The text of *Britannia Triumphans*, presented on Twelfth Night 1638, simply states that it was 'by Inigo Jones, Surveyor of his Majesty's workes, and William Davenant, her Majesty's servant'. The closing paragraph of *Salmacida Spolia* gives pre-eminence to Jones's work, though it mentions the poet and, more interestingly, contains an acknowledgement—unique in Caroline court masque texts—to the work of a composer: 'The invention, ornament, scenes, and apparitions, with their descriptions, were made by Inigo Jones, Surveyor General of his Majesty's Works. What was spoken or sung, by William Davenant, her Majesty's Servant. The subject was set down by them both. The music was composed by Lewis Richard, Master of her Majesty's Music' (ll. 473–80).[4]

Jones's control over the descriptions in the text results in his own achievements being recorded more and more emphatically. The final transformation in *Tempe Restored* 'was for the difficulty of the Ingining and number of the persons the greatest that hath beene seene here in our time' (p. 99). Of the central transformation in *Coelum Britannicum*, we learn that 'This strange spectacle gave great cause of admiration, but especially how so huge a machine, and of that great height could come from under the Stage, which was but six foot high' (ll. 968–71). *The Temple of Love* 'for the newness of the invention, variety of scenes, apparitions, and richness of habits was generally approved to be one of the most magnificent that hath been done in *England*' (p. 305). And the effects in *Salmacida Spolia* were 'generally approved of, especially by all strangers that were present, to be the noblest and most ingenuous [*sic* = ingenious] that hath been done here in that kind' (ll. 470–2).

For all that this is hyperbole, it does point to a growing complexity in what Jones set out to achieve with his scenes and machines—a development paralleled in the larger and larger sums set aside as seeding money for the Christmas and Shrovetide masques.[5] This has important musical ramifications, and not just because of the increased quantities of soap and loud music needed to cover the noise. Many transformations involved musicians performing as they travelled through the heavens. In the 'Expostulation' an exasperated Jonson had claimed that Inigo Jones wished 'To plant yᵉ Musick where noe eare can reach'. We can see what he meant—and that this tendency became more pronounced as time went on.

   [4] In the original text, each sentence here is set out as a separate paragraph. The text of *The Triumphs of the Prince d'Amour* acknowledges Henry and William Lawes—but that was a Middle Temple, not a court, masque, and—more importantly—it was designed by M. Corseilles and so lay outside Inigo Jones's control.

   [5] See Ashbee *RECM*, iii. 22 (£400 for 1627), 28 (£600 for 1628), 58 (two entries, £800 for 1631), 64 (£1,000 for 1632), 76 (£1,200 for 1634), 81, 93, and 96 (£1,400 for 1635 and 1638).

Numerous Jacobean masque texts claim rather vaguely that musicians 'descend', but descent normally implied only a movement from the stage area behind the proscenium arch down on to the dancing-area at floor level in front of the State. In *Time Vindicated* (1623) and *The Fortunate Isles* (1625) soloists were revealed in the heavens from where they sang (with a chorus beneath).[6] In *Love's Triumph through Callipolis*, '*Euclia*, or a faire Glory, appeares in the heauens, singing an applausiue song ... Which ended, the Scene changeth to a Garden, and the heauens opening, there appeare foure new persons, in forme of a *Constellation*, sitting, or a new *Asterisme*, expecting *Venus*, whom they call vpon with this song' (ll. 49–50 and 175–8). Zephyrus and Spring in *Chloridia* sing a dialogue from two clouds, while the chorus of Naiades wait below.

Soloists above/chorus below became a normal procedure in the Caroline masque. In *The Temple of Love* Divine Poesy descends on a cloud singing while the shades of the ancient Greek poets join her as a chorus from the stage area. In *Luminalia* Hesperus and Aurora sing a dialogue while moving through the air,[7] and in *Salmacida Spolia* Concord and the Good Genius of Great Britain sing a duet as their chariot descends from the heavens.

Luminalia contains Inigo Jones's most ambitious attempts at aerial music up to that time. At the end of the masque, 'a heaven full of Deities or second causes, with instruments and voices' is revealed. These join in song with the chorus of Apollo's priests ('Arch-Flamines and Flamines') at stage level. Then a final and even more spectacular transformation takes place. Zephyrs appear on a transparent cloud and perform an elaborate dance in the air:

the upper part of the heaven opened, and a bright and transparent cloud came forth farre into the Scene, upon which were many *Zephyri* and gentle breasts, with rich but light garments tuck'd about their waists, and falling downe about their knees, and on the heads girlands of flowers: These to the Violins began a sprightly dance, first with single passages, and then joyning hands in rounds several wayes. Which Apparition, for the newnesse of the Invention, greatnesse of the Machine, and difficulty of Enging-ing, was much admir'd, being a thing not before attempted in the Aire.   (p. 630)

From Jones's point of view, it was important that musicians be *seen*, that what might be called 'visual music' form part of these extraordinary tableaux. He was strongly attached to humanist theories which gave the visual arts the same philosophical basis that music had long enjoyed. The sense of identification between the arts of perspective and music is implicitly (and impressively) demonstrated by Salomon de Caus, architect to Prince Henry in the years when Jones held office as the Prince's 'surveyor'. De Caus published two very substantial treatises, the first in 1612 on perspective and the second in 1615 a massive work on speculative music—the *Institution Harmonique*.[8]

---

[6] There is some need for caution in generalizing about these tendencies since Jonson seems to have suppressed some of the detail of Jones's scenes in masque texts from about 1610 on.

[7] The text is slightly ambiguous: 'The Song ended, the morning Starre descends singing, and *Aurora* passeth through the Aire' (l. 625).

[8] *La Perspective, avec la Raison des Ombres et Miroirs . . . a Londres, 1612* (but printed in Frankfurt);

The classical division of knowledge into the seven liberal arts made no specific provision for painting, sculpture, or architecture. Renaissance artists exhibited a strong desire to find a place for their activities amongst the quadrivium—arithmetic, geometry, astronomy, and music. Music was, of course, included there because it was seen as being founded on number. Painters and architects (understandably) felt that they had an equal claim to the dignity of a place in this grouping and argued that perspective, dependent as it is on number and proportion, was a species of music. John Onians—in an article illuminatingly entitled 'On How to Listen to High Renaissance Art'— cites Luca Pacioli (a friend of Leonardo), who rather spitefully suggested that if perspective could not be admitted to the quadrivium, then music should be dropped from it:

If they say that music satisfies the hearing which is a natural sense, so does perspective the sense of sight which is more noble being the first gate of the intellect. If they say that music employs heard number and measure as expressed in the time of its continuances, so too does perspective use natural number according to any definition and measure as represented by the line of sight. If music recreates the soul by its harmony so too does perspective delight it by the measurement of distance and the narration of colour. If the one art exploits harmonic proportions, the other exploits arithmetic and geometrical ones.[9]

It seems that occasionally perspective may actually have displaced music in the enumeration of the liberal arts. A set of late sixteenth-century embroidered panels at Hardwick Hall provides a striking example of rearrangement in favour of the visual arts. The series has the trivium (grammar, rhetoric, and logic) intact, but represents the quadrivium by astrology (not yet distinguished from astronomy), arithmetic, architecture (possibly as a replacement for geometry), and perspective; this last surely occupies the place traditionally reserved for music.

Architects showed a special interest in this kind of thinking—and Jones was no exception. His allegiance to the argument which identified music and perspective and/or architecture is fascinatingly revealed by what survives from his library. Nearly fifty books have been identified as having once belonged to Jones, and in twenty-seven of these Jones has underlined key words and phrases and added his own marginal glosses.[10] Nearly all the books are Italian

Institution Harmonique Divisée en deux Parties (Frankfurt, 1615). By 1615 De Caus was in Heidelberg, but he nevertheless dedicated his music treatise to 'Anne, Royne de la Grande Bretaigne'.

[9] J. Onians, 'On How to Listen to High Renaissance Art', *Art History*, 7 (1984), 413.

[10] Jones's copy of Barbaro's translation of Vitruvius belongs to the Duke of Devonshire and his copy of Serlio's *Tutte l'opere di Architettura et prospetiva* is at Queen's College, Oxford; most of his other books are at Worcester College, Oxford. Forty-seven are listed in J. Harris, S. Orgel, and R. Strong, *The King's Arcadia: Inigo Jones and the Stuart Court* (London, 1973), 217–18. Dr Christy Anderson informs me that it is likely that other books still in the main collection at Worcester College also belonged to Jones. See also A. C. Fusco, *Inigo Jones, Vitruvius Britannicus: Jones e Palladio nella cultura architettonica inglese* (Rimini, 1985), 158. In writing this section I have profited from the helpful discussions of these annotations in R. M. Smuts, *Court Culture and the Origins of a Royalist Tradition in Early Stuart England* (Philadelphia, 1987), 164 ff.;

(often Italian translations of classical Greek or Latin works) and Jones's notes are predominantly summary translations (though, in his copy of Barbaro's Vitruvius, for example, they are often reactions to what he has read). What these show is that the spectacular visual presentation of musical harmony within the devices of Caroline court masques was underpinned by a consistent humanist theory, one which brought with it a sense of moral purpose.

Jones's copy of Vitruvius, translated with a commentary by Daniel Barbaro, is heavily annotated. Right at the beginning, where architecture's relationship to the liberal arts is considered, Jones has glossed Barbaro's summary with 'of the 7 liberall artes 3 ar concerning speech and 4 *about quantities*' (my italics). He then marks a 'Diffinition of Architecture' which emphasizes its multidisciplinary character: 'Architettura è scienza, di molte discipline, & di diversi ammaestramenti ornata, dal cui guidicio s'approvano tutte le opere, che dalle altre Arti compiutamente si fanno.'[11] Jones owned (and wrote a few marginal notes in) Vincenzo Scamozzi's *L'Idea della architettura universale* (Venice, 1615). This, like Vitruvius, begins by systematically considering the relevance of the various constituent arts of the quadrivium to architecture. Last comes music:

Finalmente, Musica Theoricale considera l'ordine, e la concordanza, & armonia de moti delle Sfere celestie, e quelle de puri elementi; mà la naturale consiste nell'intelletto, e nella ragione de componimenti, e nel senso dell'audito per via delle voci humane, e per mezo dell'artificio proportiona i suoni di varij stromenti . . .[12]

This, of course, makes the familiar distinction between speculative and practical music, something which is paralleled in architectural theory.

This division is part of a general Aristotelian categorization which Jones himself neatly summarized in the margin of another of his books: 'the rational power divided into two parts . . . Speculative and practick/The first stays in the truth found, the second accomodates the truth to human operations'.[13] Jones's most public (and elaborate) exposition of this idea was on the proscenium arch for *Albion's Triumph*:

on each side, stood two Women, the one young, in a watchet Robe looking upwards, and on her head, a paire of Compasses of gold, the poynts standing towards Heaven:

D. J. Gordon, 'Poet and Architect: The Intellectual Setting of the Quarrel between Ben Jonson and Inigo Jones', in id., *The Renaissance Imagination*, ed. S. Orgel (Berkeley, 1975), 77–101; and Per Palme, *The Triumph of Peace: A Study of the Whitehall Banqueting House* (London, 1957). See also Parry, *The Golden Age Restor'd*, 111–12.

[11] *I dieci libri dell'architettura di M. Vitruvio tradotti & commentati da Mons. Daniel Barbaro* (Venice, 1568), 5. 'Architecture is a science involving many disciplines, and graced by diverse kinds of learning by whose judgement all works produced entirely by the other arts are approved.'

[12] 'Finally, music theory considers the order, and the consonance, and harmony of the movements of the heavenly spheres, and those of the pure elements; but natural [music] consists in the intellect, and in the rationale [reasoned ordering] of parts, and in the sense of hearing through human voices, and by means of art proportions the sounds of various instruments' (I. 3).

[13] Marginal note in Jones's copy of Alessandro Piccolomini's *Della institution morale* (Venice, 1575); quoted by Smuts, *Court Culture*, 165.

the other more ancient, and of a venerable aspect, apparreled in tawney, looking downewards; in the one hand a long ruler, and in the other, a great paire of iron Compasses, one poynt whereof stood on the ground, and the other touched part of the ruler. Above their heads, were fixt compertiments of a new composition, and in that over the first, was written *Theorica*, and over the second *Practica*, shewing that by these two, all works of Architecture, and Ingining have their perfection . . .   (p. 75)

His notes on Vitruvius show that he recognized that this division was paralleled in music. Jones marks relevant sections 'Musike practick' and 'Mathematicall musike whatt'.[14] He heavily annotated the chapter entitled 'Dell'Armonia' which discusses Boethius' divisions and provides mathematical ratios and musical notation for various types of consonance—Jones showing particular interest in the idea that music, combined with poetry, had a special capacity to influence human behaviour: 'Musik into too Partes / theoryke / Practike wch helps maners by Poetry'.[15]

Jones's pupil John Webb described him as 'the *Vitruvius* of our age'.[16] The title pays tribute to his role in introducing to England the symmetry and proportion of classical architecture, the principles of which were expounded by Vitruvius in the first century and interpreted for sixteenth-century Europe by Andrea Palladio. As Graham Parry puts it, Palladian architecture

emphasised the supreme importance of symmetry and the harmony of proportions, proportions that were related on the one hand to the ideal dimensions of the human figure, and on the other to the fundamental mathematical ratios established both by the division of the musical scale and by the spacing of the planets, so that a Palladian building represented a statement in stone of basic cosmic harmonies related to the human frame . . . and serving a social function.[17]

The points of contact between this précis and my own summary of the main tenets of *musica speculativa* must be obvious. The mathematical ratios involved in the most satisfying architectural forms and in musical consonance were, it was stressed, the same.[18]

Given this background, it should hardly come as a surprise that Jones was alert to any discussion of music in what he read. One example will suffice to illustrate this. In the essay on moral virtue in the *Moralia* Plutarch argues that, just as musical perfection does not involve eliminating high and low, but of accommodating and controlling these, and medicine restores people to health not by extinguishing heat and cold but by tempering them, moderation is achieved by subjecting the affections to reason. Jones left this chapter unmarked until he reached the words 'Ma come la Musica . . .'; he underlined

[14] *I dieci libri dell'architettura di M. Vitruvio*, 19.

[15] Ibid. 227. Not surprisingly, Jones showed a similar interest in Barbaro's 'Comparison between the orator & the Architect' (36).

[16] *A Vindication of Stone-Heng Restored* (London, 1665), quoted by J. Summerson, *Inigo Jones* (Harmondsworth, 1989), 18.

[17] Parry, *Golden Age*, 111.

[18] Fusco, *Inigo Jones*, ch. 16, offers a detailed examination of the relationships between Palladian proportions and interval ratios, etc.

these, drew a pointer to them in the margin and added the comment 'exelent simile of musick and fisick'.[19] This seems characteristic—almost as if he had scanned some of these works for topics he regarded as relevant—and in this respect music seems to be on an equal footing with perspective and architecture. The essay on music in the *Moralia* is, in fact, more heavily annotated than any other. The paragraphs describing music's kinship with arithmetic and geometry are heavily underscored and Jones adds his own summary in the margin. Many other marginal annotations in this chapter might serve equally well as glosses on his Caroline masque devices. 'Harmony a heavenly thinge' (glossing 'l'harmonia è cosa celeste, & la natura di lei divina, bella, & maravigliosa . . .')[20] is an idea implicit in all his revelations of musicians in the heavens. Other marginalia (such as 'discord and disproportion all on[e]'[21]) seem directly relevant to antimasque concepts. In *Britannia Triumphans*, for example, the main set of antimasque dances begin in this way:

The whole Scene was transformed into a horrid Hell, the further part terminating in a flaming precipice, and the neerer parts expressing the Suburbs, from whence enter the several Anti-masques.

> 1. Entrie.
> Of mock musick of 5. persons.
> One with a Violl, the rest with
> Taber and Pipe,
> Knackers and bells,
> Tongs and key,
> Gridiron and shooing horne . . . (p. 194)

The conjunction of visual and musical discord here is particularly striking. (Jones's designs for this entry are shown in Pl. 4.)

There are places where Jones's interests and Jonson's coincide—even in the latter's last two masques. Jones marked and glossed the passage from the *Moralia* where Plutarch talks of the senses having a divine quality and being introduced to the body through harmony.[22] A similar idea informs Euphemus's opening song in *Callipolis* in its celebration of beauty and civil concord through a rich confusion of love, music, and the senses:

> Joy, ioy to mortals, the reioycing fires
> Of gladnes, smile in your dilated hearts!

---

[19] Plutarch, *Opuscoli morali, di Plutarco Cheronese*, translated by Gandino (Venice, 1614), 92.

[20] Ibid. 229.   [21] Ibid. 334.

[22] The relevant passage (on 230) reads (with Jones's underlining) 'Hor i sensi, li quali sono stati introdotti ne' corpi per harmonia, come celesti, & divini, con l'aiuto di Dio somministrando a gli huomini il senso . . .'; Jones glosses this 'senses brought in & to the gods in harmony'. The Loeb translation of the Plutarch original reads, 'Again, of the senses which are engendered in our bodies because of harmony those that are celestial, sight and hearing, being divine and having God as helper in providing men with sensation, reveal this harmony to the accompaniment of sound and light; and other senses too that come in their train are by virtue of being senses composed in conformity with a harmony, and while inferior to the first are not severed from them . . .'; *Plutarch's Moralia*, xiv, trans. B. Einarson and P. H. De Lacy (London, 1967), 411, § 25.

> Whilst Loue presents a world of chast desires,
>   Which may produce a harmony of parts! . . .
> Then will he flow forth, like a rich perfume
>   Into your nostrils! or some sweeter sound
> Of melting musique, that shall not consume
>   Within the eare, but run the mazes round.   (ll. 50–4, 78–81)[23]

Underscorings and summary translations elsewhere in the *Moralia* have some relevance to the various antimasque dances of Circe's victims in *Coelum Britannicum*. In the section headed 'Delle Questioni Convivali Libro VII' Jones notes the 'strange affect of lascivious musick', that 'musick hath more force to mak drunk then wyne', and that 'musick swetens ye bestiall part of ye soule' (and here Jones has another pointer to the Italian text).[24] Perhaps the most obvious dramatization of these concepts in *Coelum Britannicum* comes when Hedone presents a dance of five senses:

> Come forth my subtle Organs of delight,
> With changing figures please the curious eye,
> And charme the eare with moving Harmonie.   (ll. 805–7)

Immediately after the dance of the five Senses, Mercury attacks Hedone:

> Bewitching Syren, guilded rottennesse,
> Thou hast with cunning artifice display'd
> Th'enamel'd outside, and the honied verge
> Of the faire cup, where deadly poyson lurkes.   (ll. 809–12)

But the most interesting links between Jones's interests and musical representations in Caroline masques come through the way musical and architectural theory were seen to intersect. Architects were, in fact, especially committed to the identification of their science with music. Architecture, they emphasized, was visual music. Palladio stated in a memorandum written in 1567 about the design for the Cathedral of Brescia that 'The proportions of the voices are harmonies for the ears; those of the measurements are harmonies for the eyes. Such harmonies usually please very much, without anyone knowing why, except the student of the causality of things.'[25] Jones took a particular interest in an equivalent passage in Alberti's *L'Architettura*, underscoring the beginnings of two crucial sentences:

Quei medesimi numeri certo, per i quali auiene che il concento delle voci appare gratissimo ne gli orecchi degli huomoni, sono quegli stessi che empiono anco, & gli

---

[23] The most extraordinary aspect of this song is that it comes quite close to a positive expression of ideas which Jonson had earlier been prepared to ridicule in his caricature of Jones as the Cook in *Neptune's Triumph*: 'there is a palate of the Vnderstanding, as well as of the Senses. The Taste is taken with good relishes, the Sight with faire obiects, the Hearing with delicate sounds, the Smelling with pure sents, the Feeling with soft and plump bodies, but the Vnderstanding with all these: for all which you must begin at the Kitchin. There, the *Art of Poetry* was learnd, and found out, or no where . . .' (ll. 65–72).

[24] Plutarch, *Opuscoli morali*, glosses on 449, 458.

[25] Quoted by R. Wittkower, *Architectural Principles in the Age of Humanism* (London, 1952), 99–100.

occhi, & lo animo di piacere marauiglioso. <u>Caueremo adunque</u> tutta la regola del
finimento da Musici, a chi sono perfettissimamente noti questi tali numeri; & da
quelle cose oltra di questo, dallequali la natura dimostri di se alcuna cosa degna, &
honorata: ma non andrò dietro a quelle cose se non quanto farà di bisogno al
proposito dello Architettore . . .[26]

Alongside the first of the underlined words Jones wrote a succinct summary
of Alberti's point: 'the same numbers that pleas the eare please the eie'. And
against the next, 'Rule of the finimento [proportions] taken from musitians &
from the most worthy thinges of nature'.[27] Not surprisingly, the same ideas are
highlighted in his copy of Barbaro's Vitruvius with notes like 'in musike
equalliti of formes of the eare equalitie of spaces'. He marks approvingly
Barbaro's commentary on the usefulness of both speculative and practical
music to architects and his comparison of canon and perspective as an instance
of the parallels between the two arts.[28]

Jonson lampooned Jones's interests in *Love's Welcome at Bolsover*. There,
Vitruvius—a caricature of Jones—encourages the Mechanics (who are about
to dance to the music of a beaten anvil) with a clumsy rendition of the ideas
which so preoccupied Inigo Jones in his reading of architectural theory.
Jonson wished his audience to see it all as pedantic humbug:

Time, and *Measure*, are the Father, and Mother of Musique, you know, and your
Coronell *Vitruvius* knowes a little. . . . *Measure* is the Soule of a Dance, and *Tune* the
Tickle-foot thereof. Use Holy-day legges, and have 'hem: Spring, Leape, Caper, and
Gingle . . . Well done, my Musicall, Arithmeticall, Geometricall Gamesters! or rather
my true Mathematicall Boyes! It is carried, in number, weight, and measure, as if the
Aires were all Harmonie, and the Figures a well-tim'd Proportion.   (ll. 54–70)[29]

The idea that beauty is harmony made visible is everywhere implicit in Inigo
Jones's devices for masques of the Caroline period. Visual musical images
occupy a central place in virtually every main-masque transformation. For a
period in the mid-1630s the identification of pleasing symmetry with music is
made explicit. We have already seen that in *Coelum Britannicum* one of the
antimasque dances is presented as visual music—though without being able to
see the choreography, we can never know how the distinction between

[26] L. B. Alberti, *L'architettura de Leon Batista Alberti*, trans. C. Bartoli (Monte Regale, 1565), 259. The
finimento is described (258) as follows: 'Il finimento appresso di noi è una certa correspondentia di linee infra
di loro, con lequali son misurata la quantità, che una è la lunghezza, l'altra la larghezza, & l'altra la altezza.'
[27] See also Palme, *The Triumph of Peace*, 93.
[28] 'Dimostra Vitr. che & quanto alla pratica, & quanto alla ragione la Musica è utile allo Architetto . . . <u>La
Canonica</u> appartiene alle orecchie, come la prospettiva a gli occhi . . .' (Jones's underlining): *I dieci libri
dell'architettura di M. Vitruvio*, 19.
[29] Jonson's patron on this occasion seems to have wholeheartedly shared his views. The Earl of
Newcastle wrote a Christmas entertainment with an antimasque of tradesmen. When one asks 'What doe
you thinke of An Apolo or ann orfius singinge' a Welsh vicar replies 'What does I thinke marie I thinke
ther wantes Cloudes for himm to Coume doune In, Ande besides we wante the discretion off summ Justice
off Peace to make the Seanes therfore I utterlye deslike thatt.' Lynn Hulse, who is editing this text for *ELR*,
has kindly sent me this excerpt (from GB-NO, PwV26, fo. 147). Jones had been appointed a Justice of the
Peace for Westminster in 1630.

Hedone's self-indulgence and the chaste pleasures of the main masque was externalized in physical movement. The songs of the main masque direct the audience's attention away from the music heard towards a supposedly more eloquent harmony—visual music. Here the image is of a terrestrial reflection of the ultimate harmony:

> [3rd Kingdom] Here the Ayre and paces meet
> So just, as if the skilfull feet
> Had strucke the Vials. [All three] So the Eare
> Might the tuneful footing heare.
> CHORVS
> And had the Musicke silent beene,
> The eye a moving tune had seene.   (ll. 974–9)

A number of masque songs even assert the superiority of this visual music over what was heard. In *Tempe Restored* Harmony and her Choir first warn (in song) that their music is about to be surpassed:

> . . . there are Stars to rise,
> That farre aboue our song
> Are Musicke to all eyes.   (p. 98)[30]

What happens next is a transformation scene in which musicians appear as the ultimate heavenly music:

In the midst of the ayre the eight *Spheares* in rich habites were seated on a Cloud, which in a circular forme was on each side continued unto the highest part of the Heaven, and seem'd to have let them downe as in a Chaine.

To the Musicke of these Spheares there appear'd two other Clouds descending, & in them were discovered eight Stars. These being come to the middle Region of the skie, another greater Cloud came downe above them, which by little and little descending discovered other glistering Stars to the number of sixe. And above all, in a Chariot of goldsmithes workes richly adorned with precious Jemmes, sat divine *Beauty*, over whose head appear'd a brightnesse full of small starres that inviron'd the top of the Chariot, striking a light round about it.   (p. 99)

Divine Beauty and the fourteen stars were, of course, the queen and her masquers. The Highest Sphere ('represented by Mr *Laneere*') sings that 'When Divine Beautie will vouchsafe to stoope | And move to Earth, 'tis fit the Heavenly Spheres | Should be her Musicke . . .' (p. 100). An annotation on Jones's copy of Plato's *Republic* would serve equally well as a gloss on this part of the masque: 'The end of music [is] love of the beautiful.'[31]

---

[30] It is interesting to see these images (like so many others which originated in quite seriously considered medieval and Renaissance theory) reduced to the level of facile compliment in Edward Phillips's commendatory poem published with Henry Lawes's *Ayres and Dialogues* (1653): 'brightest *Dames*, the splendour of the Court, | Themselves a silent *Musick* to the Eye, | Would oft to hear thy solemn *Ayres* resort, | Making thereby a double Harmony: | 'Tis hard to judge which adds the most delight, | To th' Eare thy Charms, or theirs unto the Sight.'

[31] Quoted by Smuts, *Court Culture*, 167.

So the audience heard and saw the music of the spheres as attendants of Divine Beauty. Jones and Townshend place rather too much strain on their own device since they inevitably distort humanist theory in giving material form to something whose perfection resides in its intangibility. In a song performed by the Highest Sphere and a chorus, the performing musicians are made the authors of their own humiliation when they sing,

> The Musick that yee heare is dull,
> But that ye see is sweete indeed,
> In euery Part exact, and full,
> From whence there doth an Ayre proceed,
> On which th'Intelligences feed,
> Where faire and good, inseparably conjoyned
> Create a *Cupid*, that is never blind.   (p. 100)

Jones seems to have been undaunted by the difficulties of giving material form to phenomena normally regarded as lying beyond the limits of human perception. Shirley's text for *The Triumph of Peace* draws on *musica mundana* in a way which would be quite characteristic of the Jacobean masque. When the music accompanying the first transformation scene is heard, Opinion exclaims (before he and the other antimasque presenters 'go off fearfully') 'What new change | Is this? These strains are heavenly' (ll. 481–2). By having Opinion claim that the music of the main masque had an unearthly quality Shirley interprets the music for his audience: it manifestly comes closer to ultimate harmonic perfection than anything heard so far in this masque. Inigo Jones took this a step further, however, by depicting five musicians as Constellations. Heavenly music is given a literal representation.

Jones again represented the harmony of the spheres in the last court masque, *Salmacida Spolia*:

From the highest part of the Heavens came forth a cloud far in the Sceane, in which were eight persons richly attired representing the Spheares; this, joyning with two other clouds which appeared at that instant full of Musicke, covered all the upper part of the Sceane; and at that instant beyond all these, a Heaven opened full of Deities; which celestial Prospect, with the Chorus below filled all the whole Sceane with apparitions and harmony.   (ll. 442–8)

The visual spectacle must have seemed little short of miraculous (and Pl. 14 gives us some sense of this), but it is hard to imagine how Louis Richard could possibly have fulfilled the assignment implied by the device:

> So musicall as to all Eares
> Doth seeme the musick of the Sphears,
> Are you; unto each other still,
> Tuning your thoughts to eithers will.
>
> All that are harsh, all that are rude,
> Are by your harmony subdu'd;

Yet so, into obedience wrought,
As if not forc'd to it, but taught.   (ll. 451–8)

No actual musical setting, however wonderful, could realize the harmony of the spheres. By definition, *musica instrumentalis* was but an imperfect reflection of its ultimate paradigm. The whole endeavour demonstrates that for all his interest in *musica speculativa* Jones was thinking as an architect. His heavens full of musicians look beautiful but are they are not beauty; they represent beauty through the statement that musical harmony is founded on the same mathematical proportions that are the basis of visual satisfaction. What Jones is really doing is using a visual representation of music as a metaphor for an ultimate beauty which cannot be represented directly. It thus becomes an element in an allegorical tableau.

The aural representation of *musica mundana* was not without precedent. The harmony of the spheres had been represented in the 1607 *Entertainment at Ashby* (see below, p. 285). More importantly, the first of the 1589 Florentine *intermedi* had a double chorus representing 'le celeste sfere', who sang to music by Chritofano Malvezzi.[32] Jones not only knew these *intermedi* but wished to emulate them. The same complex of ideas, needless to say, exerted their influence on the *ballet de cour* in France. Guillaume Collete wrote in his preface to *Le Ballet de L'Harmonie* (performed in Paris late in 1632): 'La danse n'est autre chose qu'une Musique pour les yeux, comme les voix Harmoniques en sont une pour les oreilles, et tous les deux ensemble une Harmonie pour l'une et pour l'autre. La preuve en est evidente dans les effets de la Nature . . .'.[33]

Postscript

Inigo Jones's fascination with foreign entertainments seems to have been something else which irritated Jonson. In the antimasque of *Neptune's Triumph*, the Cook (Inigo Jones) tells the poet ('one that is vsed at least once a yeare, for a trifling instrument, of wit or so') that he should be following fashion: 'you, are to know the palate of the times: study the seuerall tasts, what euery Nation, the *Spaniard*, the *Dutch*, the *French*, the *Walloun*, the *Neapolitan*, the *Britan*, the *Sicilian*, can expect from you' (ll. 49–52). It is interesting to note in passing that Jones and his literary collaborators were only too happy to imply that the masque really was the English equivalent of Italian courtly spectacles. The text of *Tempe Restored* draws to a close with the words 'and so concluded the last *Intermedium* . . .' (p. 103), while that of *Britannia Triumphans* is introduced with the statement that for the past three years 'the King and

---

[32] See Walker (ed.), *Musique des intermèdes*, 9.

[33] P. Lacroix (ed.), *Ballets et mascarades de cour de Henri III à Louis XIV*, 6 vols. (Geneva and Turin, 1868–70; repr. 1968), iv. 208. 'Dance is nothing other than music for the eyes, as voices in harmony are music for the ears, and both together make a harmony with each other. The proof of this is clear in the effects of Nature.'

Queen's Majesties have not made Masques with shewes and intermedii' (p. 187).

Jones's interest in things French undoubtedly helped win him favour with Henrietta Maria. He was, in any case, quickly drawn into her own architectural aspirations. In 1626, he remodelled part of Somerset House for her (collaborating with French designers). Commissions for larger projects followed, notably the completion of the Queen's House at Greenwich and the construction of Henrietta Maria's chapel at Somerset House.

Jonson was not, it seems, in nearly so good a position to be patronized by the Queen. His interest in French language and culture seems not to have been strong. Although his poem commending *French Court Ayres* (1629) proposes that Filmer's union of French music and English poetry 'Recelebrates the ioyfull Match with *France*', his epigram for Joshua Sylvester on his translation of Du Bartas confesses to an inability to assess Sylvester's work:

> . . . But, as it is (the Child of Ignorance,
>   And vtter stranger to all ayre of *France*)
> How can I speake of thy great paines, but erre?
>   Since they can only iudge, that can conferre. . . .[34]

Jonson did visit France in 1612 as tutor to the young Walter Raleigh. But apart from his being present at a discussion about the doctrine of the Real Presence, all that is known of his activities there is rather unedifying—his young charge had him carried on a cart through the streets of Paris in a drunkenly comatose state.[35] Another of his Epigrams ridicules Englishmen who affect French manners:

> Would you beleeue, when you this M O V N S I E V R see,
>   That his whole body should speake *french*, not he? . . .
> That he, vntrauell'd, should be *french* so much,
>   As *french*-men in his companie, should seeme *dutch*?
> Or had his father, when he did him get,
>   The *french* disease, with which he labours yet?
> Or hung some M O V N S I E V R s picture on the wall,
>   By which his damme conceiu'd him, clothes and all? . . .[36]

Jonson's lack of enthusiasm for French fashions and his limited grasp of the language may have had nothing to do with his neglect as a masque writer in the 1630s, but it cannot have helped commend him to the queen.

The contrast with the others commissioned for court masques is striking.[37] Aurelian Townshend spoke very good French. He spent the years 1600 to

---

[34] *Epigram 132: To M*ʳ *Iosuah Sylvester*, H&S, viii. 83.

[35] See the 'Conversations with William Drummond of Hawthornden', H&S, i. 140.

[36] *Epigram 88: On English Mounsieur*, H&S, viii. 56.

[37] In 1630 Jonson wrote a number of complimentary epigrams addressed to Henrietta Maria, but these may be regarded almost as an official duty. Since 1616 Jonson had received a salary from the crown of 100 marks; this made him the first 'Poet Laureate' (although that term was not used until later). Charles I increased Jonson's salary to £100 in 1630 (in response to a request—framed as a poem—from Jonson).

1603 in Paris, sent there by Sir Robert Cecil as preparation for acting as tutor to his son. When Sir Edward Herbert (later Lord Herbert of Cherbury) went abroad in 1608–9, he took Townshend as a companion, 'a Gentleman, that spake the Languages of Frensh Italian and Spanish, in greate Perfection . . .'.[38] It seems likely that his expertise in this area, accompanied presumably by a knowledge of French tastes, led to his being commissioned to work with Inigo Jones on the two masques of the 1632 season. It has long been recognized that the treatment of the Circe myth in *Tempe Restored* has features—like the opening with its fugitive favourite—which must derive from the 1581 *Balet comique de la royne*.[39] The antimasque(s) of *Tempe Restored*, while not taken from the *Balet comique*, clearly derive from French models (see below, p. 235).

Thomas Carew, the author of *Coelum Britannicum*, is the archetypal cavalier poet. From 1612 on he spent some time in Venice where his relative Dudley Carleton was ambassador (though by the end of 1615 he was back in England—sent home, it seems, under a cloud). Like Townshend, Carew must have been well versed in French language and taste. When Herbert was appointed ambassador to France (a post he held from 1619 to 1624)[40] he took Carew with him. Presumably he must have been party to some of the diversions that Herbert describes in his *Life*: 'I had spare tyme not onely for my Booke but for Visits to divers Grandees . . . when fowle weather was they spent theire tyme in Uisits at each others houses where they interchanged civill Discourses or heard Musick or fell a dancing vsing according to the manner of that Countrey all the reasonable Libertyes they could with theire Honor . . .'.[41] That Davenant's aspirations at least ran along the same lines as his gentlemanly and Francophile colleagues is evident in his adoption of the spelling 'D'Avenant' on his title-pages (a piece of pretentiousness greatly enjoyed by his critics).[42]

Henrietta Maria's own chauvinistic preferences in drama have been well documented. Her ideas about music ran along similar lines—as the number of French musicians in her household illustrates. Bulstrode Whitelocke reported proudly that when he showed the queen his coranto (composed with help from Simon Ives) she praisèd it by expressing disbelief that it could possibly have been written by an Englishman 'bicause she said it was fuller of life and spirit than the English aiers use to be'.[43] It can hardly be surprising that French influence in some areas of the arts became pervasive.

[38] Herbert, *Life*, 41.   [39] See Welsford, *The Court Masque*, 225.

[40] He was displaced in the post when the Earl of Carlisle—formerly Lord Hay—and Viscount Kensington were sent to negotiate the marriage with Henrietta Maria.

[41] Herbert, *Life*, 102.

[42] His background was far from aristocratic: his father was a prosperous and respected Oxford innkeeper who died while holding office as mayor.

[43] Whitelocke, 'Annales', GB-Lbl, Add. MS 53726, fo. 96ʳ.

6

French Influence in the Caroline Masque

French Dancing-Masters

Madam, I did not think your ladyship
Had so little judgment . . .
As to let an Englishman draw your picture,
And such rare monsieurs in town . . .
You must encourage strangers, while you live;
It is the character of our nation, we are famous
For dejecting our own countrymen . . .
Trust, while you live, the Frenchman with your legs,
Your faces with the Dutch . . .

James Shirley, The Ball, III. iii. 33–45

Shirley's play was licensed for performance at the end of 1632 (the year in which the most sought-after Dutch portraitist, Van Dyck, took up residence in England). *The Ball*'s satire on the court and its prevailing fashions proved almost too close for comfort; Lord Herbert, the Master of the Revels, considered having the play banned because 'there were divers personated so naturally, both of lords and others of the court, that I took it ill'.[1] The word 'ball' is itself a French borrowing.[2] As its use in the title of Shirley's play might lead us to expect, learning dancing from Frenchmen is singled out for particular scorn as a fashionable affectation. Shirley's Monsieur le Frisk is a caricature who could have been based on any number of French dancing-masters in London in the 1630s. He implies that he is essentially a dance specialist (while other Frenchmen excel at violin-playing): 'My broder, my lord, know well for de litle kit—he fiddle—and me for de posture of de body.

---

[1] 18 Nov. [1632]. See Bentley, *The Jacobean and Caroline Stage*, v. 1077.

[2] Randle Cotgrave's *Dictionarie of the French and English Tongues* (London, 1611) gives a definition of 'bal' as 'a daunce; a dauncing; Reuels, or, a Reuelling'. The *OED* gives Shirley's title as the earliest English use of the word to mean 'a social assembly for dancing'. However, on 13 Jan. 1621 John Chamberlain used the word in a letter to Dudley Carleton describing the entertainment provided for the French envoy, the Marquis of Cadenet: 'That night they had a bal at Whitehall . . .': *The Letters of John Chamberlain*, ed. N. E. McClure (Philadelphia, 1939), i. 333. The court presumably thought of this as an appropriate way to honour distinguished *French* visitors. (Chamberlain's letter goes on to describe a Twelfth Night masque for which no text survives.)

Begar, de king has no two such subjects . . .' (III. ii. 55–7). (Elsewhere in the play, however, references are made to le Frisk playing the violin.)

Shirley was not alone in ridiculing the activities of French dancing-masters. Jonson's patron, William Cavendish, First Earl of Newcastle, was uneasy about what seemed to be an obsession with French fashion at the English court. Two of his plays, *The Country Captain* and *The Variety*, satirize French fashion at court, the first through the figure of Monsieur Device and the second through Galliard, another French dancing-master.[3] Galliard is particularly interesting for our purposes since he is preoccupied with preparing a masque. When asked about the preparation of the text he dismisses this as something of minimal importance: 'Aw, de write? dat is noting alamode, your speesh two, tre, yard long, pfaw? give a me de quick a spirit, de fancie, de brave scene, de varietie of de Antimasque, de nimble a foot, no matre de sense, begar it vole be de brave ting . . .'. He gives an interesting twist to the idea that the masque is a force for peace in the kingdom: 'dey are so bissey to learne a de dance, dey vil never tinke of de Rebellion, and den de reverence is obedience to Monarchy . . .'. Dancing *branles* to the music of a French kit (an instrument 'that looks like a broken fagot stick . . . and sounds as if it had got the French disease'), cutting capers, and walking splay-footed is contrasted with the traditional English values professed by the pointedly named Manly— a character who is said to resemble 'famous *Cardell* the dancing Master in Queen *Elizabeth's* time' (III. ii).[4]

By the later Caroline period, the mention of an *English* dancing-master like Thomas Cardell might indeed have aroused a sense of nostalgia. French dancing-masters became dominant quite early in the seventeenth century. Even Prince Henry's first dancing-master, Nicolas Villiard, was French (although, when he died in 1605, he was replaced by the Englishman Thomas Giles).[5] Jacques Cordier ('Bochan'), who was celebrated as both violinist and dancing-master in his native France, enjoyed favoured status in England. He was a member of Prince Henry's household by mid-1608 and a year later was given an annuity by the king of £60 (twice the salary paid to regular members of the court violin band).[6] Bochan was involved with the dances for *Love Freed* and *The Lords' Masque* (see above, pp. 36 and 39), and in the early years of

---

[3] These plays were separately printed but issued with a common title-page: *The Country Captaine, and the Varietie, Two Comedies, Written by a Person of Honor. Lately presented by His Majesties Servants, at the Black-Fryers* (London, 1649). The reference to their having been acted at Blackfriars dates them as earlier than 1642. *The Country Captain* was printed in The Hague. Martin Butler has an interesting discussion of the satire on masques in *The Variety* (and other plays); see *Theatre and Crisis*, 196 ff.

[4] Thomas Cardell (d. 1621) served both Elizabeth I and James I; see the entries in Ashbee, *RECM*, iv and vi, and Holman, *Four and Twenty Fiddlers*, 115.

[5] Ashbee, *RECM*, iii. 7 and 12. In Shakespeare's *Henry V* (written in 1599), the Duke of Britaine— claiming that the ladies of the French court have been accusing their husbands of cowardice—uses an image which suggests that even at the end of the 16th c. French dancing-masters were making their presence felt in England: 'They bid us to the English dancing-schools | And teach lavolatas high and swift corantos, | Saying our grace is only in our heels | And that we are most lofty runaways' (III. vi. 32–4).

[6] Ashbee, *RECM*, iv. 23, *et passim*.

Charles I's reign he was the recipient of a number of very substantial 'free gifts' (the last of which—£200 in February 1634—may indicate some involvement with *Coelum Britannicum*, performed that month).[7] Nicolas Confesse devised and taught dances for *Love Freed*, *The Lords' Masque* (both with Bochan), *Oberon*, and probably other masques before returning to France in 1628 (where he continued to be described as a 'musicien de la reine d'Angleterre').[8] Nicolas Picart, a member of the violins in the King's Musick throughout the Caroline period, is also called a 'M^r a danser' in a 1625 list of Henrietta Maria's household.[9] Late in 1640, George Turgis received payment for 'attending and teaching their Maties and the Maides of hono^r in the Art of dancing'. In the following year he is both listed amongst the violins and described as a 'teacher to dance'.[10]

There were other French violinists who, while not known specifically as dancing-masters, were equally important in the dissemination of French dance music and styles of dancing in England. Adam Vallet is particularly interesting for his proven association with both *ballet de cour* and masque. Before going to England in 1616 he had been active as a violinist in France. Late in 1607 he had signed a contract to perform ballet music with six colleagues. Vallet, who was to play *dessus* (treble violin), undertook to arrange and supply parts for three ballets to be performed in the New Year.[11] By the time he reached the court of James I he must have been very familiar with the music and dancing styles of the *ballet de cour*. He was, moreover, a dancer himself, for in April 1616 he received a gift from the king for dancing at Newmarket.[12] From January 1617 until his death in 1625 he held a position as a violinist in the King's Musick (and so must have played for all the later Jacobean court masques). And there are other important figures whose activities have already

[7] The other gifts were £500 in Aug. 1625 ('procured by the Duke of Buckingham'), £60 from the Queen in 1630, and £300 from the King in 1633. His name disappears from subsidy exemption lists from Michaelmas 1614 and it is clear that he must have been living in Paris in 1622–5, when three of his children were baptized. There are other entries in the Paris civic records relating to his family in 1623, 1630, 1633, 1635, 1636, 1637, and 1640. It is difficult to know how to reconcile these with his service in England in these years. See Ashbee, *RECM*, iii–v, *passim*; and Y. de Brossard (ed.), *Musiciens de Paris, 1535–1792: Actes d'état civil d'après le fichier Laborde de la Bibliothèque Nationale* (Paris, 1965), *passim*.
The Vingt-Quatre Violons were referred to as 'les disciples de Bocan' and in the later 17th c. he was called 'le Baptiste d'alors', the forerunner of Lully (see Prunières, *Le Ballet de cour*, 209).

[8] De Brossard (ed.), *Musiciens de Paris*, 68; cited by Ashbee, *RECM*, iii. 246.

[9] GB-Lpro, SP. 16. 3. 175 (1625), 'Estat des offitiers et serviteurs de la Royne'. I cannot decipher the end of this description, which begins 'M^r a danser des filles . . .'. Picart had returned to France by 1644.

[10] Ashbee, *RECM*, iii. 106, 109, and 113. His nationality is not certain, but Turgis is certainly a French name. (There was a musician of that name active in Paris in the late 18th c.; see de Brossard, *Musiciens de Paris*.)

[11] Vallet's ensemble consisted of two musicians playing *dessus*, one *haute contre*, two *taille*, and two *basse*. The ballets are identified as the Ballet de Monsieur de Nemours, called the Ballet des Espritz, the Ballet of Fillou, and the Ballet of Madame la duchesse de Roen. See M. Jurgens (ed.), *Documents du minutier central concernant l'histoire de la musique*, 2 vols. (Paris, 1967), ii. 354–6. There were several ballets by M. de Nemours performed before 1607 which could be the one referred to in the contract; the identity of the other two remains a mystery. See McGowan, *L'Art du ballet de cour*, 261 and 263.

[12] Ashbee, *RECM*, iv. 44.

been mentioned—notably the two La Pierres, Sebastian and Guillaume (see Ch. 4).

French dancing-masters active in London, and French violinists who coached and played for dance rehearsals are only the most obvious agents through which recognizably French dance structures and choreographic styles might have found their way into the English masque. The link between violin-playing and dancing is so strong that it is likely that some of the other French violinists active in London participated in this process. Amongst the servants of Queen Anne who were provided with livery for the funeral of Prince Henry, five Dutch and four French musicians were listed. No further mention of these Dutch musicians (who are not individually identified) appears in the court records, but French musicians were a regular part of Anne's establishment (seven were to take part in her funeral). These were absorbed into the even larger group of French musicians attached to the household of Charles I's queen, Henrietta Maria.

Something more than simply a broad French influence in courtly dancing is at issue here. French musicians at the English court brought first-hand practical experience of the *ballet de cour*—and this must have facilitated quite specific changes in the shape of the Caroline masque.

Masque and Ballet de Cour

The French and the English had always thought of masque and *ballet de cour* as equivalent entertainments. The terms were used interchangeably. In his report on *The Masque of Queens* the French ambassador consistently referred to it as a ballet; and Filmer in *French Court Ayres* (1629) described two *Airs de ballet* as having been sung 'in a Masque'.[13] The parallels between these two genres (even before the Caroline era) are sufficiently close for each to be regarded almost as a national variant on a single form. It should also be said that English interest in the French model ran high throughout James's reign. But in the 1630s the relationship between *ballet de cour* (already perceived as analogous to the English genre) and the masque became more active; the *ballet de cour* emerged as a dominant influence on the masque.

In order to recognize this, we need first to examine the distinguishing features of the *ballet de cour*. As with the masque, much of what is known about *ballet de cour* comes from the publications associated with specific occasions. These, however, are never quite the equivalent of masque texts. The *ballet de cour* gave rise to two distinct types of publication. First there are the *livrets*, giving descriptions of the ballet and sometimes (but not always) including the poetry sung as *récits*.[14] These are of most use in establishing where the vocal or

---

[13] For La Boderie's report see H&S, x. 497–8. E. Filmer, *French Court Ayres* (London, 1629), I ('A Panegyric: Sung by the Sunne, in a Masque of the Prince of Condies, to the now French Queen-Mother, at that time Regent') and XII ('The Aire of the Tritonides in a Masque before this Lewis the thirteenth and his Mother, at Madame his Sisters taking her leave to goe into Spaine').

[14] The *récit* was simply an *air* sung in the context of a ballet. The term does not imply any connection with *récitatif*.

dance music fitted within the overall structure of a ballet. More common than the *livrets* are little booklets of verses distributed to audience members (and sold after the event) which linked particular roles in the ballet with the persons dancing. In 1623, when Henrietta Maria danced in the *Fêtes de Junon*, Boisrobet included a 'vers de Madame représentant Iris pour la Reyne sa mère':

> Qu'on ne s'esmerveille pas
> De voir en moy tant d'appas;
> Si l'on y veut prendre garde,
> J'ay comme Iris emprunté
> Mes couleurs et ma beauté
> Du Soleil qui me regarde.[15]

The sun from whom Iris borrowed her beauty was Marie de Medici, the Queen Mother, who two years earlier had featured in the *Grand Ballet de la Reyne représentant le Soleil*. On that occasion Henrietta Maria had danced as Aurora—the dawn.[16] Louis XIV was participating in a well-established tradition when in the *Ballet de la nuit* of 1653 he danced as the glorious morning sun and so established the image which became the symbol of his reign. The *vers* for the *Ballet de la Reyne tiré de la fable de Psyché* are preceded by a note which is in effect an apology for their lack of specificity: 'Pour les vers qui suivent, la Reyne commanda à Monsieur de Gombauld de les faire, sans qu'il fust resolu quelle Deesse chacune des Dames devoit representer.'[17] The printed description of *Le Ballet de la Délivrance de Renaud* (1617) closes with a reference to the distribution of the *vers* at the end of the entertainment: 'Tandis que le grand Bal se dança, et que chacun s'amusa à lire les vers particuliers que le Roy et les seigneurs de sa suitte donnerent aux Dames, sur le personnage que chacun d'eux avoit representé aux entrées'.[18] (The tradition lived on: one of the scenes in the ballet at the conclusion of the Lully/Molière *Bourgeois Gentilhomme* has members of the audience clamouring for a copy of the *Vers*.)

For many of the more important ballets both *livrets* and *vers* would be published. But, as with the masque, there was no guarantee of any form of printed account. Of the nearly 150 ballets listed by McGowan as having taken place between 1610 and 1620, over half have neither *vers* nor *livret* surviving,

[15] Lacroix, *Ballets et mascarades*, ii. 354. 'You should not be surprised to see me so alluring; if you care to pay attention, I, like Iris, have borrowed my colours and my beauty from the sun who looks at me.'

[16] McGowan, *L'Art du ballet de cour*, 182 says that it is Louis XIII who is the sun in the *Ballet de la Reyne* of 1621. This is not the case, although the *vers* reflect some anxiety about the relationship between Louis and *this* sun. The 'Vers pour la Reyne representant le Soleil; au Roy' contains the line 'C'est de vous que ie prens ma flame'.

[17] 'The Queen ordered M. de Gombauld to write the poems which follow, before it had been decided what Goddess each of the ladies would represent.' Lacroix, *Ballet et mascarades*, ii. 207. These *vers* were printed with the *livret*.

[18] 'While the grand Ball was danced, and each one amused himself in reading the personal lines that the king and the lords of his retinue gave to the ladies, on the character that each of them had represented in their entries'. From the *Discours au vray du ballet dansé par le roy*, reprinted in Lacroix, *Ballets et mascarades*, ii. 119.

and are known only from musical sources or from diaries, memoirs, and chronicles. Forty per cent of the rest have extant *vers* and fewer than 20 per cent (twenty-six ballets altogether) have *livrets*. Quite often *livrets* and *vers* survive for the same ballet—sixteen of the sample considered here have both. Thirty English masque texts survive for the same period, a number which is comparable with the survival rate of *livrets*. This suggests that the level of full-scale dramatized court entertainments may have been quite similar on both sides of the Channel.[19]

What many of the sets of *vers* throw into relief is that audiences, like those at the English masque, were expected to perceive a link between a role and the person dancing it. But this was not followed through quite as systematically as in England, for the *ballet de cour* gave aristocrats the opportunity to play at being uncourtly. In the *Délivrance de Renaud* Count Rochefoucault danced as the spirit of vanity and—even more remarkably—in *Le Ballet du Roy représentant les Bacchanales* (1623) Louis XIII danced as a wool-spinner.[20] Such freedom ran counter to the whole ethos of the Jacobean masque. But that, as we shall see later in this chapter, began to change shortly after Henrietta Maria's arrival from France.

There is no English equivalent of the *vers*, except for three publications which, significantly, date from the early 1630s. The verses and 'subject of the masque' by Aurelian Townshend printed for *Florimène* seem, with the exception of a Pigmy's speech, intended to be read privately rather than heard as part of the entertainment. This pamphlet must be an imitation of French publishing practices. And Francis Lenton produced two booklets of anagrams describing masque participants. The first (*The Innes of Court Anagrammatist*, 1634) relates to *The Triumph of Peace*; the poems in this tiny volume are (like many of the French *vers*) mildly satirical and risqué. The second publication, *Great Britains Beauties or the Female Glory*, relates to *Luminalia* (1638). Its tone is oppressively deferential—as a few lines from the opening Anagram for Henrietta Maria (and based on Maria Stvart, 'I AM A TRV STAR') show:

> A morning *Star*, whose Rose at blush and smile,
> Shewed the dayes solace, and the nights exile;
> A radient *Star*, whose lustre, more Divine,
> By Charles (our Sun) doth gloriously shine ... (p. 2)

This (complete with its identification of Charles I as the sun king) is awful poetry, but it does relate to the masque device where Aurora declares 'that her brother the Sunne hath for this time given up his charge of lightning this

---

[19] Many of the ballets mentioned in passing in memoirs and diaries may have been little more than an evening's dancing in an aristocratic residence without necessarily a great deal of careful planning and rehearsal and not depending on elaborate sets or machinery—the sort of thing Herbert reminisced about in his account of his years as ambassador in France (see above, p. 220). For details of *livrets*, etc. see McGowan, *L'Art du ballet de cour*, 250–309.

[20] Several characters here were depicted as 'donneurs de serenades'; compare *Britannia Triumphans*.

Hemisphere to a terrestriall Beautie, in whome intellectuall and corporeall brightnesse are joyn'd' (p. 623).

It is not appropriate here to give a comprehensive account of the development and diversification of the *ballet de cour* in the period. I nevertheless wish to draw attention to features found in the *ballet de cour* of Louis XIII's reign which make it rather different from the Jacobean masque. Table 6.1 sets out schematically the structure of two of the grandest court ballets from the years preceding Henrietta Maria's departure for England. Their most striking feature is the long sequences of dances which are not separated by song or speech (as they invariably were in the English masque of the same era).[21] The *Ballet de Tancrède*, for example, has a sequence of twelve *entrées* which apparently ran on one into the next. This ballet is a danced dramatization of the incident in Tasso's *Gerusalemme liberata* (xiii. 38–46) where Tancredi in the underworld comes upon Clorinda's spirit embedded in a cypress tree. Many of its dances had a mimed quality. The climactic twentieth *entrée* (in this case, placed between two vocal pieces) is described in this way:

Le chant finy, le théâtre reprit sa clarté, et fut à l'instant changé en amphithéâtre, la forest ayant disparu. Et comme Tancrede commençoit à faire quelque cadence, il vit naistre à ses pieds un grand cyprez que s'esleva tout à coup au milieu du théâtre comme si quelque Demon l'y fust venu porter. Il estoit si bien representé, que la pluspart le creurent estre naturel. Sur l'escorce du cyprez se voyoient escrites les mesmes paroles que les voix plaintives avoient chantées. Tancrede s'approcha en dançant, et ayant leu les characteres, donna un grand coup d'espée au cyprez en cadence et en coupa une branche dont sortit du sang. Alors comme si le tronc eust esté sensible, il poussa hors une voix pitoyable chantant ces vers: 'Toy de qui la rigueur m'a fait cesser de vivre . . .'.[22]

Le Ballet de la Délivrance de Renaud (1617) presents a similar picture of a drama unfolding through continuously evolving dance. Both this and *Tancrède* have a stronger dramatic frame than many *ballets de cour*, but even where such a strong sense of an overall dramatic progression is missing, mime elements pervade the choreography. In both, the climax of the entertainment coincides with a more equal alternation between dance and sung *récits* or choruses. Typically, the concluding *Grand Ballet* was preceded by a chorus. In this respect their structure approximates to the movement from an antimasque

---

[21] I should nevertheless point out that this was not the only possible model. The *Ballet d'Apollon* performed in Feb. 1621 has alternating *récits* and *ballets* throughout until the final *Grand Ballet*. The printed text (*Suiet du Ballet du Roy Faict dans la salle du petit Bourbon ce 19. fevrier 1621*) has marginal glosses marking these divisions. (The shelf-mark of the GB-Lbl copy is C. 38. b. 21.)

[22] Lacroix, *Ballets et mascarades*, ii. 182. 'The song finished, the theatre was once again lit, and was in an instant changed into an amphitheatre, the forest having disappeared. And as Tancredi began to fall into a dance he saw born at his feet a big cypress which rose up suddenly in the middle of the stage as if some demon had drawn it out. It was so well represented that most thought it was natural. On the bark of the cypress the same words which the plaintive voices had sung were seen to be written. Tancredi went up to it dancing, and having read the letters, struck the cypress with a strong sword blow in time to the music, and he cut a branch from which blood came out. Then as if the trunk had felt this, a pitiful voice singing these lines came out: "You whose severity has made me give up my life . . ."'.

TABLE 6.1. *Structure of two French court ballets*

Le Ballet de la Délivrance de Renaud 1617

Chorus: 'Puis que les ans'
1er Entrée: Spirits of Fire [the King], Water [M. de Vendôme], Air [M. de Mompoullan]
2e Entrée: Spirit of the Hunt [Count Roche-Guyon] & Spirt of fools [M. le General de Gallères]
3e Entrée: Spirits of play [M. de Blinville], of the avaricious [M. de Challais], of the villagers [M. de Humières]; a foolish spirit [M. de Liancourt]
4e Entrée: an aerial spirit [Marquis de Courtanvault]; spirits of vanity [Count Rochefoucault], the moors [M. de Brantes], war [M. le Baron de Palluau]
5e Entrée: Renaud [M. de Luynes] and the last four spirits
6e Entrée: two knights [unidentified in the text]
Air: 'Quelle pointe de jalousie' (Boësset)
7e Entrée: the knights and the monsters [unidentified in the text]
Air: 'Deitez qui, libres d'ennuis' (Bataille)
8e Entrée: Rinaldo (flees Armide)
9e Entrée: Armide [Marais] and her Demons [led by Belleville]
Air: 'Quel subit changement' (Guédron)
10e Entrée: the Demons as old women
Chorus of soldiers—the army of Godefroy (Guédron)
Dialogue between a magician and the soldiers (Guédron)
Chorus: 'Enfin le Ciel a retiré' (Guédron)
Grand Ballet [the King as a new Godefroy]

Le Grand Ballet de Tancrède en la Forest enchantée

Récit: Ismen, 'Je suis cet enchanteur si fameux par le monde'
Ballet des dieux bocagers
    1er Entrée: the deities of the woods
    2e Entrée: four satyrs playing oboes with four sileni
    3e Entrée: six satyrs playing flutes with four dryads
Ballet des Monstres Armez
    Récit: Ismen, 'Toy, Pluton, qui regis l'infernalle caverne'
    4e Entrée: eight monsters
Ballet des puissances d'enfer
    5e Entrée: three furies
    6e Entrée: three Judges of Hell (Minos, Eaque, Rhadamante)
    7e Entrée: three Parcae
    8e Entrée: Pluto, Proserpina, Charon, and nine other powers of Hell
Ballet des Entrées
    9e Entrée: four woodcutters
    10e Entrée: four sawyers
    11e Entrée: four archers
Intermède des quatre chevaliers des aventures
    12e Entrée: three knight adventurers
    13e Entrée: Tancredi and two squires

TABLE 6.1. *Continued*

14ᵉ Entrée: Tancredi and the three knight adventurers
15ᵉ Entrée: Fencing knights and monsters (guarding the trees)
    Chorus: disembodied souls, 'Quelle estrange manie, ô cruels adversaires'
16ᵉ Entrée: Tancredi (cuts the cypress/Clorinda)
    Récit: Clorinda, 'Toy de qui la rigueur m'a fait cesser de vivre . . .'
17ᵉ Entrée: Tancredi
18ᵉ Entrée: the two squires (see 13ᶜ Entrée)
19ᵉ Entrée: Tancredi, knights, woodcutters, sawyers, and archers
Ballet des anges
    Chorus: angels, 'Puisque le Ciel propice aux armes de Tancrede'
20ᵉ Entrée: eight dancing angels
    Chorus: angels, 'L'esclat de vos beautez, si digne de louange'
21ᵉ Entrée: angels
Le Grand Ballet des seize conquerans de la Palestine
    Chorus: angels, 'Ce monstre dont l'enfer fut la noire origine'
    Grand ballet

---

with a long sequence of danced entries to a main masque where set dances are placed in a context which is defined through song.

The tendency for the *ballet de cour* to consist of extended sequences of danced *entrées* uninterrupted by song became particularly marked after the death of the Duc de Luynes in 1621 when what is now referred to as the *ballet à entrées* or the *ballet burlesque* emerged as the dominant type.[23] In the *ballet à entrées* the thematic links between the various dances and the sense of the whole entertainment building to a climax were much weaker than in, say, *Tancrède* or *Renaud*. There is nothing in the Jacobean masque quite like these extended, unbroken sequences of dances.

Before turning to see how these features of the *ballet de cour* made an impact on the developing forms of the English masque, I should point out that—well before Henrietta Maria's arrival in England—there was one ballet specifically devised for the English court. Marc de Maillet's *Balet de la revanche du mespris d'Amour* was, according to its title-page, 'Dancé devant la Royne de la grande Bretaigne. Imprimé a Londres ce 28. Ianvier 1617'. If Maillet was using the (NS) Continental calendar here, his ballet would have taken place between

---

[23] Margaret McGowan describes the *ballet burlesque* in this way: 'Il s'agit tout simplement d'une série d'entrées dansées, parfois accompagnées de chant, devant un décor plus ou moins compliqué selon les besoins du ballet et les dimensions du théâtre ou du salon . . . Une idée, un fil conducteur, lie tant bien que mal les diverses entrées qui ont le plus souvent peu de rapport entre elles' (*L'Art du ballet de cour*, 138). She adds (140): 'Le rôle de la musique et de la poésie est très réduit dans le ballet burlesque.' ('It is a matter quite simply of a series of danced *entrées*, sometimes accompanied by singing in front of a set which is more or less complicated depending on the needs of the ballet and the dimensions of the theatre or room. . . . An idea, a connecting thread, joins the diverse *entrées* after a fashion, but they often have very little relationship with each other. The role of music and poetry is very reduced in the *ballet burlesque*.')

the first performance of *The Vision of Delight* and the presentation of *Lovers Made Men* to the French ambassador in the following month.[24] If this were so, it may even have been that Jonson framed his device for the second of these masques partly as a response to the ballet. There, Love presents the perfect souls he has found in going around the earth to the queen and testifies to the joy, honour, and happiness they find in being at her service. The *livret* does not label the *entrées* or give a description of the dances but Love's sung *récits* make it clear that some of his retinue were figures of derision:

> Vous verrez des obiects plaisans
> Grand Royne, apprestez vous a rire . . .
> Ie rends deux viellards de tous espris
> De l'amour de deux ieunes femmes,
> Et iugez si le seul mespris
> N'est tout le guerdon de leurs flames . . .[25]

In *Lovers Made Men* Jonson was, of course, returning to an old theme ('Love freed from ignorance and folly'), but the way it picks up and extends Maillet's may be more than coincidence. Jonson's lovers, drinking the waters of the Lethe, are able to forget and free themselves from a demeaning love which made them objects of ridicule (demonstrated in the antimasque dance).[26]

If French influence was perceptible in the Jacobean masque, it became very much more marked after Henrietta Maria's arrival in England. This is particularly so in the displacement of Jacobean antimasque types by French-style *entrées*.[27]

---

[24] The dates do not fit perfectly, but could this have been the 'maske or antique' performed before the Queen at Somerset House on 19 Feb. 1617? See C. E. McGee and J. C. Meagher, 'Preliminary Checklist of Tudor and Stuart Entertainments: 1614–25', *RORD* 30 (1988), 46. The *Balet de la revanche du mespris d'Amour* was one of several attempts by Marc de Maillet to win favour at the English court. In Sept. 1617 he published a poem in praise of James I—actually an appeal for patronage. From the preface to this we learn that he had served Marguerite de Valois for eight years and that he had brought a letter of recommendation from the Prince de Genville; he also implied that the Lords Hay and Daubigny would be able to speak in his favour.

Enid Welsford detected French influence in *The Vision of Delight*; see *The Court Masque*, 203.

[25] Sig. A3. 'You will see some amusing things, great Queen; get ready to laugh. . . . I make two old men utterly obsessed with love for two young women, and just see if scorn alone does not reward their flames.'

[26] There is a payment to French musicians dated 6 May 1617 which has been linked to *The Vision of Delight*. It seems possible that this had something to do on the one hand with Maillet's ballet and on the other with the visit of the French ambassador, since the one person mentioned in the warrant (Pierce Parminit) is not known to have had any other connection with the English court: 'To Pierce Parminit french Musicion the some of One hundred poundes by him devided equally among the companie of the french Musicions being twelue in number for their service in the Maskes and other solemnities performed before his Matie at xmas last past . . .': GB-Lpro, E 403/2737, fo. 22^r; quoted H&S, x. 569–70. (Note, however, that this warrant describes the masque as having been performed before 'his Majesty', and that Chamberlain described the masque at Somerset House on 19 Feb. as having been presented by the Queen's French musicians.)

[27] On other aspects of French influence see John Peacock, 'The French Element in Inigo Jones's Masque Designs', in D. Lindley (ed.), *The Court Masque* (Manchester, 1984), 149–68.

The Entry in the Caroline Masque

A superficial transfer of French terminology anticipated a more significant adoption of French structural features by some years. In his early Jacobean masque texts, Jonson normally spoke of the masquers 'dancing forth' or 'descending and falling into their first dance'.[28] Beaumont, Chapman, Campion (in *The Somerset Masque*), Middleton, and the writers of *The Masque of Flowers* and *The Mountebanks Masque* occasionally had recourse to the verbal forms 'enter' or 'entered', though not in a way which seems essentially different from the use of the same words in the stage directions of play texts where no dancing is involved.[29]

In *The Lords' Masque*, however, Campion speaks of the masquers beginning 'their first new entring dance' (p. 97, ll. 1–2) and, for the first time, we seem to be dealing with an anglicization of the term *entrée* from the *ballet de cour*. It is surely significant that this usage should be introduced by someone who had studied in France and whose interest in English quantitative poetic metres may well have been prompted by the activities of Baïf's *Académie* in France. Jonson used the word 'entry' referring to a masquers' dance for the first time in *Lovers Made Men* (1617). Again, it cannot be chance that this was the production mounted for the visit of Baron de La Tour as ambassador extraordinary from France. Jonson seems conscious of introducing an unfamiliar term since he 'translates' it into normal masque idiom: 'Here they dance forth their entrie, *or first dance*' (my italics, l. 154). He chose to use and interpret the term again in *Time Vindicated* (1623), where the context makes it clear that it is being used in a technical sense—it cannot refer to the masquers coming on to the stage since they are there already: 'Here, to a loud Musique, they march into their figure, and daunce their *ENTRY*, or first *DAVNCE*' (ll. 332–3). Something very similar appears in the texts of *The Fortunate Isles* (and *Neptune's Triumph*). The masquers first 'prepare for their figure' and then 'dance their *Entry* or first dance' (l. 567). By this time there can have been little need for the added explanation since Jonson had used the word 'entry' without amplification in other masques.[30] In none of these cases is this term any more appropriate than the English expression 'first dance'. It seems, in fact, a rather confused borrowing: a fashionable French term restricted by its normal English meaning of 'arrival'. In the Caroline period, however, not only did 'entry' become the standard term, but it was used in a sense which was much more closely related to the *entrée* of the *ballet de cour*.

---

[28] See *The Masque of Blackness*, l. 266, *The Masque of Beauty*, l. 320, *Hymenaei*, l. 270, *The Haddington Masque*, ll. 343–4, *The Masque of Queens*, l. 731, *Tethys' Festival*, ll. 319–20, *Oberon*, l. 394, *The Irish Masque*, l. 184, and Chapman's *Memorable Masque*, l. 339.

[29] Beaumont's *Masque of the Inner Temple and Gray's Inn*, ll. 191, 202, Chapman's *Memorable Masque*, l. 163, *The Masque of Flowers*, l. 254, *The Masque of Heroes*, l. 180, and *The Mountebanks Masque*, p. 437.

[30] *Pan's Anniversary* (l. 190), and *The Masque of Augurs* (ll. 364–5). The word entry was used again in *Neptune's Triumph* (l. 453).

Love's Triumph through Callipolis and *Chloridia* are the first surviving court-masque texts from the Caroline period. Since these were so evidently written under a new dispensation, we should pause for a minute to consider what is known about masques and related entertainments at court during the first six years of Charles I's rule. Early in 1626 the Marquis de Racan's *Artenice*, the first of Henrietta Maria's French pastorals, was mounted at court. Each act ended with a chorus and, although the text itself does not indicate this specifically, there were obviously other masque-like elements: the Lord Chamberlain's accounts for this event include 'soape for the engines of the Pastorall'.[31] In November of that year Marshal Bassompierre was a guest at an extraordinary entertainment provided by the Duke of Buckingham at his residence, York House:

[le roy] me mena a Iorchaus cheux le duc quy luy fit le plus superbe festin que je vis de ma vie. Le roy soupa en une table avec la reine et moy, quy fut servie par des ballets entiers a casque service et des representations diverses, changemens de teatres, de tables, et de musique. Le duc servit le roy, le comte de Carlile la reine, et le comte de Holland me servit a table. Apres souper on mena le roy et nous en une autre salle ou l'assemblée estoit, et on y entroit par un tour, comme aux monasteres, sans aucune confusion; ou l'on eut un superbe ballet que le duc dansa, et en suitte nous nous mismes a danser des contredanses jusques a quattre heures apres minuit. De là on nous mena en des appartemens voutés ou il y avoit cinq diverses collations.[32]

This event attracted considerable comment. Another observer noted that 'all things came down in clouds; amongst which one rare device was a representation of the French King and the two Queens with their chiefest attendants and so to the life that the Queen's Majesty could name them'.[33] The Reverend Joseph Mead was less impressed. He reported that 'His Grace [Buckingham] took a shape upon the other Thursday night, which many thought too histrionical to become him, when in the presence of king, queen, ambassadors, and the flower of the court, he acted a master of fence, to teach the great porter to skirmish, and my Lord of Holland, a privy counsellor, also taught him the mathematics, and Sir George Goring to dance . . .'.[34] It is worth noting that the Frenchman, Bassompierre, does not appear to have been scandalized by what, according to Mead, upset many. Such roles were,

---

[31] Hill (ed.), 'Dramatic Records', 36.

[32] '[the king] took me to the duke's at Jorschau [York House], who gave him the most magnificent entertainment I ever saw in my life. The king supped at one table with the queen and me, which was served by a complete *ballet* at each course, with sundry representations—changes of scenery, tables, and music: the duke waited on the king at table, the Earl of *Carlile* on the queen, and the Earl of *Hollande* on me. After supper the king and me were led into another room, where the assembly was, and one entered it by a kind of turnstile, as in convents, without any confusion, where there was a magnificent ballet, in which the duke danced: and afterwards we set to and danced country-dances till four in the morning; thence we were shown into vaulted apartment where there were five different collations.' Translation from *Memoirs of the Embassy of the Marshal de Bassompierre to the Court of England in 1626*, 2 vols. (London, 1819), i. 93–6 (Sunday, 15 Nov. 1626). This corresponds to the *Journal* (1870–7 edn.) iii. 274.

[33] T. Birch (ed.), *The Court and Times of Charles the First* (London, 1849), i. 326.

[34] Ibid. 180; quoted O&S, i. 389.

as we have seen, quite normal in the *ballet de cour*. Bassompierre himself describes how in 1598 he had ingratiated himself with Henri IV by dancing a ballet with some of the most eminent men in the realm in which they acted as barbers (that is, surgeons).

This was not the Duke of Buckingham's only venture of this kind. In 1627, before he left on his expedition to support the Huguenots in France, he 'gave his farewell supper at York House, and a masque unto their majesties, wherein first comes forth the Duke, after him Envy, with divers open-mouthed dogs' heads, representing the people's barking; next came Fame; then Truth, &c.'[35] Other large-scale masques were presented—or at least planned. Mead reported early in 1628 that 'The gentlemen of the Temple being this Shrovetide to present a masque to their majesties, over and besides the king's own great masque, to be performed in the Banqueting House by a hundred actors'.[36] It seems possible that neither of these entertainments took place. The Lord Chamberlain's accounts for the second of these refers to 'a new Maske *intended* to haue bynne performed there'.[37]

Two points emerge. First, despite the absence of texts, the early years of Charles I's reign were not without courtly entertainments. Second, these entertainments seem to have departed from Jacobean models. Although the evidence is sparse, there are at least hints that this might have been a period of experimentation.

Love's Triumph through Callipolis is not, on the face of it, so different from earlier Jonson masques. The masquers (fourteen perfect lovers plus the king as a 'heroical' lover) arrive with fourteen Cupids: 'The Cupids dance their dance. | And the Masquers their entry' (ll. 147–8). It is not clear what distinction Jonson has in mind here between the terms entry and dance. The antimasque which has preceded all this is of twelve 'confused affections'— very obviously the opposites of the main masque's noble lovers. They are divided into four groups 'in the habits of the foure prime *European* Nations' (l. 33) who appear from the text to have danced in sequence. The national division itself—superimposed on the disordered lovers' theme—may have been borrowed from a ballet which took place in Paris in 1626. The *Grand Bal de la Douairiere de Billebahaut* (the quintessential *ballet burlesque*) was divided into ballets representing the four principal parts of the world.[38] A 'Ballet des peuples d'Europe' formed its final section. Since the *Callipolis* antimasque is entirely danced (and since it is the first Jonson antimasque ever to be like this) it looks as if its form as well as its subject-matter was tailored to Henrietta Maria's tastes. Jonson (and Jones) virtually say as much in the preface:

Wee, the Inuentors, being commanded from the King, to thinke on some thing worthy of his Maiesties putting in act . . . For the honor of his Court, and the dignity

---

[35] Ibid. 226.   [36] Ibid. 312.   [37] Hill (ed.), *Dramatic Records of the Office of Works*, 38.

[38] Ballets/antimasques of different nations remained popular; see *Florimène* (1635), with its antimasques of Canadians, Egyptians, Pantaloons from Bergamo, and Spanish, and the *Ballet des quatres Monarchies Chrestiennes* (also 1635).

of that heroique loue, and regall respect borne by him to his vnmatchable Lady, and Spouse, the Queenes Maiestie, after some debate of cogitation with our selues, resolued on this following argument.   (ll. 7–15)

Chloridia was the queen's response to *Love's Triumph*—and here the French elements stand out clearly, particularly in the antimasque section. Cupid, piqued at being treated as a child by the gods, has gone to hell to stir up mischief. The havoc he has caused is illustrated by a series of dances, performed apparently without a break, by eight different groups of characters. A dwarf Postilion's introductory speech and dance are called 'the first entry of the antimasque' and the succeeding dances—an uninterrupted sequence—are headed '2 Entry' and so on up to the '8 and last Entry'. This is the first use of the word 'entry' in an antimasque situation, and it describes something virtually identical to the danced *entrée* of the *ballet de cour*. Different characters or groups of characters come on stage, dance and leave. They are only loosely connected by the device of the antimasque and there is a significant mime element. Here, for example, are the third and fourth entries:

3 Entry.

The Queenes Dwarfe, richly apparel'd, as a *Prince* of *Hell*, attended by six infernall *Spirits*; He first danceth alone, and then the *Spirits*: all expressing their ioy, for *Cupids* comming among them.

4 Entry.

Here the *Scene* changeth, into a horrid storme. Out of which enters the Nymph *Tempest*, with foure *Windes*, they dance.   (ll. 170–8)

The consciously French element in *Chloridia* seems to be confirmed by another coining. Instead of the term 'main dance'—used consistently since 1615 for the second of the set masque dances—Jonson says that the goddess Chloris and her nymphs (the masquers) 'descend the degrees, into the roome, and dance the entry of the grand-masque' (ll. 229–31).[39] The term 'grand-masque' must be an English equivalent of the *grand ballet*, which usually concluded the *entrées* of a *ballet de cour*.

Antimasques built around an uninterrupted sequence of danced entries became standard. Aurelian Townshend adopted this structure (without taking over precisely the same terminology) in both *Albion's Triumph* and *Tempe Restored*. In the first of these (as in *Chloridia*), the antimasque is moved away from its initial position—something which in itself might derive from the freer structure of *entrées* in the *ballet de cour*. The antimasque dance (illustrating 'Such kind of pastimes as Victorious Emperors were wont to present as spectacles to the People') is described in the text as a sequence of seven entries:

The Anti-Maskes enter
  First, *Fooles* 6
  Secondly, *Saltators* or *Tumblers* 7

---

[39] For 'main dance', see above, p. 131.

Thirdly, *Pugili* or *Buffeters* 3
Fourthly, *Satyrs like Dauncers* 2
Fifthly, *One Giant, and Pigmies* 5
Sixtly, *Gladiators or Fencers* 4
Seventhly, *Mimicks* or *Morescoes* 7   (p. 82)

The seven entries offered a mixture of traditional antimasque grotesquerie, mime, and gymnastics. In obvious contrast, the description of movement in the main-masque section of *Albion's Triumph* placed enormous emphasis on dignity: the masquers moved down the steps 'in a stately pace to Musick made by the Chorus of Sacrificers' (p. 84), the High Priests and Sacrificers approached the Queen 'treading a grave Measure' (p. 85). There was only one set masque dance—and it is called 'the mayne Maske' (p. 86). This is one of only two uses of this expression in a masque text and, like Jonson's 'grand masque' the year before, it seems intended as an English equivalent of *grand ballet*. (As we shall see, Townshend and Jones move even closer to this term in their next masque.)

In *Tempe Restored* the sequence of antimasques consists of 'Indians and Barbarians, who naturally are bestiall, and others which are voluntaries, and but halfe transformed into beastes' (p. 97). The word 'entry' is not used but the text contains a numbered series of comic or grotesque dances. Mime is an important ingredient. The subjects of these entries vary from seven Indians 'adoring their . . . Pagode' to three apes and an ass 'like a Pedante teaching them Prick-song'. The seventh and last of the entries was a dance which (along the lines of a *grand ballet*) combined characters from the preceding six entries.

The antimasque section of Davenant's *Temple of Love* follows a similar pattern. It begins after a prologue in which Divine Poesy and a Chorus of Poets announce that Love's Temple is to be restored in Charles's court. Three Magicians emerge from hollow caves under ground and set out to 'hinder destiny' by frustrating the restoration of the Temple of True Love. Like the witches in *The Masque of Queens*, the magicians plot how to achieve their wicked ends. In true antimasque fashion, they themselves cannot conceive of music which is at all sophisticated: one calls Divine Poesy 'a fiddling Deity', while another says, 'Shee's one that makes the holy Jigges, | And sacred Catches for the gods . . .' (p. 292). The magicians raise up spirits of fire, air, earth, and water who are to be the agents of their mischief. These perform an 'Antimasque of the Spirits', a continuous mimed dance set out in seven 'entries'.

While the considerable amount of spoken dialogue in the antimasque section of *The Temple of Love* locates it securely in an English masque tradition, it seems—quite apart from its French structural features—full of *ballet de cour* borrowings. The entry of the magicians as presenters of the antimasque from under the stage recalls Ismen's role in *Tancrède* (1619): 'Sur le devant de la forest se vit Ismen, grand magicien, qui s'eslevoit insensiblement par un trou dessus le theâtre, comme s'il venoit du profond de l'enfer, affreux en son

aspect, la teste en feu, un livre à la main gauche, et une verge à la droicte'.[40]
And the entries by the spirits of the four elements might also derive from the
opening *entrée* of *Le Ballet de la Délivrance de Renaud* (see Table 6.1).

Luminalia is another hybrid of English and French features. The
antimasques are described in a way which reasserts the traditional function of
the antimasque within the production as a whole. The presenters of the
antimasques, Night and Sleep, are as old as the Stuart masque itself,[41] and
Jonson's expression—'a foil'—is twice used to describe the antimasque's
function. Night, we are told, 'came to give repose to the labours of mortals;
but seeing all things here tending to feasts and revels, she with her attendants
will give her assistance, though it serves but as a foile to set off more nobler
representation'. Night repeats the expression in a song which immediately
precedes the comic entries themselves: 'All that our striving mystery
presents | Will be but foiles to nobler ornaments' (p. 619). Earlier, one of
Night's attendants—a 'Vigil'—refers to the audience awaiting the music and
dancing of the main masque:

> What is the use of silence here?
> Thou see'st (great Empresse) ev'ry eyie,
> Doth watch for measures, ev'ry ear
> Doth hearken after harmony. (p. 617)

What Night and Sleep actually present is two sequences of dances which
could very easily have formed part of a *ballet burlesque*. 'The Antimasques
produced by the Attendants of Night' are set out as a series of four entries. The
first of these (the most fully described) had a strong mime element: 'The two
Thieves enter to share a booty, the watchmen and Bellman first affright them
as they are dividing their booty, but in the end they were contented to share
with the Thieves, and so they all joined in a dance' (p. 619).

At the end of this description, the text reveals that 'Most of these
Antimasques were presented by *Gentlemen of Quality*'. The intrusion of
courtiers into the world of misrule normally inhabited only by professionals
represents a quite profound erosion of Jonsonian ideals. There is a second set
of antimasque dances when 'the sons of *Sleep* bring in these Antimasques of
dreams'. This time seven entries are listed, and many participants are actually
named. These were indeed 'gentlemen of quality' and included the Earl of
Devonshire and the Duke of Lennox—both of whom had been masquers in
Coelum Britannicum. In his entry, the Duke of Lennox was joined by the Earl
of Carlisle, Lord William Hamilton, and Lord Russell, who acted as 'principall
Mariners or Master Mates in rich habits, but proper to the subject' (p. 622).
In the Jacobean masque it would have been unthinkable to have members of

---

[40] Lacroix, *Ballets et mascarades*, ii. 168. 'In front of the forest the great magician Ismen appeared, who
rose gradually through a hole underneath the stage, as if he came from the depths of hell, frightening to look
at, his head in flames, a book in his left hand, and a wand in his right.'

[41] See above, p. 77.

the court representing bird men, coiners, lackeys, and thieves. But such a situation would not have seemed at all out of place in the *ballet de cour*.[42]

Predictably, these trends reach a peak in *Salmacida Spolia*. There we find a sequence of twenty continuously danced entries (running the whole gamut of antimasque subjects) together with the names of the persons who danced them.[43] At the end of this unprecedentedly long list of entries, Davenant writes that all these antimasques 'were well set out and excellently danced, and the tunes fitted to the persons'. This brings us to our next important question. The antimasque tunes found in GB-Lbl, Add. MS 10444 belonged to a type of antimasque dance quite different from the comic entries which are such a feature of the Caroline masque. The new dramatic shape presupposes a new musical structure. What kind of music was used? Since this type of antimasque is a French borrowing, it seems likely that the musical models might also have been the dances for the *ballet de cour*.

Music for the Ballet de Cour

The dance music for the *ballet de cour* is clearly different in its overall organization from English masque dances—but the differences stand out more clearly in certain sources than in others. As with the masque, dance-music sources for the *ballet de cour* are of two kinds: dances preserved in arrangements for what we might call domestic use (outside the original ballet context), and repositories dedicated specifically to the preservation of ballet music. The principal printed sources in the first category are Ballard's two books of *Diverses Piesces* (Paris, 1611 and 1614), the two books of Nicolas Valet's *Le Secret des Muses* (Amsterdam, 1618 and 1619), and G. L. Fuhrmann's *Testudo Gallo-Germanica* (Nuremberg, 1615). (The range of publication locations here testifies to a widespread interest in this repertoire.) However, it is the second type of source—the specialized repositories—which are of more use in determining how this music fitted into its dramatic context.

By far the most comprehensive of these is the collection compiled by André Danican Philidor (Philidor *l'aîné*) at the end of the seventeenth century. In his dedication to Louis XIV he claimed that he wished to demonstrate the vast strides that music had made in the time of Lully and Lalande:

Je presente à Votre Majesté un Recüeil de presque tous les Ballets qui ont esté faits sous les derniers regnes des Rois vos predecesseurs. C'est une recherche que je n'ay entrepris que pour faire voir la différence qu'il y a des Ouurages de Musique de ces

---

[42] *Tethys Festival* (1610) is the exception which proves the rule—but Daniel was not interested in replicating the Jonsonian antimasque. See above, p. 77.

[43] They were clearly 'gentlemen of quality' but not of quite the rank as in *Luminalia* where, since the masquers were ladies, the antimasques were all that was left for gentlemen dancers. Several of the *Luminalia* antimasquers appear in the list of masquers for *Salmacida Spolia*, which had both men and women masquers. Most of the *Salmacida Spolia* antimasquers danced in several entries. Amongst them is a Mr Tartareau who had been listed as a gentleman servant in Henrietta Maria's household in 1625 (GB-Lpro, SP 16. 3. 173). The Queen's dwarf, Jeffrey Hudson, featured prominently (as he had done in other Caroline antimasques).

temps là à ce que l'on fait aujourd'huy. Je sçay bien qu'on n'y trouuera aucune de ces grandes beautez qui sont repanduës dans tout ce qu'à produit l'Incomparable M^r. de Lully, ny rien qui soit du gout sauant de ce que fait M^r. de la Lande qui luy a succedé; Mais il faut demeurer d'accord aussi que la Musique, et tous les autres Arts n'ont atteint à leur perfection, que sous le regne de Loüis le Grand, Ainsi je n'ay point fait de scrupule d'assembler tout ce que J'ay pu de Vieux Ballets qui ont esté dansez sous les Rois Henry 3. Henry 4. et Loüis 13, et de les retirer de la poussiere de quelques Cabinets, où ils estoient comme enseuelis, ayant creu que des Airs qui auoient diuerti de si grands Heros n'estoient pas indignes de reuoir encore le jour, et c'est pour les y faire paroître avec plus d'éclat que je les consacre à Votre Majesté.[44]

Two of Philidor's manuscripts, F-Pn, MS Rés. F. 496 and 497, cover the first half of the seventeenth century.[45] Although their presentation is very much more elegant and the collection altogether larger, these manuscripts communicate exactly the same kind of information for the *ballet de cour* as GB-Lbl, Add. MS 10444 does for the Jacobean masque. Philidor must have been working from something resembling Le Strange's sources for Add. MS 10444, in other words, something closely connected with the dancing-masters who wrote the tunes and devised the choreography. Both anthologies represent dance tunes awaiting, as it were, arrangement for the rich instrumental resources used in actual performances.

Michael Praetorius's *Terpsichore* (1612), in a sense, represents that next stage. It includes music for thirty-two ballets, mostly in four-part arrangements (although there are four ballets for a five-part ensemble). Praetorius says in the dedication to the Duke of Lüneburg that the treble parts only were brought to him from France by the duke's dancing-master, Anthoine Emeraud.[46] If Philidor and Add. MS 10444 stand in an analogous relationship to their parent entertainments, then Praetorius roughly parallels Adson's *Courtly Masquing Ayres* (1621). In both we find a reasonably generous selection of dances in

---

[44] 'I present to your Majesty a collection of almost all the ballets which have been composed during the reigns of the kings who were your predecessors. I undertook this research solely to show the difference between the musical works of those times and what is composed today. I am well aware that those great beauties which are displayed in all that the incomparable M. de Lully has written, or the informed taste evident in the works of his successor, M. de La Lande, will not be found here. But one must agree, too, that music and all the other arts have only attained their perfection under the reign of Louis the Great. Thus I had no hesitation in assembling all that I could of the old ballets which were danced under Kings Henri III, Henri IV, and Louis XIII, and to extract them from the dust of various cabinets where they were mouldering, believing that the Airs which had diverted such great heroes could not be unworthy of seeing the light of day again, and it is to make them appear with more brilliance that I dedicate them to your Majesty.' The dedication appears at the beginning of the third of his very substantial manuscript volumes F-Pn, MS Rés. F. 497.

[45] F-Pn, MS Rés. F. 496 is the second volume in the Philidor collection; it begins with a single five-part piece. Volume i (MS Rés. F. 495) contains predominantly 16th-c. material though it does have some 17th-c. pieces. It also has pieces in five and six parts.

[46] '. . . diese allerley Art Frantzösischer *Branslen*, Däntze und Melodien wie deroselbigen nur einige *Discant* Stimme durch E. Fürstl. G. Dantzmeister *Anthoine Emeraud ex Gallia* mitbracht und mir alhier einbehendiget worden auf fünff und vier Stimmen zu componiren und zu setzen mir billich gebühren wollen'. ('. . . these various kinds of French music, *branles*, dances, and melodies, of which only a few soprano parts were brought and given to me by your Highness's dancing-master, Antoine Emeraud from France, which I have allowed myself to compose and set for five and four voices'.)

which the original lines have been left intact and where the provision of other parts may come reasonably close stylistically to the versions actually used in performance at court by the ensembles of violins and lutes.

Of the mentioned sources, the Philidor manuscripts were, obviously, the last to be assembled. Given their late date, the compiler's avowedly evolutionary perspective, and the apparent lack of sophistication of their contents, we need to consider the quality of transmission here. Henri Prunières felt sceptical about the reliability of the Philidor manuscripts. He considered that the handful of lute solos deriving from ballet *entrées* in Ballard's two books provided firm evidence of the corrupt state of Philidor's transcriptions. Comparing an *entrée* from Ballard's first book with a concordant piece in Philidor, he commented 'l'on sera surpris de la manière dont celui-ci a alourdi et défiguré ce morceau'. He accepted Ballard as being more authoritative on the grounds of date and concluded that 'On doit donc considérer la collection Philidor plutôt comme un précieux répertoire thématique que comme un recueil d'airs copiés avec exactitude.'[47]

In fact, what has gone on here seems rather different. Ballard, in making an idiomatic lute piece, has invested the original dance with an interest which the basic two-part version in Philidor does not disclose. A few bars shown as a *petite reprise* in Philidor are placed by Ballard at the octave below the original statement, providing quite a suave ending for the *entrée*. The same dance occurs in Praetorius, and this version—where again the hand of a first-rate musician has intervened between the source and the printed copy—seems to confirm that Philidor probably transcribed what he found. In Ex. 6.1 the bass lines of the three extant versions of the *entrée* discussed by Prunières are compared (and I have added figures to indicate what goes on in inner parts). No version seems particularly distinguished, but together they provide no justification for thinking that Philidor has disfigured a beautiful original which had been respected by Ballard. The bass lines coincide in a random way—and the points of agreement seem explicable entirely in terms of the restricted possibilities of the upper line. In other words, all that these versions share is a dancing-master's tune, and they are in virtually complete agreement about that. What they did with it reflects their destination, not their origin.

Ex. 6.2 illustrates that the lute miscellanies have priorities very different from the preservation of a dramatic record. In Ballard's first book, the 'Second [Chant]' in the 'Entrée de Luth' corresponds in Philidor to the second *entrée* in the *Ballet de la Reine dansé l'an 1606*.[48] Other instrumental versions of the same *entrée* occur in both Vallet and Fuhrmann. Each of these shows a simple *entrée* excerpted from a longer sequence and developed as an instrumental solo. Ballard characteristically writes out decorated repeats and, in the second

---

[47] *Le Ballet de cour*, 211. 'It is surprising to see the way in which the latter [Philidor] has spoilt and disfigured this piece. . . . The Philidor collection should therefore be regarded more as a precious thematic repertoire than as a collection of faithfully copied airs.'

[48] F-Pn, MS Rés. F. 496, p. 40.

Ex. 6.1. *Ballet des paysans et des grenouilles*, bars 1–5, from (*a*) Praetorius, *Terpsichore* (1612); (*b*) Philidor, F-Pn, MS Rés. F. 496; (*c*) Ballard, F-Pm, Ms. Réserve B. 4761

(*c*) Note-values have been halved
Based on transcription in Prunières, *Le Ballet de cour*, 211; here transposed up a tone

strain, uses his favourite device of placing the repeat in a different octave. Vallet decorates the repeat of the second strain, while Fuhrmann does not write out the repeat at all. Interestingly, the continuation in Fuhrmann (after double bars enclosing the word 'Suite') follows on into the next strain of Philidor—probably a new *entrée*, but not labelled as such.[49] The example points towards an inverse relationship between an interest in dramatic context and the drive to produce attractive, self-sufficient lute solos. Fuhrmann, by far the plainest of the lute versions, retains much more of a sense of how these two strains formed part of a larger musical event. Together, the three versions serve as an important reminder that apparently self-sufficient balanced pieces found in instrumental collections at this time may be disguising their origins.[50]

[49] The 'Premier' and 'Troisième Chant' in Ballard have no connection with the *Ballet de la Reine*.

[50] This example is complicated by the fact that it occurs as a vocal piece ('Belle qui m'avés blessé') in G. Bataille, *Airs de différents auteurs*, ii (Paris, 1608) and (in a four-part version) in P. Guédron, *Airs de cour à 4 et 5 parties* (Paris, 1613). See A. Verchaly (ed.), *Airs de cour pour voix et luth (1603–1643)* (Paris, 1961), 26 (and commentary, pp. xxxvi–xxxvii).

Ex. 6.2. *Ballet de la Reine dansé l'an 1606*: 2ᶜ Entrée, from (*a*) Philidor, F-Pn, MS Rés. F. 496

(*b*) Fuhrmann, *Testudo Gallo-Germanica* (1615)

(c) Valet, *Le Secret des Muses* (1619)

It would be folly, however, to claim too much authority for Philidor as an informant. As we shall see, it is often difficult to correlate his *entrées* with information provided by the texts (or *livrets*). There are many places where his manuscripts need emendation. Again, they resemble Add. MS 10444, where it is often hard to decide whether solecisms arise from an error in transcription or the limited musical competence of the dancing-master composers. The music for the *grand ballet* of the *Ballet des Trois Ages* (1608) provides an interesting case either of Philidor (who presumably worked from a source without bar-lines) recording (or introducing) a corrupt version of a dance or of Praetorius intervening to make better sense of an unsophisticated original (see Ex. 6.3).[51] The last of three strains in Philidor continues the 3/2 metre of

[51] F-Pn, MS Rés. F. 496, pp. 74–5; Praetorius, no. 256.

(d) Ballard, *Premier Livre* (1611), ed. Souris, Spycket, and Rollin

Ex. 6.3. *Ballet des Trois Ages* (1608), from (*a*) Praetorius, *Terpsichore*; (*b*) Philidor, F-Pn, MS Rés. F. 496

the previous two, whereas Praetorius changes to an alla breve time signature. Both rhythmically and harmonically Praetorius makes more sense, and it seems likely that the dance was conceived this way.

There was once another dedicated repository of dance music for the *ballet de cour*. Michel Henry, one of the *Violons du chambre du roi*, compiled an annotated collection of ballet music from 1597 to *c*.1620, and his notes make it clear that he had performed in at least some of the entertainments represented in the manuscript. Unfortunately all that survives of this collection is a very full listing of its contents. In many cases, the list itemizes the *entrées* for a particular ballet and sometimes adds details about instrumentation or the performers.[52] Henry and Philidor do not cover exactly the same ballets for the period in which their contents overlap—and where they do both list music from the same entertainment, there are discrepancies between them. These discrepancies are themselves interesting since, rather than proving, for example, that the later Philidor manuscripts must be corrupt, they probably tell us something quite important about the character of the music.

The *Ballet des Coqs* (1603) is a case in point. Henry lists this as 'Ballet des coqs, fait le dimanche gras par M. Richaine' and says that it contained '4 airs'.[53] Philidor's heading is identical with Henry's and he adds that the ballet was danced before Henri IV; but Philidor gives only one *entrée* and a *Grand Ballet*. Praetorius also includes music for the same ballet. This—transposed down a tone—is the same music as in Philidor except that two strains are missing at the end of the ballet. Praetorius, however, indicates the start of a new *entrée* at the beginning of the third strain. The situation could be summarized as follows:

Philidor		Praetorius
1ᵉʳ *Entrée*	Strain 1	= 1. [Entrée] Strain 1
	Strain 2 [with *petite reprise*] =	Strain 2 [no *petite reprise*]
	Strain 3 [with *petite reprise*] =	2. [Entrée] Strain 1 [no *petite reprise*]
Grand Ballet	Strain 1	= 3. [Entrée] one strain only
	Strain 2	
	Strain 3	

Henry's '4 airs' could be account for in the Praetorius score simply by counting each strain as a separate air. Philidor, however, is apparently the more complete source. Conceivably, it could be described as three strains plus a *grand ballet* (or '4 airs'). Rather than defend this very odd arithmetic as a way of explaining away obvious discrepancies between these sources, I should like to stress that different sources identify the end of one strain and the beginning of the next at different points. The interest of this goes beyond simple counting of *entrées*. We might expect a slight gap between separate *entrées*, but

[52] F-Pn, MS fr. 24357; see F. Lesure, 'Le Recueil de ballets de Michel Henry', in J. Jacquot (ed.), *Les Fêtes de la Renaissance* (Paris, 1956), 205–19.
[53] Ibid. 210.

not between the constituent strains of a single dance. The lack of agreement about where different *entrées* begin, however, reinforces the impression given by so many texts, that much of this music was performed almost continuously—in other words, that without seeing the dance, it would be impossible to tell whether a particular section of music consisted of two *entrées* of two strains each, four of one strain, or some other configuration.

Ex. 6.4 illustrates a similar case. It juxtaposes the upper lines of the opening *entrées* of the *Ballet des Paysans et des Grenouilles* (1607) from Philidor and Praetorius.[54] The two versions are essentially the same (though Praetorius writes out in full a repeat indicated only by a sign in Philidor). But Philidor identifies the second *entrée* at a point where Praetorius does not even have a double bar. In other words, the Praetorius version gives us no reason to expect that there was any break at all between Philidor's first and second *entrées*. (Admittedly, the appearance of continuousness is not often as strong as this. Philidor writes the second *entrée* after a double bar and he restates the ¢ time signature, but here and with the next *entrée* he departs from his normal procedure of beginning a new line.) Henry also included this ballet in his collection, and the list of contents speaks of '5 airs dont le 4ᵉ entrée des grenouilles' and a 'Grand Ballet des Grenouilles, 4 airs'. This nearly matches the subdivision of the music in Praetorius, where we find five *entrées* and a *grand ballet* with only three *entrées* (but four strains). The music in Philidor is identical, but set out as six *entrées* plus a single *entrée* of one strain for the *grand ballet*. Here we have at least two and probably three descriptions of exactly the same music.

It is often not easy to see precisely how the dances in Philidor fit into a particular production. Prunières presents an integrated reconstruction of text and music for the *Ballet de la Délivrance de Renaud* using the vocal music from the *livret* and dance music from the *Ballet du Roy Dansé au Louvre L'an 1617* in Philidor. This reconstruction works quite convincingly, although there are a few problems.[55] The other great ballet whose structure is set out in Table 6.1 is similarly problematic when an attempt at reconstruction is made.

Philidor's music for the *Ballet du Roy Dansé L'an 1619* might, for example, be some of the music for the *Ballet de Tancrède*. There are, however, only two *entrées* and a *Grand Ballet* where the text calls for twenty-one plus a *Grand Ballet*. The 2ᵉ *Entrée* is divided into three parts, the second and third being called 'Air pour les Flustes' and 'Air pour les Hautbois' respectively. Although the order of these airs reverses that in the text, it seems possible that these are,

---

[54] Praetorius, *Terpsichore*, no. 252 'Ballet de Grenouille'; F-Pn, MS Rés. F. 496 (Philidor, vol. ii), pp. 61–2.

[55] See *Le Ballet de cour*, 250–65. Philidor has only seven *entrées* before the *Grand Ballet* while the text provides for eight. Prunières allocates no music for the fifth *entrée*, where two knights entered and danced to a trumpet tune. The *entrée* preceding this in Philidor is unusually long, and it is possible that the last one or two strains were used for the knights' dance. There are other problems, however. Philidor's 6ᵉ *Entrée* has its final two strains labelled 'Bourée', yet there is nothing in the text to explain the introduction of one of the standard social dances at this point.

Ex. 6.4. *Ballet des paysans et des grenouilles* (1607), from (a) Praetorius, *Terpsichore*; (b) Philidor, F-Pn, MS Rés. F. 496

in fact, the *entrées* in the first part for four sileni accompanied by satyrs playing oboes, and four dryads accompanied by satyrs playing flutes.[56]

The *Ballet de M. le Prince de Condé dansé l'an 1620* provides a good example in Philidor of a very extended group of *entrées*.[57] There are twenty-six altogether (including those of the *grand ballet*) and three other similar tunes labelled 'air'. Their structure is summarized in Table 6.2. The *livret* proposed by Margaret McGowan as belonging with this sequence of dances does not seem to fit, but it is interesting to note a number of popular subjects recurring in the titles of the *entrées* themselves. I have identified some of these correspondences in the notes column of the table, but other more familiar themes—peasants, and *entrées* depicting different nationalities, for example— feature in the list. The norm, quite clearly, is for each *entrée* to consist of two strains which are, of course, repeatable. Most of those *entrées* written out as a single strain turn out in fact either to have written-out internal repeats or to consist of antecedent–consequent phrases (often identical except for the move to an imperfect cadence at the end of the first phrase). In other words, most of the single-strain *entrées* are, in fact, completely symmetrical.

I have summarized tonal planning by giving the opening chord (or occasionally, the tonality clearly established by the first few chords) and the concluding chord in each strain.[58] The overall picture is one of very static harmonies. Most *entrées* do not even move to the dominant at their mid-point and the whole ballet scarcely moves outside a D major/minor–F major zone. (I am, incidentally, struck by the blandness of these *entrées* in comparison with the more striking Jacobean antimasque dances.) There are a couple of places where Philidor departs from his usual practice of writing a new set of clefs and a new time signature at the beginning of each *entrée*. Here the sense of one *entrée* leading without any pause at all into the next is—visually at least—particularly strong (see Pl. 15). Between the fifth and sixth strains, Philidor actually uses a tie across the double bar—his normal way of indicating first and second time bars—thus ensuring that the music continues without interruption.

The *Ballet du Triomphe de la Beauté* danced at Saint-Germain on 19 February 1640 allows us to see the relationship between an even more extended sequence of *entrées* and an actual production. The informativeness of the surviving sources makes this a particularly useful example—even though its date is a little later than ideal for making comparisons with English practices

---

[56] In her list of 'Sources des Ballets de 1581 à 1643' McGowan assumes that the music in Philidor described as being from the 'Ballet de madame sœur du Roy Louis 13' is from the *Ballet de la Reyne tiré de la fable de Psyché*. But four of the *entrées* in Philidor have descriptions ('Ardens avec des flambeaux', 'Les Sibilles', 'Bergeres', and 'Tritons') which do not fit with the text of *Psyché*. The dates do not agree either; the ballet in Philidor was performed on 19 Mar. 1619 whereas *Psyché* took place a month earlier on 17 Feb. 1619.

[57] F-Pn, MS Rés. F. 496, pp. 155–61.

[58] Where a confused original needs emendation, or where the tonality is clear only after the initial chord, chord designations appear in brackets.

TABLE 6.2. *Structure of* Ballet de Mᵣ le Prince de Condé Dansé L'an 1620

Title	New clef or new line	Length	Tonality	Notes
				Philidor, vol. ii (Rés. F. 496), pp. 155–61
1ʳᵉ Entrée les Peintres	✓	¢ 10 10	D A D	repeats written out
2. Entrée les Cuisiniers	✗	36	D D	
3ᵉ Entrée les Sauetiers	✓	¢ 10	D D	
4ᵉ Entrée les Charlatans	✓	¢ 12 5	F d d	
5ᵉ Entrée les Basques	✓	¢ 8 4	F F F	
6ᵉ Entrée les Crocheteurs	✗	14 5	F F F	see *Le Balet du Hazard*
7ᵉ Entrée les Brélandiers	✓	¢ 16	D D	*petite reprise*
8ᵉ Entrée les Gaspador	✓	¢ 13	b D	
9ᵉ Entrée les Suisses	✓	¢ 8 10	D D D	
10ᵉ Entrée les Paysans	✓	¢ 8 8	b D D	
11ᵉ Entrée ie Marchand Flamand	✓	¢ 15 9	D D D	
12ᵉ Entrée les Tirelaines	✓	¢ 16 8	(C) d	repeat written out
13ᵉ Entrée les Princes Allemands	✓	¢ 8 8	D D D	
14ᵉ Entrée les Pipeurs	✓	¢ 12	D D	*petite reprise*
15ᵉ Entrée les Bourgeois	✓	¢ 18	(E) A	*petite reprise*
16ᵉ Entrée les Coupeurs de Bourse	✓	¢ 8 4	A A A	see *Le Balet du Hazard* and *Le Ballet de Tancrède*
17ᵉ Entrée les Joüeurs d'Espadon	✓	¢ 4 3	d F F	
18ᵉ Entrée le Commissaire	✓	¢ 10	d d	
2ᵉ [*sic*] Air	✓	³₂ 14	D D D	(antecedent–consequent phrases)
19ᵉ Entrée les Archers	✓	¢ 8 8	D D D	see *Le Ballet de Tancrède*
20ᵉ Entrée les Sergens	✓	¢ 8 5	D D D	
21ᵉ Entrée Maitre Martin	✓	¢ 15	F d	
22ᵉ Entrée les Foux	✓	¢ 10 6	A f♯ A	
23ᵉ Entrée les grandes Bouffonneries	✓	¢ 26	a d	written-out repeats
2ᵉ Air	✓	¢ 4 13	(D) A (A)	confused tonality
24ᵉ Entrée le grand Ballet	✓	¢ 9 9	d A d	
25ᵉ Entrée	✓	22	d d	*petite reprise*
26ᵉ Entrée le grand Ballet	✓	³₂ 23	d d	(antecedent–consequent phrases)
Dernier Air	✓	¢ 8	A d	

in the 1630s. This string of more than thirty *entrées* is loosely connected thematically. The overall shape of the entertainment is summarized at the beginning of the *livret*:

La Beauté supreme, cette aymable puissance, à qui rien ne peut resister, et qui donne à ses sujets la felicité sous une apparence de servitude, desirant faire paroistre aux yeux de l'univers les plus illustres marques de sa gloire comme un superbe triomphe, despesche de tous costez les Amours pour assembler tout ce qui peut y contribuer; ... La Perfection commande à la Nature et à l'Art de faire trouver auprès d'elle tous les agreables presens qu'elle a faits à la Beauté par leur ministere et qui lui servent d'armes ordinaires pour vaincre; l'Admiration prend à sa suitte tous les moyens qu'elle employe dans les occasions où la Beauté fait reverer sa puissance; et la Victoire fait traisner après elle les plus nobles captifs qui peuvent honorer ce triomphe. Ces trois merveilleuses troupes estant assemblées, la Beauté s'y mesle dans un char magnifique, et fait mettre les Amours à la teste pour en faire la conduite. Mais comme elle a favorisé nostre incomparables Reine des plus nobles caracteres de ses merites, elle a voulu paroistre devant elle en ce glorieux appareil avant que de passer outre, afin de s'admirer elle-mesme dans son image la plus parfaite, et d'apprendre à tout l'univers par les hommages de ceste celebre pompe, que Sa Majesté nous doit tenir lieu sur terre de cette souveraine et celeste Beauté qui triomphe avec tant de gloire.[59]

Volume iii of the Philidor manuscript identifies many of the *entrées* for this ballet by name (and not just by number) and hence it is a relatively straightforward matter to match these with the descriptions given in the very informative *livret*. Finally, a full set of *vers* helps settle some of the ambiguities which remain after comparing the other two sources. Table 6.3 shows the relationship between the description of the ballet in the *livret* and the dances which survive for this production in Philidor. The left-hand column summarizes the *entrées* as they appear in the *livret*; the right-hand column lists the *entrées* from Philidor (and the notes add clarifying information from the *vers*).

The literary and musical sources fit together remarkably well. Philidor has the division between the first and second parts of the ballet marked one *entrée* too soon. He also lists seven more *entrées* than the text, but these can easily be accounted for. No. 1 is an Ouverture—an interesting development in itself—but clearly not a danced *entrée* which would figure in the text. Philidor's three *entrées* for the *Grand Ballet* seem accounted for in the text by the focus given

[59] Lacroix, *Ballets et mascarades*, ii. 277. 'Supreme Beauty, that benign power that nothing can resist and who gives happiness to all her subjects under the appearance of servitude, wishing to display the most illustrious marks of her glory as a superb triumph to the eyes of the universe, sends out Cupids from all sides to gather together all that could contribute to the festivity ... Perfection orders Nature and Art to collect all the agreeable presents which she has given Beauty through their agency and which serve her as weapons of conquest. Admiration takes into her retinue all the means which she uses on the occasions when Beauty makes her power revered. And Victory makes all the noble captives who can honour this triumph follow her. These three marvellous troupes being assembled, Beauty comes into their midst in a magnificent chariot with the Cupids at the front to lead the way. But as she has favoured our incomparable Queen with the most noble qualities at her disposal, she wished to appear before her in this glorious display before passing beyond, in order to admire herself in her most perfect image and to teach the whole world through this renowned ceremonial, that on earth her Majesty must occupy the place of this sovereign and heavenly Beauty who triumphs in such glory.'

TABLE 6.3. *The Ballet du Triomphe de la Beauté: comparison of livret and dance music*

Livret	Dance music in F-Pn, MS Rés. F. 497 (Philidor, vol. iii)		
Balet du Triomphe de la Beauté	*Ballet de Mademoiselle*		
Premiere Partie de la Perfection	Dansé devant le Roy A St. Germain l'An 1640		
Récit: 'La beauté de qui nos appas'	Ouverture 1er Air	C ¢	g B♭ g D
1er et 2e Entrées: Six des plus parfaictes personnes des siecles passez; les quatres Elemens	2e Entrée, les Dames	C 3	G A D
	3e Entrée les Elemens	¢ ¢	g D g
3e Entrée: La Nature et l'Art	4e Entrée, la Nature	¢ ¢	g B♭ g
4e, 5e, et 6e Entrées: le Maistre des mines; cinq ouvriers; deux demons[a]	5. Entrée, Mr de la Roche-Guyon, Maistre des Mines	¢ ¢	g B♭ B♭
	6e Entrée, le Mineur	¢ ¢	G D G
	7e Entrée, les Folets	¢ ¢	G G
7e Entrée: un vendeur de pouldre de Chypre	8. Entrée, Un Vendeur de poudre	3 3	G D G
8e Entrée: les trois Graces	9e Entrée, la Grace	C 3	G D G
9e Entrée: Une Biscaïenne avec six petits sauteurs[b]	10e Entrée, l'Humeur	¢ ¢	G D G
10e Entrée: Un maistre à danser, un maistre de luth, un maistre de guitare et un maistre de musique	11e Entrée, la Musique	C C	g B♭ g

TABLE 6.3. *Continued*

Seconde Partie

11ᵉ Entrée: trois Indiens
  Seconde Partie de l'Admiration
Récit: 'Ministres des plaisirs'
12ᵉ et 13ᵉ Entrées: Admiration; cinq Muses; quatre vents
14ᵉ, 15ᵉ, et 16ᵉ Entrées: deux apprentifs en peinture; deux vieilles femmes; le maistre plus serieux; Mercure^d
17ᵉ Entrée: Mercure; six galans de cour
18ᵉ & 19ᵉ Entrées: Circe comme puissante magicienne d'amour; deux statues qu'elle anime; deux rustiques/hommes de cour; deux vieillards/verds galans
20ᵉ Entrée: Un poëte; un chanteur et une chanteuse du Pont-Neuf
21ᵉ Entrée: cinq desesperez
22ᵉ Entrée: quatre Amants temeraires^e
23ᵉ Entrée: trois Inquietez^f

Entrée	Meter	Keys
12ᵉ Entrée, les Indiens	¢	G G
13ᵉ Entrée, Mademoiselle de Bourbon	¢ ¢	e, D G
14ᵉ Entrée	¢ ¢	d, F d
15ᵉ Entrée	¢ ¢	G, D
16ᵉ Entrée	¢ ¢	g, B♭ g
17ᵉ Entrée, Mad^lle de la Barre	¢ ¢	g, B♭ g
18ᵉ Entrée	¢ ¢	B♭, B♭ B♭
19ᵉ Entrée	C C	B♭, F B♭
20ᵉ Entrée	C C	B♭, F B♭
21ᵉ Entrée, la Magie	C 3, ¢	g, D g
22ᵉ Entrée, les Paysans	¢ ¢	g, B♭ g
23ᵉ Entrée, Les Poetes	C 3/2, ¢	G G
24ᵉ Entrée, les Deseperez	¢ ¢	D G
25ᵉ Entrée, Mr de Maulevrier	¢ ¢	G D G
26ᵉ Entrée, Mr Chabot	¢ ¢	g, B♭ B♭

Entrée	Mesure	Ton
24e Entrée: six Chevaliers enflammez	¢	g
27e Entrée, les Enfans	¢	a
Troisième Partie		g
28e Entrée, Mademoiselle		

Troisième Partie de la Victoire

Récit: 'Image des divinités'

Entrée	Mesure	Ton
25e Entrée: la Victoire[g]; six Amazones	**¢3**	D A D
26e Entrée: les quatres parties du monde	**¢**	G D G
27e Entrée: La Force	**C**	gg g
28e Entrée: Achille, Hercule, Marc-Anthoine, Roland	**¢**	gg B♭ B♭
29e Entrée: La Sagesse et la Fortune	**¢**	B♭ F B♭
30e Entrée: Polypheme avec trois satyres	**¢**	gg B♭ gg
31e Entrée: Trois hommes et trois femmes insensez d'amour	**¢**	gg B♭ gg
32e Entrée: un gentilhomme de campagne, un juge de village, un bourgeois, et un paysan	**C, 3/2, ¢**	gg D B♭
Récit: 'Je suis un beau recueil de ces divines choses'	**¢**	G D G
Grand Balet: les Princesses et les Damoiselles qui ont fait separement les trois principales et plus agreables entrées de ce triomphe		
37e Entrée, le Grand Ballet	**C, ¢, 3/2**	D D
38e Entrée	**3/2 3/2**	d A d
39e Entrée	**3/2 3/2**	d F d

Fin du Ballet de Mademoiselle

Fin

---

[a] Vers 'pour messieurs le Duc de Lynes et le Comte de Randan, representans deux Folles'.

[b] Vers 'pour le Sieur Lalun et cinq petits garçons representans la Belle Humeur et les Agrémens'.

[c] Vers 'pour Mademoiselle de Bourbon, representant l'Admiration'.

[d] Vers 'pour le sieur de la Barre, representant Mercure'.

[e] Two *vers* identify Monsieur le marquis de Maulevrier as one of the Temeraires.

[f] Vers 'pour Massieurs les comtes de Roussillon, de Coligny et de Chabot, representans des Inquietés'.

[g] Vers 'pour Mademoiselle de Vandosme, representant la Victoire'.

there to the three principal groups who had danced the opening *entrées* in each section of the ballet: 'et nous asseure, que pour cognoistre au vray les plus grands effects de son [Beauty's] pouvoir, il ne faut que voir les Princesses et les aimable Damoiselles qui paroissent après elle, et qui dansent le *grand Ballet* composé des trois belles troupes qui ont fait separement les trois principales et plus agreables entrées de ce triomphe'.[60] Philidor has four *entrées* (numbers 19–22) for the little episode involving Circe where the text describes all that happens under the heading 'dix-huict et dix-neufviesme entrées'. Circe's solo *entrée* is described as coming at the beginning of the episode in the *livret* but appears to come in the middle of the same episode in Philidor (where 'La Magie' is followed by 'Les Paysans'). Here we seem to be confronting an example of the kind mentioned earlier where exactly the same episode has been subdivided in two different ways.

What interests me most is the question of continuity. Each of the three sections of the ballet began with a sung *récit*, and another *récit* preceded the *grand ballet*. Apart from this small amount of punctuation, the entire entertainment consisted of thirty-eight uninterrupted *entrées*. The sense of one *entrée* leading into another is strongly conveyed by the text through its describing up to three *entrées* as part of a single incident. The mining scene near the beginning is a case in point:

Quartriesme, Cinquiesme et Sixiesme Entrées

Le parterre n'est pas plustost vuide qu'il y paroist une roche qui renferme en son sein une miniere de pierres precieuses, dont *deux ouvriers* conduits par *leur maistre* s'approchant pour y travailler, elle s'ouvre comme une profonde caverne sombre et toute brillante; et *trois autres ouvriers* en sortent chargez des richesses qu'ils y ont trouvées, ce qui augmente le desir des premiers, mais qui sont bien deçeus, quand de ceste mesme caverne ils voyent sortir *deux demons* qui les ayant bien tourmentez les y emportent contre leur volonté.[61]

The three *entrées* involved more interaction of the three groups of characters than the summary headings in Philidor suggest. But clearly one *entrée* here must have led straight to the next.

In the right-hand columns of Table 6.3, time signatures are used to show the number of strains in each *entrée* (and where there are changes within a strain, I have used commas between the various signatures). Tonal direction is again summarized by indicating the first chord of an *entrée*, and the final

---

[60] Lacroix, *Ballets et mascarades*, v. 288. 'And we assure you that truly to know the greatest effects of her [Beauty's] power, you would only have to see the Princesses and the aimiable young women who appear after her, and who dance the Grand Ballet made up of three lovely groups who have separately danced the three most enjoyable principal *entrées* in this triumph.'

[61] Lacroix, *Ballets et mascarades*, v. 280. 'Fourth, Fifth, and Sixth Entries. The dancing area is no sooner cleared than a rock appears enclosing a mine of precious stones. When two workers led by their master approach it to work there, it opens, revealing a deep, dark, and shining cavern. Three other workers come out loaded with the riches they have found, and this increases the craving of the first. But they are utterly disabused when they see two demons coming out of this same cave who, having tormented them, carry them off against their will.'

chord of each strain within it. For the most part this presents an unremarkable picture of predominantly two-strain *entrées* which move to the dominant or relative major in the middle and back to the tonic for the end. Given the dramatic continuity in the group of *entrées* just discussed, it might seem surprising that there is a jump from the Bb major ending of the fifth *entrée* to the submediant G major for the sixth *entrée*. This is not, of course, a particularly violent change, but it is as strongly articulated a harmonic shift as any in the Philidor collection.

The broad picture is clear. Extended sequences of short *entrées* performed continuously or with only very slight breaks were normal in the *ballet de cour*. This type of musical structure, episodic and extendable, would have been equally appropriate for Caroline antimasques of the comic-entry type. The long lists of entries in the antimasque sections of Caroline court masques parallel exactly what was happening in the equivalent French entertainments. The problem, however, is that no sources of instrumental music for the Caroline masque provide anything remotely resembling what we find in the Philidor manuscripts (or even in Praetorius). So can we point to any English music from the period which might have had its origins in Caroline antimasque dances?

English Musical Sources

In Chapter 4 we surveyed some of the instrumental sources for Caroline masques in our quest for lost symphonies. At this point, a little more needs to be said about Playford's *Court Ayres* (1655) and *Courtly Masquing Ayres* (1662) since their titles have raised hopes that they might be harbouring a rich repository of instrumental music for Caroline masques.[62] *Court Ayres* contains 245 items which Playford claims to have received mostly 'from the hands of those Excellent Masters who were their Composers'.[63] Seventy-one pieces are

---

[62] Murray Lefkowitz, *Trois Masques*, 184, writes: 'Les historiens n'ont pas accordé suffisamment d'attention à ces *Court Ayres* et *Courtly Masquing Ayres*. Pourtant leur importance, comme sources des danses originales, des "symphonies" et des chansons en forme de danse des masques caroléens et peut-être aussi des pièces de théâtre, est primordiale. Une étude plus poussée de ces publications fournirait sans doute des renseignements précieux sur les danses, les chansons, les masques et les pièces de théâtre de cette période. Il est possible aussi que des suites entières figurant dans ces recueils, et dont les morceaux déjà identifiés ne constituent qu'une partie, soient tirées des mêmes masques. Ainsi ce qui peut à première vue passer pour des recueils, sans grand intérêt, d'airs de danse à deux parties constitue peut-être la collection la plus complète de musique dramatique que nous possédions pour le règne de Charles Iᵉʳ.' ('Historians have not paid sufficient attention to *Court Ayres* and *Courtly Masquing Ayres*. They are, however, of fundamental importance as sources of original dances, of "symphonies", and of songs in dance form from Caroline masques and possibly also theatrical plays. A thorough study of these publications would probably provide precious information on the dances, songs, masques, and plays of this period. It is also possible that some of the complete suites found in these collections, of which already identified pieces constitute a part, are drawn in their entirety from the same masques. Thus what might at first sight appear to be collections of two-part dances without any great interest perhaps constitute the most complete repository of dramatic music which we possess from the reign of Charles I.')

[63] *Court Ayres*, 'To all Understanders and Lovers of Musick'.

by Charles Coleman and fifty-five by William Lawes (and I suspect that the Lawes pieces reached Playford through Coleman). There is also a single 'Simphony' (or, according to its bass part, 'Almaine') by Simon Ives, but the rest of the collection is made up of dances by composers with no known masque associations who, in many cases, were active after the cessation of masques at court. As we have seen in Chapter 4, a number of the Lawes pieces and the Ives clearly originate in masques. Many of the remaining 'Pavins, Almains, Corant's and Sarabands' (to quote from the title-page) may well have been used in Caroline masque revels, but there is nothing about either their structure or their titles to suggest that they formed part of set masque or antimasque dances.

Courtly Masquing Ayres presents a similar picture, not surprisingly, since Playford explicitly offered it as a sequel to the earlier volume (and about one-third of its contents overlap). Lawes and Coleman are again well represented with forty-seven and forty-one pieces respectively. There are, however, sixty-four pieces by Benjamin Rogers and—more interestingly—a group of fifty-four dances by Davis Mell. Could these include any of his antimasque dances for *The Triumph of Peace*? Unfortunately, the answer almost certainly has to be negative. Mell's dances are all arranged in suites (Ayre, Corant, Saraband, Country Dance) and the individual dances show none of the characteristics associated with antimasque dance tunes.[64] (Interestingly, Mell's Ayre–Corant pairings are almost always thematically linked.)

Where, however, might we look for the dance music by the French dancing-masters—musicians like Nau and La Pierre who, as we have seen, contributed to *The Triumph of Peace*? In Sebastian La Pierre's case very little survives. GB-Ob MS Mus. Sch. d. 220 is the bass part from what was once a two-part set of 'Pavanes, Galliardes, Ayres, Almains, Coranto's, Sarabands, Morisca's, Maskes & Contry Dances'.[65] This anthology clearly had been very much along the same lines as Playford's *Court Ayres*, but it includes an Ayre (on p. 39) by 'Mr Sebastian'. This is a very unremarkable piece with two balanced seven-bar strains; it is in A major and moves to the dominant at the end of the first strain. While the Ayre might well have been like any number of individual *entrées*, the piece on its own provides no evidence to confirm the hypothesis that dancing-master composers like La Pierre must have been writing French-style dance music for the court masque. Of slightly more interest in MS Mus. Sch. d. 220 is a piece in G minor on p. 27 entitled 'Grand Maske'. This ends on the dominant and is followed—beginning on a new line and with a separate heading—by 'the Second strain of the Grand Mask'. There is not much to go on here, but this starts to look just a little bit like the labelling of separate *entrées* or *airs* in the *grand ballets* of the Philidor Collection. The terminology corresponds to that introduced by Jonson in *Chloridia*.

---

[64] These same suites appear in GB-Och, Mus. 433 with preludes.

[65] From the manuscript's title-page.

The sources which look most like ballet music by dance-music composers at the English court are, unfortunately, not English. There are two manuscripts associated with Queen Christina's Swedish court. The first, in the Uppsala University Library, contains music principally by the French violinists

Ex. 6.5. 'Ballet à 5' (treble part only), from D-Kl, MS Mus. fol. 61

Ex. 6.5. *Continued*

attracted to Queen Christina's court in 1646.[66] This includes eight dances by Nicolas Picart, all of them very short two-strain pieces, like separate *entrées* but some bearing the names of regular social dances—*bransle, gavotte,* etc. Picart got out of England in the early 1640s, spent some time in the *Vingt-quatre Violons,* and was one of six violinists recruited for the Swedish court in 1647.

The Uppsala manuscript also contains nearly a dozen pieces by Étienne Nau, including an extended five-part 'Pavan de Mons Nau' with a structure so idiosyncratic that it seems to need choreography to explain it. Music attributed to Étienne Nau also features in the Kassel manuscript (D-Kl, MS Mus. fol. 61).[67] A 'Ballet à 5' has six numbered entries, all of which have two strains (see Ex. 6.5). Their structure could be summarized as follows:

1.	₵5 6		F C F
2.	7 7		F F F
3.	38 ₵4		d F d
4.	₵6 6		F C F
5.	6 6		d A d(♯)
6.	38 12		F C F

[66] S-Uu, IMhs 409. For this manuscript (which is written in new German keyboard tablature) see Mráček, *Seventeenth-Century Instrumental Dance Music.*

[67] For this manuscript, complete with facsimile, see J. Écorcheville (ed.), *Vingt Suites d'orchestre du XVII* *siècle français* (Paris, 1906).

This would function perfectly well in a French *ballet*; but it must also represent the kind of structure composed for Caroline antimasque dances. Nau and his colleagues must have been composing music like this for the antimasques of the 1630s. We do not know how Nau's music ended up in these collections. He died in England in March 1647—too early probably for him to have contributed to Queen Christina's stock of ballet music. Nau's music must have been taken to Sweden by Picart, or perhaps later by Bulstrode Whitelocke on his embassy to the Swedish court in 1653–4. There is an outside chance that some of the Nau pieces (and possibly even some of Picart's) are music for Caroline masques. Given the complete absence of any real dance music which fits the structures indicated by the texts, what is interesting about these pieces is that they demonstrate that the composers who were involved in masque productions were, when occasion demanded, capable of turning out extensible, episodic dance music of the kind which pervaded the *ballet de cour*.

7

Masques away from Whitehall

The Jacobean masque was an invention specifically tailored to the tastes, aspirations, propaganda goals, and—not least—the resources of the court at Whitehall. But a great number of masques were in fact devised for perform- ance elsewhere. All of these were inevitably adaptations of the Whitehall form—but they are so various (some grandiose, some technically modest yet intellectually sophisticated, some naïve) that they seem at first to form a confusingly miscellaneous group. Much of the interest (and especially the musical interest) of these productions lies in their varying responses to con- ditions very different from those at Whitehall. With private masques this was most obviously a matter of scaling down the requirements to fit smaller budgets, smaller musical establishments, and smaller rooms. Inventors of widely varying imagination and skill had to adapt the court masque to all kinds of performance conditions.

We cannot simply divide masques into court and private. On the one hand, some court productions which took place away from Whitehall (*The Enter- tainment at Richmond*, for example) seem to have more in common with masques in provincial private houses than they do with the parent forms. On the other hand, a number of masques which took place under the auspices of the nobility were extravagantly produced and honed to serve regional political interests as complex as those which preoccupied the court (the Earl of Newcastle's entertainments are an obvious case). For this reason, I have organized the following survey into categories designed to move—albeit haphazardly, given the diversity of the material—from types which are vir- tually indistinguishable from masques sponsored by the court at Whitehall to entertainments which are manifestly domestic. Hence we begin with Inns of Court masques (which on occasions were so much in line with what went on in the Banqueting House that they were simply transferred there for a second performance), and then consider masques presented to royalty away from Whitehall, and finally 'private' masques—non-royal occasions in the houses of the nobility. *A Maske at Ludlow Castle* is left until last, not because it belongs at the more homely end of this spectrum (indeed, it was virtually a state occasion) but because it is illuminating to come to it with a sense, not just of its court models, but of other provincial masques and family entertainments.

The Inns of Court

Not all Inns of Court masques were so grand that they could be absorbed into the Whitehall court's own programme. Their better-known enterprises grew out of a context of regular in-house revels which in themselves throw light upon the expectations and conventions which suffuse dancing in the courtly masque. Even when a full masque was not prepared, the Inns traditionally held revels during the Christmas season. Their duration and magnificence varied, but they could extend from All Hallows Eve (31 October) until Candlemas Night (2 February) and embrace performances of masques and plays presented either by students from the Inns or by professional companies.

The revels found their justification in a view of what constituted a balanced education. As such, they formed part of an informal training programme in a gentlemanly ideal which could without exaggeration be described as the *sine qua non of* all masques. The place of dancing in the curriculum of the Inns of Court was described approvingly as early as the fifteenth century in Sir John Fortescue's *De Laudibus Legum Angliae*. This work had the status of an official history of the Inns; it was published in an English translation by R. Mulcaster (not the schoolmaster) in 1567 and in this version went through numerous editions. The positive attitude to dance tuition expressed by Fortescue was endorsed in the seventeenth century. As late as 1663 Edward Waterhouse, in his commentary on Fortescue, expatiates on the importance of 'that which besides the study of the Law is learned in the *Inns of Court*, to wit, Exercises of manhood, or ornament, and delicacy, of Learning and activity'. What he has to say about the value of musical instruction is completely in accord with the concept of the moral influence of musical harmony implicit in all masque texts: 'if this be the effect of Harmony, to incline the eye to kindness, the hand and foot to agility, the ear to attention, the whole man to grace of behaviour, Our *Inns of Court-man* is to be accomplished therewith . . .'.[1]

While there were many other apologists for the broadening of the law student's curriculum, not all who observed young men devoting so much time to music and dancing could see its positive side. Francis Lenton wrote satires in both verse and prose on the subject. The 'yong Innes of Court Gentleman' in his *Characters* (1631) is depicted as one whose

greatest case now, is how to carry himselfe according to the dancing Art, and [who] holds it a greater disgrace to be Nonsuit with a Lady, than Nonplus in the Law. . . . When he aspires once to be a Reueller, he then reueals himselfe to the full, and when he should bee mooting in the Hall, he is perhaps mounting in the Chamber, as if his father had onely sent him to Cut Capers, and turne in the Ayre till his braines bee addled . . . His Recreations . . . (as Plaies, Dancing, Fencing, Tauerns,

---

[1] E. Waterhouse, *Fortescutus Illustratus* (London, 1663), 532–4; quoted in Wienpahl, *Music at the Inns of Court*, 170, 172. Waterhouse's views on the kinds of dancing which should be cultivated in such a context have been cited above (see p. 119).

Tobacco) . . . Amorous Sonnets, warbled to the Vyall, are his Coelestiall Harmony . . .[2]

On the other hand, there were some who, far from feeling that activities like dancing were mere frivolity, criticized what they saw as a decline in standards. In one extended description written in the mid-1630s of the customs and protocol observed in the Inns of Court revels a note of regret is sounded: 'Theis measures were wont to be trulie danced, it beinge accounted a shame for an Innes of Court man not to have learned to dance, especially the measures, but nowe their dancing is tourned to bare walking.'[3] Perhaps this amounts to little more than the sense of decline endemic amongst older generations contemplating the institutions around them.

As a young member of Middle Temple in 1628, Bulstrode Whitelocke felt enormously proud of the high standards of their revels. When elected to the position of Master of the Revels, he took his responsibilities very seriously

Allholland day came, which by the custom of those societies is reckoned the beginning of their Christmas, in the evening the M[r] entered the Hall, with about 16 revellers, proper hansome young gentlemen, habited in rich suits, shoes and stockings, hats and great feathers, the M[r] led them in his bar gowne with a white staffe in his hand, the musique playing before them. They began with the old measures, after that they daunced the Branles, then the M[r] took his seat, & the Revellers daunced Galliards, Corantoes, & french daunces, then countrey daunces till it grew very late.

The newes of these Revells & the excellent dauncers in them, being knowne, there resorted to them every Satterday night, being the time of the Revells, very much company of gentlemen & Ladyes, and some of them of great quality, & when they had done dauncing in the Hall, the M[r] brought the Ladyes to S[r] Sidney Montagues chamber, which he had borrowed for that purpose, & there treated them with wine, sweetmeats, & a fresh bout att dauncing.

Sometimes to Court Ladyes & other Grandesses did them the honor to come to the Revells, & were no small charge to the M[r], and being so much noted and frequented, there was a great striving for places to see them . . .

A forrein Great L. of Germany, had a desire to see these Revells, the M[r] intertained him in the Hall & chamber with no small ceremony & charge, & was able to discourse in Latin with him, and the Grave was highly pleased with his treatment, affirming that there were no such Noble Colledges in christendome.[4]

It is not difficult to see in his arrangements for the Christmas 1628–9 season some continuity with the full masques mounted by the Inns of Court. It was surely the tradition of the revels that gave the Inns of Court the experience, expertise, and confidence which enabled them to undertake more ambitious projects.

---

[2] F. Lenton, *Characterismi: or Lentons Leasures Expressed in Eassayes and Characters* (London, 1631), Sig. [F5].

[3] From the Brerewood manuscript c.1635–8 in the Middle Temple library; quoted by Cunningham, *Dancing at the Inns of Court*, 9.

[4] Whitelocke, 'Annales', GB-Lbl, Add. MS 53726, fos. 45[v]–46[r].

In our period the Inns of Court presented a number of impressive (and costly) masques at Whitehall. In February 1613 they provided two of the three masques for the Palatine wedding celebrations: first *The Memorable Masque of the Middle Temple and Lincoln's Inn* and then (a few days later than planned because the king felt tired) *The Masque of the Inner Temple and Gray's Inn.* The following year, Grays Inn contributed *The Masque of Flowers* to the Somerset wedding celebrations. (Sir Francis Bacon, whose essay 'On Masques and Triumphs' bristles with cryptic personal observations about what works in a masque, was deeply involved in the promotion of the two last-mentioned masques.) The most notable Inns of Court masque at court is, of course, *The Triumph of Peace*, the response of all four Inns to a prompt from the king that they should demonstrate their implicit opposition to the views expressed by William Prynne in *Histrio-Mastix* (1633). The financial burden of this production was enormous; levies on Inns of Court members were increased as costs escalated.

The Triumphs of the Prince d'Amour was performed at the Middle Temple, but it was nevertheless intended for royalty. It took place in February 1636 in honour of the visiting Palatinate Princes, accompanied by Queen Henrietta Maria and members of her court (who, for amusement, dressed as citizens). This masque fits into the Middle Temple's revelling tradition—with its election of a 'Prince d'Amour'—and it formed the climax of their 1635–6 season. It probably differed most from court masques in its designs since these were executed, not by Inigo Jones, but by a M. Corseilles. The vocal music by the Lawes brothers was, as we have seen, of a quality and extensiveness unsurpassed in the period. Unfortunately, nothing of any detail survives to indicate the numbers or kind of musicians involved.

In addition to productions specifically devised for performance at court, there were others which were prepared for the Inns' own halls but then given a second performance, by invitation, at Whitehall. It was under such circumstances that the 1618 Gray's Inn masque (*The Mountebanks' Masque*) was performed at court. Dudley Carleton received two letters about this event. The first, from his friend, John Chamberlain, rather dismissed it as a 'show, for I cannot call yt a Maske, seeing they were not disguised nor had visards'.[5] The other letter, from Sir Gerard Herbert, was more enthusiastic and mentioned some rather novel musical features: 'Grayes Inne maske . . . was very well liked and the dances well performed of the Gentlemen: the ayres and dances well devised. Some of the dances danct by the voices of boyes instead of musick which songe excellently well, and which gave more content then musicke . . .'.[6] There had, in fact, been dances performed to vocal music in Campion's *Lord Hay's Masque*, but the idea did not, on the whole, catch on. It can hardly be coincidence that this feature resurfaced in a masque at Francis Bacon's Inn, given his enthusiasm for 'dancing in song' (see above, p. 68).

[5] Chamberlain, *Letters*, ii. 136.

[6] Quoted by D. S. Bland (ed.), *Three Revels from the Inns of Court* (Trowbridge, 1984), 75–6.

Other Inns of Court masques are more obviously in-house productions. There are in particular two Jacobean texts which emphasize their character as private entertainments. Middleton's *Inner Temple Masque or Masque of Heroes* (1619) was—as its title-page declares—'presented . . . as an Entertainment for many worthy Ladies'. (We learn from the text that the gentlemen of the Inner Temple were assisted by actors from Prince Charles's Men). More interesting still is William Browne's 1615 *Inner Temple Masque*—or *Ulysses and Circe*—which was performed 'to please ourselves in private' (l. 8). No attempt was made to print this text (which survived in two manuscript copies).[7] The absence of a royal guest and the less formal occasion may have allowed the author greater freedom; he clearly did not feel constrained by established masque patterns and conventions. He produced an engaging text (an unusual treatment of the Circe myth) with a rather play-like narrative interest. (Browne even divides his masque into 'scenes'.)

This masque contained considerable musical variety. Its ingenious echo songs have been mentioned in Chapter 2. An antimasque of creatures who have been transformed by Circe's spells rush in and dance to an instrumental group which, like that in the first antimasque of *The Masque of Flowers* (performed twelve months earlier), is a distorted mixed consort: 'The music was composed of treble violins with all the inward parts; a bass viol, bass lute, sagbut, cornemuse, and a tabor and pipe' (ll. 259–60). There was, too, a strong mime element in the antimasque dancing: 'These together dancing an antic measure, towards the latter end of it missed Grillus who was newly slipped away, and whilst they were at a stand wondering what was become of him, the Woodman stepped forward and sung this song . . .' (ll. 260–4).

Browne merges masque and antimasque to such an extent that for a second *antimasque* of Circe's nymphs eight musicians appear looking very like the Orphic priests of so many main masques, 'in crimson taffeta robes, with chaplets of laurel on their heads, their lutes by them' (ll. 138–9). This antimasque scene concludes with a dance by the nymphs which was clearly not a 'spectacle of strangeness' but something quite dignified. Browne describes it as 'a most curious measure to a softer tune than the first anti-masque, as most fitting . . .' (ll. 379–80).

The masque opens with a Siren luring passing mariners. There is an anonymous setting of her song in GB-Ob, Tenbury MS 1019—though (predictably) without the parts for the full chorus who joined in 'as from a grove near' in the repeat of the final couplet. Browne described the song as being 'lascivious proper to them'. It *is* a beguiling setting—enhanced in the surviving score by extensive written-out ornamentation. Not unlike Ferrabosco's masque songs, it has a chordal lute accompaniment, a vocal line that often leaps within the framework of the common chord and that has some declamatory characteristics—but without a complete subordination of

---

[7] The title *Ulysses and Circe* derives from, *The Works of William Browne*, ed. T. Davies (London, 1772); for details of the text see *BM*, 200.

melody to the accent and inflection of the spoken voice. The basic tonality is C minor, although it frequently draws on the major colourings of mediant and submediant chords (Ex. 7.1).

Browne's *Inner Temple Masque* is a subtle expression of the period's fascination with the potential of sophisticated art to deceive. In a masque, we expect decadence to be ridiculous or grotesque. But the sirens sing attractive (alluring) music and Browne has his main masque and antimasques taking place in essentially the same environment. The confusion between a virtuous world and a seeming paradise is complicated further when Circe vindicates her actions. Browne's purposes seem quite amoral—this is pure entertainment. (His gently ironic treatment of masque conventions provides an interesting analogue for Milton's Circe masque nearly twenty years later.)

There is one masque which might be mentioned here since, although it was not an Inns of Court production, it was inspired by a similar view of the place of such activities as part of a complete education. Sir Francis Kynaston contrived *Corona Minervae* in 1636 for the launching of his academy, the Musaeum Minervae. It was, according to its title-page, 'presented before Prince Charles, His Highnesse the Duke of York his Brother, and Lady Mary his Sister, the 27th of February, at the Colledge of the Museum Minervae'. Kynaston's *Constitutions of the Musaeum Minervae*—a prospectus for the academy—indicate that music was to occupy its traditional place in the curriculum and that dancing would also be encouraged. Teaching positions, based primarily on the division of the liberal arts, were established; 'The Professour of Musick shall teach these: Skill in singing and Musick to play upon Organ, Lute. Violl &c.' (and we may note the emphasis on respectable instruments here—the violin, the instrument of dancing-masters and professionals, is conspicuously absent). At the end of this outline of the formal curriculum we read 'Also *Riding* shall be taught, and *Dancing* and behaviour, *Painting, Sculpture, Writing* . . .'.[8] A masque would clearly have been seen as an appropriate way of marking the College's foundation.

The text describes an antimasque of contending seasons, followed by a main masque in which the positive qualities of each season and a spirit of co-operation amongst them is celebrated. The antimasque dance is outlined in a way which makes a rather curious distinction between 'enter' and 'dance': 'Here enter to dance, 1. a *Frog* followed by a *Fisher-man*. To them, 2. a *Sheepsherer* leading a *Ram*. To them, 3. a *Drunken Butcher* holding a *Pig* by the taile. 4. To them a *Chimney-sweeper* and a *Cat*. All to severall straines of agreeing musicke. At length all being entred, they joyne in a Dance.' The description of the music is tantalizingly vague, here. In describing the music for the main masque, Kynaston implies that he had (or wanted?) something comparable with what Lawes was composing for masques just at this time— 'severall Songs by severall voices, with Symphanies betwixt, and a Chorus'.

---

[8] F. Kynaston, *The Constitutions of the Musaeum Minervae* (London, 1636), 5.

Ex. 7.1. Anon., 'Steer hither', from GB-Ob, MS Tenbury 1019

Ex. 7.1. *Continued*

All accidentals in the vocal line are editorial except for the raised *b'* in bar 10. In addition to the lute tablature, the manuscript has a stave-notation bass part written using (an octave transposing) soprano clef (but which also has other internal octave transpositions). This linear bass line has a number of errors; the bass line in Ex. 7.1 is that of the lute tablature.

2: *a'* is not marked flat

6: quintuplet group written as demisemiquavers

8: crotchet tied to semiquaver on 'pray' is written as a dotted quaver

10: quintuplet group written as demisemiquavers

11: crotchet tied to semiquaver on 'than' is written as a dotted quaver; *a'* is not marked flat

21: crotchet on 'dyes' written as dotted quaver

The main masque, however, has more talking (lecturing, almost) than any other. The entertainment culminated in a banquet and the text makes no explicit provision for revels.

Royal Entertainments

Royal entertainments away from Whitehall were often devised by the very people who worked on full court masques. Given this common genesis, it is striking how these productions nevertheless declare their difference from the Whitehall model. Amongst the productions which Jonson included in the masque section of his *Works*, a few stand out as not conforming to the classical pattern he did so much to establish. In almost all these cases, they are entertainments created for venues other than Whitehall.

Jonson's early entertainments are of this kind. *The Entertainment at Althorp* was presented by Sir Robert Spencer to Queen Anne and Prince Henry on their progress from Scotland in June 1603. *The Entertainment at Highgate*—described by Jonson as 'a private entertainment'—was hosted by Sir William Cornwallis on May Day 1604 in honour of the king and queen.[9] These are essentially garden entertainments (even though sections of both did take place indoors). Their kinship with the entertainments offered to Elizabeth I on her progresses is clear—entertainments designed for a peripatetic court, not for a burgeoning Whitehall-centred establishment.[10] At the end of his career Jonson returned to forms in which antimasque-like dramatization and musical interlude punctuate a royal visit to a country house. His last entertainments (*The Entertainment at Welbeck* and *Love's Welcome at Bolsover*) took place on the estates of William Cavendish, first Earl of Newcastle, during Charles I's progresses of 1633 and 1634.[11] Leah Marcus observes that these entertainments had a deliberately retrospective character, emphasizing continuity with the past in Charles I's return to the kingdom of his forefathers: 'Even when it came to the choice of poets in 1633, Charles's journey recapitulated the past. . . . Jonson's work [*The Entertainment at Welbeck*] is a piece of antiquarianism, a conscious replication of the popular pastimes that had embellished a royal entertainment more than fifty years earlier.'[12]

Campion's *Entertainment at Caversham* was performed in April 1613. It was devised for Lord Knollys, who was host to the queen as she progressed from Gravesend (where she had farewelled her daughter Elizabeth and the Count Palatine) to Bath (where she sought treatment for gout). Like most such entertainments, it is in three parts: a welcome in the gardens, a masque held after supper on the night of her arrival, and a farewell which took place out in the gardens again. The masque itself, like others performed away from court, has no spectacular scenic transformations and required less lavish musical resources than any of Campion's other masques. No details are given in

[9] H&S, vii. 136. The three-part song 'See, see, O see, who here is come a Maying' (ll. 93–112) was set by Martin Pearson and was published in his *Private Musicke, or the First Booke of Ayres and Dialogues* (London, 1620).

[10] For Elizabethan entertainments of this kind see J. E. Wilson (ed.), *Entertainments for Elizabeth I* (Woodbridge, 1980), and B. R. Smith, 'Landscape with Figures: The Three Realms of Queen Elizabeth's Country-house Revels,' *RD* 8 (1977), 110–15.

[11] The Welbeck entertainment took place on the king's progress to Scotland in May 1633, the Bolsover entertainment during his progress through England in July 1634. William Lawes's setting of the opening song in *The Entertainment at Welbeck* is found in his autograph, GB-Lbl, Add. MS 31432, fos. 20ᵛ–21ʳ. There has been considerable doubt about whether this setting was written for Welbeck, however, since there are marked discrepancies between text and score in the allocation of lines. Since, however, Lawes seems to have departed from his given text quite freely in the music for *The Triumph of Peace* and (especially) *Britannia Triumphans* (see above, pp. 197 and 200), it seems to me not unlikely that the Lawes setting is the one used in the performance.

[12] *The Politics of Mirth* (London, 1986), 129. On Newcastle's own criticism of the prevailing fashions in court masques, see above, p. 215 n. 29 and Butler, *Theatre and Crisis*, 196–7.

the published account of the instruments used in the masque itself, although members of the King's Musick had accompanied the queen to Caversham. We are told that when she dined privately 'the Kings Violins attended her with their sollemnest musick, as an excellent consort in like manner did the next day at dinner' (p. 242).

The emphasis in the text is on the antimasque section, a continuation from the previous day's garden entertainment of a comic conversation between a traveller, a gardener, and a cynic. This exchange leads into 'A Song of three Voyces with diuers Instruments' beginning 'Night as well as brightest day hath her delight. | Let vs then with mirth and Musicke decke the night . . .' (p. 244). This is not intrinsically antimasque material, but it is given a parodic dimension by the traveller, who promises to keep time with his gestures 'A la mode de France'. The masquers are preceded by torch-bearing pages who come in to 'a great noise of drums and phifes' (p. 245). Of the main masque itself we learn only that eight masquers came in who

instantly fell into a new dance, at the end whereof they tooke forth the Ladies, and danced with them; and so well was the Queene pleased with her intertainment, that shee vouchsafed to make her selfe the head of their Reuels, and graciously to adorne the place with her personall dancing: much of the night being thus spent with varietie of dances, the Maskers made a conclusion with a second new dance.   (p. 246)

This is typical of masques away from court: scenic display is reduced and the antimasque (dependent on personnel rather than machines) given greater importance. The same tendency can be seen in the masques at Coleoverton, Bretby, Knowsley, and—the most extreme case—in *The Gypsies Metamorphosed*.

It is ironic that no text survives for the entertainment presented to James I at Brougham Castle in August 1617 since not only is it very fully documented but, as we have seen, it is the only masque in the entire period to have a publication completely given over to its music.[13] Ian Spink deduced the masque's device from the songs themselves, and in doing so he drew attention to the remarkable parallels between this entertainment and *The Gypsies Metamorphosed*.[14] This took place in similar circumstances to the Welbeck and Bolsover entertainments of 1633–4; James I broke his journey between Edinburgh and London as the guest of Francis Clifford, fourth Earl of Cumberland. In a fascinating article on this progress, R. T. Spence presents a vivid picture of its scale—'A rough estimate', he writes, 'would put the household officers and servants on this progress at between 700 and 800, with followers extra.'[15] The Clifford family, notable patrons of the arts, retained Thomas Campion to prepare the text and oversee the production. A payment

---

[13] *The Ayres that were sung and played, at Brougham Castle in Westmoreland, in the King's Entertainment.* See above, p. 24.

[14] Spink, 'Campion's Entertainment at Brougham Castle, 1617', 61.

[15] Spence, 'A Royal Progress in the North', 44.

of 100 marks (£66. 13s. 4d.) was made 'to Doctor Campion whoe Composed the whole matter, Songs etc. for paines therein, Coming downe to prepare, order it, and see all Acted . . .'.[16] 'Composed' here meant writing the words of the songs, not setting them to music. The latter task was left in the hands of two musicians associated with the Earl's household—George Mason and (possibly for just one song) John Earsden.[17] The basic device seems to have been worked out by the earl's son, Lord Henry Clifford. In a fascinating letter to Henry Clifford in which these relationships are implicit, the earl betrays considerable anxiety about the cost of it all:

Sonn, I have till now expected y'r l'res, according to your promis at y'r departure: so did Geo. Minson [Mason] y'r directions touching the musick. whereupon he mought the better have writt to doctor Campion. . . . For my own opinion, albeit I will not dislyke y'r device, I fynde plainly, upon better consideration, the charge for that entertaynment will grow very great, besyde the musick; and that, instead of less'ning, my charge in gen'all encreaseth, and newe paim'ts come on, w'ch, without better providence hereafter, cannot be p'formed.[18]

This was another tripartite entertainment. The music was performed at supper on the first night of the king's visit, at the masque on the second night, and at his farewell from Brougham Castle. The masque must have taken place in the Great Chamber of the castle, a room which measured 54 feet by 23 feet (approximately one quarter the area of the Whitehall Banqueting House). The antimasque section begins with a bass song performed the gypsies' leader. This, declamatory in style, with a very unobtrusive bass line, is characterized by frequent leaps of a fourth, fifth, or octave, giving the whole a kind comic robustness. The song describes the antimasque dancing which, typically, is full of movements specifically described as being unsuitable for normal society:

> . . . Yet bend you low your curled tops.
> Touch the hallowed earth,
> And then rise agen
> With anticke hops vnus'd of men.

Another of the antimasque songs (entitled 'The Dance') has solo sections for a soprano, two basses, and three tenors. These performers must have danced as they sang words describing something very like a country dance:

---

[16] Quoted ibid. 59.

[17] George Mason had been a member of the Earl's household since at least 1610. Lynn Hulse writes, 'strictly speaking, George Mason was no longer a member of Cumberland's household. He had left the earl's employment towards the end of 1612 when he moved to York, but he continued to serve the Cliffords on a temporary basis until at least December 1619. . . . John Earsden joined the Cumberland household as a page to the earl's wife, Lady Grissell Abergavenny, some time before April 1610 and served out a musical apprenticeship until December 1613 when he received an adult wage. He remained in the family's employment until the late 1650s. Earsden's background may not have been as humble as the other musicians who served in the earl's band as he is referred to as gentleman to the earl, a mark of respect not accorded to Hingeston, Mason, Cressett or Pendrie. Earsden played on the lute, theorbo and viol.' (private communication).

[18] Spink, 'Campion's Entertainment', 58. Spink points out that the original of this letter is missing and that the earliest extant source for it is T. D. Whitaker, *History and Antiquities of the Deanery of Craven* (London, 1805), 263–4.

Let us in a louer's round
Circle all this hallowed ground.
Softly, softly, trip and goe,
The light foot fairies iet it so.
    Forward then,
    and back againe;
    Here and there,
    and euery where;
Winding to and winding fro,
Skipping hye and lowting low
And like louers hand in hand,
March around and make a stand.

The last couplet is marked 'Chorus', though only a unison line is provided. Mason manages some rhythmic interest through the use of mixed rhythms to underline the shifts in the text (see Ex. 7.2).

An altogether more serious mood is established by the two main masque songs. The first is a dignified declamatory setting. The second has solo sections for the same six singers who performed in the antimasque. They are quite explicitly gypsies metamorphosed ('unmasked now and clear') but the masque device must also have allowed these same singers to appear as rustics. Each singer presents attributes of James's reign—Truth, Peace, Love, Honour, Long-Life, and (unnamed) Fame. A short declamatory solo from each leads into a harmonized cadential phrase. The song ends with twenty bars of chorus

Ex. 7.2. Mason, 'The Dance', bars 25–33, from *The Ayres that were Sung and Played at Brougham Castle* (1617)

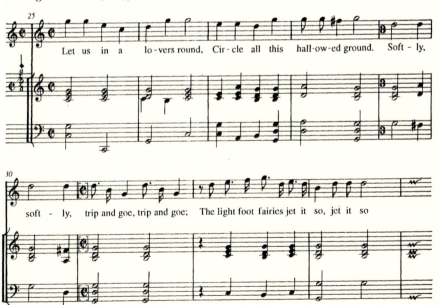

which (puzzlingly, given the four-part harmonizations of the first part of the song) is in two parts only.

The surviving accounts give a good picture of the performing arrangements. The Earl borrowed from other households to supplement his own very respectable group of musicians, some of whom held positions whose designations do not indicate a specifically musical function. Spence's analysis of the accounts presents a picture which must be reasonably typical of the arrangements made by other aristocrats faced with the problem of trying to furnish a courtly masque from a permanent establishment very much smaller than Whitehall's:

Mason himself and 'Mr Johnson, a schoolmaster of York' . . . were the leading lights judging by their rewards of £13 6s. 8d. each. Three of the Lord President's men shared £30 for their performing. Two of the players, Mr John Hillie and Mr Thomas Holte, were the Earl's gentlemen in waiting . . . The latter could dance as well as sing and play the viol, and this may have been the range of accomplishments expected of all of them . . . John Earsden and Charles Pendrie would take part, likewise Earl Francis's youngest musician, Edward Cresset.

The others were men of musical talent employed by the Earl's relatives and friends. His son-in-law Sir Gervase Clifton of Clifton, Nottinghamshire had his own group of five players, and Mason borrowed one of them, Charles of Hodsock, who received £5 in reward. Corbett, who was paid £3 6s. 8d., was employed by Sir Timothy Hutton of Marske, whom James had knighted at York. Another member was the servant of Sir Thomas Wentworth's officer Mr Fletcher. His reward of £1 was not necessarily for a minor role. Wentworth, the Earl's other son-in-law, would express his own appreciation in cash. Mason also procured a Hull man to play the lute at Brougham, but as there was no occasion to use him he was went back with 6s. for his expenses. Fourteen men, including Campion, himself a singer as well as a lutenist, should have sufficed. But it is always possible that Clifton's other musicians, who travelled about, were on hand at the Feast, though they are not mentioned.[19]

In August 1621 the Duke of Buckingham entertained the king at Burley-on-the-Hill (the beautiful country house he had recently acquired in Rutland) with 'great prouision of playes maskes and all maner of entertainment'.[20] This included on 3 August Jonson's *Gypsies Metamorphosed*. The following day the court moved on to Belvoir Castle, about fourteen miles away, where the masque was repeated on 5 August in a slightly adapted version. Early in the following month, the masque was performed a third time at Windsor Castle. Clearly James enjoyed this most coarse of Jonson's entertainments. John Chamberlain, on the other hand, was not impressed. In October, after the Windsor performance, he wrote to Dudley Carleton 'for lacke of better newes here is likewise a ballet or song of Ben Iohnsons in the play or shew at the lord Marquis at Burly, and repeated again at windsor . . . ; there were other songs and deuises of baser alay . . .'.[21]

[19] Spence, 'A Royal Progress', 60.   [20] Chamberlain to Carleton, 4 Aug. 1621, *Letters*, ii. 396.
[21] Chamberlain to Carleton, 27 Oct. 1621, ibid., 404–5.

As with *The Mountebanks' Masque* three and a half years earlier, Chamberlain was not sure how to describe this production; he calls it a 'play or shew'—the term 'masque' was not actually applied to *The Gypsies Metamorphosed* until the 1640 editions.[22] In this entertainment Jonson was writing for performance conditions quite unlike those of his court masques, and what he prepared was structurally very unusual, a work *sui generis*. The text makes no mention of revels or set masque dances. The main masque contains five songs which make no reference to dancing, but instead are all addressed directly to the king as a complimentary epilogue. Measured against court models, *The Gypsies Metamorphosed* is like an antimasque followed by a sung valediction. The antimasque section (which occupies more than nine-tenths of this 1,500-line text) is unusual in more than its bulk. As in the Brougham Castle entertainment, the gypsies of the antimasque are played by the nobles who, 'chang'd', preside over the final (main masque) section. Buckingham himself was the Captain or First Gypsy. (As we have seen, such characterization runs counter to Jonson's normal sense of decorum.) The 'dressing down' aspect of this entertainment may have allowed Buckingham—in assuming a very uncourtly persona—to indulge in the kind of virtuoso display that was frowned upon in other situations.

The antimasque is punctuated by dancing. What is described by the text as 'Dance 2' is broken up into six strains interspersed throughout the dialogue and songs of the antimasque. Each strain was performed as a separate short dance.[23] Whatever tune was used (and the promisingly titled 'Gypsies Maske' in Add. MS 10444 is one strain too short), this treatment of the constituent strains of one dance as separate short dances seems unique.[24] The country dance (at l. 799) is presented very much as a distorted reflection of the preoccupations of the court. It is introduced in a conversation between two characters who discuss how to entertain the newly arrived gypsies. One exclaims, 'Wee must haue some Musique then, and take out the wenches' (l. 769). The idea of 'taking out' the women turns this dance, accompanied by pipes and drum, into a mock-revels, a low imitation of the social dances which climaxed all court masques.[25]

There are four seventeenth-century settings of songs from *The Gypsies Metamorphosed*, and all belong to the antimasque (rather than to the concluding section). Two (including the ballad 'Cock-Lorell') are anonymous, one is by Robert Johnson, and a fourth is attributed to Edmund Chilmead (1610–54), an attribution which, if correct, means that this song could not have been

---

[22] H&S, vii. 552, 555.

[23] The material between the various strains of Dance 2 differed in each of the performances. This is most easily seen in W. W. Greg, *Jonson's Masque of Gipsies in the Burley, Belvoir and Windsor Versions* (London, 1952), which sets out the Burley/Belvoir and Windsor versions as parallel texts.

[24] GB-Lbl, Add. MS 10444 has quite a number of 6-strain antimasque dances, but no. 60, 'The Gypsies Masque' (S 111), has only five.

[25] A stage direction in the 1640 folio repeats the idea of 'taking out' the wenches. See H&S, vii. 592, critical commentary on ll. 798–9.

used for the original performances.[26] All are written in a simple, popular style, but the Robert Johnson song, 'From the Famous Peak of Derby', is musically the most satisfying. Like the mountebanks' song in *The Mountebanks' Masque*, it advertises the wares and talents of the antimasquers:

> Knacks we haue that will delight you,
> Slightes of hand that will invite you
> To indure o' tawney faces ...   (ll. 133–5)

It is sung by the 'first leading Gipsie . . . being the Jackman' (servant), presumably to the accompaniment of his 'guittara', since a few minutes earlier he had called for it. The guitar, which was not widely known in England at that time, must have been thought suitably exotic for the gypsy's song.[27] The freshness of Johnson's setting comes mainly from the constant alternation between a 3/2 and a 3/4 metre. Where a phrase is largely in 3/2, Johnson always switches to a ♩♩ (3/4) group for the phrase ending; the abruptness of this rhythm gives the whole song a robust character which is obviously suited to the antimasque (see Ex. 7.3a). The anonymous song, 'To the Old, Long Life and Treasure', which was sung later in the masque, has a similar type of phrase ending, although this time it is a matter of syncopation within a duple rhythm. (The syncopation is governed by the natural rhythm of words like 'treasure', 'pleasure', and 'leisure'; see Ex. 7.3b.[28])

The coarsely satirical 'Cock-Lorell' fits into a discussion about history and degree amongst gypsies which mirrors absurdly the rank and quality of the courtly audience. Having a ballad as the chronicle of the gypsies' history underlines the comedy of this inverted hierarchy. A minstrel is called in to 'chaunt out the farce' (which runs to twenty stanzas in the Folio text). Its simple tune was printed in Playford's *Dancing Master* of 1651.[29] Like all such ballads, the whole interest of the song lay in the comic narrative carried on from stanza to stanza.

Ben Jonson was paid £100 for *The Gypsies Metamorphosed*. Nicholas Lanier, on the other hand, received £200. It is not obvious how to account for such a generous payment to this favoured musician, particularly given that one of the antimasque settings likely to have originated in the masque performances is by Robert Johnson. The involvement of several composers is, of course, completely standard; it is the size of the payment which is puzzling. Lanier could have set all the main-masque songs—and sung them. He may, too, have taken care of whatever scenic effects were used (as he had for *Lovers Made Men*). Three payments to instrumentalists are recorded and even these (with a generous payment of £2. 11s. to a drummer) seem to emphasize the

---

[26] Sabol suggests (*Four Hundred Songs and Dances*, 556) that Chilmead may have been only the copyist of the song in GB-Lbl, Add. MS 29396.

[27] The *OED* lists this as the first example of the use of the word in English.

[28] This setting for 'To the old, long life and treasure' was probably used for 'The fairy beam upon you' (ll. 262 ff.) since both share the same (slightly unusual) verse form.

[29] See C. M. Simpson, *The British Broadside Ballad and its Music* (New Brunswick, NJ, 1966), 129–33.

EX. 7.3. (*a*) Johnson, 'From the famous peak of Derby', bars 1–4, from Playford, *The Musical Companion* (1673)

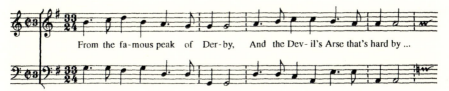

From the fa-mous peak of Der-by, And the Dev-il's Arse that's hard by ...

(*b*) anon., 'To the old, long life and treasure', bars 1–4, from US-NYp, MS Drexel 4257

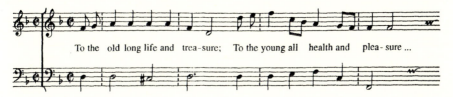

To the old long life and trea-sure; To the young all health and plea-sure ...

domination of antimasque elements. A cornett-player received 11s. and a group of violins £12. 16s. Given that the figures cited in Chapter 1 varied between £1 and £2 for a violinist performing in a masque, this last payment could imply any number of players between six and twelve. (Interestingly, it would provide for five violinists—with just a shilling to spare—paid at the same rate as the drummer. Perhaps they formed a five-part ensemble without any instrumental doubling.)

In *The Gypsies Metamorphosed* Jonson—responding to unique performance conditions—came up with something quite unlike any of his other masques.[30] It is instructive to realize that *Lovers Made Men* was also performed under unusual circumstances—as part of an entertainment presented by Lord Hay in honour of the Baron de la Tour, ambassador extraordinary from the French

---

[30] The so-called *Masque of Owls* is even less like its courtly namesakes. Presented to Prince Charles at Kenilworth in Aug. 1624, it consists of one extended rhyming speech by the Ghost of Captain Cox introducing six 'owls' who, Herford and Simpson suggest, 'probably . . . were rustic actors who danced out as Captain Cox sprung them one by one upon the company' (H&S, x. 700). It should be noted that there are two Jonson 'masques' which took place at Whitehall and which seem almost as irregular as *The Masque of Owls*. *Christmas his Masque* was 'presented at court, 1616' and, again, is very like a mummers' play. It was not printed until the 1640 Folio, but an earlier manuscript copy calls it 'Christmas his Showe', a title which Herford and Simpson note 'Jonson might have retained with advantage'. *The Irish Masque*, which does have a regular structure but with a very truncated main-masque section (and no mention of revels), was Jonson's contribution to the Somerset wedding at Christmas 1613. In comparison with Campion's *Somerset Masque* and the Gray's Inn *Masque of Flowers*, Jonson is remarkably reticent about the occasion for this masque; one passing reference to a marriage is made in the antimasque (l. 69), while the main masque stresses the virtue of obedience to the king. The author of *Hymenaei* manages to avoid the charge of hypocrisy in carrying out the commission for this masque by ignoring the wedding itself and concentrating (albeit obliquely) on the dissent it had aroused. Campion confronts these issues more directly in his masque by having Error, Rumour, Curiosity, and Credulity represented as having prevented the enchanted knights reaching the nuptial celebrations at court.

court.[31] It is not clear whether the king attended the performance, though it seems likely. This is a particularly attractive Jonson text and its musical significance has been explored in Chapter 3. It is worth noting here, however that (as in the Brougham Castle masque and *The Gypsies Metmorphosed*, but unlike the standard court masque) there is not a separate cast of antimasquers—they are simply lovers in a besotted state before their transformation into the alert and courteous nobles of the main masque. Lanier's scene—though apparently finely executed—did not require any machinery for transformations. All these features seem explicable as a response to Essex House (Lord Hay's residence) as a venue rather than the Banqueting House. Perhaps it was the different circumstances which encouraged Jonson and Lanier to experiment in other directions as well.[32]

Robert White's *Cupid's Banishment: a Maske*—a remarkable early seventeenth-century antecedent for Purcell's *Dido and Aeneas* (and Blow's *Venus and Adonis*)[33]—was presented to Queen Anne by the young gentlewomen of the Ladies' Hall at Deptford in Greenwich in May 1617. It appears from Occasion's introductory speech (ll. 106–9) that such entertainments were an annual event. Towards the end of the masque, the queen is presented with needlework by two of her goddaughters—pupils at the Hall. Like the Middle Temple with its Prince d'Amour, the Ladies' Hall had a 'Kinge and Queene of Fortunes choice' to preside over their celebrations. *Cupid's Banishment* exploits the combined presence of both the real queen and these monarchs of the revels.

The title of the masque is slightly misleading. At its culmination the young women masquers are presented by Diana (and so are to be seen as embodiments of chastity) and the final song refers to what has been happening as 'Cynthia's Triumphs'. In the extended first section of the masque, Cupid (wanton love) is indeed banished, though Bacchus is allowed to stay for a time to entertain the young ladies. Diana is first revealed when a mountain opens (ll. 160–4). This resembles *Pleasure Reconciled to Virtue* (performed eight months later) and even more striking anticipations of this court masque follow. Robert White's Bacchus was clearly the inspiration for Jonson's Comus, and his children—dancing in barrels—are very like Comus' retinue (especially as described by the Venetian chaplain). Did the Queen encourage

---

[31] Lord Hay is said to have spent a total of £22,000 on the ambassador's entertainment. See H&S, x. 566.

[32] This was not Lord Hay's only masquing venture. In Jan. 1618 he, or rather his wife, planned a masque which had to be abandoned because it displeased the king and queen. The incident attracted quite a lot of comment. John Chamberlain (*Letters*, ii. 125–6) is most informative about it: 'There was a maske of nine Ladies in hand at theyre owne cost, whereof the principall was the Lady Haye as Quene of the Amazons . . . They had taken great paines in continuall practising, and were almost perfet and all theyre implements provided, but whatsoever the cause was, neither the Queene nor King did like or allow of yt and so all is dasht.'

[33] It is unlikely, however, that either of these productions received its *first* performance at Josiah Priest's school. See (on *Dido*) B. Wood and A. Pinnock, ' "Unscarr'd by turning times"?: The Dating of Purcell's *Dido and Aeneas*', *EM* 20 (1992), 372–91; and R. Luckett, 'A New Source for *Venus and Adonis*', *MT* 130 (1989), 76–9.

Jonson to develop White's idea (just as she had made suggestions about an antimasque for *The Masque of Queens*)?[34]

The manuscript of *Cupid's Banishment* is of unique interest since it includes the setting of Bacchus' song at the point in the text where it is to be sung. This is an appropriately sturdy, strophic setting. The song itself is made up of five stanzas, each of which contains four lines with three stresses and four with four stresses. In the setting, the three-stress lines are in common time, while the four-stress lines are set as a lively tripla section (with a *petite reprise* for the last couplet in each stanza).

The range of musical resources deployed in this masque is both impressive and modelled on court practice. The antimasque music is characteristically burlesque—a hammer and kettle (for a tinker), and a drunken fiddler—though Bacchus accompanies himself on a bass lute. 'Lowde musicke playes' as the mountain opens (l. 163), Hymen 'enters singinge . . . his followers attendinge him, with lutes and theorboes and excellent voices, the Musicions all in greene taffaty Robes' (ll. 227–32), and the masquers dance to violins (l. 537). The set dances all seem to have been elaborately choreographed. The final masque dance, in particular, created alphabetical figures as ingenious as anything described in court-masque texts: 'Twelue Nymphs descend from the mount . . . they pace with maiesty towards the presence and after the first strayne of the violins they daunce Anna Regina in letters their 2 maskinge daunce Iacobus Rex theire departinge daunce is Charolus P with many excellent figures fallinge off. by Mr Ounslo, tutor to the La: hall . . .' (ll. 523–40). The text gives the names of the participants. The young women masquers seem predominantly to have been the daughters of prominent officials in the Jacobean court.[35] Hymen, a singing role, was played by Charles Coleman (aged about 12 at the time), who was to become prominent as a musician in court circles during the Caroline period.

It was Coleman who took charge of the vocal music for *The Entertainment at Richmond* presented in September 1636 before Charles I and Henrietta Maria—a masque of considerable musical interest. The king and queen were returning to London from Oxford where they had been entertained with several plays (including *The Royal Slave*). The printed text is unusually informative about the process of putting the masque together. The suggestion came from Henrietta Maria who, we are told, wished to see her 6-year-old son (the future Charles II) in a dance. The Prince's servants and 'others in the

[34] On the links between this masque and *Pleasure Reconciled* see P. Walls, 'Jonson's Borrowing', *Theatre Notebook*, 28 (1974), 80–1.

[35] See C. E. McGee, '*Cupid's Banishment*: A Masque Presented to Her Majesty by Young Gentlewomen of the Ladies Hall, Deptford, May 4, 1617', *RD* 19 (1988), 259–60 (commentary on ll. 1–22). McGee gives the following information about Mr Ounslo: 'Judith Edwards of Wadhurst, Sussex, hired a dancing teacher with the same name for her daughters in 1627. Regular quarterly payments to him of £3 are registered in her personal account book until August of 1628 . . . In addition an Amaria Oneslowe undertook on October 21, 1618 "to serve this howse Gary's Inn with musike for the next yeare following for the ould wages . . ." ' (263–4).

family' had the idea of preceding this courtly dance with a country dance 'and some other rude ones, that might the better set off the Princes . . .'. Around this, and apparently in great haste, the author built his drama, making use, he tells us, of the accents of the locals for his antimasque.[36] Charles, given a Spenserian characterization as Prince Britomart, was joined by other youthful masquers: Lord Buckhurst and Edward Sackville (the two teenage sons of his governess, the Countess of Dorset), the 9-year-old Duke of Buckingham and his younger brother, Lord Francis Villiers (who since their father's assassination had been brought up with the royal children at Richmond), and Lord Carr.[37]

The author begins by claiming anonymity for himself and the music master:

> Scarse is the Author: what he meanes lesse knowne
> None will the words, none will the Musique owne. (ll. 3–4)

It is, thankfully, not the case that the person in charge of the music remained unknown. The text, while remaining silent on its authorship, ends with a tribute, first to Prince Charles for his varied steps, and then to Coleman. This begins with a wistful glance at the 'insubstantial pageant' theme:

Then was the Curtain let fall, and this folly (as all others doe) had consum'd it selfe, and left no impression in the spectators, or hearers, had it not bin that much admiration was conceau'd at the great quicknesse, and aptnesse of the *PRINCE*, who varying figures so often, was so farre from being out that he was able to lead the rest.

The speaking and action (which grac'd the words) was perform'd by my *Lord* of *Buckhurst*, and *M. Edward Sackvile*, shew'd that genuine action, was not so much confin'd to the stage, but a Gentleman might reach it, if not transcend it. The rest had its support from the Musique, which prepar'd, and commended the numbers, to the eares of the Auditors, and was excellently compos'd by Master *Charles Coleman*. (ll. 621–36)

Coleman had a house in Richmond; but he was also a member of The King's Musick. He is first listed in 1625 as part of 'The Consort' at the coronation of Charles I. From then on his name appears regularly with the Lutes (and Voices).[38] Two years before the Richmond entertainment he had been a lutenist/singer in *The Triumph of Peace* and he was highly esteemed as a song composer. Lucy Hutchinson (whose husband had lodged with Coleman before their marriage) described Richmond as a place where 'a greate deale of good young company, and many ingenious persons, that by reason of the court, where the young princes were bred, entertain'd themselves in that place'. Coleman, she continues, 'being a skilful composer in musick, the rest

---

[36] He actually describes them as Wiltshire accents (though Richmond is, of course, in Surrey).

[37] Lord Buckhurst's year of birth is unknown, but his brother was 14 at the time of the masque. Bentley points out that a painting of the two brothers done in 1637 makes them seem very close in age, possibly even twins. Their father, the fourth Earl of Dorset, was Lord Chamberlain to Henrietta Maria and so would also have been involved in the preparation of this masque. Van Dyck painted the Duke of Buckingham's two young sons in 1635, the year before *The Entertainment at Richmond*; they are dressed in what appears to be masquing costume.

[38] See Ashbee *RECM*, iii. 3, 33, 35, 38, and 109.

of the king's musitians often met at his house to practise new ayres and prepare them for the king; and divers of the gentlemen and ladies that were affected with musick came thither to heare; others that were not, tooke that pretence, to entertain themselves with the companie'.[39] For the Richmond masque, Coleman apparently set three main-masque songs (see below). The first antimasque, however, builds up to a performance of the pastoral dialogue 'Did not you once, Lucinda, vow', which survives in GB-Lbl, Add. MS 22582 and in various Playford songbooks published in the 1650s and 1660s.[40] A Shepherd (doubtless Coleman) and Shepherdess enter. Tom, the principal rustic character, having told the story of the pair's betrothal—the shepherdess 'was led away with his singing vorzooth'—produces a theorbo (a 'Viddle . . . aumost as long as a May-pole') and invites them to sing. Coleman's composition is typical of the pastoral dialogues being set in the Caroline period: seventeen lines of declamatory interchange, a shift to three lines of melodious triple-time solo, and a concluding four-line stanza set as a duet. This was doubtless an already composed piece inserted into the antimasque.

Coleman must, however, have written new music for the main-masque songs and choruses. The musicians are represented as the Priests of Apollo, and they are introduced by a Druid in terms which proclaim a continuity with mainstream court masques:

> Great *Apollo*,
> That know'st to heale wth thy sweet harmony
> The fierce rude minds of men, as well as bodies
> W[th] thy try'd medicines shew thy power now,
> Inspire thy *Priests* that may restraine this people,
> Come forth you sacred Ministers of peace
> And with your well tun'd *Lutes* and sweeter voice
> Make this disordred route to learne some measure. (ll. 406–13)

The person responsible for working out the dances is identified by the text as Simon Hopper. His part in facilitating Prince Charles's display of dancing skills at Richmond may have won him favour; in December 1638 he was granted an annual salary of £30 in the Prince of Wales's household 'for playing on music to the prince and the Duke of York'.[41] The country dance which forms part of the antimasque (like the sung dialogue) would not have been devised for this occasion. Elsewhere Hopper again used a standard dance in a contrived context: a Spaniard enters absorbed in reading 'when on the suddaine the Violin playes a Pavin, at which amaz'd he leaues off reading, the Violin stops, and as soone as he falls to reading againe it begins a Saraband, which makes him leasurely to take off his Rapier, and his Cloake, and fold it

---

[39] Lucy Hutchinson, *Memoirs of the Life of Colonel Hutchinson . . . Written by his Widow Lucy*, ed. J. Hutchinson (London, 1806), 38.

[40] Playford, *Select Musicall Ayres* (1652 and 1653), *Select Ayres* (1659), and *The Treasury of Musick* (1669). Modern editions in Sabol, *Four Hundred Songs and Dances*, S 48, and Spink, *English Songs 1625–1660*, 120 ff.

[41] In Jan. 1642 Hopper was appointed to a place in the violins in the King's Musick. See Ashbee, *RECM*, iii. 100, 114, 115 and—for his reappointment an the Restoration—129.

up gently, and in this measure to fall into a dance' (ll. 509–16). Elsewhere, however, Hopper clearly did have to work out new dances. One antimasque dance illustrated soldiers' warlike instincts being tamed by the queen's presence: 'Then rush in fiue totter'd Souldiers who begin wildly at first to dance, but conclude with a kinde of timorousnesse, and lay down their weapons at the *Queenes* feete' (ll. 440–3).

There were no revels in the course of this 'masque' (a term used on its title-page). It must have been decided that the child masquers should not have to do more than dance their two carefully prepared items. The Post who announces the arrival of Prince Britomart and his very young Cavaliers explicitly warns the audience not to attempt to dance with the principal masquer: 'But by the way, I am to signifie to you, Ladies, that you must not hope to dance with him; Pray do'nt vrge him to't. Hee'le be angry if you doe . . .' (ll. 480–2). (Perhaps that jocular prohibition was based on a genuine fear of a little boy's tantrum!)

The Richmond masque conforms to the pattern of court masques: responsibility for the dances—both composing the music and devising the choreography—lay with a violinist while the vocal music was the work of a lutenist-singer. The description of Coleman's contribution suggests that the dances were not thought of as part of the 'music'. Coleman and Hopper had had first-hand experience of the grandest form of such entertainments—both had performed in *The Triumph of Peace* (and possibly other less well documented court masques). Everything about *The Entertainment at Richmond*, however, was on a domestic scale.

In the early 1620s James I was entertained with a masque presented by Sir John Croft at Little Saxham, his house in Suffolk. This was very much a family affair. The masquers—nine goddesses—were mostly accounted for by Croft's eight daughters, four of them unmarried and all renowned beauties.[42] This seems to have been relatively modest in its scope: the surviving text has no antimasque section and gives no indication that changeable scenery was used. The main masque is itself very short—excluding a lengthy closing speech from Pan, it is entirely sung and runs to only fifty lines. But it follows the classical court pattern. Songs from Apollo introduce two set masque dances (described as 'measures'), the revels ('. . . they take out men to daunce Currantos and other dances'), and the concluding measure. Its form and modest scope suggest that the distinction between masques presented to royalty and truly 'private masques' could, on occasions, become very blurred.

Private Masques

How many masque-like entertainments took place in the houses of the nobility we shall never know, but it is becoming increasingly clear that those

[42] See C. E. McGee, 'The Visit of the Nine Goddesses: A Masque at Sir John Croft's House,' *ELR* 21 (1991), 371–84. The goddesses were Juno, Venus, Pallas, Diana, Flora, Fortuna, Thetis, Ceres, and Natura.

with surviving texts represent only a small proportion of the total.[43] These ranged from the astonishingly ambitious *Entertainment at Ashby* at the beginning of the period to the emphatically domestic *Masque at Knowsley* at its end. All, however, are directly modelled on the court form.

The context in which many of these entertainments took place was one of intense interest in what had been going on at court. Masque performances were eagerly reported in correspondence—though often it was the attempts of ambassadors not to be humiliated by omission from the guest list rather than details of the production which attracted comment. Members of the aristocracy who could not attend particular masque performances often went out of their way to obtain copies of the text. The seventh Earl of Shrewsbury was one of those who took a lively interest in masque performances. He was sent the text of *The Vision of the Twelve Goddesses* and his daughter, the Countess of Arundel, promised him a copy of *The Masque of Beauty* (in which she had danced). Shrewsbury, though, was so impatient to read about the event that he wrote off directly to the Queen's lord chamberlain, Viscount Lisle, for a copy.[44] Amongst the fifth Earl of Cumberland's household accounts for the 1630s there are several entries recording the purchase of masque books (at 6*d.* each).[45] As we have seen, a few days after the performance of *Chloridia* in February 1631, Sir John Ashburnham sent Elizabeth of Bohemia a copy of the text.[46] In 1634 Viscount Conway paid 1*s.* 6*d.* to have the text of a masque (*Coelum Britannicum?*) copied out.[47] All this suggests a readership eager to share vicariously in the splendours of the court masque—and to emulate them in so far as their means would allow.

A network of familial connections links court and private entertainments. Sir Robert Spencer, who entertained James I at Althorp in 1603, was the father of Alice, Countess-Dowager of Derby, for whom the *Entertainment at Ashby* was performed in 1607.[48] In the early 1630s she received a similar tribute when Milton's *Arcades* was presented on her estate at Harefield.[49] Her daughter Frances married Sir John Egerton, the future Earl of Bridgewater, for whom the Chirk Castle Entertainment and the *Maske at Ludlow Castle* were presented. In February 1634 their sons danced at court in *Coelum Britannicum*.

[43] See C. E. McGee and J. C. Meagher, 'Preliminary Checklist of Tudor and Stuart Entertainments: 1603–1613', *RORD* 29 (1984), 47–126; and '. . . 1614–1625', *RORD* 30 (1988), 17–128.

[44] See H&S, x. 459.

[45] 8 Nov. 1633, 'two masque books, 1s' and 28 Jan. 1635, 'For a masque book, 6d'; GB-Llp. MS 3201, fo. 182ᵛ, cited in Woodfill, *Musicians in English Society*, 259.

[46] See H&S, x. 680, and above, p. 22.

[47] *CSPD* 1634–5, 591; and see Butler, *Theatre in Crisis*, 106 (and, for Conway's interest in other dramatic texts, 112).

[48] C. C. Brown, *John Milton's Aristocratic Entertainments* (Cambridge, 1985), says that Alice, Countess-Dowager of Derby was one of the masquers in *The Vision of the Twelve Goddesses* (1604) and *The Masque of Blackness* (1605). However, the person identified as the Countess of Derby in the annotations on the British Library copy of Daniel's masque, and in Antimo Galli's *Rime* describing *The Masque of Beauty* (and in the texts of the masques of *Blackness*, *Beauty*, and *Queens*) must be Elizabeth de Vere, who married the sixth Earl of Derby in 1594. See H&S, x. 441.

[49] John Egerton was the son of Lady Alice's second husband by an earlier marriage.

Similarly, the Duke of Buckingham, one of the most prominent figures in the court masque, was active (as we have seen) in the 1620s as a sponsor of his own private masques.[50] And various members of the extended Cavendish/Talbot family, whose estates in Nottinghamshire and Derbyshire were the scene of a number of courtly entertainments, had taken part in masques at Whitehall.[51] David Price, in describing the musical interests of the various branches of this family, suggests that the surviving correspondence gives 'only a glimpse of the possible cultural exchanges between the various related families and the court'.[52]

The overlap in personnel between court and private masques was not confined to those privileged enough to participate as masquers (or be invited as audience). In many instances, the writers and musicians engaged by the nobility for their own entertainments were the very people who were responsible for masques at court. Ben Jonson, Thomas Campion, Henry Lawes, John Dowland, and James Shirley all provided texts or music for entertainments away from court and all, of course, had been involved with the parent form.

No matter how aware of court masques those who contrived to put on masques away from court may have been, however, their resources were utterly different. The Clifford family accounts (the sole source of information about the masque at Skipton Castle in April 1637) show that the York Waits—six musicians altogether—were brought to Skipton for the occasion to supplement their own three household musicians.[53] Apart from payments to the waits (one described only as 'for the Musick of the Citty' and one 'to the boy wch danced') there are no other clues about musical performance. It is, of course, possible that other musicians were involved; as at Brougham Castle, members of the Earl of Cumberland's household would not necessarily appear in a list of special payments.

That having been said, it is worth turning to the exceptional case of Robert Cecil, first Earl of Salisbury, who maintained one of the largest private musical

[50] See James Knowles, 'Change Partners and Dance', *TLS*, 9 Aug. 1991, 19; and Parry, *The Golden Age Restor'd*, 136, 142. Buckingham took part in *The Golden Age Restored*, *The Vision of Delight*, *Pleasure Reconciled to Virtue*, *For the Honour of Wales*, *News from the New World in the Moon*, *Time Vindicated*, and *The Fortunate Isles*.

[51] Lady Anne Herbert, the widow of Francis Talbot, took part in the *Masque of Blackness*; William Herbert, the third Earl of Pembroke (and husband of Mary Talbot) danced in the *Haddington Masque*; Alathea Talbot, Countess of Arundel, danced in *The Masque of Queens*.

The motives of William Cavendish, Earl of Newcastle, in trying to win favour with Charles I by presenting the entertainments at Welbeck and Bolsover in 1633 and 1634 are described by Lynn Hulse in her Ph.D. thesis 'The Musical Patronage of the English Aristocracy, *c*.1590–*c*.1640' (King's College, University of London, 1992), 204–10 and 250–7.

[52] D. C. Price, *Patrons and Musicians of the English Renaissance* (Cambridge, 1981), 108.

[53] The musicians John Earsden, John Hingeston, and William Hudson were employed by the Cliffords in 1637 (information from Lynn Hulse). The relevant accounts are reproduced in full by M. Butler, 'A Provincial Masque of Comus, 1636', *RD* 17 (1986), 149–73. Lynn Hulse has pointed out that the Skipton Castle entertainment took place in Apr. 1637 (not 1636 as Butler states). Woodfill, *Musicians in English Society*, 256–60 gives a partial transcription of the Skipton masque accounts and excerpts from other Clifford accounts relating to music. J. Merryweather, *York Music* (York, 1988), shows that the York waits regularly employed six musicians from 1611 on.

establishments in early seventeenth-century England.[54] Cecil hosted a number of very opulent masque-like entertainments. James I stayed at Theobalds, Cecil's first Hertfordshire residence, on his progress from Scotland in 1603 and was there provided 'with entertaynment such and so costly as hardly can be expressed'.[55] When the Earl of Salisbury exchanged Theobalds for Hatfield House (having been put under some pressure by the king to do so), the occasion was again marked by a masque-like entertainment at which, according to Ben Jonson's text, the gallery was 'fill'd with rare and choise Musique to which was heard the following Song, deliuer'd by an excellent voice, and the burden maintain'd by the whole Quire'.[56] Over the next few years, the Earl presented other similar entertainments; one in 1608 at Salisbury House celebrated his appointment as Lord Treasurer and in the following year another marked the opening of the new exchange.

Where did Cecil get his 'rare and choice music'? During the early years of the seventeenth century he retained half a dozen musicians (including Nicholas Lanier), and employed about an equal number on an occasional basis (including Coprario and other members of the Lanier family). There were also a number of apprentices in the household.[57] Since the masques held under his auspices took place in London, they offered the possibility of adding to his own substantial establishment any number of first-rate musicians. It would, in fact, be very surprising if there were not a two-way exchange going on between Cecil's establishment and the royal households. For its part, the court made use of the talent Cecil had gathered around him; in 1606 Queen Anne's Receiver General recorded a payment of £5 'unto the Erle of Salisburies musytians'.[58] As Lynn Hulse has pointed out, Coprario and Lanier's first experience of writing for masques must have been in Cecil's entertainments—and it is interesting to note that they both contributed to *The Lords' Masque* (1613) and (in Lanier's case) *The Somerset Masque* (1614) before their appointments to the King's Musick and while still enjoying Cecil's patronage.[59] The musical resources for the Earl of Salisbury's entertainments may well have approached those at court in scale.

But, as we have said, this picture cannot have been typical. No other wealthy and musically interested masque patron seems to have maintained so large and distinguished a musical establishment. Some masques held away from court in aristocratic houses probably got by with, say, six to eight musicians—perhaps a five-part violin and/or viol consort plus one or two

[54] Cecil's establishment was rivalled by that of Thomas Sackville, first Earl of Dorset. See below, n. 62.

[55] Stow, *Annales*; quoted in H&S, x. 400.

[56] *An Entertainment of the King and Queen at Theobalds*, H&S, vii. 158, ll. 126–8.

[57] See Hulse, 'The Musical Patronage of Robert Cecil'; also Charteris, 'Jacobean Musicians at Hatfield House'.

[58] Ashbee, *RECM*, iv. 197.

[59] Hulse, 'The Musical Patronage of Robert Cecil', 32. Lanier was still in Cecil's service in Apr. 1614; he was appointed to a place in the King's Musick in Jan. 1616. Coprario was connected with Cecil's household until Apr. 1613.

lutes and, of course, at least one singer. An ensemble like this could cope with
all the music needed for the masques at Coleoverton, Knowsley, Bretby, and,
for that matter, at Ludlow Castle. Moreover, such a scaling-down would have
been acoustically appropriate in the smaller venues involved. No country-
house room could have rivalled the Whitehall Banquetting houses and special
masquing hall. The Earl of Westmorland, whose masque *Raguaillo d'Oceano*
was just one in a series of dramatic entertainments presented at Apethorpe in
the period, was able to use a gallery which was virtually identical with the
Inigo Jones Banqueting House in length, but it was only half as wide.[60] The
great hall at Ludlow Castle was less than a quarter the size of Inigo Jones's
Banqueting House.[61]

The texts of private masques are often unspecific about the number and
kind of musicians involved. This is the case, for example, with the entertainments held at Coleoverton (1618), Chirk (1634), Bretby (1640), and
Knowsley (1641). A few imply quite lavish musical resources. This is notably
so with *The Entertainment at Ashby* (1607), a masque which merits close
attention. The Countess-Dowager of Derby was treated to something which
was musically rich. How did the Earl of Huntingdon manage to assemble such
a varied palate of instrumental colours? His household accounts record small
payments to musicians, but there is no evidence that he retained a musical
establishment of any size. Moreover, Huntington's financial position at this
time was not good; hiring the number of musicians implied by the text would
have seemed an unjustifiable luxury to many.[62] It seems likely, as Lynn Hulse
has suggested, that the Countess of Derby contributed her own musicians and
that Huntingdon may also have been able to borrow the first Earl of Dorset's
'company of violins'.[63]

This *Entertainment* was on a royal scale and conforms to the tripartite pattern
discussed above. The Countess was given a dramatized welcome—with

[60] For plans and a detailed historical description of Apethorpe see The Royal Commission on Historical
Monuments, *An Inventory of the Historical Monuments in the Country of Northampton*, vi (London, 1984), 5 ff.
The *external* dimensions of the long gallery are 113' × 21'.

[61] It is not always possible to establish the dimensions of the rooms used for private entertainments.
Pevsner—noting that the Strange family's motto is '*sans changer*'—ruefully observes that virtually nothing
earlier than the second half of the 17th c. remains at Knowsley; see N. Pevsner, *The Buildings of England:
South Lancashire* (Harmondsworth, 1969), 132. The great chamber at Brougham Castle measured 63' × 23';
the Whitehall Banqueting House measures 110' × 55'; the new (temporary) masquing room built at
Whitehall in 1637 measured 112' × 57' (and reached a height of 59' 'to the raising plate'. See Hill, 'Dramatic
Records', 51. The great hall at Ludlow Castle was *c.*58' × *c.*30'; see Brown, *Milton's Aristocratic Entertain-
ments*, 36.

[62] Excerpts from the Huntingdon accounts are reproduced in Woodfill, *Musicians in English Society*,
262–3. And see Brown, *Milton's Aristocratic Entertainments*, 19, 22.

[63] 'The Countess of Derby or her husband Thomas, Lord Ellesmere may have supplied musicians for the
entertainment. Both husband and wife maintained musicians and later patronized a number of well-known
composers including Henry and William Lawes and John Attey, though none of these could have been
responsible for setting Marston's text to music. Taking into consideration Sir William Skipwith's involvement in entertaining the Countess of Derby during her summer progress, I wonder if the musicians of
Thomas, first Earl of Dorset were employed by Huntingdon' (private communication). For details of the
Earl's musical establishment see Holman, *Four and Twenty Fiddlers*, 126–7.

elaborate musical effects. As she approached the grounds of Ashby Castle 'a full noise of cornets winded; and when she entered the Park, treble cornets reported one to another'. On entering the house 'a consort softly played'. The end of her visit was marked by another pastoral entertainment as she made her way out through the grounds. A masque forms the centre-piece of these celebrations; no other private entertainment in the period rivalled it in musical splendour. The opening was announced by loud music: 'At the approach of the countesses into the great chamber the hoboys played until the room was marshalled; which once ordered, a traverse slided away; presently a cloud was seen . . . upon which Cynthia was discovered riding . . .' (p. 394). The masque has a preliminary section like the proems in court masques before the development of the antimasque proper. Cynthia, 'looking down and earnestly surveying the ladies', is indignant that earth could boast lights so illustrious as to outshine the heavens; she is placated by Ariadne, who protests that they are seeing the lustre of true virtue. Cynthia decides to help and joins Ariadne as a presenter of the main masque. Announcing her changed intentions, Cynthia makes a direct link between speculative and practical music, commanding the spheres to 'sound':

> Let's visit them and slide from our abode:
> Who loves not virtue leaves to be a god.
> Sound, spheres, spread your harmonious breath,
> When mortals shine in worth gods grace the earth.

The clouds descend; while soft music soundeth, Cynthia and Ariadne dismount from their clouds . . . (p. 396)

Jacobean masque texts often suggest that earthly (heard) music is an imitation of divine harmony, but here we have the implication that what is heard *is* that harmony.

The transformation scene, prepared for in song, is accompanied by loud music: 'Suddenly, upon this song, the cornets were winded, and the traverse that was drawn before the masquers sank down. The whole show presently appeareth . . .' (p. 398). Ariadne then goes on to introduce the set masque dances, drawing attention to the way the dances illustrate the masquers' virtue, and paying tribute to the beauty of the ladies of honour in the audience. The text describes the first set dance as a 'new measure', played by the violins. The revels are introduced by a song which insists on the identification of courtly dancing with social virtue:

> Audacious night makes bold the lip,
> Now all court chaster pleasure,
> Whilst to Apollo's harp you trip,
> And tread the gracing measure   (p. 400)

The metaphor of Apollo's harp (symbol of divine control) implies that those who dance to it are co-operating in the divinely ordained order of the universe. A relatively full listing of the revels is given: 'During this song, the masquers presented their shields, and took forth their ladies to dance. After they had danced many measures, galliards, corantos, and levaltos, the night being much spent, whilst the masquers prepared themselves for their departing measure, Cynthia spake . . .' (p. 401). And what Cynthia has to say draws attention to the coming dawn:

> Now pleasing rest; for, see the night
> (Wherein pale Cynthia claims her right)
> Is almost spent; the morning grows,
> The rose and violet she strows
> Upon the high celestial floor,
> 'Gainst Phoebus rise from paramour   (p. 401)

Every detail in this can be paralleled in court masques: the use of loud music at the beginning and at the transformation scene, the use of violins to accompany the dances, and the forms of the dances themselves. The song introducing the revels is a conventional masque song, and Cynthia's speeches introducing the set dances and bringing the masque to a close deal with conventional masque topics which in (later) court masques were to be expressed in song, rather than in spoken verse. In its overall structure and balance, too, this masque is worthy of the early Jacobean court. The text was by John Marston (who had been a member of the Middle Temple and probably gained masque experience there).

The small-scale *Maske presented on Candlemas Nighte at Coleoverton* (1618) is perhaps a more typical example of a provincial masque. Coleoverton (Cold Overton) in Leicestershire was the fine and very recently built house of Sir William and Lady Francis Seymour. The twelve masquers—six masculine and six feminine virtues[64]—were led by the Earl of Essex. He, and another of the Coleoverton masquers, Lord Willoughby, had danced in *Hymenaei* in 1606. (The Essex wedding had, in fact, provided the occasion for that masque.) The women masquers have one set dance to themselves, and the men possibly none since after they are revealed we read only that 'the Men and Women dance together, and at the last maskinge dance, as they went to their Places, was song this 3 Songe' (p. 335). There seems to be a conflation here of set masque dances and revels.

Bretby in Derbyshire, the seat of the first Earl of Chesterfield, was the scene of a Twelfth Night masque in 1639 written by the earl's nephew, Sir Aston Cokayne. It, too, follows court patterns. An antimasque in which a satyr is persuaded to give up his rude ways,

> But for my last farewell unto the woods,
> I'll show you a wild dance of nimble Satyrs;

---

[64] The masculine virtues are identified as Nobility, Valour, Wisdom, Justice, Temperance, and Courtesy. Predictably, the opposing feminine virtues posit an ideal of female behaviour which is passive and retiring: Meekness, Simplicity, Truth in Love, Modesty, Silence, and Chastity.

For we do dance as much as they that live
In princes' courts and tissue palaces.   (p. 10)

In a transition between the antimasque and the main masque, the two sons of
the Earl enter looking for their father and mother. The dialogue between the
two boys and the Lar—the household god—is direct eulogy of the Earl and
his wife. The masquers, mixed men and women again ('the ladies dress'd like
the ancient goddesses'), are introduced in song. And—just as in masques at
court—song is used to interpret the set masque dances, or at least to suggest
that they are laden with meaning:

> Come, ladies, rise, and let us know,
> Now you have seen, what you can do.
> Hark! how the music doth invite
> All you to solemnize this night;
> Then let the sounds that you do hear
> Order your feet unto your ear.
>   O rise! rise altogether,
>   And let us meet;
>   Musick's divine, and well may join
>   Our motions rude into a sweet.
>
>   II
> The figures of the magic art
> We'll equal in a better part;
> Judicial astrology
> Cannot cast such an one as we . . .   (pp. 13–14)

Cokayne's text is essentially a plan for a masque rather than a description of
one.[65] Where dances are called for, he roughs out the kind of thing he
expected to see. Hence the 'Anti-Masque' of satyrs is introduced with the
sentence 'Satyrs rudely but decently attired . . . dance in as many several
shapes as shall be necessary' (p. 11). Cokayne is equally open-minded about his
main-masque dances: 'Here they dance what or as many set dances as they
please, the MASQUERS being men and women, or only women. When they
have danced all they intended, the LAR, or one of the MASQUERS, invites
the spectator-ladies with this song to join with them . . .' (p. 13).

A year later a Twelfth Night masque was performed at Knowsley Hall in
Lancashire, the home of James Stanley, Lord Strange (who in 1642 became
seventh Earl of Derby). It is not surprising to find masques being organized by
a family with such a strong interest in drama—plays by Shakespeare and
Marlowe received their first performances by Strange's Men in the late 1580s
and 1590s. In 1631 Lord Strange had been one of the masquers in *Love's
Triumph through Callipolis* and his wife had danced in the Queen's companion

---

[65] John Ward, 'Newly Devis'd Measures', 135–42 discusses and transcribes (from GB-Ob MS Rawl. c.
799) a masque which Robert Bargrave planned for a wedding at the British Embassy in Constantinople
sometime between 1647 and 1652.

piece, *Chloridia*. The text for their own masque was written by Sir Thomas Salusbury, a distant cousin of Lord Strange.[66] Salusbury, as a former member of the Inner Temple, had had first-hand experience of such entertainments and may well have had Middleton's *Masque of Heroes* in mind when he wrote the Knowsley entertainment.[67] Just the year before the Knowsley masque, Salusbury had devised 'A Show or Antimasque of Gypseys' for Chirk Castle.[68] Then and with the Masque at Knowsley, he boasted that the composition was completed in the space of six hours. The text is, in fact, rather sketchy. It is not possible to work out, for example, at what point the main-masque dances or revels took place. There are some very familiar features, however. The transformation scene (in which a temple opens) is heralded by a song performed by a chorus of Priests and beginning 'Hence all prophane . . .' (p. 13). One of the antimasque dances (Salusbury uses the term 'antemasque') is said to be 'in way of a Matichine' (a sword dance; see above, p. 117). But there is no specific information in this text about the numbers or kinds of musicians Lord Strange's household could muster for such an occasion. The masque was very much a household affair. An antimasque device of a personified Christmas making his will enables specific mention to be made of various servants in the house, while the concluding section of the main masque—in which masquers characterized as the Twelve Months offer New Year wishes to Lord Strange and his wife—draws in other friends and family members (including Strange's son).

The second Earl of Westmorland, Mildmay Fane, wrote *Raguaillo d'Oceano* for the entertainment of his family in 1640. The whole production is divided into a series of fifteen 'entries' (here meaning scenes with spoken dialogue and, sometimes, song and dance) and an apparently sung epilogue. This text is crammed with musical references which convey an enthusiasm for music not quite matched by understanding. The first song in the epilogue sets the audience some rather forbidding aural tests:

> Now let ye Spheares
> Contend
> W^ch to our Ears
> More Melody Commend
> For good
> Yet Soe distinctly play
> We may
> W^th Ease distinctly play
> We may
> W^th Ease distinguish of their mood

---

[66] Salusbury's grandfather had married the natural daughter of Lord Strange's great-grandfather, Henry Stanley, 4th Earl of Derby.

[67] See Bentley, *Jacobean and Caroline Stage*, v. 1041–2.

[68] See C. C. Brown, 'The Chirk Castle Entertainment of 1634', *Milton Quarterly*, 11 (1977), 79. Both the Masque at Knowsley and the Antimasque of Gypsies are preserved in GB-AB, MS 5390 D—described by Bentley as a Salusbury family commonplace book. Brown argues persuasively that Salusbury was probably the author of the Chirk Castle Entertainment in 1634.

And Key
Wither to flat or Sharp
The Tunes are Set Command Oryons Harpe   (pp. 93–4)

This kind of misapplication of musical terminology is typical. After accompanying an antimasque dance on their harps, Arion and Orpheus, 'raysing
their Ayer to a higher Key . . . play a Solemne Maskinge daunce' (p. 67). Later
these same two musicians play 'a Madrigall or Some Solemn graue Tune to
wch ye Princes[s] descends Maiestically out of ye Scene . . .' (p. 91). Even so,
Fane's idiosyncratic descriptions sometimes convey quite a vivid picture of the
sort of thing he wanted: 'Heer as if Enchanted by ye Lowd Musiks high Strain
They All fall into a Morrice & Mad Iomping Phantastike Daunce . . .' (p. 91).
The Earl's musical resources, if the text itself is any indication, were varied
rather than large and not terribly well balanced. The two harpists carry the
main burden of the entertainment. It is they who 'Play ye Mayn Masking
Daunce wch ye Six YONG PRINCES & Six LADIES attired in Starrs performe
in a New composed figure . . .' (p. 93). Three Syrens 'of rare voyces' sing 'to
Theorbo & Lute'. (Interestingly, these perform from three music rooms
above.) There was also a consort of recorders, described as 'the stillest of wind
Instruments' (p. 65). And finally he makes quite extensive use of a loud-music
ensemble whose composition is described in detail: 'two *Tritons* . . . with their
shell Trumpets awaken the *foure* WINDES (*viz:*) the Lowde Musicke–a
Hautboy, a Cornett, a Sagbutt, and a double Curtault, which Tempest rais'd
the *Skyper* strikes Saile and departs . . .' (p. 64).

The overall picture is of the Earl of Westmorland indulging in the kind of
entertainment that he and his household obviously enjoyed, and making
imaginative use of the musical resources around him in his splendid long
gallery at Apethorpe. Clifford Leech comments about *Raguaillo d'Oceano* that
'Fane borrowed from the court something of the masque form, and used it to
provide a festivity for his household at Apthorpe. As, however, Apthorpe was
somewhat remote from the ceremonials of Whitehall, the form of the ritual
was used without much trace of its spirit: no very obvious tradition or
principle was being honoured.'[69] I should wish to describe the situation rather
differently. Fane's departures from the formal structures of the court masque
were at least as great as any liberties he took with its spirit. In *Raguaillo
d'Oceano* we see him, as it were, remixing the elements of the masque, to
produce something quite unique.

A Maske Presented at Ludlow Castle

As a masque away from court, Milton's *Comus* is especially remarkable.
Recent criticism has demonstrated—in a variety of ways—that *Comus* estab-

---

[69] M. Fane, *Raguaillo d'Oceano 1640 and Candy Restored 1641*, ed. C. Leech, Materials for the Study of the
Old English Drama, NS 15 (Louvain, 1938), 30. On the threatrical connections of Fane and, more
particularly, his relative Sir Humphrey Mildmay, see Butler, *Theatre in Crisis*, 114–18.

lishes a kind of critical dialogue with its courtly paradigm. While managing to avoid anything which could be challenged as subversive, *Comus* scutinizes the values of the court, engages in the debate about the nature and availability of grace, and challenges the moral validity of the assumptions underlying the masque's emblematic mode. Milton's skill in relating more enduring moral questions to present occasions is also clear. The occasion itself—an official celebration of the Earl of Bridgewater's appointment as Lord President of the Council of the Marches—has rightly been described as one of viceregal importance.[70] Hence *Comus* is many things. It has, like the true court masque, a ceremonial, public significance; it was also, like some of the more domestic entertainments considered earlier in this chapter, a family affair with the Earl's children as protagonists. Its use of music, like the drama, proves to be an original and sure-footed response to the expectations established by the genre and the possibilities offered by the occasion. In this Milton had an extremely able—but perhaps slightly condescending—collaborator in Henry Lawes.

Lawes was a trusted presence in the Egerton household. He accompanied the family when they travelled in the months immediately before *Comus*, and in the dedicatory epistle for its publication in 1637 he describes himself to John Egerton, Lord Brackley, as having been 'by many favours . . . long oblig'd to your most honour'd Parents'. The masque's description of Thyrsis as 'a Swain, | That to the service of this house belongs' (ll. 84–5) conflates (in a typically masque fashion) Lawes's dramatic role with his actual relationship to the Egerton family. Valued for his skills by Milton on the one hand and the Earl of Bridgewater on the other, there seems good reason for attributing to Lawes the final decisions about the shape and content of *Comus* as it was performed at Ludlow. (It was, of course, Lawes who was instrumental in having the masque published in 1637.)

The story of the presentation of the text for performance at Ludlow provides an interesting supplement to the discussion in Chapter 1 of the character of masque texts and their value as sources of information about music. *Comus* is the greatest literary legacy of the masque tradition—and nowhere is the relationship between text and performance more interesting. The standard modern text of *Comus*, in line with traditional principles of textual criticism, transmits Milton's final thoughts about the work; it is based, in other words, on the text printed in 1673 with Milton's *Poems*. The other sources, however, tell a fascinating tale of the masque's literary genesis, adaptation for the actual performance, and further revision for its form as a printed literary artefact.[71]

---

[70] See Orgel, *The Jonsonian Masque*; Brown, *Milton's Aristocratic Entertainments*; Marcus, *The Politics of Mirth*, ch. 6; M. C. McGuire, *Milton's Puritan Masque* (Athens, Ga., 1983); J. Creaser, 'The Present Aid of this Occasion: The Setting of *Comus*', in Lindley (ed.), *The Court Masque*, 111–34; and D. Norbrook, 'The Reformation of the Masque'; ibid., 94–110.

[71] My summary of this history (or rather, those parts of it which are relevant to our specifically musical concerns) is based on Milton, *'A Maske': The Earlier Versions*, ed. S. E. Sprott (Toronto, 1973). Readers are referred to Sprott's introduction for a detailed account of the interrelationship of these sources. When

Milton's autograph in Trinity College, Cambridge is a working copy; its numerous emendations log Milton's compositional process. From this manuscript Milton must have made a fair copy (now lost) for use at Ludlow. This version was extensively adapted, probably by Henry Lawes, for the performance. Some of the changes were made for practical dramatic reasons, while others seem to arise out of a sense of respect for the sensitivities of the Egerton family. The Bridgewater manuscript was prepared close to the performance date, to be used (like the manuscripts of *The Masque of Queens* and *Pleasure Reconciled to Virtue*) as a presentation copy for the Earl of Bridgewater or his son. It is this manuscript which comes closest to an account of the actual performance. (Milton, however, cannot have approved of all the revisions it contains since they were not adopted in the later printed texts.[72]) The 1637 edition of *A Maske presented at Ludlow Castle* seems (despite its being 'not openly acknowledg'd by the Author'[73]) to have been set from a copy which was further revised by Milton. The printed text is altogether closer to his original intentions (as deduced from the Trinity College autograph) than to the version presented at Ludlow.

This text is often so reticent about dramatic action that it seems to invite reception as something read rather than something acted. (In this it is distinct from both manuscripts—the Bridgewater manuscript and Milton's autograph—which convey the sense that the text is intended to be dramatically realized.) When the Elder Brother calls for help, the Bridgewater manuscript has '*he hallowes* and is answered, the guardian dæmon comes in habited like a shepheard'.[74] But the printed sources have simply 'The attendant Spirit habited like a shepheard' (at l. 488). It is left to the reader to infer from the Elder Brother's lines that he calls out and is answered by the Guardian Demon (or, Attendant Spirit, as he is called in the later sources). Similarly, where Comus and his crew sense the Lady's approach, both manuscripts have the stage direction 'they all scatter' (at l. 147), while the printed text allows Comus' speech to imply the action. At the end of the Lady's song, both manuscripts introduce Comus' speech of wonderment at her beauty with the direction 'Comus looks in & speakes' (at l. 243); this, too, has been excised from the printed text.

One of the changes designed to make the text more self-sufficient reduces the amount of reported musical detail. The printed texts describe the dances at the end of the masque as follows: 'The Scene changes, presenting *Ludlow* Town and the Presidents Castle; then com in Countrey-Dancers, after them the attendant Spirit, with the two Brothers and the Lady' (at l. 957). The text

referring to manuscript readings, I have given in-text line references to the equivalent point in the standard text.

[72] For an interesting discussion of the these revisions see Brown, *Milton's Aristocratic Entertainments*, 171–80.

[73] According to Henry Lawes's dedicatory epistle.

[74] The autograph manuscript has: 'he hallows the guardian Dæmon hallows agen & enters in the habit of shepheard'.

of the song following this goes on to suggest that, after some time, the country dancers must make way for more dignified participants. The manuscripts' directions give a much more vivid sense of these people actually dancing, of an active performance. Here is the Bridgewater manuscript's reading (though the autograph's phrase 'countrie dances & such like gambols' is worth noting): 'The sceane changes then is p^rsented Ludlow towne and the Presidents Castle, then come in Countrie daunces, and the like &c, towards the end of those sports the demon with the 2 brothers and the ladye come in. the spiritt singes'.

A number of the textual changes directly affect the music itself (rather than just what we can learn about the music through the text), and in one instance, Milton seems to have left to Lawes the decision about musical setting. In the Bridgewater manuscript, the Epilogue is preceded by the direction '*They daunce, the daunces all ended the Dæmon singes or sayes.*'[75] But Milton's original epilogue (as seen cancelled in the autograph[76]), has had four lines cut and been divided into two. The first of these parts was transferred to the beginning of the entertainment and set by Lawes as a sung prologue—with a consequential change in the wording of the opening line, 'To the Ocean now I fly' (l. 975) becoming in the sung version 'From the heavens nowe I flye'. Thus the masque is framed by two songs from the Attendant Spirit, both of which describe the blessed realm from which he comes. This rearrangement corresponds to the order in which the *Comus* songs appear in the musical sources.

In the Bridgewater manuscript the Attendant Spirit's song invoking Sabrina's aid (ll. 858 ff.) is followed by a rubric 'The verse to singe or not' (contradicting the autograph's 'to be said'). 'Listen and save', the concluding line of the previous song, is repeated at the end of this potentially sung passage, but otherwise it is in the functionally indeterminate four-stress rhyming couplets of this masque. In addition to introducing the possibility of singing here, the Bridgewater manuscript divides the passage very symmetrically between the two brothers and the Attendant Spirit. If Lawes intended setting it, it would have been as a dialogue.

Milton's intentions in undoing these revisions may have come quite close to Jonson's in his initial decision to publish the texts of *Blackness* and *Beauty*— to allow an invention for a particular occasion to have a more enduring life as literature. Perhaps he succeeded too well: Dr Johnson, while acknowledging that 'a work more truly poetical is rarely found', declared that 'as a drama it is deficient. The action is not probable.'[77] Thomas Warton expressed similiar views, seeing *Comus* as a compendium of incidental *literary* delights:

---

[75] This direction originates in the autograph, but there it has been cancelled and replaced by a new rubric which nevertheless leaves open the question of how the lines which follow are to be delivered: 'The Dæmon sings or says.'

[76] It is replaced there by the longer version prepared for the 1637 edn.; see Sprott, 180–91.

[77] S. Johnson, *Lives of the English Poets*, 1779–81, ed. G. B. Hill, 3 vols. (Oxford, 1905), i. 168.

We must not read *Comus* with an eye to the stage, or with the expectation of dramatic propriety . . . *Comus* is a suite of speeches, not interesting by discrimination of character; not conveying a variety of incidents, not gradually exciting curiosity: but perpetually attracting attention by sublime sentiment, by fanciful imagery of the richest vein, by an exuberance of picturesque description, poetical allusion, and ornamental expression.[78]

To these writers, *Comus* seemed to have found its rightful place amongst the *Poems*. Although Warton responded to one element in *Comus*, his view of it ignores any sense of progression through the work, and his lack of sympathy with the workings of the 'old English Mask' suggests an incapacity to view *Comus* in terms of that genre—an incapacity which, until recent years, seems to have been fairly general.[79]

In fact, a perfectly regular courtly masque could be extracted from *Comus*. This 'regular' masque—adapted by its avoidance of spectacular transformations and by its quite modest musical requirements to the conditions at Ludlow Castle—follows the usual progression from antimasque to main masque. The antimasque would begin at line 93 with the entry of Comus and his 'rout of Monsters, headed like sundry sorts of wilde Beasts . . . making a riotous and unruly noise' (or—in the autograph manuscript's more masque-like vocabulary—'in a wild and antick fashion'). It would continue without a break until line 147, thus including Comus' initiation of the 'midnight shout and revelry' and the climax of these rites in the rout's 'measure (in a wild, rude & wanton antick)'. This antimasque section would conclude with Comus' exclamation:

> Break off, break off, I feel the different pace,
> Of som chast footing near about this ground.   (ll. 145–6)

Then we would move straight to line 813 (the entry of the brothers as Comus flees) or even further on to line 958 (where the scene changes to Ludlow Town) for a transition to the transformation scene followed by a main masque which is complete with songs, set dances, revels, and concluding song. (I shall pass over the non-sequiturs in the dialogue at lines 813–958, since my point is not to to claim that it *is* a regular masque but to draw attention to an aspect of *Comus*'s structure.)

My hypothetical masque would be very like a domesticated *Pleasure Reconciled to Virtue*. The Egerton children would not have had speaking parts, but courtly masquers never did anyway. The Attendant Spirit's songs in this part of *Comus*, like the songs of many masque presenters, underline the emblematic significance of the set dances. After the simple, innocent, and joyous country dancing, he sings

[78] J. Milton, *Poems upon Several Occasions*, ed. Thomas Warton (London, 1785), 262.
[79] See the critical views quoted at the beginning of my '*Comus*: The Court Masque Questioned', in J. Caldwell, E. Olleson, and S. Wollenberg (eds.), *The Well Enchanting Skill: Music, Poetry, and Drama in the Culture of the Renaissance* (Oxford, 1990), 107–13.

> Back Shepherds, back, anough your play,
> Till next Sun-shine holiday,
> Here be without duck or nod
> Other trippings to be trod
> Of lighter toes, and such Court guise
> As *Mercury* did first devise
> With the mincing *Dryades*
> On the Lawns and on the Leas.   (ll. 957–64)

The song makes a familiar distinction between the kind of dancing country dancers perform (with 'ducks and nods') and the more courtly steps of the three masquers. These masquers are presented to the Earl and his wife in the Attendant Spirit's next song, a song which draws the conventional contrast between the main-masque dances (which embody the virtue of the dancers) and the disorder of the antimasque:

> Noble Lord, and Lady bright,
> I have brought ye new delight,
> Here behold so goodly grown
> Three fair brances of your own
> Heav'n hath timely tri'd their youth,
> Their faith, their patience, and their truth.
> And sent them here through hard assays
> With a crown of deathless Praise
>   To triumph in victorious dance
> O're sensual Folly, and Intemperance.   (ll. 965–75)

The Attendant Spirit's final song, like Daedalus' in *Pleasure Reconciled to Virtue*, exhorts the hearers to pursue the virtue that has been vindicated in the masque:

> Mortals that would follow me,
> Love vertue, she alone is free,
> She can teach ye how to clime
> Higher than the Spheary chime;
> Or if Vertue feeble were,
> Heav'n it self would stoop to her.   (ll. 1017–22)

In these sections of *Comus*, music and dance are used in a way which is thoroughly typical of the courtly masque. Antimasque dances and masque dances are sharply contrasted, and the virtuous nature of the masque dances is emphasized by the masque songs. Hence we are presented with a miniature but complete courtly masque.

But this accounts for only about one-eighth of the total text of *Comus*. With the exception of the Attendant Spirit's prologue,[80] the excluded part of

---

[80] A prologue preceding the antimasque and presented by characters who belong primarily in the world of the main masque was not unusual in Caroline court masques; see e.g. Ben Jonson's last masque, *Chloridia* (1631), and Aurelian Townshend's *Albion's Triumph* (1632).

the text all lies *between* the antimasque and main masque sections of the buried 'regular' masque. None of this central section is particularly masque-like (although Sabrina's intervention to free the Lady from Comus' spell does have a precedent in the Muses' Priests' intervention to free Love from the Sphynx in *Love Freed from Ignorance and Folly*).

Given that the one hundred and twenty odd lines discussed above do form a short but perfectly regular masque, Milton's procedure could be described as follows: he has replaced the transformation scene (normally of cardinal importance) by an extended dramatic sequence which takes place in the antimasque world. This long section is fundamentally un-masque-like, although it has a few masque elements. It is framed by a real antimasque and a real main masque.

The transformation scene in a 'normal' masque separates the antimasque from the main masque: it is the key moment when, as if by natural necessity, virtue overcomes vice or wisdom and civilized behaviour displace folly and vulgarity. In the regular masque extracted from *Comus* this relationship between masque and antimasque and the dramatized assertion that virtue must overcome vice is preserved; but the extended middle section of Milton's text calls these fundamental structural and thematic rules into question.

The Elder Brother describes the significance of Minerva's emblems in a way which is thoroughly in accord with the iconography of the courtly masque:

> What was that snaky-headed *Gorgon* sheild
> That wise *Minerva* wore, unconquer'd Virgin,
> Wherewith she freez'd her foes to congeal'd stone?
> But rigid looks of Chast austerity,
> And noble grace that dash't brute violence
> With sudden adoration, and blank aw.   (ll. 446–51)

Noble grace dashing brute violence with sudden adoration and blank awe is an almost perfect description of what happens at the transformation scene in the typical Jonsonian masque. But it does not happen quite so readily in *Comus*. The Elder Brother's confidence, if not entirely misplaced, is at least not completely endorsed by Milton. The whole middle section of *Comus* works partly by setting up emblematic expectations in a context where, for most of the time at least, realistic conditions prevail. In other words, we expect to watch an allegorical presentation of moral victory, but instead we are faced with a dramatization of moral uncertainty and danger.

Dramatic tension is created by the possibility that virtue will not automatically overcome vice, and much of the action depends upon the inability of a virtuous but frail human to recognize vice for what it is. The Lady addresses Comus as 'gentle shepherd' (l. 270), and 'gentle villager' (l. 303); he may not even look obviously different from the Attendant Spirit 'habited like a shepherd' (l. 489). The Lady tells Comus,

> Shepherd I take thy word,
> And trust thy honest offer'd courtesie,
> Which oft is sooner found in lowly sheds
> With smoaky rafters, then in tapstry Halls
> And Courts of Princes, where it first was nam'd,
> And yet is most pretended   (ll. 320–5)

This might seem a rather unusual comment to find in a masque (from which the possibility of a wicked prince was usually excluded), but what is perhaps more significant is that the Lady is substituting for a normal masque assumption an equally conventional stereotype; her mistake is to accept any appearances (emblematic or otherwise) as an indication of reality. Stephen Orgel, discussing Jonson's depiction of Comus in *Pleasure Reconciled*, makes in passing a nice comparison with Milton's work: 'The audience at Ludlow Castle was being taught to mistrust appearances. In contrast, the spectators at Whitehall in 1618 had more faith that the aesthetic judgement was the right one. Merely by looking at Jonson's Comus, they knew who and what he was.'[81] Milton's Comus boasts of the power 'to cheat the eye with blear illusion | And give it false presentements' (ll. 155–6); Inigo Jones might have made the same claim—but Jonson always insisted that the illusions in his masques expressed a higher reality or moral truth.

There are yet more surprising reversals of normal masque assumptions. Comus' banquet, for which 'The Scene changes to a stately Palace, set out with all manner of deliciousness' (following l. 657), is a main-masque tableau which could have come, for instance, from Jonson's *Oberon*, where we find 'There the whole *Scene* opened, and within was dicouer'd the *Frontispice* of a bright and glorious *Palace*, whose gates and walls were transparent' (ll. 138–40). In Milton's masque, however, this tableau has been usurped by the forces of the antimasque. Moreover, in this scene Comus puts forward a traditional masque argument:

> Wherefore did Nature powre her bounties forth,
> With such a full and unwithdrawing hand,
> Covering the earth with odours, fruits and flocks,
> Thronging the Seas with spawn innumerable,
> But all to please and sate the curious taste?
> And set to work millions of spinning Worms,
> That in their green shops weave the smooth-haired silk
> To deck her Sons . . .
> Beauty is natures brag, and must be shown
> In courts, at feasts, and high solemnities
> Where most may wonder at the workmanship   (ll. 709–16, 744–6)

---

[81] Orgel, *The Jonsonian Masque*, 153. A related point is made by Brown in *Milton's Aristocratic Entertainments*, 88: 'Here the audience is being invited to a mixture of reactions unusual in the self-conscious devices of comedy or masque, for Milton's technique with the masque has a way of reasserting a realism, a moral realism, through the celebratory gestures.'

Words like 'sate' and 'brag' undermine his otherwise exalted tone, but apart from these indications of a different authorial attitude, the speech seems fit for a main masque. It presents, after all, a perspective implied by titles like *The Masque of Beauty*, and the speech itself comes close in content to one of the masque songs in *Neptune's Triumph*:

> Why doe you weare the Silkwormes toyles;
> Or glory in the Shellfish spoyles? . . .
> Why do you smell of Amber-gris,
> Of which was formed *Neptunes* Neice
> The Queene of Loue; vnlesse you can,
> Like Sea-borne *Venus*, loue a man? . . .
> Your lookes, your smiles, and thoughts that meete,
> *Ambrosian* hands, and silver feete,
>   Doe promise you will do't.   (ll. 484–503)

The key phrase in the Jonson song is 'and thoughts that meete' since it points to the masque's dependence on emblem: fair must be good and ugly must be foul, and there can be no disparity between the ladies' physical beauty and their inner dispositions. The Elder Brother's statement that 'he that hides a dark soul, and foul thoughts | Benighted walks under the mid-day Sun' (ll. 382–3) could have no place in one of Jonson's masques. Thus in Milton's *Comus* the traditional masque pattern is established and in some measure preserved, while its structural and thematic identity as an animated emblem is exposed to alien pressures. Although Milton preserves the basic movement from disorder and intemperance to the virtuous pleasures of the main masque, his treatment of the genre makes the point that this process is far from being automatic.

In the long middle section of *Comus* music sometimes participates in the untrustworthiness of appearances. When the scene changes for Comus' banquet, for example, soft music complements the other seemingly main-masque features. Earlier, Comus attempts to confuse the natural order by claiming that his retinue are like the rest of natural creatures in imitating the cosmic dance:

> We that are of purer fire
> Imitate the Starry Quire,
> Who in their nightly watchfull Sphears,
> Lead in swift round the Months and Years.
> The Sounds, and Seas with all their finny drove
> Now to the Moon in wavering Morrice move,
> And on the Tawny Sands and Shelves,
> Trip the pert Fairies and the dapper Elves;
> By dimpled Brook, and Fountain brim,
> The Wood-Nymphs, decked with Daisies trim,
> Their merry wakes and pastimes keep . . .   (ll. 111–21)

There are, too, one or two instances where *musica instrumentalis* takes on a significance which is ambiguous to human ears. The Attendant Spirit as Thyrsis

> . . . with his soft Pipe and smooth dittied Song
> Well knows to still the wilde winds when they roar,
> And hush the waving Woods . . .   (ll. 86–8)

These lines—in part a personal compliment to Lawes—affirm the power of *musica instrumentalis* to restore the harmony of nature (*musica humana*).[82] The fact that it is a spirit (and not really Thyrsis) who produces the music dignifies this pastoral music even further. But in *Comus*, not just the Attendant Spirit plays a pastoral pipe. When the Lady hears Comus and his crew she recognizes the sounds 'of Riot, and ill manag'd Merriment' (l. 171) but the instruments mentioned are 'the jocund Flute or gamesom Pipe'. Hence the usual clear distinction in instrumentation between antimasque and masque does not apply, and the hearer must rely on more subtle differences to distinguish between 'wanton dance' and the honest 'jigs and rural dance' which take place at the end of the masque.

By and large, however, the use of music and dance corresponds to normal masque usage. Comus and his retinue are associated with 'barbarous dissonance' (l. 549). The antimasque, as we have seen, contains a 'wild, rude, and wanton antick' while the main-masque dances are described by the songs which introduce them as dignified and courtly. Most importantly, nobody of Comus' party ever sings. Song has a power and dignity above that of ordinary speech. It is reserved for the Lady and the Attendant Spirit to seek help ('Sweet Echo' and 'Sabrina Fair'), for Sabrina, the goddess of the river, to introduce herself ('By the rushy-fringèd bank'), and for introducing the main-masque dances. The Attendant Spirit's songs at the end of the masque emphasize that he has more than mortal vision and that he resides above the confusion of this world. All the songs move beyond the human uncertainties which inform so much of the spoken verse, and they are all either sung by or addressed to an immortal being.

The words of the Lady's song, 'Sweet Echo', sustain this special position given to song, especially in its final couplet:

> So maist thou be translated to the skies,
> And give resounding grace to all Heav'ns Harmonies.   (ll. 241–2)[83]

The consonance of this music with the *musica mundana* is underlined. In the Bridgewater manuscript and in Lawes's setting, the final line reads 'And hold a counterpoint to all Heaven's harmonies', thus making less abstract the

---

[82] The Elder brother also draws attention to Thyrsis' musical abilities, saying that his 'artfull strains have oft delaid | The hudling brook to hear his madrigal, | And sweeten'd every muskrose of the dale . . .' (ll. 493–5).

[83] This song is discussed fully by Hollander, *The Untuning of the Sky*, 319–23.

interlocking of worldly and heavenly music. Both Comus (ll. 244 ff.) and the Attendant Spirit (ll. 555 ff.) hear the song and comment on the heavenly quality of the music. In both cases, they make comparisons between the perfection of the lady's song and other kinds of music, thus suggesting links with various kinds of musical expression at every point on the spectrum of viciousness and virtue. As the song ends, Comus comments in wonderment on the way in which the Lady's music indicates a soul communing with heaven. He goes on to compare this with the misapplied, seductive harmonies of his mother Circe's music. Later, the Attendant Spirit tells the brothers that his own pastoral music-making was interrupted by the discordant sounds of Comus' rout, but that this was then silenced by the mystical sound of the lady's singing:

> I sate me downe to watch upon a bank
> With Ivy canopied, and interwove
> With flaunting Hony-suckle, and began
> Wrapt in a pleasing fit of melancholy
> To meditate my rural minstrelsie
> Till fancy had her fill, but ere a close
> The wonted roar was up amidst the Woods,
> And fill'd the Air with barbarous dissonance
> At which I ceas't, and listen'd them a while
> Till an unusual stop of sudden silence
> Gave respit to the drowsie frighted steeds
> That draw the litter of close-curtain'd sleepe;
> At last a soft, and solemn breathing sound
> Rose like a stream of rich distill'd perfumes
> And stole upon the Air, that even Silence
> Was took e're she was ware, and wisht she might
> Deny her nature, and be never more
> Still to be so displac't. . . . (ll. 542–59)

The use of discrete songs in *Comus* is similar to the early Jacobean court masque, but quite different from the more extended musical structures found in contemporary masques performed at court such as *The Triumph of Peace*. In this more than in any other musical details, *Comus* can be seen as an adaptation of the courtly masque to the smaller musical resources available to the Earl of Bridgewater. What is most interesting is the way in which the music partly participates in Milton's ironic or critical treatment of the masque form, and partly fulfils traditional masque functions. Masque expectations are satisfied often enough to confirm that this is a real masque, but beyond that, they are manipulated in a way which calls into question the assumptions on which the form depends.

Quite sophisticated settings were required to sustain the elevated position given to the songs by Milton's text. Henry Lawes was, in fact, inspired by the text and the occasion to write some of his most successful and attractive ayres.

The Lady's song, and the song to Sabrina are both excellent examples of Lawes matching the natural rhythms and accents of the verse. Milton has provided two sestets and a couplet with verse of the most delicately malleable kind; line-lengths and stress-patterns are varied, and half rhyme mediates between full rhymes. This is particularly obvious in the second sestet:

> Canst thou not tell me of a gentle Pair
> That likest thy *Narcissus* are?
> O if thou have
> Hid them in some flowry Cave,
> Tell me but where
> Sweet Queen of Parly, Daughter of the Sphear . . .   (ll. 235–42)

Lawes makes good use of the fluidity of the verse (Ex. 7.4). He takes the opening 'Sweet echo, sweetest Nymph' and treats it as a repeated apostrophe, and then—responding to the enjambment at the end of the first line—moves straight through to the end of line three in a single sweep. Wherever words or syllables are extended very far beyond normal speech patterns, there is always an expressive justification. This is most obvious perhaps in the phrase 'her sad song mourneth well', where the long note on 'sad' followed by a descending diminished fourth communicates a sense of pathos. The leaps of a seventh to '*Sweet* Queen of Parly' and '*Daugh*ter of the sphere' give emphasis to the Lady's cries. The melodic contour of the climactic final couplet, with its hint of illustration in rising up to 'skies', and the emphatic approach to the last cadence, with the essential cadential notes framed again by a diminished fourth, confirms that this is a beautifully expressive setting.

The song to Sabrina has a similarly varied and supple stanza form and Lawes displays a characteristic sensitivity to its rhythmic qualities (Ex. 7.5). He extends the first line from four to seven syllables by repeating the word 'Sabrina', but then balances this by introducing a repetition ('Listen, listen and save') into the final line of the stanza (also four syllables in Milton's text). The symmetry in these phrases extends even further: the first 'listen' recalls the melodic pattern of 'Sabrina'; 'Sabrina fair' carries the melody into dominant harmonies and thence on into the piece, while 'listen and save' brings the melody to rest on the tonic. The one rhyming couplet in the stanza is given two rhythmically identical balanced phrases, the second leading emphatically to the dominant before the final 'Listen, listen and save'. The musical rhythms reproduce the natural scansion of the words; this is especially noticeable in the line 'Under the glassy, cool, translucent wave'.

No setting survives for Sabrina's own song, 'By the rushie fringed bank' (ll. 889 ff.), which has a rather more regular metre than the Lady's or Thyrsis' invocations. The songs which interrupt the dance music in the main-masque section are even more regular metrically, having the same seven-syllable, four-stress rhyming couplets used for the Epilogue and some sections of the spoken text.

Ex. 7.4. Henry Lawes, 'Sweet Echo', from GB-Lbl, Add. MS 53723

Ex. 7.4. *Continued*

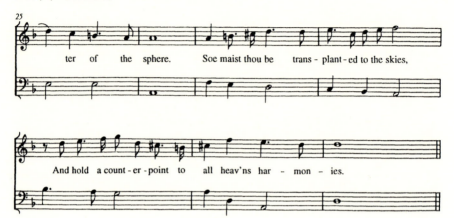

ter　of　the sphere.　Soe maist thou be　trans-plant-ed to the skies,

And hold a count-er-point to　all heav'ns har — mon — ies.

Ex. 7.5. Henry Lawes, 'Sabrina fair', from GB-Lbl, Add. MS 53723

Sa-brin — — a,　Sa-brin-a fayre, Lis-ten where thou　art sit-tinge

Un-der the glass-y coole　translucent wave,　In twist-ed brades　of lil-yes knit-ting The

loose trayne of　thy am-ber droppinge haire; List — en for deer　hon — or's sake,

God — dess of the　sil — ver lake,　Lis — ten,　lis — ten and　save.

Milton selected for special praise the most notable aspect of Lawes's song style—his ability to accommodate the accent and inflection of English poetry naturally:

> *Harry* whose tuneful and well measur'd Song
> First taught our English Musick how to span
> Words with just note and accent, not to scan
> With *Midas* Ears, committing short and long . . .[84]

He was glad to acknowledge that in Henry Lawes he had a musician whose worth and skill as a composer (and—in *Comus*—as a performer) could help establish these aesthetic/moral distinctions in his work.

[84] Sonnet 13, 'To Mr. *Henry Lawes*, on his Aires'.

8

Realizations

In the preceding chapters a number of basic points about the function of music in the masque have emerged. We have seen that the dances of the main masque are presented as models of the happy peace, co-operation, and order characterizing a wisely governed commonwealth. While this is made explicit by the words of the songs which introduce them, the choreography and the clear formal structure of the music itself supports the idea. The masque songs themselves are stylistically sophisticated—worthy vehicles for (and illustrations of) the ideas they convey. The special importance of music and song is underlined in many ways, but most obviously through the characterization of musicians as priests, deities, or ancient poets.

The antimasque stands in deliberate contrast to all this. Its characters are either musically unsophisticated or completely lacking in musical sensibility (a sure sign that they are not to be trusted). Antimasque dances, with their vigorous, eccentric movements, based on tunes with unpredictable structures, give expression to the vulgarity or viciousness of the characters who dance them. The language of antimasques often tends towards chaotic prose, and singing rarely has any place.

These features suggest a broad measure of co-operation between music, choreography, and device. But they do not necessarily imply detailed inter-connections between specific compositions and literary text. Nor do they reveal how concepts like those outlined here survived in performance. It is this last question which, by way of conclusion, I wish to pursue a little further by examining three apparently rather disparate topics. In each the ideals of the texts are examined in the light of actual performance. The first returns to the territory explored in Chapter 5 in looking at the links between a visual image with musical implications and its aural realization. The second attempts to integrate the concern with song, dance, and instrumental music explored separately in Chapters 1 and 2 by seeing how these came together in a single production. The final section examines the revels—the section of the masque in which the audience were incorporated into the whole device, where the ideal might finally be realized—or forgotten.

The Music of Fame

Musical imagery is omnipresent in the literature of this period. Poets and playwrights drew on a reservoir of ideas which was part of a common intellectual heritage. The theories of *musica speculativa* alone furnish an enormous range. What makes reference to such images rather different in masque texts is the simple fact that music was not just talked about but performed. In various ways, the relationship between the music heard about and the music heard has been a central concern of this book.

It is striking that the masque on the whole avoided too literal an interpretation of musical images. The point is illustrated by the treatment of the figure of Fame (who appears in many different masques) since one of her standard properties is a musical instrument, the trumpet. In *The Masque of Queens* the twelve masquers were revealed sitting on a triumphal throne in the House of Fame. After a long speech by Heroic Virtue, Fame herself was revealed:

Here, the Throne wherein they sate, being *Machina versatilis*, sodaynely chang'd; and in the Place of it appeared *Fama bona*, as she is describ'd, in Iconolog. di Cesare Ripa. attir'd in white, wᵗh white Wings, hauing a collar of Gold, about her neck, and a heart having at it; wᶜh *Orus Apollo* in his *Hieroglyp.* interprets the note of a good fame. In her right hand she bore a trumpet, in her left an oliue-branch, and for her state, it was as *Virgil* describes her, at the full, her feete on the Ground, and her head in the Cloudes. She, after the Musique had done, wᶜh wayted on the turning of the *Machine*, calld from thence to *Vertue*, and spake . . .   (ll. 446–56)

Here, presumably, we see an example of genuine co-operation between Jonson and Inigo Jones. Both are concerned to relate their Fame to a well-established iconographic tradition—Ripa, Horapollo, and Virgil are all cited as authorities. Of all her attributes it is, needless to say, the trumpet that interests me here. It is the first object mentioned by Ripa, whose Fama Buona is a 'Donna con vna tromba nella mano dritta . . .'.[1] A winged figure with a trumpet is readily identifiable as Fame. On the frieze at the top of the proscenium arch for *Salmacida Spolia* Fame was shown 'with spreaded wings, in act, sounding a Trumpet of gold' (l. 44).

In *The Masque of Queens* Fame calls on Virtue, her father, to help her in presenting the twelve Queens. Her speech ends by initiating the humiliation of the antimasque witches:

And, let those *Hagges* be led, as Captiues, bound
Before theyʳ wheeles, whilst I my trumpet sound.   (ll. 472–3)

The text then reads, 'At wᶜh, the loud *Musique* sounded, as before; to giue the *Masquers* time of descending' (l. 474). Whatever Fame did with the trumpet she was holding in her hand, what the audience heard was not, apparently, trumpet music but the 'loud music'. A wind consort is, of course, not inappropriate, but it is only what we might expect to hear at the equivalent

---

[1] C. Ripa, *Iconologia* (Padua, 1611; repr. New York, 1976), 154.

point in any court masque. In other words, no attempt seems to have been made to give a more specific realization of the idea that Fame sounded her trumpet. The practical function of this loud music, first to cover the noise of Inigo Jones's machine and then to give the masquers time to descend to their chariots, is at least as obvious as any emblematic significance.

While the masquers ride in triumph about the stage, a 'full triumphant music' sings

> Helpe, helpe all Tongues, to celebrate this wonder:
> The voyce of FAME should be as loud as Thonder.
>   Her House is all of *echo* made,
>   Where neuer dies the sound . . .   (ll. 723–6)

Now a new musical attribute of Fame is introduced: her house is made of echoes. This idea, too, has a distinguished literary tradition—one which stretches back through Chaucer's *House of Fame* to Ovid's *Metamorphoses*.[2] We have no way of knowing how much word-painting went on in this chorus, but there is no indication in the text of any musical echoes. Given the number of times echo effects were used in masque songs, this might seem surprising. Evidently a literal, aural representation of an allegorical concept was not sought here.

The final song in *News from the New World* is performed by Fame:

> Looke, looke alreadie where I am,
>   bright Fame,
>   Got up unto the skie,
>   thus high,
>   Vpon my better wing,
>   to sing
>   The knowing King,
>   And make the musicke here,
>   With yours on earth the same.   (ll. 365–73)

The text does not include an independent description of Fame's appearance, though the song obviously presupposes the winged figure. (Note, too, that the song mentions both wings and musical attributes.) Jonson may have intended his short, two-syllable rhyming lines in this final song to be realized as echoes—but he certainly does not say so (nor does he include anything which would prompt the audience to interpret such echoes as allegorically significant). The most basic point about the nature of Fame is made, not by specific musical effects, but simply by having her sing at all. Her theme (a flattering inversion of the accepted order) is that celestial music should be 'tuned' to the music of the king's peace (a phrase actually used earlier in this masque).

Fame sings again in *Chloridia*, where she is revealed in one of several transformations within the main masque. The description here makes refer-

---

[2] See H&S, x. 508. The editors point out that Jonson/Jones have introduced their own variants. It was, in fact, Chaucer who had brought the figure of winged fame with (two) trumpets into the English tradition.

ence to her iconographic attributes: 'Here, out of the Earth, ariseth a Hill, and on the top of it, a globe, on which *Fame* is seene standing, with her trumpet in her hand . . . *Fame* begins to mount, and moouing her wings, flyeth, singing, vp to Heauen' (ll. 275–81). The trumpet functions as a purely visual emblem; Fame's actual music (the music we hear) is vocal.

Britannia Triumphans presents a similar case. Fame has a trumpet, mentioned in the antimasque when Action tells Imposture that Fame 'intends | Her triumphs all of Truth; her Trumpet she | Hath chosen new and cleane, lest it should taint | Her breath' (p. 189). At the transformation scene, Fame appears—as in the Ripa emblem—holding her trumpet: 'Fame in a Carnation garment trimd with gold, with white wings and flaxen haire, In one hand a golden Trumpet, and in the other an Olive Girland' (p. 203).[3] Again, the trumpet remains a visual emblem only; Fame's actual music is vocal. Her second song is performed as her palace sank out of sight and she, 'remaining hovering in the air, rose on her wings singing, and was hidden in the clouds' (p. 205). What she sings is the Lawes Ciacona (examined in Ch. 4)—an innovative and appealing piece which is thoroughly appropriate in mood here. But Lawes does not attempt to create a musical emblem. Once again, we are confronted with an example of a musical icon being (very deliberately) left as a visual symbol.[4]

Kynaston's *Corona Minervae* contains yet another example of Fame's trumpet being left unplayed. Time claims that he will make Minerva's virtues widely appreciated: 'I by fames Trumpet will make understood | Her reason through the world . . .' (sig. C1ᵛ). Again, there is no suggestion that this was to be realized as a musical effect.

In all of these cases (with the possible exception of *News from the New World*, where her appearance is not actually described), Fame was recognizable because she carried a trumpet, yet in none is she associated with music which attempts to translate this emblem into aural terms with any kind of specificity. The loud music in *The Masque of Queens* is the closest we ever get to such an idea. As we have seen, Fame's music in the masques is virtually always vocal. It may be worth noting that the emblem of Fame's trumpet stands for, more than anything else, human speech (the means by which a reputation is created). But since all masques are full of vocal music, the fact that Fame articulates her concerns in song leaves her musically undifferentiated from all the other figures who give voice to main-masque themes. The music masters

---

[3] It is clear that for his Palace of Fame in *Britannia Triumphans* Jones imitated designs for the first of the intermedi which had accompanied *Il Giudizio di Paride* in Florence in 1608. Fame was, in fact, personified in numerous Florentine court entertainments—always with the trumpet and often holding an olive branch (as in *The Masque of Queens* and *Britannia Triumphans*). On several occasions her robe was decorated with a motif of eyes, ears, and tongues. See Nagler, *Theatre Festivals*, 41 (for the 1569 festivities), 100 (for *Il Rapimento di Cefalo*, 1600), 105 (for *Il Giudizio di Paride*, 1608), and 199 (for *Eros and Anteros*, 1613).

[4] Understandably—given the obvious possibilities the image offered for musical realization—some have found this hard to believe: alongside the line 'Fame's universal voice I hear' (Bellerophon heralding Fame's arrival), Lefkowitz added an editorial stage-direction 'a trumpet within': *Trois Masques*, 203.

had an obvious opportunity to realize an emblematic concept in sound, but they consistently did not do so.

The contrast with the Restoration period brings home the point. Here I shall cite just two well-known examples. In Act IV of Purcell's *Dioclesian* 'Sound, Fame, thy Brazen Trumpet Sound' is introduced by a 'Tune for the Trumpets', and the song itself has a prominent trumpet obbligato. There is a solo trumpet too in the chorus of Fame's 'I come to sing Great Zempoalla's Story' in *The Indian Queen*.

The example of Fame's music illustrates a crucial point about the relationship between music and imaginative device in the masque. There is usually a congruity between the two, but often this is a matter of *general* stylistic appropriateness. In only a few instances can the nuances of the music be illuminated by specific detail in a text. The composers who created this music are from a generation who, on the one hand, avoided the excesses of madrigalian word-painting (Campion is on record as finding it absurd) and, on the other, showed scant interest in the purely theatrical exploitation of these images such as we find in later music.[5] There seem to me to be two possible reasons for this. The first is that allegory and emblem were still so current as ways of articulating abstract ideas that illustration of the kind we have envisaged would have seemed superfluous, naïve, a distraction even. The other is that the whole process of putting together a masque—the co-ordination of different departments almost, rather than the collaboration and dynamic interaction of a small intimate group of creative artists—may have provided for broad rather than specific agreement, a general stylistic congruity rather than detailed interconnections between musical composition and literary text.

Oberon

Let us turn to *Oberon: The Faery Prince* (1611) as an example of how these different departments related in a single production. What we can know about music in this masque is—quite typically—a matter of drawing together information from a diverse range of sources. The starting-point, obviously, is Jonson's text. This is usefully supplemented by observers' accounts, most notably a Spanish description found amongst the papers of William Trumbull, who at the time of the performance was the British envoy in Brussels.[6] Surviving financial records (for *Oberon* rather more than for most masques) contribute significantly to our knowledge of the musical resources used. Last but not least, there is the music itself—confined in this case to two songs (in

---

[5] For Campion's remarks on word-painting see the preface to *A Booke of Ayres . . . by Philip Rosseter* (1601); *Thomas Campion*, ed. Davis, 15.

[6] GB-Lbl, MS Trumbull Misc XIV. There are inaccuracies in the treatment of musical and dancing terms in the translation of this report reproduced in H&S, x. 522–3. In this chapter, I have used the published translation as the basis for quoted excerpts; where I have had to depart from it, the original Spanish has been noted in brackets.

GB-Ob, MS Tenbury 1018) and two dances (plus, as so often, a whole range of other dance music which might very well have been used). The financial records are reproduced above (pp. 37–8) and the relationship between the other kinds of sources are set out schematically in Table 8.1.

In a way, the modern perspective on the masque reflects the state of these sources. It is not simply that the text is intact while the music consists only of fragments, but that the text projects a partisan view of the work's significance. Despite the title-page's description of *Oberon* as 'a Masque of Prince Henries', by 1616 it was well on its way to becoming 'a masque by Ben Jonson', given a different kind of dignity and status by inclusion in his *Works*. The *Oberon* text is ostensibly a report, though it might more accurately be described as a dramatic poem pretending to be a report. It is emphatically not a script or libretto. In relation to music, every detail recorded contributes to the sense of structure or enhances a thematic idea Jonson is working to articulate. The Spanish account—less discriminatory in its interests—supplies musical detail which does not form part of Jonson's text.

The role of the wind band—the thirteen 'Holt boyes' mentioned in the financial records—is a case in point. As we have seen in Chapter 3, such an ensemble always played at the beginning of masque performances. The Spanish account proves that *Oberon* was no exception, although the text is silent on the matter. This is typical; in all his masque texts, Jonson mentions this use of loud music only once, and then rather obliquely—the description of *Neptune's Triumph* gets under way with the words 'His Matie being set, and the loude Musique ceasing . . .'. Jonson *was* interested, however, in the wind band's playing at transformation scenes where, over and above its practical function of covering the noise of stage machinery, it evoked a sense of awe. As we shall see, in the *Oberon* text the reference to 'Lowd triumphant music' provides a context for the transformation song.

Prince Henry, whose investiture as Prince of Wales seven months earlier had been marked by the performance of *Tethys Festival*, danced in *Oberon* as the principal masquer—the 'fairy prince' of the title. He took an active role in planning the masque. Many would have seen him as an ideal sponsor; his own interests and the interests of his court were perfectly attuned to everything the masque could offer. Sir Francis Bacon called the prince 'a lover both of antiquity and arts', while Sir John Harrington described his household as a place where a young nobleman might 'learne to fashion himselfe'.[7] To begin with, the component arts of the masque were fostered there in forms which evince a desire to assimilate all that the avant-garde of continental Europe had to offer. The prince's own interest in music was genuine, well informed, and open to innovation. His household included John Bull, Robert Johnson, the

---

[7] Bacon, quoted in Roy Strong, *Henry Prince of Wales* (London, 1986), 133. Strong also quotes John Holles: 'For good men of all professions were welcome to him . . . All men of learning, countryman or stranger, of what virtue soever, military or civil, he countenanced and comforted' (ibid. 8). For Harrington, see Parry, *Golden Age*, 69.

TABLE 8.1. *Relationship of musical sources, text, and observer's report in Oberon*

Extant music	Jonson, *Oberon, The Faery Prince*, in *Works* (1616) (line numbers from H&S, vii)	GB-Lbl, MS Trumbull Misc XIV: 'Relacion breue de la mascara que hizo el Principe de Gales a los onze de Hen. 1611 en Londres'[a]
		When their Majesties entered accompanied by the princess and the ambassadors of Spain and Venice, shawms played [tocaron chirimias] and the curtain was drawn discovering a great rock with the moon showing above through an aperture . . .
	11 [Satyr 1] *wound his Cornet, and thought himselfe answer'd; but was deceiued by the Echo.*	
? Playford, *Catch that Catch Can* (1667), attrib. Edmund Nelham	209 *At which the Satyres fell sodainely into this catch* [Buz, quoth the blue Flie']	
	259 [Satyr 1] Brothers, sing then, and vpbraid (As we vse) yond' seeming maid. SONG: 'Now, my cunning lady, Moone . . .',	
GB-Lbl, Add. Ms 10444, no. 56 (S 107); 'The Satyres Masque'; Simpson, *Taffel Consort* (1621), no. 24, Robert Johnson (untitled)	282 *The song ended: They fell sodainely into an antique dance, full of gesture, and swift motion, and continued it, till the crowing of the cock: At which they were interrupted by* SILENVS.	They then danced a ballet [vn bailete] in their wild fashion, with appropriate music and with a thousand gestures and strange grimaces [a su modo saluaje, con musica appropriada y con mil meneos y Visajes estrannos], affording great pleasure.

291 *There the whole palace open'd, and the nation of Faies were discouer'd, some with instruments, some bearing lights; others singing; and within a farre off in perspective, the knights masquers sitting in their seuerall sieges: At the further end of all,* OBERON, *in a chariot, which to a loud triumphant musique began to moue forward, drawne by two white beares, and on either side guarded by three. Syluanes, with one going in front.*

This done the rock opened discovering a great throne with countless lights and colours all shifting, a lovely thing to see. In the midst stood the prince with thirteen other gentlemen chosen as famous dancers of the Court. Before passing into the hall ten musicians appeared playing lutes [con sendos laudes] . . .

299 SONG: 'Melt earth to sea, sea flow to ayre . . .'

314 *By this time, the chariot was come as far forth as the face of the scene. And the Satyres beginning to leape, and expresse their ioy, for the vn-vsed state, and solemnitie . . . .*

369 *The* SONG, *by two Faies* ['Seeke you maiestie, to strike?']

. . . and two boys who sang very well some sonnets [sonetes] in praise of the prince and his father.

382 *Then, the lesser Faies dance forth their dance*

Then ten little pages dressed in green and silver with flat bonnets à l'antique danced another ballet with much grace.

384 *which ended a full song followes, by all the voyces.* ['The solemne rites are well begunne']

? Add. MS 10444, no. 57 (S 108), 'The Fairey Masque', Add. MS 38539, fo. 10ᵛ, 'the fayris Daunce'; GB-Cu, MS Dd.6.36, fo. 24ᵛ, 'The fayris Daunce'

        Realizations

T A B L E 8.1. *Continued*

Extant music	Jonson, *Oberon, The Faery Prince*, in *Works* (1616) (line numbers from H&S, vii)	CB-Lbl, Trumbull Misc XIV: 'Relacion breue de la mascara que hizo el Principe de Gales a los onze de Hen. 1611 en Londres'[a]
	394 *There* OBERON, *and the knights dance out the first masque-dance*	. . . They entered dancing two ballets intermingled with varied figures and many capers [con muchas cabriolas], extremely well done by most of them.
GB-Ob, MS Tenbury 1018, fo. 36ᵛ, Alfonso Ferrabosco II	395 *which was follow'd with this song.* ['Nay, nay,	You must not stay']	
	407 *After which, they danced forth their second masque-dance*	
	408 *and were againe excited by a song* . . . [(Dialogue) 'Nor yet, nor yet, O you in this night blest']	
	420 *Then follow'd the measures, coranto's, galliards, &c. till* PHOSPHORVS, *the day-starre, appear'd, and call'd them away;*	The prince then took the queen to dance, the Earl of Southampton the princess, and each of the rest his lady. They danced an English dance called the measures which is like a pavan [y danzaron una danza ynglesa que llaman las mesuras que es como pabana]. When the queen returned to her place the prince took her for a

coranta which was continued by others, and then the galliard began, which was something to see and admire. The prince took the queen a third time for *los branles de Poitou*, followed by eleven others of the masque. As it was about midnight and the king somewhat tired he sent word that they should make an end.

So the masqueraders performed the exit dance [danzaron las mascaras el baileto de la salida] in which the satyrs and fauns joined.

With vocal . . .

. . . and instrumental music the masquers approached the throne to make their reverence to their Majesties.

GB-Ob, MS Tenbury 1018, fos. 37ᵛ–38ʳ, Alfonso Ferrabosco II

422 *but first they were inuited home, by one of the Syluanes, with this song.* ['Gentle knights']

444 *After this, they danc'd their last dance, into worke.*

445 *And with a full song, the starre vanish'd, and the whole machine clos'd.* ['O yet, how early, and before her time']

ᵃ Translation adapted from *Historical Manuscripts Commission Report on the Manuscripts of the Marquess of Downshire preserved at Easthampstead Park, Berks*, iii, 'Papers of William Trumbull the Elder 1611–12', ed. A. B. Hinds, 1–2.

lutenist Thomas Cutting, Thomas Lupo (appointed as the first Composer for
the Violins in the King's Musick in 1622), Thomas Ford, and Angelo Notari
(composer of *Prime musiche nuove*). Of most immediate interest here, at the
beginning of 1604 Ferrabosco was given an annual pension of £50 'in regard
to his attendance uppon the Prince and instructing him [in] the art of
musick'.[8] In dedicating the 1609 *Ayres* to the Prince, Ferrabosco indicates that
his patron and pupil both appreciated his work and was capable of an
intelligent critical response to it. Finally, as we saw in Chapter 6, Thomas
Giles had been employed as a dancing-master in Prince Henry's household
since the beginning of 1606.

Prince Henry was also intensely interested in masques themselves, in their
potential to project an image of princely and state priorities through the
combined arts of music, poetry, and perspective. A few months after *Oberon*,
his architect Constantine de Servi (who was under pressure from the prince to
produce something very sophisticated) wrote to Florence to try to obtain
copies of the engravings of intermedi designs (which he clearly intended to
use as a model).[9] It was Prince Henry who undertook the co-ordination and
planning of the entertainments—including three masques—for the wedding
of Princess Elizabeth and the Count Palatine (though he died before these
plans were brought to fruition).

The prince had originally wanted to have his 1611 masque presented on
horseback (perhaps emulating the horse ballet which had formed part of the
1608 Medici wedding celebrations in Florence),[10] but James I forbade this.
(He had only reluctantly given permission for Prince Henry's Barriers the year
before.) In the end, the prince's chivalric ambitions had to be satisfied by a
device in which the Fairy Prince and his knights pay homage to a king who
is 'the matter of vertue' and who teaches his subjects 'by the sweetnesse of his
sway, | And not by force' (ll. 341–6).

Serious planning for *Oberon* began about six weeks before the performance.
Marc'Antonio Correr, the Venetian ambassador, wrote on 25 November
1610 that the King 'will leave for Royston on Saturday, and the Prince will
go with him for a couple of weeks, as he must come back to arrange a Masque
for Christmas . . .'.[11] This was about the usual lead-up time; we know that
similar intervals elapsed between conception and performance for both *The
Masque of Queens* and *Pleasure Reconciled*.[12]

---

[8] Ashbee, *RECM*, iv. 11.

[9] See Strong, *Henry Prince of Wales*, 91 (and see 95). De Servi's designs for *The Somerset Masque* were
generally felt to be very disappointing; see above, p. 18.

[10] *Ballo e Giostra di Venti* (see GB-Lbl, 114. b. 13). This formed part of the same celebrations in which
the intermedi for *Il Giudizio di Paride* were performed. At least one horse ballet took place in France, the
Ballet de M. de Vendosme fait pour le Carrousel (1612). Prince Henry's Barriers may have inspired the *Ballet
du Combat à la Barrière* in 1610.

[11] Quoted in H&S, x. 518.

[12] On 14 Nov. 1608 John Donne had reported to Sir Henry Goodyere that the King 'hath left with the
Queen a commandment to meditate upon a Masque for Christmas, so that they grow serious about that
already' (see H&S, x. 491). On that occasion the result was, of course, *The Masque of Queens*. John

This mid- to late-November start with the planning for early-January masques is interesting, since it seems that musical preparations—and even rehearsing for the set dances—must have got under way at virtually the same time. The warrant authorizing a supplementary payment of £20 to Ferrabosco, Herne, and Confesse speaks of their 'paines having bene imployed in the Princes late Mask by the space almost of sixe weekes' (see above, p. 37). It seems unlikely that Jonson handed over a completed text to the composers before the production was put into rehearsal. In other words, the different departments seem to have worked in parallel. As noted earlier, this helps explain why the relationship between music and other aspects of the masque is one of general—not particular—correspondence. It may be that initially Nicolas Confesse, Robert Johnson, and Thomas Giles (all of whom contributed to *Oberon*) knew little more than how many of each kind of set dance would be needed. Equipped with their own and Robert Johnson's tunes, and with choreographies in their heads—or in 'brachygraphy'—Confesse and Giles must have begun working with the Prince, the Earl of Southampton, and the other masquers (whose names are not known but who, according to the Spanish account, were 'chosen as famous dancers of the court'). They used rehearsal violinists for this—presumably Thomas Lupo, Alex Chisan, and Rowland Rubidge, who were paid separately. At some later point Thomas Lupo and Robert Johnson arranged the dance tunes for the violins and the lutes.

The Spanish account makes it clear that the Banqueting House was set up in the customary way with the dancing-area—covered with a green cloth—enclosed by the State at the lower end, degrees for the audience along both sides, and a raised stage behind a proscenium arch at the upper end. Over the years the green cloth gets numerous mentions in the Lord Chamberlain's accounts—it must have saved dancers from slipping and muffled the sound of their steps.

After the loud music, the antimasque opens as gradually, by the light of the moon, a satyr is revealed. He first calls out to his fellows and then 'wound his Cornet, and thought himselfe answer'd; but was deceiued by the Echo' (l. 11). He sounds his cornett a second time and is again answered by an echo. On the third cornett call, another satyr responds to the sound and appears on stage. The episode is an ingenious variation on the convention of musical echoes within pastoral masques, an indoor variant of the device favoured in garden pastoral entertainments of having cornetts reporting to each other from different parts of a park.[13] Most pastoral echoes imply that the whole environ-

---

Chamberlain wrote to Dudley Carleton on 29 Nov. 1617 telling him that the preparations for *Pleasure Reconciled* were under way: 'The Prince went three dayes since towards Newmarket to the King: he is practising for a maske at Christmas which they say shalbe at the Earle of Buckinghams charge.' *Letters*, ii. 120.

[13] See e.g. Jonson's *Entertainment at Althorp* (ll. 3 ff.), Marton's *Entertainment at Ashby* (p. 387), and Campion's *Entertainment at Caversham* (p. 230, and p. 239).

ment shares the joy of the occasion, but in this genial antimasque the nymph Echo teases the simple satyr. Glossing a line in which the satyr suggests that all his fellows may be in a drunken sleep, Jonson refers to the Casaubon engraving reproduced as Pl. 9 'wherein is described the whole manner of the *Scene, and Chori, of Bacchus*, with *Silenus*, and the *Satyres*'.[14] The emblem points to an iconographic tradition which makes it seem right for a satyr to have a cornett as an approximation of the classical aulos—the reed instrument with divergent pipes shown in the Casaubon engraving. When the satyrs discuss how they can honour Oberon and his knights, they make it clear that pipes and percussion instruments are their chosen means of expression:

> SATYRE 2
> And to answere all things els,
> Trap our shaggie thighes with bels;
> That as we do strike a time,
> In our daunce, shall make a chime
> SATYRE 3
> Lowder, then the rattling pipes
> Of the wood-gods;
> SATYRE 1
> Or the stripes
> Of the *Taber*, when we carrie
> BACCHUS vp, his pompe to varie.   (ll. 121–31)

The satyrs sing twice. The first time—at Silenus' command to 'strike a charme into their eares'—they wake the two sleeping sylvans supposed to be guarding Oberon's palace. What they sing, 'Buz, quoth the blue Flie', is a catch—a popular and unsophisticated vocal form.[15] Later, to fill in the time until Oberon is due to appear, the satyrs sing a wanton song to the moon:

> Now, my cunning lady; Moone,
> Can you leaue the side, so soone,
> Of the boy, you keepe so hid?
> Mid-wife IVNO sure will say,
> This is not the proper way
> Of your palenesse to be rid . . .   (ll. 262–7)

Immediately after this, the satyrs 'fell sodainely into an antique dance, full of gesture, and swift motion' (ll. 282–3). The Spanish account calls this a wild dance 'with appropriate music' and 'a thousand sudden movements and strange gestures, affording great pleasure'. Both author and observer emphasize that the dance was characterized by the vigorous movement and extravagant gestures so typical of antimasque-dancing. We can for once be reasonably

---

[14] Gloss on line 17.

[15] Playford was to publish a version of this (with an extra line of verse) in *Catch that Catch Can* (1667), where it is attributed to Edmund Nelham. It is far from certain that this version was used in the performance of the masque. Any catch would, however, have been in a similarly uncomplicated and popular style.

confident that in this case the 'appropriate music' can be identified: Add. MS 10444, no. 56, 'The Satyr's Masque' (S 107) appears in Simpson's *Taffel Consort* without a title but ascribed to Robert Johnson, who was paid for 'making Daunces' in *Oberon*. The piece is a superb example of its kind (Ex. 8.1). It is long (six strains) and has virtually all the defining characteristics of antimasque dances: several changes of metre, triple rhythms before the final section, and the use of the fast duple time signature. There is a continuous alternation between straight and hemiola rhythms in the first triple strain, the second strain juxtaposes sustained notes and moving crotchets (like 'the First Witches Dance'), and the fast duple strain uses lots of syncopation. The final strain is rhythmically ambiguous. It begins with a motif deriving from the opening of the piece now adjusted to a 3/2 metre; on some of its abbreviated repetitions this motif assumes a 2/2 character, and a couple of bars before the end of the piece, the dotted rhythm from the original motif is subsumed into a 6/4 pattern. These ambiguities are reflected in the way Simpson and Add. MS 10444 use different time signatures. The only information about who might have played this dance is the rather unspecific line in the accounts 'xvj other instrumentes, for the Satires & faeries'. We might assume (cautiously—given Fame's treatment in the masques of the period) that these included the tabors, bells, and shawms claimed by the satyrs as personal attributes.

Satyrs playing wind instruments and dancing antic dances are part of a well-established literary and iconographic tradition.[16] The audience may have recognized the instrumental sounds they were hearing as suitable for a scene of satyrs and sylvans. The musical compositions used here—eccentric dance and trivial catch—fit perfectly. Words, spectacle, and music work together to produce an appropriately comic prelude of 'light and skipping sport' (l. 321) to the rites of the Fairy Prince.

Unlike some, the antimasque in *Oberon* is not in hostile opposition to the main masque. Silenus and his satyrs acknowledge that the king to whom Oberon and his knights come to pay their annual vows

> . . . stayes the time from turning old,
> And keepes the age vp in a head of gold.   (ll. 350–1)

The front of Oberon's castle is revealed during the antimasque when the first *scena ductilis* (flats sitting in grooves on the stage) slides away. The satyrs remain on stage for a short time after the full transformation scene, and when Oberon's chariot approaches they begin to 'leape, and expresse their ioy, for the vn-vsed state, and solemnitie' (ll. 315–16).[17] The Spanish account's remark that the satyrs' antics 'excited great laughter' serves as a reminder that those professional actors and dancers who took part in the antimasques were skilled comedians. Here Thomas Giles and Nicholas Confesse must have been joined

---

[16] See e.g. Spenser's *Faerie Queene*, III. x. 44–6.

[17] Trumbull's correspondent says that 'the fauns danced about joyfully exciting great laughter' *before* the full antimasque dance; he may have mixed up the sequence of events.

Ex. 8.1. Robert Johnson, The Satyrs' Masque, from GB-Lbl, Add. MS 10444, no. 56 (S 107)

8: 1st and 2nd time bars indicated by ○ |ↀ.‖

9, 10: dots under slurs added editorially

12T: *g″* tied over from bar 11

17T: *a′* tied over from bar 16

Ex. 8.1. *Continued*

by the 'Players imployed in the Maske' who are mentioned as a group in the financial records.

The musicians so splendidly revealed in Oberon's palace (see Table 8.1) are, for once, not priests or deities. They appear as part of the nation of fairies, and as such they share in the masquers' spiritual perfection. The Spanish account describes them as 'ten musicians each with a lute' ('diez musicos con sendos laudes'). The financial records make it clear that there were in fact ten singers and six lutenists provided by Ferrabosco.

The transformation song, like the Satyrs', is a splendid example of its kind. Its constant imperatives are, as we have seen, typical of such songs; the singers seem to be initiators rather than observers of the wondrous change:

> Melt earth to sea, sea flow to ayre,
> 　　And ayre flie into fire,
> Whilst we, in tunes, to ARTHVRS chayre
> 　　Beare OBERONS desire;
> 　　　Then which there nothing can be higher,
> Saue *IAMES*, to whom it flyes:
> But he the wonder is of tongues, of eares, of eyes.　(ll. 300–6)

That last line (which is repeated as a refrain) takes its immediate significance from the unique conditions of the court masque—an entertainment in which all the arts unite.

After the transformation song and before the first dance of Oberon and his knights, the satyrs leave the scene and the lesser Faies (pages) perform. First there is the 'Song, by two Faies', a dialogue which extols (in successive couplets) the majesty, glory, wisdom, knowledge, and piety of the king. Next came the Faies' dance, which was so different from the Satyrs' that it clearly did belong in the world revealed through the transformation scene. The Spanish account says that it was performed 'with much grace', and it is introduced by the foremost Sylvan in a way which suggests that—like so many main-masque dances—its choreography worked towards alphabetical and geometric patterns:

> Stand forth, bright *Faies*, and *Elues*, and tune your layes
> Vnto his name: Then let your nimble feet
> Tread subtle circles, that may alwayes meet
> In point to him; and figures, to expresse
> The grace of him, and his great empresse.   (ll. 360–4)

Since the tune called 'The Fairey Masque' immediately follows 'The Satyres Masque' in Add. MS 10444, it seems likely that this dance would also have come from *Oberon* and been used for the lesser Faies. (We have seen that the instruments for the satyrs and fairies were treated as a single item in the financial accounts.) But this tune (as the fragment of information about instrumentation might lead us to expect) is structurally much more like an antimasque dance than one from a main masque. It has five strains with eight changes of metre, twice uses the fast duple signature (both times as a change within a strain), and includes a triple strain early on in the piece (see Table 3.2 above).[18] It also shifts abruptly (and temporarily) from C major to B♭ major at the beginning of the second strain. If it was used, it must have made this part of the masque seem very much an intermediate zone between antimasque and main masque.

Although the broad distinction between antimasque and main masque is clear, the initiation of 'the solemn rites' of the masque proper is gradual. The difference between antimasque and masque is expressed by a stratification of the various ranks of fairy creatures who do honour to the king; the noble 'lesser Faies' stand between the naïve and naughty satyrs on the one hand and Oberon and his attendant knights on the other. Who, then, were these lesser Faies? The two singers may have been choirboys or (like the boys who were later to participate in *The Triumph of Peace*) apprentices being trained by

---

[18] The virtually identical lute versions of this dance in GB-Lbl, Add. MS 38539, fo. 10ʳ, and GB-Cu, MS Dd. 6. 36, fo. 24ᵛ do not use the fast duple time signature but continue both strains 2 and 4 in a regular ¢ metre.

members of the King's Musick. The dancing pages were probably children of courtiers—like those who were to dance in *Coelum Britannicum.*

Following the pages' dance, 'a full song . . . by all the voyces' is performed, introducing the first masque dance by Oberon and his knights. Little is said in the text about the two set dances which precede the revels, but the Spanish account mentions both 'varied figures' and 'many capers'. The latter phrase underlines the difficulty now of trying to judge exactly where the line was drawn between praiseworthy virtuosity and unbecoming flamboyance. It serves as a useful reminder that set masque dances, for all that they remained within the bounds of decorum, were not staid. They drew on the masquers' real skill, built up over a number of years and deployed in each new court masque in a specially worked-out choreography which itself would be rehearsed for several weeks. The results must have been satisfyingly attractive and impressive.

The *Oberon* main-masque dances were accompanied by Robert Johnson's twenty lutes, an ensemble which must have done a great deal to give a magical aura of opulence and excitement. No tunes can be identified with any certainty for these main-masque dances. Any of the dances called 'The Prince's first/second/third Masque' in Add. MS 10444, for example, could have been used. And any of these would have seemed models of musical order in comparison with 'The Satyrs Masque'; all but one of the twelve dances with this title have a regular ₵ ₵ or ₵ ₵ 3 metrical structure.

The main-masque songs all fulfil conventional masque functions. The first set dance is followed by a song urging the masquers to continue dancing. Linking these exhortations to the device of the masque, the song protests that, as fairy knights, the dancers should have more than mortal agility and grace:

> Knottie legs, and plants of clay
> Seeke for ease, or loue delay.
> But with you it still should fare
> As, with the ayre of which you are.   (ll. 403–6)

In the final line the assertion of the masquers' incorporeal nature is made through the almost homophonous word pair, 'ayre' and 'are'; ayre is also a musical pun which identifies the masquers and their dancing with the music to which they perform. Ferrabosco's setting of this song—extant in GB-Ob, MS Tenbury 1018—seems perfectly adjusted to its context.[19] With its crisp rhythms and jaunty vocal line, it is itself like dance music.

The song which follows the second masque dance introduces the revels (in a way which we have seen to be typical) by encouraging the masquers to take partners:

[19] Ferrabosco's settings of 'Nay, nay you must not Stay' and 'Gentle Knights' are in GB-Ob, MS Tenbury 1018, fos. 36ʳ and 37ᵛ–38ʳ respectively. Both songs are published in Sabol, *Four Hundred Songs and Dances*, nos. 15 and 16; and Alfonso Ferrabosco II, *Manuscript Songs*, ed. I. Spink, ELS, II, 19 (London, 1966), nos. 6 and 7.

> And these beauties will suspect
> That their formes you doe neglect,
>   If you doe not call them forth . . .   (ll. 414–16)

The revels themselves are followed by two concluding songs; the first is performed by one of the sylvans when Phosphorus, the day-star, appears:

> Gentle knights,
> Knowe some measure of your nights.
> Tell the high-grac'd O BERON,
> It is time, that we were gone.
>   Here be formes, so bright, and aery,
>   And their motions so they vary
>   As they will enchant the *Faery*,
>   If you longer, here, should tarry.   (ll. 425–32)

Ferrabosco's setting is arguably his most beautiful masque song. Declamatory traits are perfectly reconciled with a quite different kind of expressive melody, and even the tendency to write vocal lines with wide leaps is accommodated without awkwardness. The basic tonality is G minor, but with the characteristic major/minor ambiguity. The initial declamatory calls to the 'gentle knights' rise up on notes from a G major chord, so that when the $e^{b'}$ and $b^{b'}$ are introduced in the second half of the opening phrase they have an expressive edge (Ex. 8.2). The next phrase takes up the rising motif from the opening (extending it to an octave) and draws on the new harmonic colouring of B flat major, which is given extra warmth by taking the voice down to a low B^b. The vocal range is wider than in any other Ferrabosco masque song except 'How Near to Good', and it is used most expressively. The highest note is reserved for 'here be forms so *bright* and airy',[20] a phrase which is given additional lightness through the use of two crotchets (instead of minims) on the *e* of 'airy'. There is extensive (and on 'motions' partially descriptive) use of melisma. The second half of the song is repeated, but the second time the last line of the poem is given a more ornate treatment.

   The song is followed by a speech from Phosphorus introducing the final set dance, which took the masquers back into the scene. The Spanish account informs us that the antimasque creatures participated in this dance. Since Jonson does not mention this, he may have felt uncomfortable with this departure from normal masque decorum. It does, however, seem to be in line with the overall thrust of the masque's device—each section of *Oberon* points in the same direction. The antimasquers may come from a different world but they are not hostile to Oberon's knights.

   The chorus which ends the masque protests at the approach of the morning and underlines the ephemeral nature of all that has just happened; the sun approaches 'lest, taken with the brightnesse of this night, | The world should wish it last, and neuer misse his light' (ll. 454–5).

---

[20] MS Tenbury 1018 reads 'light and airy'.

Ex. 8.2. Ferrabosco, 'Gentle Knights', from GB-Ob, MS Tenbury 1019

Ex. 8.2. *Continued*

There is an obvious practical justification for the type of music used throughout *Oberon*: the loud music at the transformation, the style of the solo songs, and the size of the instrumental ensembles could be accounted for simply in terms of the acoustic conditions. But a more important justification for these lies in the overall artistic design of the masque. The impact of the different types of music is apparent from the Spanish account of the performance, but in addition, the use of cornetts in the antimasque and lutes in the main masque is iconographically appropriate. Similarly, the contrast in dance styles evident in the production, combined with the impact of costume and set, link the various sections of the masque to values which are implicit in much visual art of the period.[21] At every stage of *Oberon* musical, literary, and visual elements shared a unity of purpose. Jonson's contrasting worlds of rude satyrs and fairy knights were delineated musically. The antimasque uses popular song and eccentric dance, while the main masque includes beautiful and sophisticated solo songs, choruses, and dances, all performed to a noble accompaniment.

So far I have said nothing about the revels, yet the Spanish account provides one of the fullest descriptions in the period of this section of the masque. There is an irony about the revels which we must now confront; in doing so, we must again widen our focus beyond *Oberon*.

The Revels

Ever since Epiphany night 1512 when the king with eleven others entered in disguise ('after the manner of Italy, called a maske') and asked the ladies to

[21] See R. Strong, *Van Dyck: Charles I on Horseback* (London, 1972), esp. chs. 3 ('One Imperial Prince') and 6 ('A Well-wrought Landscape').

dance with them, revels have been the defining feature of entertainments classed as masques. The masque grew around the revels, providing a dramatic framework for them. It is salutory to recognize this, since approaching the masque through texts (as we must) can make the revels seem quite peripheral. While in the Jacobean masque the revels are often carefully integrated into the imaginative device, in some Caroline masques (*Chloridia*, *The Temple of Love*, and *Luminalia*, for example) they are simply tacked on to the end of an essentially completed structure.

As with set dances, the amount of information given in the texts about the composition of the revels decreases from the beginning to the end of the period (see Table 8.2). At first they are introduced by sentences like, 'They take forth the Ladies and the Revels follow',[22] but from about 1620 onwards this is reduced to a bare heading: 'The Revels'. Fortunately, a few documentary accounts give quite a vivid picture of how this section of the evening was conducted.

All the descriptions—both in the texts and in more anecdotal sources—make it clear that the revels began with the most sedate and dignified dances (the measures) and then moved to lighter, more vigorous dances (most obviously corantos and galliards). This same progression can be seen in Inns of Court revels. In the Middle Temple revels for 1628–9 (see above, p. 262), the Master of the Inn—wearing his bar gown and carrying a white staff in his hand—led the dancing of the old measures and branles but then took his seat once the galliards, corantos, French dances, and country dances got under way. A bipartite structure—solemn revels and lighter dances—was recognized at the Inns of Court by the use of the terms 'Revels' and 'Post Revels'; there is even some evidence that different groups of musicians were used at the Inns for each of these types (and that one could take place without the other).

In January 1604 Dudley Carleton wrote to John Chamberlain describing two Christmas season masques, one with a device of Indian and Chinese knights performed on New Year's night and the other *The Vision of the Twelve Goddesses* given on Twelfth Night. He uses the expressions 'ordinary measures' and 'common measures' to distinguish the set dances performed by the masquers on their own from the dignified opening dances of the revels. In each masque the normal progression from measures to lighter dances was observed. Carleton took note of who was honoured by the sense of social precedence in the conduct of the revels and he revealed a keen interest in the grace and skill of the various dancers. What he says about the second of these masques provides an interesting amplification of the passages in Daniel's text mentioning the set dances and the revels (see above, pp. 156–7):

Then after the walking of two rounds fell into their measure, which for variety was nothing inferior but had not the life as the former. For the common measures they

---

[22] This phrase is from *Lovers Made Men* (l. 181); almost identical wording is used in *Pleasure Reconciled*, and very similar wording in *The Vision of Delight* and *The Masque of Heroes*.

TABLE 8.2. *The Dances of the Revels*

	measures	galliards	corantos	durets	moriscos	brawls/branles	lavoltas	canaries	passamezzi	Spanish dances	country dances
The Vision of the Twelve Goddesses (1604)	★	★	★								
The Masque of Blackness (1605)	★		★								
Hymenaei (1606)	★	★	★								
The Lord Hay's Masque (1607)	★	★	★				★				
The Entertainment at Ashby (1607)	★	★	★				★				
The Masque of Beauty (1608)		★	★								
The Masque of Queens (1609)		★	★								
Tethys Festival (1610)	★	★	★								
Oberon (1611)	★†	★†	★†								
The Masque of the Inner Temple and Gray's Inn (1613)		†	★	★		†					
The Somerset Masque (1614)		†	†		†						
The Masque of Flowers (1614)		★	★	★	★						
The Golden Age Restored (1615)		★	★			★					
The Masque of the Inner Temple (1615)	★	★	†								
Pleasure Reconciled to Virtue (1618)	†	†	†					†	†	†	
Time Vindicated (1623)	†	†	†			†			†		†

★ dance mentioned in a masque text
† dance mentioned in observers' reports

took out the earl of Pembroke, the duke, the lord chamberlain, Lord Henry Howard, Southampton, Devonshire, Sidney, Nottingham, Monteagle, Northumberland, Knollys, and Worcester. For galliards and corantoes they went by discretion, and the young prince was tossed from hand to hand like a tennis ball. The Lady Bedford and Lady Susan took out the two ambassadors and they bestirred themselves very lively, especially the Spaniard, for his Spanish galliard shewed himself a lusty old reveller. The goddesses they danced with did their parts, and the rest were nothing behindhand when it came to their turns; but of all for good grace and good footmanship Pallas bore the bell away. They retired themselves toward midnight in order as they came and quickly returned unmasked but in their masking attire.[23]

There are two further descriptions which give welcome information about the individual dances performed and convey a very strong sense of an almost ritual progression, a movement into informality. The first is the Spanish account of *Oberon* (see Table 8.1) where all, it seems, was as it should have been. The right people are respected in the etiquette of the occasion and they were obviously very capable participants. The Agent of Savoy at *The Somerset Masque* recorded similar, though perhaps more personal, impressions. He noticed particularly the social hierarchy respected in the revels and a level of competence in the dancing which seemed admirable (more so, in fact, than anything else he saw that night):

[the enchanted bough] fu portato al Conte di Pambroch in segno di dover cominciar le danze, come fece, dando mano alla Regina, e gli altri Cav^{ri} dil balletto alla sposa et altre dame, e danzorono passeggiando solamente una gagliarda, che durò mezo quarto d'hora. Finito questo e posate le dame, il detto Conte tornò pigliar la Regina e la fece danzare una corrente; danzorono ancor l'istessa corrente gli altri Cav^{ri} con altre dame. Finito, il detto Conte tornò dar di mano alla Regina; fu cominciato un brando alla francese, che fu tutto il bello e degno di esser lodato in tutta la festa, per esservi la persona della detta Regina, et il vederla ballare con tanta maestà e grandezza quanto si possi imaginare. Il Prencipe non ballò. Finito questo brando, tornò la musica nell'istesso luoco . . .[24]

What is especially interesting here is the sense that some of these dances were very extended and intricate.

The specific dances mentioned in the text are not, of course, a random selection of what was available in the early seventeenth century. Jonson

[23] Letter of 15 Jan. 1604, GB-Lpro, SPD 14. 6. 21; from D. Carleton, *Dudley Carleton to John Chamberlain, 1603–1624: Jacobean Letters*, ed. M. Lee (New Brunswick, NJ, 1972), 56.

[24] Quoted by Orrell, 'The Agent of Savoy at *The Somerset Masque*', 304 (from GB-Lbl, Add. MS 32023 B, fos. 152^r–159^v). Orrell gives a translation (modified here): 'it [the enchanted bough] was carried to the Earl of Pembroke as a sign that he ought to begin the dances, which he did, offering his hand to the queen. The other lords from the masque gave their hands to the bride and the other ladies, and passing up and down they danced only a galliard which lasted a half-quarter of an hour.

When that was done and the ladies had sat down, the Earl went back to the queen and led her out to dance a corranto; the other gentlemen danced the corranto with other ladies. When that was over, the Earl again offered his hand to the queen, and they began a French brando [branle], which was by far the most beautiful and praiseworthy thing in all of the festivity, because of the participation of the queen and the sight of her dancing with as much majesty and grandeur as one could imagine. The prince did not dance.

When this brando was over the music returned to the same place . . .'.

himself never admits that anything other than the most regular courtly dances had a place in the revels. No doubt such dances did occupy a lot of the time (all the evidence points to this), but Jonson's references to 'measures, galliards, and corantos' or just 'galliards and corantos' can be regarded virtually as standard ways of referring to a conventional selection of courtly dances. As a historical record they should not be taken too literally.

We might deduce as much from the slightly different emphasis, first in texts of masques not by Jonson, and secondly in the accounts (often written by foreigners) which augment the information provided by texts. There we get a slightly wider range of dances mentioned. Apart from measures, galliards, and corantos, *The Entertainment at Ashby* mentions lavoltas, which were also included amongst the 'lighter dances' in *The Lord Hay's Masque*. Beaumont's *Masque of the Inner Temple and Gray's Inn* and *The Masque of Flowers* include 'durets' or 'durettos', *The Masque of Flowers* mentions moriscos, and Browne's *Inner Temple Masque* the brawl. To these we can add the *Oberon* account's *los branles de Poitou*. Busino mentions passamezzi, canaries, and Spanish dances in the revels of *Pleasure Reconciled*, and the Office-book of the Master of the Revels contains a rather extraordinary account of what took place in *Time Vindicated*: 'The measures, braules, corrantos, and galliards, being ended, the Masquers with the ladyes did daunce 2 contrey daunces, namely The Soldiers Marche, and Huff Hamukin, where the French Embassadors wife and Medemoysala St. Luke did [dance].'[25]

Most of these dances are unremarkable, though one or two had an aura not quite in accord with the high moral tone adopted in Jonson's texts. The duret appears to be the name of a tune for a coranto.[26] The term 'brawl' is simply an English version of 'branle' and although some branles were mimed dances, the 'common branle' would have been familiar in courtly gatherings—it is the dance we saw Aurelia trying to remember at the beginning of Chapter 3. In the *Branles de Poitou* the women made a noise with their shoes on the floor.[27] Busino's passamezzi were probably just what are normally called the measures in masque texts. As we saw in Bassompierre's reminiscences of the entertainment at York House in 1626, dancing country dances was a popular court pastime.[28] In the planned part of the masque, both country dances and

[25] Quoted H&S, x. 649. For Busino's account see ibid. 583.

[26] J. E. Knowlton points out that in *Terpsichore* Praetorius says that the '*Courantes de Perichon* und *La Durette*: haben den Namen von ihren Meistern' ('The courantes of *Perichon* and *La Durette* have the names of their masters'). She also notes that a 'Duretto' attributed to Gibbons appears in GB-Lbl, MS Royal 23. L. 4 ('Benjamin Cosyn's Virginal Book') and a 'Courant. La Duretta' in D-Lr, MS KN. 146. See 'Some Dances of the Stuart Masque Identified and Analyzed', 42–3.

[27] 'Pas coupé'; see De Lauze, *Apologie*, trans. Wildeblood, 144.

[28] Country dances were certainly enjoyed by the court. Woodfill, *Musicians in English Society*, 189 cites an account which says that in the year 1600 Queen Elizabeth was in the habit of coming out into the presence almost every night 'to see the ladies dance the old and new country dances, with the taber and pipe'. Thomas Morley in *A Plain and Easy Introduction to Practical Music* discusses the English country dance in the same passage in which he describes courants and voltas—among dances which are 'more light' than branles, etc. (p. 297). See also Walter Sorell, 'Shakespeare and the Dance', *Shakespeare Quarterly*, 71 (1957), 373.

moriscos were confined to low inductions. Arbeau describes the canaries in a way which suggests that they would fit very uncomfortably into a Jonsonian view of the revels' function: 'gaillards, & neantmoins estranges, bizares, & qui resentent fort le sauuage . . .'.[29] In the context of a movement towards lighter dances within the revels, however, there is nothing untoward about the inclusion of dances like canaries. Most dances performed in the revels were accepted as appropriate for courtiers and ladies. What fitted less well with the Jonsonian ethos was the behaviour of some of the revellers.

But this does bring us to a very interesting aspect of masque performances. They were social occasions, not self-contained works of music drama. It is worth remembering that by far the greatest part of the entertainment was effectively beyond the control of its inventors. *Oberon* was, we know, a very orderly affair—all over by twelve o'clock. We have just seen that *The Vision of the Twelve Goddesses* also ended at about midnight, but many masques seem to have continued much further into the night. One observer (probably Sir John Finnet) wrote of *Tethys Festival*: '. . . it was high time to go to Bed, for it was within half an hour of the sun's not setting but rising. Howbeit a further time was spent in viewing and *scrambling* at one of the most magnificent Banquets that I have ever seen . . .'.[30] Busino says that *Pleasure Reconciled* ended at two in the morning and the Venetian ambassador reported that *News from the New World* 'lasted more than three hours'.[31] Later masque texts often emphasized the length of the revels (possibly as a way of indicating the success of the entertainment): Townshend claimed that the revels in *Tempe Restored* 'continued all the night' (p. 69), Carew that those in *Coelum Britannicum* lasted 'a great part of the night' (l. 1049), and Davenant that those in his *Temple of Love* 'continue[d] the most part of the night' (p. 305).

Since masques normally began somewhere between eight and ten o'clock at night, these accounts suggest that on average the entire entertainment would have lasted about four hours, of which probably three would have been absorbed by the revels.[32] And though the songs which introduce the revels habitually point to the dancing of masquers and audience as the most perfect manifestation of the masque's social ideals, this is the one part of the masque which could not be shaped by the inventor's imagination. Despite Jonson's best efforts, the beneficiaries of his aesthetics of power did not always behave in a way which allowed the ideal to work.

[29] See Arbeau, *Orchésographie*, fo. 95ʳ: 'gay and nevertheless strange, bizarre, and which have a markedly wild atmosphere'. Middleton, *Women Beware Women*, III. iii. 218 mentions the canaries in a passage which (as Ray Lurie pointed out on the 'rendance' e-mail network) puns on 'canary wine' rather than explaining anything about the licentiousness of the dance: 'Plain men dance the measures, the sinque pace the gay, | Cuckolds dance the hornpipe, and the farmers dance the hay; | You soldiers dance the round, and maidens that grow big; | You drunkards the canaries; you whore and bawd, the jig.' See also O. Gombosi, 'Some Musical Aspects of the English Court Masque', *JAMS* 1 (1948), 3–19.

[30] Winwood, *Memorials of Affairs of State*, iii. 181.

[31] See H&S, x. 584 (for *Pleasure Reconciled*) and 597 (for *News from the New World*).

[32] On starting times: *Mercury Vindicated* began shortly after 8 p.m. and *Pleasure Reconciled* about the sixth hour of the night (10 p.m.?). See H&S, x. 547 and 582.

The sense of social degree which lay at the heart of court-masque devices was equally obvious in the revels (though for slightly different reasons). Who got invited to the masque and who danced with whom gets a lot more attention in letters about masque performances than descriptions of their music. It would almost be possible to trace the shifts of power and influence at court through reported gossip about these matters. Dudley Carleton gives a cynical account of the Spanish ambassador's obsequious behaviour during the revels of *The Masque of Blackness*: 'He took out the Queen, and forgot not to kiss her Hand, though there was Danger it would have left a Mark on his Lips.'[33] John Pory, writing to Sir Robert Cotton about *Hymenaei*, quickly turned in his description to important people who were seen to dance:

They danced all variety of dances, both seuerally and promiscuè; and then the weomen took in men, as namely the Prince (who danced wth as great perfection and setled a Ma^{ty} as could be deuised) the Spanish ambassado^r, the Archidukes ambassado^r, the duke, etc. And the men gleaned out the Queen, the bride, and the greatest of the ladies.[34]

The French ambassador, La Boderie, reported with some satisfaction in his memoirs that at *The Haddington Masque* and *The Masque of Queens* the King and Queen had paid considerable attention to his family, and that on both occasions the young Duke of York had danced with his daughter during the revels.[35] Sir John Astley's account of the performance of *Time Vindicated*, cryptic though it is, notes that the Prince led the measures with the French ambassador's wife.

Sometimes, it seems, all went smoothly; we find comments about the excellence of the dancing which allow us to think that the courtly masquers did manage to do justice to the ideals of the device. On 22 February 1618, after the *second* performance of *Pleasure Reconciled* Sir Gerard Herbert wrote to Carleton: 'the tuesday night the Prince his maske was very excellent well performed of the prince, & dansinge his dances with much applause & Commendations: & the rest of his maskers doynge there partes very well.'[36] (It is interesting to see how prominently dancing features in his account.)

But clearly it was not always so edifying. Sometimes dancers were simply incompetent. Dudley Carleton wrote to John Chamberlain of the masque honouring the wedding of Sir Philip Herbert and Lady Susan Vere in 1605, '. . . theyr dancing full of life and variety: onely Sr Thos: Germain had lead in his heeles and sometimes forgott what he was a doing'.[37] Sometimes, it was a case of virtue resigned for pleasure. Carleton obviously enjoyed telling his friends about some of the scandalous behaviour that went on at *The Masque of Blackness*:

---

[33] H&S, x. 448.   [34] Ibid. 466–7.   [35] Ibid. 486 and 498.
[36] GB-Lpro, SP 14 96 27; quoted ibid. 577.
[37] GB-Lpro, SP 14 12 6; see Nichols, *Progresses*, i. 470–6.

... and in the cumming owt, a banquet wch was prepared for the k: in the great chamber was overturned table and all before it was scarce touched. It were infinit to tell you what losses there were of chaynes, Jewels, purces, and such like loose ware. and one woeman amongst the rest lost her honesty, for wch she was caried to the porters lodge being surprised at her busines on the top of the Taras.[38]

The entertainment provided for the King of Denmark at Theobalds in 1606 has become famous for its lack of decorum. According to Sir John Harrington's amused and disgusted account:

His Majestie then got up, and would dance with the Queen of Sheba; but he fell down, and humbled himself before her, and was carried to an inner chamber and laid on a bed of state; which was not a little defiled with the presents of the Queen, which had been bestowed on his garments; such as wine, cream, jelly, beverage, cakes, spices, and other good matters.[39]

And then there is Busino's description of the revels in *Pleasure Reconciled*:

Ballarono finalm^{te} un'alla uolta la spagnoletta con la sua Dama, et perche erano quasi stracchi andauano sorrando; il Rè come di natura colerica diede in una impacienza, et gridò forte, perche non si balla, à che fine m'hauete fatto uenir qua? che'l Diauolo ui porti quanti, che sete, ballate. Subito saltò fuori il sign. Marchese de Bocchingha[m] Mignon fauoritiss^o. di S. Ma^{tà}., con una mano di molto alte, et minutiss^{me} capriole, accompagnate con tanta gratia, et leggiadria, che fece ammirar et inamorar ciasched^{no}. della sua persona, non che habbia forza di placar l'ira del suo alterato Sig^e. Innanimiti gli altr[i] Mascherati seguitarono à far le lor prodezze un doppo l'altro, con differenti Dame, concludendo pur con capriole, et col leuar da terra la sua Diua. furono numerate sino 34. capriole tagliate una dopp[o] l'altra da un Cau^{re}. tuttauia niuno arriuò alla compita maniera del Marchese.[40]

What is interesting here is not just the king's bad behaviour, but the way in which a sycophantic favourite and his probably frightened acolytes seem to have abandoned all notions of unostentatious decorum.

David Lindley has pointed out how often the songs introducing the revels have a rather anxious, warning note to them.[41] As we know, not all masque writers shared Jonson's sense of moral seriousness. Some acknowledge and

---

[38] Letter to John Chamberlain, 7 Jan. 1605; GB-Lpro, SP 14 12 6, quoted in H&S, x. 449.

[39] Nichols, *Progresses*, ii. 72–3.

[40] Text from I-Vnm, Cl. VII, Cod. MCXXII, fos. 72–5, quoted in H&S, x. 581; translation from *CVSP*, xv. 114: 'Last of all they danced the Spanish dance, one at a time, each with his lady, and being well nigh tired they began to lag, whereupon the king, who is naturally choleric, got impatient and shouted aloud Why don't they dance? What did they make me come here for? Devil take you all, dance. Upon this, the Marquis of Buckingham, his Majesty's favourite, immediately sprang forward, cutting a score of lofty and very minute capers, with so much grace and agility that he not only appeased the ire of his angry lord, but rendered himself the admiration and delight of everybody. The other masquers, thus encouraged, continued to exhibit their prowess one after another, with various ladies, also finishing with capers and lifting their goddesses from the ground. We counted thirty-four capers as cut by one cavalier in succession, but none came up to the exquisite manner of the marquis.'

[41] Paper given to joint Viola da Gamba and Lute Societies meeting, Nov. 1992. Since writing this chapter I have read Keith Sturgess, *Jacobean Private Theatre*; he makes a similar point on p. 165.

even condone the insincere gallantry that went on; Beaumont introduced the
revels in *The Masque of the Inner Temple and Gray's Inn* with the following
song:

> More pleasing were these sweet delights,
> If Ladies mov'd as well as Knights;
> Runne ev'ry one of you and catch
> A Nymph in honor of this match;
> And whisper boldly in her eare,
> *Jove* will but laugh if you forsweare.
> *All*: And this dayes sinnes he doth resolve
> That we his Priests should all absolve.   (ll. 308–16)

All this suggests a gap between the Jonsonian vision and the realities of
masque performance. The assertion that it presented an image of good and
happy government and its fruits must sometimes have seemed either hollow
or nobly defiant. Jonson himself acknowledged the pitfalls of the kind of
normative eulogy on which his masque texts are based:

> Though I confesse (as every Muse hath err'd
> And mine not least) I have too oft preferr'd
> Men past their termes, and prais'd some names too much,
> But 'twas with purpose to have made them such.[42]

The masque, far from being a form in which all the arts combined to represent
the integrity, wisdom, and benign character of the Stuart court, must frequently have become an emblem of its own opposite.

---

[42] 'An Epistle to Master Iohn Selden', H&S, viii. 159.

Epilogue

Charles I left London in March 1642. Six months later a satirical pamphlet described the changed atmosphere at Whitehall. Amongst the manifestations of courtly extravagance and pretension which it exposed, the masque featured prominently. The kind of imagery which suffused masque texts was put to the service of irony:

... Majesty had wont to sit inthron'd within those glorious Walls, darting their splendour with more awfull brightnesse then the great Luminaries in the Firmament. And with the same life and vigour Cherishing the hearts of their admiring followers, And creating to those Favourites on whom their beames of grace reflected, names of honour, and estates to maintaine it till the Worlds end ...

In the Cockpit and Revelling Roomes, where at a Play or Masque the darkest night was converted to the brightest Day that ever shin'd, by the luster of Torches, the sparkling of rich Jewells and the variety of those incomparable and excellent Faces, from whence the other [sic] derived their brightnesse, Comparative whereunto to paralell [sic] the refulgencie of their bright-shining splendor, Now you may goe in without a Ticket, or the danger of a broken-pate, you may enter at the Kings side, walke round about the Theaters, view the Pullies, the Engines, conveyances, or contrivances of every several Scaene And not an Usher o' th' Revells, or Engineere to envy or finde fault with your discovery, although they receive no gratuitie for the sight of them.[1]

The envy and resentment that the élite had aroused is palpable. In what is yet another variant on the 'insubstantial pageant' theme, this pamphlet reminds us that the civil war determined that the fully developed court masque was to be a short-lived genre.

Two dramatists prominent in the writing of Caroline masques did not, however, entirely give up on the stage. For both William Davenant and James Shirley the masque seemed a way around Puritan restrictions. There were two reasons for this. First, the masque's allegorical tradition meant that it could be represented as morally improving rather than—as the Parliamentary ordinance

---

[1] *A Deep Sigh Breathed Through the Lodgings at White-Hall, Deploring the Absence of the Court, and the Miseries of the Pallace* (Wing D812); 'Printed for N. V. and J. B. 1642' sigs. A2 and [A3ᵛ]. The British Library copy (in the Thomasson Tract collection) has a handwritten date 'Octob: 4ᵗʰ'. The existence of this fascinating pamphlet, in which a satirical description of court life is mixed with regret at its passing, was first noted by G. Thorn-Drury, 'Whitehall in 1642', *RES* 1 (1925), 462.

banning plays put it—'too commonly expresing laciuious Mirth and Levitie'.[2] Secondly, masques, unlike plays, were not open to whoever was prepared to pay the penny admission price; they had, in a sense, always been private entertainments given to invited audiences. (Even for the performance of *The Masque of Blackness* in 1605 James I had insisted that 'a Masque is not a public function, and . . . his Majesty is quite entitled to invite any Ambassador he may choose, not as an Ambassador, but as a friend'.[3])

Anthony à Wood described James Shirley's response to the new situation: 'Afterwards following his old trade of teaching school, which was mostly in White-friers, he not only gained a comfortable subsistence (for the acting of plays was then silenced) but educated many ingenious youths . . .'.[4] But he did not totally renounce dramatic writing. Sometime before the death of William Lawes (1645) and almost certainly after the closing of the theatres, Shirley wrote *The Triumph of Beauty*. This, published with Shirley's *Poems* in 1646, was described as 'A Masque . . . personated by some young Gentlemen, for whom it was intended as a private Recreation.'[5] The young gentlemen were probably his pupils (and so *The Triumph of Beauty* takes its place in the seventeenth-century list of masque-like dramas for schools).[6] On the dramatic level, *The Triumph of Beauty* shifts away from the animated emblem of the masque towards something much more play-like. Its music, however, retains much more contact with masque traditions.

The Triumph of Beauty—like the masque in Act V of Shirley's *Constant Maid*—is a dramatization of the judgement of Paris.[7] It begins, however, with a scene which, it has long been recognized, is heavily indebted to the mechanicals' episode in *A Midsummer Night's Dream*.[8] Bottle, Crab Clout, Toadstool, Shrub, Scrip, and Hobbinoll discuss 'some rare and pleasant device' they will prepare for Paris, son of Priam. This section contains bagpipe music and culminates in an antic dance which is performed before an exasperated Paris. Then, 'On the sudden, other music is heard'; Mercury descends and sings Paris to sleep. William Lawes's setting for Mercury's song 'Cease warring thoughts' (examined in Ch. 4) is for three voices—though the text gives no indication that anyone other than Mercury is on stage with Paris.

Next Juno, Pallas, and Venus present themselves and put their case in song. Paris's decision in favour of Venus initiates a short main masque with much singing and some dancing. The first song in this section introduces the Graces and the Hours, who are the masquers (altough they are never actually *called*

---

[2] From the parliamentary order 2 Sept. 1642 suppressing the theatres; the full text of this order is reproduced by Bentley, *The Jacobean and Caroline Stage*, ii. 690.

[3] *CVSP*, x, no. 332; quoted by H&S, x. 447.

[4] Quoted by Bentley, *The Jacobean and Caroline Stage*, v. 1070.

[5] Title-page; a similar description occurs on the title-page of Shirley's *Contention of Ajax and Ulysses for the Armour of Achilles* (published in 1659).

[6] See above, p. 276 for *Cupid's Banishment*.

[7] *The Constant Maid* was published in 1640 and is thought to have been written in the late 1630s.

[8] See G. Langbaine, *An Account of the English Dramatic Poets* (Oxford, 1691), 485.

such). The songs, like conventional masque songs, encourage and direct the actions of the masquers, and one draws the classical analogy between the masquers' movements and the motions of the spheres:

> How dully all your joys do move?
> Delight is crippled here;
> Your motion should be like to that above;
> This is too thick a sphere . . .   (p. 341)

It is, in fact, in its use of music that *The Triumph of Beauty* comes closest to the court masque. Nearly all the songs have court-masque precedents, there is an obvious contrast between the mechanicals' antic dance and the dance of the main masque, and the one reference to instruments (bagpipes in the antimasque) suggests that this contrast extended to the kind of musical sounds heard in the two parts of the production. Despite these features, which suggest continuity with the court masque, the interaction between the characters is un-masque-like. Moreover, there is no provision for revels, and the masquers do homage to a stage 'queen of love and beauty' (Venus) rather than a real one.

In 1659 John Gamble published settings for all but one of the songs in this masque.[9] Except in a few very minor details, these settings follow the distribution of the voice-parts indicated in the text. It thus looks likely that these settings were written for a revived production. The whole character of this 'masque' is such that revivals would present no problems. This is not a text formed around a particular occasion. What we see beginning to happen here is the developed musical tableaux of the masque being absorbed into a more conventional drama.

This process is taken a stage further in Shirley's other private masque, *Cupid and Death*—the only pre-Restoration masque for which a complete musical score survives. The 1653 edition of the text makes it clear that, like *The Triumph of Beauty*, it was not written with an eye on a 'present occasion': 'This Masque was born without ambition of more than to make a good private entertainment, though it found, without any address or design of the authority an honourable acceptation from his Excellency, the ambassador of Portugal, to whom it was presented by Mr. Luke Channen & c . . .'.[10] Its revival six years later confirms the point. Matthew Locke's autograph score (GB-Lbl, Add. MS 17799) gives much less prominence to the term 'masque' than the printed editions of the text; instead it uses the descriptions 'Moral Representation' and 'private Entertainment'—both redolent of the stance which served to justify dramatic productions in the Commonwealth era.[11]

The score represents the work of Christopher Gibbons and Matthew

---

[9] In Gamble, *Airs and Dialogues* (1659).

[10] 'The Printer to the Reader'; see M. Locke and C. Gibbons, *Cupid and Death*, ed. E. J. Dent, MB 2 (London, 1951), p. xii. Dent points out that Mr. Luke Channen is probably Mr. Channell, the dancing-master.

[11] Fos. 2ʳ and 2ᵛ. (The words 'A Masque' appear in brackets on fo. 2ᵛ.)

Locke. Locke, it seems, retained in his 1659 score some of the music Gibbons had composed for the 1653 performance (when it is likely that only the sections of the text entitled 'song' were actually sung). Locke's additional vocal music for the 1659 performance results in the first really extensive examples of recitative in an English staged drama.

As in *The Triumph of Beauty*, the entrance of Mercury divides the entertainment into antimasque and main masque. But while this basic structural division is preserved, the dramatic progression is plot-oriented in quite an unmasque-like way. Again, however, it is the music which declares the strongest allegiance with the court masque. The antimasque ends with a dance of satyrs and apes, and Locke's music for this is very much in the traditional antimasque manner. It has the characteristic alternation in metre from ¢ to 3/2 to 3/4 to 3/2 (for two bars) and finally to ₡ (the time signature which is a hallmark of earlier antimasque dances). Moreover, there is the same kind of alternation between long sustained notes and fast running passages in the first two strains of this dance that we find in such early antimasque dances as 'The first witches dance' and 'The Satyres Masque' (see Ex. E1). The contrast between this dance and the 'solemn music' for Mercury's descent which follows is made quite beautifully with three lines interweaving in a dignified contrapuntal texture (see Ex. E2).

Like the music, the final revelation of the grand masquers in an Elysian scene is deliberately reminiscent of earlier masques. Mercury's first words are those which had banished the antimasquers in *The Triumph of Peace*, 'Hence ye profane'. Despite these links with the court masque, *Cupid and Death* is an essentially different kind of production.

Like Shirley, Davenant also saw the masque as a way past the Commonwealth's restrictions on the presentation of plays in public. He gained permission to put his 'operas' on the stage provided they were 'morall representations . . . without obscenenesse, profanenesse, and scandall'.[12] This policy produced initially *The First Day's Entertainment at Rutland House* (1656) and then, more significantly, the production which has traditionally been considered the first English opera, *The Siege of Rhodes* (first performed 1656).

At the Restoration 'ordinary' drama again thrived. Charles II licensed two acting companies, but—with some notable exceptions like Blow's *Venus and Adonis* and now, it seems, Purcell's *Dido and Aeneas*—neither he nor his successor attempted to emulate their father and grandfather by regularly sponsoring masques and plays at court.[13] The masque moved into the theatre. It is striking that inserted masques in plays in this period were quite clearly modelled on the court masques of the previous age (just as the rather vestigial masques in Jacobean and Caroline plays recalled Elizabethan models). The masques which form the main structural blocks of Restoration semi-operas

---

[12] See Butler, *Theatre and Crisis*, 99.

[13] The limited sense in which court masques were revived in the Restoration is described by Holman, *Four and Twenty Fiddlers*, ch. 15.

Ex. E1. Matthew Locke, dance of satyrs and apes (*Cupid and Death*), bars 1–6, from GB-Lbl, Add. MS 17799

Ex. E2. Matthew Locke, descent of Mercury (*Cupid and Death*), bars 1–5, from GB-Lbl, Add. MS 17799

strive to recapture the splendour of pre-Commonwealth courtly extravagance within the confines of the small indoor theatres. The description of trans-formation scenes in, for example, the Purcell/Betterton *Dioclesian* (admittedly one of the grandest of these productions) makes an instructive comparison with its pre-Commonwealth models:

While a symphony is playing, a machine descends, so large it fills all the space from the frontispiece of the stage to the further end of the house, and fixes itself by two ladders of clouds to the floor. In it are four several stages, representing the Palaces of two Gods and two Goddesses. The first is the Palace of *Flora*: the columns of red and white marble breaking through the clouds; the columns fluted and wreath'd about with all sorts of flowerage, the pedestals and fluting inrich'd with gold. The second is the Palace of the Goddess *Pomona*: the columns of blue marble, wound about with all kinds of fruitage, and inrich'd with gold as the other. The third is the Palace of *Bacchus*: the columns of green marble, wreath'd and inrich'd with gold, with clusters of grapes hanging round them. The last is the Palace of the Sun; it is supported on either side by rows of *termes,* the lower part white marble, the upper part gold. The whole object is terminated with a glowing cloud, on which is a chair of state, all of gold, the Sun breaking through the cloud, and making a glory about it; as this descends, there rises from under the stage a pleasant prospect of a noble garden, consisting of fountains, and orange trees set in large vases; the middle walk leads to a Palace at a great distance. At the same time enter *Silvanus, Bacchus, Flora, Pomona, Gods of the Rivers, fauns, Nymphs, Heroes, Heroines, Shepherds, Shepherdesses,* the *Graces,* and *Pleasures,* with the rest of their followers. The Dancers place themselves on every stage in the machine: the Singers range themselves about the stage.

The specificity of emblematic reference may have gone, but the list of characters on stage seems like a roll-call of masque *dramatis personae*—even the Sun king is there.

Dioclesian is an interesting case. The externals of the masque survive with a vengeance, but they are put to the service of an ideal which is the very antithesis of that projected in the masques of the early Stuart court. Its concluding masque (a gigantic inflation of the pastoral celebration at the end of its parent play, Fletcher's *Prophetess*) exults in the victory of rustic honesty over the corrupting influence of the court. But musically (as theatrically) the masque did give English writers and composers an indigenous tradition upon which they could draw in creating large-scale music drama. It is not unreasonable to see a line of development here from Ferrabosco through William Lawes to Matthew Locke and on to Blow and Purcell.

A nostalgia for early Stuart court masques was still evident in the eighteenth century, when a number were adapted for the opera-house. The best known and most successful of these was Thomas Arne's *Comus*, a 1738 adaptation of Milton's text by James Dalton in which airs are allotted indiscriminately to good and bad characters. The use of song as an indicator of moral authority is completely forgotten here.[14] Arne also composed the music for an adaptation by George Colman of *Oberon* performed at the Theatre Royal in Covent Garden. As the 'Advertisement' which precedes the text states, 'The greater part of this Masque is borrowed with some variations, from *Ben Jonson.* The same liberty has been taken with a few passages of Shakespeare, and a Chorus of the late *Gilbert West* Esq. The final Chorus is from *Dryden.*'[15] After the antimasque of satyrs, the rock opens to reveal, not Oberon's palace, but St

[14] Arne's *Comus* (1738) had been preceded in 1737 by an operatic version with libretto by Paul Rolli; the composer of this version is not known. See Thomas Arne, *Comus*, ed. J. Herbage, MB 3 (London, 1951), p. x.

[15] G. Colman, *The Fairy Prince* (London, 1771), sig. A3.

George's Chapel at Windsor. Jonson's songs find a new context in a scene depicting the installation of the Knights of the Garter in Windsor Castle. The music is set out in a series of recitatives and airs. In November 1774 'a Pastoral Masque and Pantomime' called *The Druids* was presented at Covent Garden with music by John Abraham Fisher. This was in part a conflation and adaptation of *Hymenaei* and *The Haddington Masque*.[16]

In 1887 *The Masque of Flowers* was revived by the gentlemen of Gray's Inn (whose forebears, as it were, had presented the original performance). The text (given an old-world appearance through the use of the long 's') explains that, 'by a few alterations (very slight and not in any way affecting the spirit of the play) the Maske has been rendered . . . not inappropriate to the celebration of Her Most Gracious Majesty's Jubilee . . .'.[17] A conventional string orchestra with added viola da gamba was conducted by J. A. Fuller-Maitland.

A performance of *The Vision of Delight* to celebrate the coronation of George V in 1911 ended with Dame Clara Butt stepping forward to the front of the stage at His Majesty's Theatre in London to lead the audience in 'God Save the King'. It was preceded by a series of entertainments which Herford and Simpson describe as 'a riot of fun'—antimasque merged with royal variety show.[18] A 1928 performance of *Pan's Anniversary* included an antimasque of robots.[19] *Chloridia* and *Comus* were performed in 1935 in the Open Air Theatre in Regents Park; 'Before the masque began King Charles and attendant Lords walked in and occupied the front row of seats.'[20] In 1948 the Oxford University Dramatic Society decided to honour a visit of the then Princess Elizabeth by presenting a masque. Instead of reviving a Stuart Masque, Glynne Wickham and Neville Coghill devised *The Masque of Hope*. Performed in the front quadrangle of University College, this 'masque' depicts the banishment of Fear and the triumph of Hope in post-war Britain.[21]

These productions all recognize in one way or another the importance of a relationship between occasion and device. Where no pretext (like Queen Victoria's jubilee) could be found for adapting a Stuart masque to a contemporary celebration, player kings and queens were incorporated: the historical context as well as the masque itself had to be dramatized.

In more recent years, music has often been the motivating force behind numerous masque reconstructions. I shall mention only a few. A version of *Britannia Triumphans* was performed at the Juilliard School of Music in 1953.[22] Years later John Hollander devised a masque-like *Entertainment for Elizabeth* for the pioneering early music group, the New York Pro Musica.[23] In

---

[16] See H&S, x. 525 and R. Fiske, *English Theatre Music in the Eighteenth Century* (London, 1973), 382.
[17] *The Maske of Flowers* (London, 1887), 4.   [18] H&S, x. 570.
[19] Performed at Avery Hill College, Eltham; see H&S, x. 608.   [20] Ibid. 686.
[21] G. Wickham and N. Coghill, *The Masque of Hope* (Oxford, 1948), 5.
[22] Lefkowitz, *Trois Masques*, 185.
[23] John Hollander, *An Entertainment for Elizabeth*, English Literary Renaissance Monographs ([Storrs], Conn., 1972). The musical directions in the printed text indicate, however, that the musical reconstruction was not very masque-like: Dowland's 'Flow my Tears' is used as a contrafactum for one song, and a 'doleful

November 1974 a musical reconstruction of three masques—*Oberon, The Somerset Masque*, and *The Triumph of Peace*—was given a concert performance in the Whitehall Banqueting House.[24] For that performance an impressive number of lutenists and baroque string players had been assembled. In March 1993 a reconstruction of *Oberon*, beautifully danced and involving some fine musicians, formed the centre-piece of a conference on the masque in Cleveland, Ohio.

The masque embraces so much that is of intense interest to those involved in what is often called the 'early music movement' that in recent years there have been quite a number of reconstructions. Given that there is not a complete set of music for any one pre-Commonwealth masque, all reconstructions demand ingenious cuts and/or ingenious pastiche.[25] Some have provided a glimpse of just how exciting masques at court must have been. I have myself been involved in a good few masque reconstrutions—mostly at vacation early music courses where a project has been needed which could occupy singers, dancers, and a disparate group of performers playing period instruments. Hopefully, these have been satisfying and illuminating. But working in a school hall on a budget which barely stretches to providing instant coffee for participants can make a Whitehall Banqueting House lit by thousands of candles and containing the best lutenists England has ever known seem very distant. The experience helps to bring home the point that this was a form dependent on the early Stuart court—not just for its reckless willingness to spend vast amounts of money on a single evening's entertainment, but for its culture's way of thinking which made it seem natural to have their own lives and policies writ large as heroic allegory. T. S. Eliot commented of Jonson's masques that they 'can still be read, and with pleasure, by any one who will take the trouble—a trouble which in this part of Jonson is, indeed, a study of antiquities—to imagine them in action, displayed with the music, costumes, dances, and the scenery of Inigo Jones'.[26] We need not always be confined to reading; but even in the most professional reconstructions the imagination must play a role in allowing present realizations to evoke more removed occasions.

dump' on the harpsichord is called for. Early in 1974 a version of *The Triumph of Peace* using staging reconstructed from Inigo Jones's drawings was performed at the Davis campus of the University of California, but the instrumental resources there seem to have been basically modern.

[24] This was directed by Peter Holman, who arranged most of the music. Tim Crawford set the dances to the lutes (an exercise which led eventually to the splendid recording of three masque dances on the CD *Three, Four and Twenty Lutes*, BIS-CD-341). I edited some of the vocal music.

[25] Andrew Sabol has published two reconstructed scores for Jacobean masques: *A Score for 'Lovers Made Men'* (Providence, RI, 1963) and *A Score for 'The Lords' Masque'* (1993). Both, however, distort the court masque in quite fundamental ways. I have reviewed the more recent volume in *ML* 76 (1995), 467–70.

[26] T. S. Eliot, *Elizabethan Dramatists* (London, 1963), 82.

A Calendar of Masque Texts

There is a problem in referring to masques, particularly those performed in the earlier part of the period covered by this book. Often the original texts have general titles which could apply to a range of similar productions. Not surprisingly, these titles tend to have been replaced in later editions (and discussions) with something better able to identify the particular production—usually through incorporating a reference to a characteristic feature of the device or a unique aspect of the occasion. Occasionally, however, commentators have seized upon different identifying marks—so, for example, Campion's *The Description of a Masque: presented at the Mariage of the Right Honourable the Earle of Somerset* (London, 1614) has been called both *The Squires' Masque* and *The Somerset Masque*. (I have used the latter.)

This appendix is primarily meant to fix an unambiguous link between the working titles used throughout the book and the productions to which they refer. Since quotations from masque texts have been identified by line or page references given in the text, the appendix also serves to indicate which editions have been used for this purpose. Because of a policy of retaining original spelling and orthography wherever possible, quotations are sometimes drawn from seventeenth-century editions while line/page references are given to an accessible, modern-spelling edition.

Since this appendix is intended as a key to using this book, only masques with extant texts are listed. It is not, in other words, a comprehensive calendar of known masque performances (such as those prepared by C. E. McGee and J. C. Meagher listed in the Bibliography). The folio editions of Jonson's *Works* (1616 and 1640) are listed only where they are the earliest surviving printed text. Where several early texts of a particular masque exist, this is noted in the table with an indication of where to look for a full bibliographical account.

Appendix

Date	Author	Original title/source	Working title/edition used
1604, 8 January	Samuel Daniel	*The Vision of the Twelve Goddesses* (London, 1604)	*The Vision of the Twelve Goddesses*, in T. J. B. Spencer and S. Wells (eds.), *A Book of Masques* (Cambridge, 1967)
1605, 6 January	Ben Jonson	'The Twelfth Nights Revells' GB-Lbl, MS Royal 17. B. xxxi	*The Masque of Blackness*, in H&S, vii
		The Characters of Two royall Masques. The one of Blacknesse, The other of Beautie (London, 1608)	
1606, 5 January	Jonson	*Hymenaei* (London, 1606)	*Hymenaei*, in H&S, vii
1607, 6 January	Thomas Campion	*The Discription of a Maske, Presented on Twelfth Night last, in honour of the Lord Hayes and his bride* (London, 1607)	*The Lord Hay's Masque*, in *The Works of Thomas Campion*, ed. W. R. Davis (London, 1969)
1607, August	John Marston	'The Honourable Lord & Lady of Huntingdons Entertainment of theire right Noble Mother Alice: Countesse Dowager of Darby', US-SM, MS EL. 34. B9	*The Entertainment at Ashby*, in Marston, *Works*, ed. A. H. Bullen (London, 1887)
1608, 10 January	Jonson	*The Characters of Two royall Masques. The one of Blacknesse, The other of Beautie* (London, 1608)	*The Masque of Beauty*, in H&S, vii
1608, 9 February	Jonson	*The Description of the Masque, with the Nuptiall Songs. Celebrating the happy Marriage of Iohn, Lord Ramsey, Vicount Hadington* (London, 1608)	*The Haddington Masque*, in H&S, vii

1609, 2 February	Jonson	GB-Lbl, MS Royal 18. A. xlv *The Masque of Queenes celebrated from the House of Fame* (London, 1609)	*The Masque of Queens*, in H&S, vii
1610, 5 June	Daniel	*The Order and Solemnitie of the Creation of the High and mightie Prince Henrie . . . Whereunto is annexed the Royal Maske* (London, 1610)	*Tethys Festival*, in *The Complete Works in Verse and Prose*, ed. A. B. Grosart, 5 vols. (London, 1885–6; repr. New York, 1963), iii
1611, 1 January	Jonson	*Oberon, the Faery Prince*, in *Works* (London, 1616)	*Oberon*, in H&S, vii
1611, 3 February	Jonson	*Love Freed from Ignorance and Folly*, in *Works* (London, 1616)	*Love Freed from Ignorance and Folly*, in H&S, vii
1612, 6 January	Jonson	*Love Restored, In a Masque at Court*, in *Works* (London, 1616)	*Love Restored*, in H&S, vii
1613, 14 February	Campion	*A Relation of the Late Royall Entertainment at Cawsome House . . . . Whereunto is annexed the Description, Speeches and Songs of the Lords Maske presented in the Banquetting-house on the Mariage night of the High and Mightie, Count Palatine, and the Royally descended the Ladie Elizabeth* (London, 1613)	*The Lords' Masque*, in *The Works of Thomas Campion*, ed. Davis
1613, 15 February	George Chapman	*The Memorable Maske of the two Honorable Houses or Inns of Court; the Middle Temple, and Lyncolns Inne* (London, 1613)	*The Memorable Masque of the Middle Temple and Lincoln's Inn*, in *The Plays of George Chapman: The Comedies*, ed. A. Holaday, M. Kiernan, and G. B. Evans (Urbana, Ill., 1970)

Date	Author	Original title/source	Working title/edition used
1613, 20 February	Francis Beaumont	*The Masque of the Inner Temple and Grayes Inne* (London, 1613)	*The Masque of the Inner Temple and Gray's Inn*, in *The Dramatic Works in the Beaumont and Fletcher Canon*, ed. F. Bowers (Cambridge, 1966)
1613, 27 April	Campion	*A Relation of the Late Royall Entertainment at Cawsome House . . .* (London, 1613)	*The Entertainment at Caversham*, in *The Works of Thomas Campion*, ed. Davis
1613, 26 December	Campion	*The Description of a Masque: presented at the Mariage of the Right Honourable the Earle of Somerset* (London, 1614)	*The Somerset Masque*, in *The Works of Thomas Campion*, ed. Davis
1613, 29 December 1614, 3 January	Jonson	*The Irish Masque at Court*, in *Works* (London, 1616)	*The Irish Masque*, in H&S, vii.
1614, 6 January		*The Maske of Flowers* (London, 1613)	*The Masque of Flowers*, in Spencer and Wells (eds.), *A Book of Masques*
1615, 6 and 8 January	Jonson	*Mercurie Vindicated from the Alchemists at Court*, in *Works* (London, 1616)	*Mercury Vindicated from the Alchemists at Court*, in H&S, vii
1615, 13 January	William Browne	'The Inner Temple Masque', GB-Ce, MS 68	*The Inner Temple Masque*, in Spencer and Wells (eds.), *A Book of Masques* (where it is called *Ulysses and Circe*)
1616, 1 and 6 January	Jonson	*The Golden Age Restored*, in *Works* (London, 1616)	*The Golden Age Restored*, in H&S, vii
1616, 25 December	Jonson	*Christmas his Masque*, in *Works* (London, 1640)	*Christmas his Masque*, in H&S, vii
1617, 6 and 19 January	Jonson	*The Vision of Delight*, in *Works* (London, 1640)	*The Vision of Delight*, in H&S, vii

1617, 22 February	Jonson	*Lovers Made Men* (London, 1617)	*Lovers Made Men*, in H&S, vii
1617, 4 May	Robert White	'Cupid's Banishment', US-NYpm, MS M. A. 1296	*Cupid's Banishment*, ed. C. E. McGee, *RD* 19 (1988), 227–64
1618, 6 January	Jonson	'Pleasure Reconcild to Virtue', Devonshire, Chatsworth MS	*Pleasure Reconcild to Virtue*, in H&S, vii
1618, 2 February		'A Maske presented on Candlemas nighte at Coleoverton', GB-Lva, MS Dyce 36	*A Masque at Coleoverton*, in R. Brotanek, *Die englischen Maskenspiele* (Vienna and Leipzig, 1902), 328–37
1618, 2 and 19 February		'The Antemaske of Mountebankes', various MSS; see McGee and Meagher, 'Preliminary Checklist 1614–1625', 60–3	*The Mountebanks' Masque*, in D. S. Bland (ed.), *Three Revels from the Inns of Court* (Trowbridge, 1984)
1618, 17 February	Jonson	*For the Honour of Wales*, in *Works* (London, 1640)	*For the Honour of Wales*, in H&S, vii
1619, 6 January 2 February	Thomas Middleton	*The Inner-Temple Masque, or Masque of Heroes* (London, 1619)	*The Masque of Heroes*, in Spencer and Wells (eds.), *A Book of Masques*
1620, 17 January 29 February	Jonson	*Newes from the New World discover'd in the Moone*, in *Works* (London, 1640)	*News from the New World Discovered in the Moon*, in H&S, vii
1620, 19 June	Jonson	*Pan's Anniversary; of the Shepherds Holy-day*, in *Works* (London, 1640)	*Pan's Anniversary*, in H&S, vii
1621, 3 and 5 August 9 September	Jonson	various MSS and printed texts; see H&S, vii. 541–6, and W. W. Greg, *Jonson's Masque of Gipsies* (London, 1952)	*The Gypsies Metamorphosed*, in H&S, vii

Date	Author	Original title/source	Working title/edition used
1621, c.22 December		[A Masque at Sir John Croft's House]	in C. E. McGee, 'The Visit of the Nine Goddesses: A Masque at Sir John Croft's House', ELR 21 (1991)
1622, 6 January 5 or 6 May	Jonson	The Masque of Augures (London, 1621)	The Masque of Augurs, in H&S, vii
1623, 19 January	Jonson	Time Vindicated to Himself and to His Honors (London, 1622)	Time Vindicated, in H&S, vii
1624, (planned for 6 January)	Jonson	Neptune's Triumph for the Return of Albion (London, 1624)	Neptune's Triumph for the Return of Albion, in H&S, vii
1624, 19 August	Jonson	The Masque of Owls, in Works (London, 1640)	The Masque of Owls, in H&S, vii
1625, 9 January	Jonson	The Fortunate Isles and their Union (London, 1624)	The Fortunate Isles, in H&S, vii
1631, 9 January	Jonson	Loves Triumph through Callipolis (London, 1630)	Love's Triumph through Callipolis, in H&S, vii
1631, 22 February	Jonson	Chloridia (London, [1630])	Chloridia, in H&S, vii
1632, 8 January	Aurelian Townshend	Albion's Triumph (London, 1631)	Albion's Triumph, in The Poems and Masques of Aurelian Townshend, ed. C. C. Brown (Reading, 1983)
1632, 14 February	Townshend	Tempe Restored (London, 1631)	Tempe Restored, in The Poems and Masques of Aurelian Townshend, ed. Brown
1633, 21 May	Jonson	'The King's Entertainment at Welbeck', GB-Lbl, MS Harley 4955	The Entertainment at Welbeck, in H&S, vii

Date	Author	Title	Edition
1634, 3 and 11 February	James Shirley	*The Triumph of Peace* (London, 1634)	*The Triumph of Peace*, in Spencer and Wells (eds.), *A Book of Masques*
1634, 18 February	Thomas Carew	*Coelum Britannicum* (London, 1634)	*The Poems of Thomas Carew with his Masque Coelum Britannicum*, ed. R. Dunlap (Oxford, 1949)
1634, 29 September	John Milton	*A Maske Presented at Ludlow Castle, 1634: On Michaelmasse night, before the Right Honorable John Earle of Bridgewater, Viscount Brackly, Lord President of Wales* (London, 1637)	*Comus*, in *The Works of John Milton*, i: *The Shorter English Poems*, ed. F. A. Patterson (New York, 1931)
1634, 31 July	Jonson	'Love's Welcome at Bolsover', GB-Lbl, MS Harley 4955	*Love's Welcome at Bolsover*, in H&S, vii
1634, August	Thomas Salusbury	[no title], GB-Lbl, MS Egerton 2623	'The Chirk Castle Entertainment'; see C. C. Brown, 'The Chirk Castle Entertainment of 1634', *Milton Quarterly*, 11 (1977), 76–86
1635, 10 February	William Davenant	*The Temple of Love* (London, 1635)	*The Temple of Love*, in *William Davenant: Dramatic Works*, ed. J. Maidment and W. H. Logan (Edinburgh, 1873–4)
1636, 12 September		*The King and Queenes Entertainment at Richmond. After their Departure from Oxford: In a Masque, presented by the most Illustrious Prince, Prince Charles Sept. 12. 1636* (Oxford, 1636)	*The Entertainment at Richmond*, ed. W. Bang and R. Brotanek (Louvain and Leipzig, 1903)
1636, 24 February	Davenant	*The Triumphs of the Prince d'Amour* (London, 1636)	*The Triumphs of the Prince d'Amour*, in M. Lefkowitz (ed.), *Trois Masques à la cour de Charles 1er d'Angleterre* (Paris, 1970)

Date	Author	Original title/source	Working title/edition used
1638, 7 January	Davenant	*Britannia Triumphans* (London, 1638)	*Britannia Triumphans*, in Lefkowitz, *Trois Masques*
1638, 6 February	Davenant	*Luminalia, or The Festivall of Light, Personated in a Masque at Court* (London, 1638)	*Luminalia*, in *William Davenant: Dramatic Works*, ed. Maidment and Logan
1640	Mildmay Fane	'Raguaillo d'Oceano', GB-Lbl, Add. MS 34221	*Raguaillo d'Oceano*, ed. C. Leech (Louvain, 1938)
1640, 6 January	Aston Cokain	*A Masque at Bretbie* (London, 1639)	*A Masque at Bretbie*, in *The Dramatic Works of Sir Aston Cokain*, ed. J. Maidment and W. H. Logan (London, 1874)
1640, 21 January	Davenant	*Salmacida Spolia* (London, 1640)	*Salmacida Spolia*, in Spencer and Wells (eds.), *A Book of Masques*
1641, 6 January	Thomas Salusbury	'A Masque as it was presented at ye right hon^{ble} ye Lord Strange his [house] at Knowsley on Twelfth night 1640 … Designed & written in six hours space by S^r Th. Salusbury'; GB-AB, MS 5390 D	*A Masque at Knowsley*, ed. R. J. Broadbent, *Transactions of the Historic Society of Lancashire and Cheshire*, 41 (1925), 8–16
after 1642	Shirley	*The Triumph of Beauty. A Masque* (London, 1646)	*The Triumph of Beauty*, in *The Dramatic Works and Poems of James Shirley*, vi (New York, 1833; repr. 1966).
1653, 26 March, 1659	Shirley	*Cupid and Death* (London, 1653)	*Cupid and Death*, in Spencer and Wells (eds.), *A Book of Masques*

Bibliography

PRINTED MUSICAL SOURCES

ADSON, J., *Courtly Masquing Ayres* (London, 1621), ed. P. Walls, 3 vols., English Instrumental Music of the Late Renaissance (London, 1975–6).

ARNE, T., *Comus*, ed. J. Herbage, MB 3 (London, 1951).

BALLARD, R., *Premier Livre*, ed. A. Souris, S. Spycket, and M. Rollin (Paris, 1963).

—— *Deuxième Livre*, ed. A. Souris, S. Spycket, and M. Rollin (Paris, 1976).

BRADE, W., *Newe ausserlesene liebliche Branden* (Hamburg, 1617), ed. B. Thomas, 3 vols. (London, 1974).

BRETT, P. (ed.), *Consort Songs*, MB 22 (London, 1967).

BULL, J., *Keyboard Music*: i, ed. J. Steele and F. Cameron, MB 14 (London, 1960), and ii, ed. R. T. Dart, MB 17 (London, 1963).

CACCINI, G., *Le nuove musiche* (Florence, 1601); ed. H. Wiley Hitchcock (Madison, 1970).

CAMPION, T., *The Discription of a Maske . . . in honour of the Lord Hayes* (London, 1607; repr. Menston, 1970).

—— *Two Bookes of Ayres* (London, *c*.1613; repr. Menston, 1967); ed. E. H. Fellowes, ELS, II, 2 (London, 1925).

—— *The Description of a Maske . . . at the Mariage of the Right Honourable the Earle of Somerset* (London, 1614; repr. Menston, 1970).

CUTTS, J. P. (ed.), *La Musique de scène de la troupe de Shakespeare* (Paris, 1972).

DART, R. T., and COATES, W. (eds.), *Jacobean Consort Music*, MB 9 (2nd edn., London, 1962).

DOWLAND, J., *A Pilgrimes Solace* (London, 1612; repr. Menston, 1970); ed. E. H. Fellowes and R. T. Dart, 2 vols., ELS, I, 12 and 14 (London, 1960).

—— *Collected Lute Music*, ed. D. Poulton and B. Lam (London, 1974).

DOWLAND, R., *A Musicall Banquet* (London, 1610); ed. P. Stroud, ELS, II, 20 (London, 1968).

—— *Varietie of Lute Lessons* (London, 1610).

ÉCORCHEVILLE, J. (ed.), *Vingt Suites d'orchestre du XVIIe siècle français* (Paris, 1906).

EDWARDS, W. (ed.), *Music for Mixed Consort*, MB 40 (London, 1975).

EYCK, J. VAN, *Der Fluyten lust-hof, vol psalmen, paduanen, allemanden, couranten, balletten, airs & c.*, 3 vols. (Amsterdam, 1646–54); ed. G. Vellekoop, 3 vols. (Amsterdam, 1957).

FARNABY, G. and R., *Keyboard Music*, ed. R. Marlow, MB 24 (London, 1965).

FERGUSON, H. (ed.), *Anne Cromwell's Virginal Book* (London, 1974).

FERRABOSCO II, A., *Ayres* (London, 1609; repr. Menston, 1970); ed. E. H. Fellowes, ELS, II, 16 (London, 1926).

—— *Manuscript Songs*, ed. I. Spink, ELS, II, 19 (London, 1966).

FILMER, E., *French Court Ayres* (London, 1629).

FUHRMANN, G. L., *Testudo Gallo-Germanica* (Nuremberg, 1615).

GAMBLE, J., *Ayres and Dialogues* (London, 1659).

GIBBONS, O., *Keyboard Music*, ed. G. Hendrie, MB 20 (2nd edn., London, 1967).

JACKSON, R. (ed.), *A Neapolitan Festa a Ballo* (Madison, 1978).

JOHNSON, R., *Robert Johnson: Ayres, Songs and Dialogues*, ed. I. Spink, ELS, II, 17 (2nd edn., London, 1974).

LAWES, H., *Ayres and Dialogues* (London, 1653).

—— *Second Book of Ayres and Dialogues* (London, 1655).

LAWES, W., *Select Consort Music*, ed. M. Lefkowitz, MB 21 (London, 1963).

—— *Consort Sets in Five and Six Parts*, ed. D. Pinto (London, 1979).

LEFKOWITZ, M. (ed.), *Trois Masques à la cour de Charles Ier d'Angleterre* (Paris, 1970).

LOCKE, M., and GIBBONS, C., *Cupid and Death*, ed. E. J. Dent, MB 2 (London, 1951).

MAITLAND, J. A. F., and SQUIRE, W. B. (eds.), *The Fitzwilliam Virginal Book*, 2 vols. (Leipzig, 1899; repr. New York, 1963).

MASON, G., and EARSDEN, J., *The Ayres that were Sung and Played at Brougham Castle* (London, 1618; repr. Menston, 1962); ed. I. Spink, ELS, II, 18 (London, 1962).

MATTHYSZ, P., *'t Uitnement Kabinet* (Amsterdam, 1649, and c.1655); ed. R. A. Rasch, 4 vols. (Amsterdam, 1973).

MORLEY, T., *The First Book of Consort Lessons* (London, 1599 and 1611); ed. S. Beck (New York, 1959).

MRÁČEK, J. J. S. (ed.), *Seventeenth-Century Instrumental Dance Music in Uppsala University Library Inst. mus. hs 409* (Stockholm, 1976).

NOTARI, A., *Prime musiche nuove* (London, 1613).

Parthenia (London, c.1613); ed. R. T. Dart (London, 1962).

Parthenia In-Violata (London, c.1624); ed. R. T. Dart (New York, 1961).

PLAYFORD, J., *The English Dancing Master* (London, 1651); ed. M. Dean-Smith (London, 1957).

—— *Court Ayres* (London, 1655).

—— *Courtly Masquing Ayres* (London, 1662).

—— *Catch that Catch Can: or the Musical Companion* (London, 1667).

PRAETORIUS, M., *Terspichore, in Gesamtausgabe der musikalischen Werke von Michael Praetorius*, xv, ed. F. Blume (Wolfenbüttel and Berlin, 1929).

ROSSETER, P., *Lessons for Consort* (London, 1609).

SABOL, A. (ed.), *A Score for 'Lovers Made Men'* (Providence, RI, 1963).

—— *Four Hundred Songs and Dances from the Stuart Masque* (Hanover, NH, and London, 1978, with supplement 1982).

—— *A Score for 'The Lords' Masque' by Thomas Campion* (Hanover, NH, and London, 1993).

SARGENT, G. (ed.), *Elizabeth Rogers' Virginal Book* ([American Institute of Musicology], 1971).

SIMPSON, T., *Taffel Consort* (Hamburg, 1621).

SPENCER, R. (ed.), *The Board Lute Book*, facs. (Leeds, 1976).

SPINK, I. (ed.), *English Songs 1625–1660*, MB 33 (London, 1971).

THOMAS, B., and WALLS, P. (eds.), *Twenty-one Masque Dances* (London, 1974).

—— *Twenty-five Masque Dances* (Brighton, 1985).

VALET, N., *Paradisus Musicus Testudinis (Le Secret des muses)* (Amsterdam, 1618).

—— *Le Second Livre de tablature de luth, intitulé le secret des muses* (Amsterdam, 1619).

VERCHALY, A. (ed.), *Airs de cour pour voix et luth (1603–1643)* (Paris, 1961).

WALKER, D. P. (ed.), *Musique des intermèdes de 'La Pellegrina'* (Paris, 1963).

WILSON, J., *Cheerful Ayres or Ballads* (Oxford, 1660).

BOOKS, ARTICLES, AND EDITIONS OF MASQUE TEXTS

ALBERTI, L. B., *L'architettura de Leon Batista Alberti*, trans. C. Bartoli (Monte Regale, 1565).

ALLSOP, P., *The Italian 'Trio' Sonata* (Oxford, 1992).

ANON. [I. G., W. D., and T. B.], *The Maske of Flowers* (London, 1614).

ARBEAU, T., *Orchésographie* (Langres, 1588), trans. M. S. E. Evans and J. Sutton, as *Orchesography* (New York, 1967).

ASCHAM, R., *The Scholemaster* (London, 1570), ed. L. V. Ryan as *The Schoolmaster* (New York, 1967).

ASHBEE, A., *Records of English Court Music*, 6 vols. (i–iv, Snodland, 1986–91; v–vi, Aldershot, 1991–2).

BACON, F., *Essays* (London, 1625; repr. Menston, 1971).

BAILDON, W. P., and ROXBURGH, R. F. (eds.), *The Records of the Honourable Society of Lincoln's Inn: The Black Books* (London, 1897–8).

BANG, W., and BROTANEK, R. (eds.), *The King and Queenes Entertainment at Richmond 1636* (Louvain and Leipzig, 1903).

BASSOMPIERRE, F. DE, *Mémoires du Mareschal Bassompierre* (Paris, 1665).

—— *Memoirs of the Embassy of the Marshal de Bassompierre to the Court of England in 1626*, 2 vols. (London, 1819).

—— *Journal de ma vie: mémoires*, 4 vols. (Paris, 1870–7).

BEAUMONT, F., *The Masque of the Inner Temple and Grayes Inne* (London, 1613).

—— and FLETCHER, J., *The Dramatic Works in the Beaumont and Fletcher Canon*, ed. F. Bowers (Cambridge, 1966).

BENTLEY, G. E., *The Jacobean and Caroline Stage*, 7 vols. (Oxford, 1941–68).

BERTOLOTTI, A., *Musici alla Corte dei Gonzaga in Mantova* (s.l., 1890; repr. Bologna, 1969).

BIRCH, T. (ed.), *The Court and Times of Charles the First* (London, 1849).

BLAND, D. S. (ed.), *Three Revels from the Inns of Court* (Trowbridge, 1984).

BOSTON, J. L., 'Priscilla Bunbury's Virginal Book', *ML* 36 (1955), 365–73.

BOSWELL, E., and CHAMBERS, E. K. (eds.), 'Dramatic Records: The Lord Chamberlain's Office', *MSC* 2.iii (1931).

BRAITHWAIT, R., *The English Gentleman* (London, 1630).

BRENNECKE, E., 'The Entertainment at Elvetham, 1591', in J. H. Long (ed.), *Music in English Renaissance Drama* (Lexington, Ky., 1968), 32–56.

BROADBENT, R. J., 'A Masque at Knowsley', *Transactions of the Historic Society of Lancashire and Cheshire*, 41 (1925), 8–16.

BROSSARD, Y. DE (ed.), *Musiciens de Paris, 1535–1792: Actes d'état civil d'après le fichier Laborde de la Bibliothèque Nationale* (Paris, 1965).

BROTANEK, R., *Die englischen Maskenspiele* (Vienna and Leipzig, 1902).

BROWN, C. C., 'The Chirk Castle Entertainment of 1634', *Milton Quarterly*, 11 (1977), 76–86.

—— *John Milton's Aristocratic Entertainments* (Cambridge, 1985).

BURNEY, C., *A General History of Music* (London, 1776–89), ed. F. Mercer, 2 vols. (London, 1935; repr. 1957).

BUTLER, M., *Theatre and Crisis 1632–1642* (Cambridge, 1984).

—— 'A Provincial Masque of Comus, 1636', *RD* 17 (1986), 149–73.

CAMPION, T., *The Discription of a Maske, Presented . . . on Twelfth Night last, in honour of the Lord Hayes and his bride* (London, 1607; repr. with an introduction by P. Holman, Menston, 1973).

—— *A Relation of the Late Royall Entertainment . . . at Cawsome House* (London, 1613). This volume contains the *Description, Speeches and Songs of the Lords Maske . . . on the Mariage night of the High and Mightie, Count Palatine, and the Royally descended the Ladie Elizabeth* (London, 1613).

—— *The Description of a Masque: presented at the Mariage of the Right Honourable the Earle of Somerset* (London, 1614; repr. with an introduction by P. Holman, Menston, 1973).

—— *Campion's Works*, ed. P. Vivian (Oxford, 1909).

—— *The Works of Thomas Campion*, ed. W. R. Davis (London, 1969).

CAREW, T., *Coelum Britannicum* (London, 1634).

—— *The Poems of Thomas Carew with his Masque Coelum Britannicum*, ed. R. Dunlap (Oxford, 1949).

CARLETON, D. *Dudley Carleton to John Chamberlain, 1603–1624: Jacobean Letters*, ed. M. Lee (New Brunswick, NJ, 1972).

CAROSO, F., *Il Ballarino* (Venice, 1581).

—— *Nobiltà di Dame* (Venice, 1600), trans. by J. Sutton, music ed. F. M. Walker (Oxford, 1986).

CARTWRIGHT, W., *The Plays and Poems of William Cartwright*, ed. G. B. Evans (Madison, 1951).

CAVENDISH, W. (first Earl of Newcastle), *The Varietie, A Comœdy lately presented by His Majesties Servants at the Black-Friers* (London, 1649).

CHAMBERLAIN, J., *The Letters of John Chamberlain*, ed. N. E. McClure, 2 vols. (Philadelphia, 1939).

CHAMBERS, E. K., *The Elizabethan Stage*, 4 vols. (Oxford, 1923).

CHAPMAN, G., *The Memorable Maske of . . . the Middle Temple, and Lyncolns Inne* (London, 1613).

—— *The Plays of George Chapman: The Comedies*, ed. A. Holaday, M. Kiernan, and G. B. Evans (Urbana, Ill., 1970).

CHARTERIS, R., 'Jacobean Musicians at Hatfield House, 1605–1613', *RMARC* 12 (1974), 115–36.

COGHILL, N., and WICKHAM, G., *The Masque of Hope* (London, 1948).

COHN, A., *Shakespeare in Germany in the Sixteenth and Seventeenth Centuries* (London, 1865).

COKAIN, A., *A Masque at Bretbie* (London, 1639).

—— *The Dramatic Works of Sir Aston Cokain*, ed. J. Maidment and W. H. Logan (London, 1874).

CREASER, J., 'The Present Aid of this Occasion: The Setting of *Comus*', in D. Lindley (ed.), *The Court Masque* (Manchester, 1984), 111–34.

CUNNINGHAM, J. P., *Dancing at the Inns of Court* (London, 1965).

CUTTS, J. P., 'Jacobean Masque and Stage Music', *ML* 35 (1954), 185–200.

DANIEL, S., *The Vision of the Twelve Goddesses* (London, 1604).

—— *Tethys Festival* (London, 1610).

—— *The Complete Works in Verse and Prose*, ed. A. B. Grosart, 5 vols. (London, 1885–6; repr. New York, 1963).

DART, T., 'The Repertory of the Royal Wind Music', *GSJ* 11 (1958), 93–106.

DAVENANT, W., *The Temple of Love* (London, 1635).

—— *The Triumphs of the Prince d'Amour* (London, 1636).

—— *Britannia Triumphans, a Masque* (London, 1638).

—— *Luminalia, or The Festivall of Light, Personated in a Masque at Court* (London, 1638).

—— *Salmacida Spolia* (London, 1640).

—— *Dramatic Works*, ed. J. Maidment and W. H. Logan (Edinburgh, 1873–4).

—— *The Siege of Rhodes*, ed. A.-M. Hedback, Acta Universitatis Upsaliensis, 14 (Uppsala, 1973).

DE CAUS, S., *La Perspective* (London, 1612).

—— *Institution Harmonique* (Frankfurt, 1615).

DE LAUZE, F., *Apologie de la Danse* (s.l., 1623), trans. J. Wildeblood (London, 1952).

DE MAILLET, M., *Balet de la revanche du mepris d'Amour* (London, 1617).

DOUGHTIE, E. (ed.), *Lyrics from English Airs 1596–1622* (Cambridge, Mass., 1970).

DRYDEN, J., *The Works of John Dryden*, xv, ed. E. Miner, G. R. Guffey, and F. B. Zimmerman (Berkeley, 1976).

DUCKLES, V., 'Florid Embellishment in English Song of the Late 16th and Early 17th Centuries', *AM* 5 (1957), 329–45.

—— and ZIMMERMAN, F. B., *Words to Music* (Los Angeles, 1967).

DUFFY, J., *The Songs and Motets of Alfonso Ferrabosco, the Younger (1575–1628)* (Ann Arbor, 1980).

ELIOT, T. S., *Elizabethan Dramatists* (London, 1963).

EMSLIE, McD., 'Nicholas Lanier's Innovations in English Song', *ML* 41 (1960), 13–27.

EVANS, H. A., *English Masques* (London, 1897).

EVANS, W. M., *Ben Jonson and Elizabethan Music* (New York, 1929; repr. 1965).

—— *Henry Lawes: Musician and Friend of Poets* (New York, 1941).

—— 'Cartwright's Debt to Lawes', in J. H. Long (ed.), *Music in English Renaissance Drama* (Lexington, Ky., 1968), 103–16.

FANE, M., *Raguaillo d'Oceano 1640 and Candy Restored 1641*, ed. C. Leech, Materials for the Study of the Old English Drama, NS 15 (Louvain, 1938).

FELLOWES, E. H., STERNFELD, F. W., and GREER, D. (eds.), *English Madrigal Verse 1588–1632* (Oxford, 1962).

FINNEY, G. L., *Musical Backgrounds for English Literature: 1580–1650* (New Brunswick, NJ, 1962).

FISKE, R., *English Theatre Music in the Eighteenth Century* (London, 1973).

FLECKNOE, R., *Ariadne deserted by Thesus, and found courted by Bacchus* (London, 1654).

FULLER, D., 'The Jonsonian Masque and its Music', *ML* 14 (1973), 440–52.

FUSCO, A. C., *Inigo Jones, Vitruvius Britannicus: Jones e Palladio nella cultura architettonica inglese* (Rimini, 1985).

GOMBOSI, O., 'Some Musical Aspects of the English Court Masque', *JAMS* 1 (1948), 3–19.

GORDON, D. J., *The Renaissance Imagination*, ed. S. Orgel (Berkeley, 1975).

GREG, W. W., *Jonson's Masque of Gipsies in the Burley, Belvoir and Windsor Versions* (London, 1952).

GURR, A., *Playgoing in Shakespeare's London* (Cambridge, 1987).

—— *The Shakespearean Stage 1574–1642* (3rd edn., Cambridge, 1992).

HALLIWELL-PHILLIPPS, J. O., *Dictionary of Old English Plays* (London, 1860).

HARRIS, J., ORGEL, S., and STRONG, R., *The King's Arcadia: Inigo Jones and the Stuart Court* (London, 1973).

HAWKINS, Sir JOHN, *A General History of the Science and Practice of Music* (London, 1776), ed. C. Cudworth, 2 vols. (New York, 1963).

HAZLITT, W. C., *Manual for the Collector of Old English Plays* (London, 1892).

HERBERT, E., *The Life of Edward, First Lord Herbert of Cherbury, Written by Himself*, ed. J. M. Shuttleworth (London, 1976).

HILL, R. F. (ed.), 'Dramatic Records in the Declared Accounts of the Office of Works 1560–1640', *MSC* 10 (1977).

HOBY, Sir THOMAS, *The Book of the Courtier*, ed. W. Raleigh (London, 1900).

HOLLANDER, J., *The Untuning of the Sky: Ideas of Music in English Poetry 1500–1700* (Princeton, 1961).

—— *An Entertainment for Elizabeth*, English Literary Renaissance Monographs ([Storrs], Conn., 1972).

HOLMAN, P., 'The Harp in Stuart England: New Light on William Lawes's Harp Consorts', *EM* 15 (1987), 188–203.

—— *Four and Twenty Fiddlers: The Violin at the English Court 1540–1690* (Oxford, 1993).

HOWES, E., *The Annales or Generall Chronicle of England, begun first by maister John Stow* (London, 1614).

HULSE, L., 'The Musical Patronage of Robert Cecil, First Earl of Salisbury (1563–1612)', *JRMA* 116 (1991), 24–40.

—— 'The Musical Patronage of the English Aristocracy, *c.*1590–*c.*1640' (Ph.D. diss., King's College, University of London, 1992).

HUTCHINSON, L., *Memoirs of the Life of Colonel Hutchinson . . . Written by his Widow Lucy*, ed. J. Hutchinson (London, 1806).

HUTTON, J., 'Some English Poems in Praise of Music', *English Miscellany*, 2 (1951), 1–63.

JOHNSON, J. T., 'How to "Humour" John Jenkins' Three-part Dances: Performance Directions in a Newberry Library MS', *JAMS* 20 (1967), 197–208.

JOHNSON, S., *Lives of the English Poets, 1779–81*, ed. G. B. Hill, 3 vols. (Oxford, 1905).

JOINER, M., 'British Museum Add. MS. 15117: An Index, Commentary, and Bibliography', *RMARC* 7 (1969), 51–109.

JONSON, B., *Hymenaei* (London, 1606).

—— *The Characters of Two royall Masques. The one of Blacknesse, The other of Beautie* (London, 1608).

—— *The Description of the Masque, With the Nuptiall Songs. Celebrating the happy Marriage of Iohn, Lord Ramsey, Vicount Hadington* (London, 1608).

—— *The Masque of Queenes* (London, 1609).

—— *The Workes of Beniamin Jonson* (London, 1616).

—— *Louers made Men* (London, 1617).

—— *The Masque of Augures. With the Several Antimasques* (London, 1621 (1622 NS)).

—— *Time Vindicated to Himselfe, and to his Honors* (London, 1622 (1623 NS)).

—— *Neptunes Triumph for the Returne of Albion* (London, 1623 (1624 NS))

—— *The Fortunate Isles and their Vnion, celebrated in a Masque design'd for the Court on Twelfth night 1624* (London, 1624 (1625 NS)).

—— *Chloridia. Rites to Chloris and Her Nymphs. Personated in a Masque, at Court* (London, 1630 (1631 NS)).

—— *Loves Triumph Through Callipolis* (London, 1630 (1631 NS)).

—— *The Workes of Beniamin Jonson. The second Volume* . . . (London, 1640).

—— *Ben Jonson*, ed. C. H. Herford and P. and E. Simpson, 11 vols. (Oxford, 1925–52).

JURGENS, M. (ed.), *Documents du minutier central concernant l'histoire de la musique*, 2 vols. (Paris, 1967).

KNOWLES, J., 'Change Partners and Dance', *TLS*, 9 Aug. 1991, 19.

KNOWLTON, J. E., 'Some Dances of the Stuart Masque Identified and Analyzed' (Ph.D. diss., Indiana University, 1966).

KRUMMEL, D. W., 'Venetian Baroque Music in a London Bookshop: The Robert Martin Catalogues 1633–50', in O. Neighbour (ed.), *Music and Bibliography* (London, 1980), 1–27.

KYNASTON, S. F., *Corona Minervae or a Masque Presented before Prince Charles his Highness* . . . *the 27th of February at the College of the Museum Minervae* (London, 1635).

—— *The Constitutions of the Musaeum Minervae* (London, 1636).

LACROIX, P. (ed.), *Ballets et mascarades de cour de Henri III à Louis XIV*, 6 vols. (Geneva and Turin, 1868–70; repr. 1968).

LANGBAINE, G., *An Account of the English Dramatic Poets* (Oxford, 1691).

LAWRENCE, W. J., 'Early Substantive Theatre Masques', *TLS* 8 Dec. 1921, 814.

—— 'Notes on a Collection of Masque Music', *ML* 3 (1922), 49–58.

—— 'The Origins of the Substantive Theatre Masque', *Pre-Restoration Stage Studies* (1927), 325–39.

LEFKOWITZ, M., 'New Facts Concerning William Lawes and the Caroline Masque', *ML* 40 (1959), 324–33.

—— *William Lawes* (London, 1960).

—— 'The Longleat Papers of Bulstrode Whitelocke; New Light on Shirley's *Triumph of Peace*', *JAMS* 18 (1965), 42–60.

LENTON, F., *Characterismi: or Lentons Leasures Expressed in Essayes and Characters* (London, 1631).

LESURE, F., 'Le Recueil de ballets de Michel Henry', in J. Jacquot (ed.), *Les Fêtes de la Renaissance* (Paris, 1956), 205–19.

LIMON, J., *Gentlemen of a Company: English Players in Central and Eastern Europe, 1590–1660* (Cambridge, 1985).

—— 'Neglected Evidence for James Shirley's *The Triumph of Peace* (1634)', *REED Newsletter*, 13 (1988), 2–9.

LINDLEY, D. (ed.), *The Court Masque* (Manchester, 1984).

—— *Thomas Campion* (Leiden, 1986).

LODGE, E., *Illustrations of British History*, 3 vols. (London, 1791).

LONG, J. H. (ed.), *Music in English Renaissance Drama* (Lexington, Ky., 1968).

LUCKETT, R., 'A New Source for *Venus and Adonis*', *MT* 130 (1989), 76–9.

MACE, T., *Musick's Monument* (London, 1676; repr. Paris, 1968).

McGEE, C. E., '*Cupid's Banishment*: A Masque Presented to Her Majesty by Young Gentlewomen of the Ladies Hall, Deptford, May 4, 1617', *RD* 19 (1988), 227–64.

—— ' "Strangest consequence from remotest cause": The Second Performance of *The Triumph of Peace*', *Medieval and Renaissance Drama in England*, 5 (1991), 309–42.

—— 'The Visit of the Nine Goddesses: A Masque at Sir John Croft's House', *ELR* 21 (1991), 371–84.

—— and MEAGHER, J. C., 'Preliminary Checklist of Tudor and Stuart Entertainments: 1603–1613', *RORD* 29 (1984), 47–126.

—— 'Preliminary Checklist of Tudor and Stuart Entertainments: 1614–1625', *RORD* 30 (1988), 17–128.

McGOWAN, M., *L'Art du ballet de cour en France 1581–1643* (Paris, 1963).

McGUIRE, M. C., *Milton's Puritan Masque* (Athens, Ga., 1983).

MANIFOLD, J. S., *The Music in English Drama from Shakespeare to Purcell* (London, 1956).

MARCUS, L., *The Politics of Mirth* (London, 1986).

MARK, J., 'The Jonsonian Masque', *ML* 3 (1922), 358–71.

MARSTON, J., *Works*, ed. A. H. Bullen, 3 vols. (London, 1887).

MARTIN, R., *Catalogus Librorum* (London, 1633, 1635, 1639, 1640).

The Maske of Flowers (London, 1614).

MEAGHER, J. C., *Method and Meaning in Jonson's Masques* (Notre Dame, Ind., 1966).

MERRYWEATHER, J., *York Music* (York, 1988).

MIDDLETON, T., *The Inner-Temple Masque, or Masque of Heroes* (London, 1619).

—— and ROWLEY, W., *A Courtly Masque: The Device called the World Tost at Tennis* (London, 1620).

MILTON, J., *A Maske Presented at Ludlow Castle* (London, 1637).

—— *Poems upon Several Occasions*, ed. T. Warton (London, 1785).

—— *The Works of John Milton*, i: *The Shorter English Poems*, ed. F. A. Patterson (New York, 1931).

—— '*A Maske*': *The Earlier Versions*, ed. S. E. Sprott (Toronto, 1973).

MORLEY, T., *A Plain and Easy Introduction to Practical Music* (London, 1597), ed. R. A. Harman (London, 1952).

NAGLER, A. M., *Theatre Festivals of the Medici 1539–1637* (New Haven and London, 1964).

NEGRI, C., *Le Gratie d'Amore* (Milan, 1600).

—— *Nuove Inventioni di Balli* (Milan, 1604).

NICHOLS, J. (ed.), *The Progresses, Processions, and Magnificent Festivities of King James the First*, 4 vols. (London, 1828).

NORBROOK, D., 'The Reformation of the Masque', in D. Lindley (ed.), *The Court Masque* (Manchester, 1984), 94–110.

ONIANS, J., 'On How to Listen to High Renaissance Art', *Art History*, 7 (1984), 411–37.

ORBISON, T., and HILL, R. F. (eds.), 'The Middle Temple Documents Relating to James Shirley's *The Triumph of Peace*', *MSC* 12 (1983), 31–84.

ORGEL, S., *The Jonsonian Masque* (Cambridge, Mass., 1965).

—— 'Florimène and the Ante-Masques', *RD* 4 (1971), 135–53.

—— and STRONG, R., *Inigo Jones: The Theatre of the Stuart Court*, 2 vols. (London, 1973).

ORRELL, J., 'The Agent of Savoy at *The Somerset Masque*', *RES* 28 (1977), 301–4.

—— 'Antimo Galli's Description of the Masque of Beauty', *Huntington Library Quarterly*, 43 (1979), 13–23.

PALME, P., *The Triumph of Peace: A Study of the Whitehall Banqueting House* (London, 1957).

PARRY, G., *The Golden Age Restor'd* (Manchester, 1981).

PEACHAM, H., *The Compleat Gentleman* (London, 1622), ed. V. B. Heltzel (Ithaca, NY, 1962).

PEACOCK, J., 'The French Element in Inigo Jones's Masque Designs', in D. Lindley (ed.), *The Court Masque* (Manchester, 1984), 149–68.

PETERSON, R. S., 'The Iconography of Jonson's *Pleasure Reconciled to Virtue*', *Journal of Medieval and Renaissance Studies*, 5 (1975), 123–51.

PEVSNER, N., *The Buildings of England: South Lancashire* (Harmandsworth, 1969).

POULTON, D., *John Dowland* (2nd edn., London, 1982).

PRICE, D. C., *Patrons and Musicians of the English Renaissance* (Cambridge, 1981).

PRUNIÈRES, H., *Le Ballet de cour en France avant Benserade et Lully* (Paris, 1914).

PRYNNE, W., *Histrio-Mastix: The Players Scourge, or Actors Tragedie* (London, 1633; repr. New York, 1974).

RICHE, B., *Riche his Farewell to the Militarie Profession* (London, 1581).

RIPA, C., *Iconologia* (Padua, 1611; repr. New York, 1976).

SABOL, A., 'New Documents on Shirley's Masque "The Triumph of Peace"', *ML* 47 (1966), 10–26.

SCAMOZZI, V., *L'Idea della architettura universale* (Venice, 1615).

SHIRLEY, J., *The Triumph of Peace* (London, 1634).

—— *Cupid and Death* (London, 1653).

—— *The Triumph of Beauty. A Masque* (London, 1646).

—— *The Dramatic Works and Poems of James Shirley* (New York, 1833; repr. 1966).

SIBLEY, G. M., *The Lost Plays and Masques 1500–1642* (Ithaca, NY, 1933).

SIMPSON, C. M., *The British Broadside Ballad and its Music* (New Brunswick, NJ, 1966).

SMITH, B. R., 'Landscape with Figures: The Three Realms of Queen Elizabeth's Country-house Revels', *RD* 8 (1977), 110–15.

SMITH, G. (ed.), *Elizabethan Critical Essays*, 2 vols. (London, 1904).

SMITH, J., and GRATISS, I., 'What did Prince Henry Do with his Feet on Sunday 19 August 1604?', *EM* 14 (1986), 198–207.

SMUTS, R. M., *Court Culture and the Origins of a Royalist Tradition in Early Stuart England* (Philadelphia, 1987).

SORELL, W., 'Shakespeare and the Dance', *Shakespeare Quarterly*, 71 (1957), 367–84.

SPENCE, R. T., 'A Royal Progress in the North: James I at Carlisle Castle and the Feast of Brougham, August 1617', *Northern History*, 27 (1991), 41–89.

SPENCER, T. J. B., and WELLS, S. (eds.), *A Book of Masques in Honour of Allardyce Nicoll* (Cambridge, 1967).

SPINGARN, J. E. (ed.), *Critical Essays of the Seventeenth Century*, 3 vols. (London, 1908–9).

SPINK, I., 'English Cavalier Songs 1620–1660', *PRMA* 86 (1959–60), 61–78.

—— 'The Musicians of Queen Henrietta-Maria: Some Notes and References in the English State Papers', *AM* 36 (1964), 177–82.

—— 'Campion's Entertainment at Brougham Castle, 1617', in J. H. Long (ed.), *Music in English Renaissance Drama* (Lexington, Ky., 1968), 57–74.

—— *English Song, Dowland to Purcell* (London, 1974, rev. 1984).

STEELE, M. S., *Plays and Masques at Court during the Reigns of Elizabeth, James, and Charles* (New Haven, 1926).

STERNFELD, F. W., 'Écho et répétition dans la poésie et la musique', in J.-M. Vaccaro (ed.), *La Chanson à la Renaissance* (Tours, 1981), 242–53.

—— 'A Note on Stile Recitativo', *PRMA* 110 (1984), 41–4.

—— *The Birth of Opera* (Oxford, 1993).

STRONG, R., *Van Dyck: Charles I on Horseback* (London, 1972).

—— *Henry Prince of Wales* (London, 1986).

STRUNK, O., *Source Readings in Music History* (New York, 1950).

STURGESS, K., *Jacobean Private Theatre* (London, 1987).

SUMMERSON, J., *Inigo Jones* (Harmondsworth, 1989).

THORN-DRURY, G., 'Whitehall in 1642', *RES* 1 (1925), 462.

TILL, D., 'Ornamentation in English Song Manuscripts 1620–1660' (B.Litt. diss., Oxford University, 1975).

TOFT, R., *Tune thy Musicke to thy Hart* (Toronto, 1993).

VITRUVIUS POLLIO, M., *I dieci libri dell'architettura di M. Vitruvio tradotti & commontati da Mons. Daniel Barbaro* (Venice, 1568).

WALKER, K., 'New Prison: Representing the Female Actor in Shirley's *The Bird in a Cage*', *ELR* 21 (1991), 385–400.

WALLS, P., 'Jonson's Borrowing', *Theatre Notebook*, 28 (1974), 80–1.

—— 'New Light on Songs by William Lawes and John Wilson', *ML* 57 (1976), 55–64.

—— 'Insubstantial Pageants Preserved: The Literary and Musical Sources for the Jonsonian Masque', in I. Donaldson (ed.), *Jonson and Shakespeare* (London, 1983), 202–18.

—— 'The Origins of English Recitative', *PRMA* 110 (1983–4), 25–40.

—— ' "Music and *Sweet* Poetry"? Verse for English Lute Song and Continuo Song', *ML* 65 (1984), 237–54.

—— '*Comus*: The Court Masque Questioned', in J. Caldwell, E. Olleson, and S. Wollenberg (eds.), *The Well Enchanting Skill: Music, Poetry, and Drama in the Culture of the Renaissance. Essays in Honour of F. W. Sternfeld* (Oxford, 1990), 107–13.

—— 'The Influence of the Italian Violin School in Seventeenth-Century England', *EM* 18 (1990), 575–87.

—— 'London, 1603–49', in C. Price (ed.), *The Early Baroque Era*, Man and Music Series (London, 1993), 270–304.

WARD, J. M., 'The English Measure', *EM* 14 (1986), 15–21.

—— 'Newly Devis'd Measures for Jacobean Masques', *AM* 60 (1988), 111–42.

WEDGWOOD, C. V., 'The Last Masque', in *Truth and Opinion* (London, 1960), 143–55.

WELSFORD, E., *The Court Masque* (Cambridge, 1927; repr. New York, 1962).

WESTRUP, J., 'The Nature of Recitative', *Proceedings of the British Academy*, 42 (1956), 27–44.

WHENHAM, J., *Duet and Dialogue in the Age of Monteverdi*, 2 vols. (Ann Arbor, 1982).

WHITELOCKE, B., *Memorials of English Affairs* (London, 1682).

—— *The Diary of Bulstrode Whitelocke 1605–1675*, ed. R. Spalding (Oxford, 1990).

WIENPAHL, R. W., *Music at the Inns of Court during the Reigns of Elizabeth, James, and Charles* (Ann Arbor, 1979).

WILLETS, P. J., 'Sir Nicholas Le Strange's Collection of Masque Music', *British*

Museum Quarterly, 29 (1965), 79–81.

——— *The Henry Lawes Manuscript* (London, 1969).

WILSON, J. E. (ed.), *Entertainments for Elizabeth I* (Woodbridge, 1980).

WINWOOD, R., *Memorials of Affairs of State in the Reign of Queen Elizabeth and King James I*, 3 vols. (London, 1725).

WOOD, B., and PINNOCK, A., ' "Unscarr'd by turning times"?: The Dating of Purcell's *Dido and Aeneas*', *EM* 20 (1992), 372–91.

WOODFILL, W. L., *Musicians in English Society* (Princeton, 1953).

Index